W9-ARN-112

☀

Presented To

From

Date

☽

MOMENTS of **PEACE** in the **PRESENCE** of **GOD**

MORNING AND EVENING MEDITATIONS FOR EVERY DAY OF THE YEAR

BETHANYHOUSE

a division of Baker Publishing Group
Minneapolis, Minnesota

© 2010 by GRQ, Inc.
Published by Bethany House Publishers
11400 Hampshire Avenue South
Bloomington, Minnesota 55438
www.bethanyhouse.com

Bethany House Publishers is a division of Baker Publishing Group, Grand Rapids, Michigan.

This edition published 2016
ISBN: 978-0-7642-1849-1

Scripture quotations noted AMP are from *The Amplified Bible, Old Testament*. Copyright ©1965, 1987 by The Zondervan Corporation. *The Amplified New Testament*. Copyright ©1954, 1958, 1987 by The Lockman Foundation. Used by permission.

Scripture quotations noted CEV are from *THE CONTEMPORARY ENGLISH VERSION*. Copyright © 1991 by the American Bible Society. Used by permission.

Scripture quotations noted ESV are from *The Holy Bible, English Standard Version*, copyright © 2001 by Crossway Bibles, a division of Good News Publishers. Used by permission. All rights reserved.

Scripture quotations noted GNT are from the *Good News Translation*, Second Edition, copyright © 1992 by American Bible Society. Used by permission. All rights reserved.

Scripture quotations noted GOD'S WORD are from *God's Word*. Copyright © 1995 by God's Word to the Nations. Used by permission of Baker Publishing Group. All rights reserved.

Scripture quotations noted HCSB are from the *Holman Christian Standard Bible*®, copyright ©1999, 2000, 2002, 2003 by Holman Bible Publishers. Used by permission. Holman Christian Standard Bible®, Holman, CSB®, and HCSB® are federally registered trademarks of Holman Bible Publishers.

Scripture quotations noted KJV are from the KING JAMES VERSION.

Scripture quotations noted MSG are from *THE MESSAGE: The New Testament, Psalms and Proverbs*. Copyright ©1993, 1994, 1995 by Eugene H. Peterson. All rights reserved.

Scripture quotations noted NASB are from the *NEW AMERICAN STANDARD BIBLE*®. Copyright ©1960, 1962, 1963–1968, 1971, 1973–1975, 1977, 1995 by the Lockman Foundation. Used by permission.

Scripture quotations noted NCV are from *The Holy Bible, New Century Version*, copyright ©1987, 1988, 1991 by Word Publishing, a division of Thomas Nelson, Inc. All rights reserved. Used by permission.

Scripture quotations noted NIV are from the *Holy Bible: New International Version* (North American Edition)® Copyright ©1973–1978, 1984, by the International Bible Society. Used by permission of Zondervan. All rights reserved.

Scripture quotations noted NKJV are from *THE NEW KING JAMES VERSION*. Copyright ©1979, 1980, 1982, Thomas Nelson, Inc., Publishers.

Scripture quotations noted NLT are from the *Holy Bible, New Living Translation*, copyright ©1996. Used by permission of Tyndale House Publishers, Inc., Wheaton, Illinois 60189. All rights reserved.

Scripture quotations noted NRSV are from the NEW REVISED STANDARD VERSION of the Bible. Copyright © 1989 by the Division of Christian Education of the National Council of The Churches of Christ in the U.S.A. All rights reserved.

Scripture quotations noted TLB are from *The Living Bible*, copyright © 1971. Used by permission of Tyndale House Publishers, Inc., Wheaton, Illinois 60189. All rights reserved.

Editor: Lila Empson Wavering
Associate Editor: Natasha Sperling
Writers: The writers for GRQ, Inc.
Interior Design: Whisner Design Group

16 17 18 19 20 21 22   7 6 5 4 3 2 1

CONTENTS

INTRODUCTION

You show me the path of life. In your presence there is fullness of joy; in your right hand are pleasures forevermore.
Psalm 16:11 NRSV

When Jesus went to his disciples on the evening of his resurrection, the first thing he said to them was, "Peace be with you."

That has not changed. When you are in the presence of God, you are in a place of peace. Peace comes from the presence of someone who made you in love and keeps you in grace, someone you can count on to be with you in all things. When you are in God's presence, you are with one who knows you and wants you to have the best life has to offer. In such a presence you have an inner calm that exceeds human understanding and measurement.

This book invites you into the presence of God, where the gift of peace awaits. In its pages you can discover that God is nearer to you than you are to yourself. To know God's presence in this way is to be at peace.

There are morning and evening meditations for every day of the year. You can begin where and when you choose.

Morning meditations—"Let the morning bring me word of your unfailing love, for I have put my trust in you. Show me the way I should go, for to you I lift up my soul" (Psalm 143:8 NIV).

The morning meditations are a good way to begin your day with God. Just as when you nourish your body with a hearty, healthy breakfast, feeding your soul with God's grace will renew and refresh you for the hours ahead. Nothing will affect your life in such a powerful and satisfying way as seeking God first thing in the morning.

These brief meditations have been fashioned to encourage you and give you hope. Some days, your faith will be reassured. Other days, you will be emboldened to live it out. Yet every morning you will experience the wonderful goodness of God.

Though it is impossible to describe the profound depth of God's love for you, you will grow to understand and appreciate it more as you spend time with your beloved Creator. He will empower you in difficult times, inspire you to meet challenges, and support you when you simply need to trust him. Undoubtedly, the Bible will guide you, his grace will comfort you, and his love will provide you with the strength to make it through the day.

Evening meditations—"GOD, my shepherd! I don't need a thing. You have bedded me down in lush meadows, you find me quiet pools to drink from" (Psalm 23:1–2 MSG).

The evening meditations are from the book of Psalms. Throughout the ages, the Psalms have been an inspiration to countless people. Not only do they hold some of the most beautiful verses ever written about the joys and sorrows of the human heart, but they also bring you to the very throne of heaven as it describes your loving God.

Originally a worship book for the people of Israel, the book of Psalms was compiled during a time period of more than a thousand years—from the time of the exodus from Egypt until after the Babylonian captivity. Seventy-three of the psalms were composed by King David; however, Moses, Solomon, Asaph, and possibly King Hezekiah also contributed to this exquisite book of hymns, prayers, and poetry. Their insights are recorded to encourage you and bring you closer to God.

These meditations on the Psalms were put together with you in mind. They connect the daily struggles you face with the profound wisdom of the Bible. Throughout the Psalms, you will discover the intimate relationship God wants to have with you—how he can be your Defender, Provider, Healer, and King no matter what you face.

God is waiting to fill you with joy and to comfort you with his presence morning and evening and throughout the day. Read the inspirational verses, pray, worship God, and enjoy your journey.

This book invites you to turn up the quiet in your life, to be still and know God immediately and intimately.

Quiet your body as you sit still; hush the nudge to be somewhere else.

Quiet your mind as you shake off the pressures of agenda and schedule.

Quiet your heart as you make God's presence your priority and relegate anything else to lesser importance.

God is waiting to fill you with joy and assure you that he is with you on every step of your journey. So read the inspirational verses, pray, and enjoy your moments of grace each morning and evening. May your daily meetings with God completely bless your soul.

You have made known to me the ways of life;
you will make me full of gladness with your presence.
Acts 2:28 NRSV

The LORD gives his people strength.
The LORD blesses them with peace.
Psalm 29:11 NLT

January

☀

GOD said,
"My presence will go
with you. I'll see the
journey to the end."

Exodus 33:14 MSG

TO SHARE HIS LOVE

*In the beginning God created the
heavens and the earth.*
GENESIS 1:1 NLT

*Let them all praise
the name of the
LORD! He com-
manded, and they
were created.*

PSALM 148:5 GNT

In the beginning, God—who is limitless in power, wisdom, and love—wanted one thing. He wanted someone with whom to share his love. So he set about creating the universe.

Words flowed from his mouth, forming planets and stars, continents and oceans. Yet as detailed and amazing as they were, they were only the stage for his dearest and best creation: you.

God created everything needed for you to live and for him to express his love to you. And he created you in his image—with a heart that could accept his love and reciprocate it.

God wants to share himself with you. Today, open your heart to him.

*Dear God, thank you for creating such an amazing
universe and for loving me. Help me to know your love
and show you love in return. Amen.*

TO BE BLESSED

Happy are those who . . . love the LORD's teachings,
and they think about those teachings day and night.
PSALM 1:1–2 NCV

When you have a wounded heart, you may find it difficult to know where to turn. You look outwardly to loved ones and those who purport to know the answers to your hurt, but there is no real comfort. You look into yourself and find pain and confusion there. Where can you go to soothe your soul?

He will be like a tree firmly planted by streams of water, which yields its fruit in its season and its leaf does not wither; and in whatever he does, he prospers.

PSALM 1:3 NASB

Friend, it is no coincidence that your search has brought you here. It is not in looking out or in, but *up* to God that you will find what you are seeking. God promises you blessing when you read and embrace the Bible. God promises that you will be filled with love, joy, purpose, and peace. Isn't that what your heart has been aching for, after all?

God, I need you. Thank you for revealing yourself
to me through the Psalms and for healing my heart.
Only you can truly bless me. Amen.

GOD UNDERSTANDS

*We do not have a High Priest who cannot
sympathize with our weaknesses.*
HEBREWS 4:15 NKJV

*We are people of
flesh and blood.
That is why Jesus
became one of us.*

HEBREWS 2:14 CEV

Some days you may feel that no one appreciates the unique pressures you face. And perhaps you are in such an exceptional situation that very few really could. God, however, knows you intimately and cares about what concerns you.

God knows the hidden thoughts of your heart and can see your circumstances from an all-encompassing viewpoint. He also knows how you feel when you are emotionally spent.

Always remember that God understands you very well—even better than you know yourself—and can help you overcome any challenge you face. Take heart today by trusting in him.

*Dear God, thank you for understanding and loving me.
Help me to always remember that—no matter what
happens—you will help me through. Amen.*

DEEP ROOTS

They are strong, like a tree planted by a river. The tree produces fruit in season, and its leaves don't die. Everything they do will succeed.

PSALM 1:3 NCV

Looking for peace in the Psalms is not a random choice on your part. There's a reason you've come here. Perhaps you're seeking understanding in a difficult situation. Or maybe you don't know where else to turn. Either way, you're looking in the right place—the only place peace can be found: in God. You'll always find God in his Word.

They delight in the law of the LORD, meditating on it day and night.

PSALM 1:2 NLT

Like river waters nourishing a tree's roots, when you drink in God's Word, it goes deep into your heart and makes you strong. God's nurturing truth gives you the courage and wisdom for whatever you're facing.

Allow God's Word to take root deep in your heart.

God, I know that I haven't come here by chance. Thank you that the Psalms strengthen my heart and nourish my soul. Amen.

GREETING THE SAVIOR

Blessed is He who comes in the name of the Lord!
Hosanna in the highest!
MATTHEW 21:9 NKJV

You make known to me the path of life; in your presence there is fullness of joy; at your right hand are pleasures forevermore.

PSALM 16:11 ESV

When Jesus entered Jerusalem during that last week of his life, the crowds welcomed him with palm branches and cheers. They happily greeted him as the answer to their hopes. They did not know that their joy would lie in the grave with him for three days. It was not until Jesus rose from the dead that they truly saw their hopes gloriously fulfilled.

Today you may be disappointed that some exciting opportunities—things you praised God for—look like they've taken a turn for the worst. Yet continue to greet God with gladness. He will bring your dreams to life again in a way that will make you truly joyful.

Dear God, I greet you with joy. I praise you that no matter how it may look, you are breathing life into my dreams. Amen.

SURRENDERING TO SENSE

Serve the Lord with reverent fear,
and rejoice with trembling.
PSALM 2:11 NLT

Sometimes no matter how hard you try, you cannot understand what is happening to you. The more details you discover, the more confused you become. None of the information you are receiving fits together, and you feel as if your mind just can't wrap itself around the situation.

Blessed are all those
who put their
trust in Him.
PSALM 2:12 NKJV

Yet there is One who is great enough to make sense of your circumstances—and wise enough to know what you should do.

When you worship God, focusing on his almighty power and trembling in awe of his wisdom, you realize that there is nothing too big for him to handle. Surrender the situation to God's care.

God, I come into your presence in worship, adoration,
and surrender. You are truly wise and make sense
of all that concerns me. Amen.

THE DELIGHT OF BLESSING

*I will make of you a great nation, and I will bless you and
make your name great, so that you will be a blessing.*
GENESIS 12:2 ESV

*Scripture foresaw that
God would justify the
Gentiles by faith and
foretold the good news
to Abraham, saying,
All the nations will be
blessed in you. So those
who have faith are
blessed with Abraham.*

GALATIANS 3:8–9 HCSB

God knew that what Abraham
wanted most was a son—
someone to love and teach and to
carry on his name. Yet God wanted
to do more than just provide Abraham with an heir—he wanted to give
Abraham the joy of blessing others.
So God made Abraham into a wonderful example of faith.

God delights in providing your
heart's desires as well. Yet he often
allows you to wait because he wants you to be a blessing—and
nothing blesses others more than a real, joyful trust that God
works on behalf of those who love him.

Today, rejoice that God is making you a blessing to others.
Your faith is absolutely delightful.

*Dear God, thank you for blessing me. Strengthen my faith in your
promises, and make me a joyful blessing to others. Amen.*

TIME IN HIS PRESENCE

Blessed (happy, fortunate, and to be envied) are all those who seek refuge and put their trust in Him!
PSALM 2:12 AMP

Knowing God is a privilege. Although some have the good fortune of meeting with presidents and prime ministers, few are invited into their inner sanctuary—and no one is eternally changed by the encounter.

Worship God in adoring embrace, celebrate in trembling awe.

PSALM 2:11 MSG

Yet God invites you to know him in the most profound way possible and to embrace his best for your life. The Creator of the universe beckons you to be transformed by his divine mercy, wisdom, and provision, and to know the unlimited power and love that have been made available to you.

Spending time in God's presence is a precious gift—one that you have been given to enjoy at any moment, no matter the hour or the reason. Therefore, do not decline his invitation. It is the best appointment you will keep all day.

God, thank you so much for inviting me into your presence, transforming my life, and loving me. I praise and worship you with all of my heart. Amen.

THIS IS YOUR TIME

*Who knows but that you have come to the kingdom for
such a time as this and for this very occasion?*
ESTHER 4:14 AMP

*We ask our God to
make you worthy of
the life he has called
you to live. May he
fulfill by his power
all your desire for
goodness and complete
your work of faith.*

2 THESSALONIANS 1:11 GNT

After the Babylonian captivity—when there were still Israelites in Persia—there arose an evil man named Haman who wanted to destroy the people of God. God, through various circumstances, placed Esther in King Xerxes' household, and she alerted him to Haman's plans. Esther trusted God, and God worked through her to save his people.

You can have peace today knowing that God has also placed you in your unique situation to have an extraordinary impact for him. He is not surprised at where you are. Rather, he put you there, gave you the gifts necessary for your circumstances, and will give you victory if you place your trust in him.

*Dear God, I do trust you. Thank you for the peace
of knowing that you are fulfilling a victorious
plan in my circumstances. Amen.*

AN IMPENETRABLE DEFENSE

You, O LORD, are a shield for me, my glory
and the One who lifts up my head.
PSALM 3:3 NKJV

King David always had plenty of enemies. However, this time, his adversary represented the greatest betrayal, knew David's most profound weaknesses, and pierced the deepest part of his heart. This time, the enemy was David's own son Absalom.

Real help comes from
GOD. Your blessing
clothes your people!
PSALM 3:8 MSG

Are you facing a problem that's a lose-lose situation no matter how you look at it? You aren't sure whom to trust, and you're heartbroken about the way you've been betrayed? It's difficult to know what to do.

You can always do as David did—count on God as your impenetrable defense, who not only protects your body but also guards your heart. Do not despair. Trust God to shield you.

God, I know that you can turn this lose-lose
situation into a victory. Thank you for being
my merciful defender. I trust you. Amen.

THE BATTLE BELONGS TO GOD

All this assembly shall know that the LORD does not save
with sword and spear; for the battle is the LORD's.
1 SAMUEL 17:47 NKJV

He had great success in everything he did because the LORD was with him.

1 SAMUEL 18:14 NCV

The idea was to pit Israel's strongest warrior against the champion of the enemy. But even the bravest of Israel's soldiers were terrified of the mighty Goliath. That is, all except young David, who was there to deliver bread to his brothers. He knew that the battle wasn't about human strength; it was about the divine power of God.

This morning, are your thoughts on the Goliaths that challenge you today? If you are living for God, you can have triumphant confidence like David's, because no earthly threat can match the power of your heavenly champion. As you prepare for the day, trust him and relax. All your battles belong to God.

Dear God, thank you that I never have to
fear the Goliaths in my life. I praise you for
your power that wins every battle. Amen.

A SURE DEFENDER

*With my voice I cry to the Lord, and He hears
and answers me out of His holy hill.*
PSALM 3:4 AMP

As King David considered his options, he realized that there could be no good resolution to the conflict. His son Absalom had rallied forces to take the throne of Israel away from him. It was an impossible situation—either David would lose his kingdom and his life, or he

*You are my shield,
and you give me
victory and
great honor.*
PSALM 3:3 CEV

would lose his son. No matter the outcome, his heart and his nation would be broken. Psalm 3 is the prayer that flowed from the anguish within him.

Are you facing a situation that seems completely hopeless? Go to God. Even if you cannot see a constructive way out, he can, and he knows exactly what is best for everyone involved. Therefore, trust him. He is your Shield and Defender, and if you obey him, he will surely lead you to triumph.

*God, thank you for not only hearing me but also for
understanding my situation better than I do. I will
trust you to guide me to the best solution. Amen.*

FOR THE RIGHT MOMENT

In the shadow of His hand He has concealed Me; and He has also made Me a select arrow, He has hidden Me in His quiver.
ISAIAH 49:2 NASB

As for me, I trust in You, O LORD, I say, "You are my God." My times are in Your hand.

PSALM 31:14–15 NASB

The excellent marksman does not waste his ammunition. He waits for the right opportunity and then sends his arrow flying at the precise moment for maximum effect.

You are far too important to God for him to squander your talents or misplace you. In fact, you are so precious to him that he has hidden you close to him, to polish and perfect your spiritual gifts. He is waiting for the right moment—the right assignment—to send you soaring.

Today, be patient about what God is doing in you, and thank him for his timing and expertise. He has wonderful things for you to accomplish. Praise his name.

Dear God, it is hard to be patient, but I know I can trust your timing and skill. Thank you for your excellent assignments. Amen.

JANUARY 7 * EVENING

TRUE HEALING

*O God of my righteousness! You have given
me relief when I was in distress.*
PSALM 4:1 ESV

Whether it is pain or paralysis in your limbs or an illness that affects you internally, health problems can severely limit what you can accomplish. The same is true for emotional and spiritual difficulties. Fears and regrets can torment you to the point that you feel trapped in your situation.

> *You have given me
> greater joy than those
> who have abundant
> harvests of grain and
> new wine.*
>
> PSALM 4:7 NLT

In your own power, you can do nothing to set yourself free, yet God can overcome whatever you are facing. In fact, God will work through your affliction to make you genuinely complete and help you fulfill your purpose in life.

Therefore, trust him to heal you to the depths of your soul. He will turn your limitations into opportunities for surprising fruitfulness and teach you how to live in his comfort and abundance.

*God, thank you for truly healing my distress and giving
relief to my troubled soul. I trust you to turn this place
of pain into a reason for praising you. Amen.*

PREPARED, NOT FORGOTTEN

Wheat is threshed and milled, but still not endlessly. The farmer knows how to treat each kind of grain.
ISAIAH 28:28 MSG

This also comes from the LORD of hosts, who is wonderful in counsel and excellent in guidance.

ISAIAH 28:29 NKJV

Isn't it wonderful that wheat is not ground forever? Eventually the milling process ends, and the grain is perfect for baking into bread.

As you awoke this morning, you may have felt like the grain—threshed and milled by trials. You may even feel that God has forgotten you. The moment will come, however, when the threshing ends, and you will be prepared with the patience, faith, and humility that only milling can create in your life.

Just as the farmer knows what is required for each type of grain, God knows what preparation is essential for each person. He knows exactly what you need, so be patient and trust him.

Thank you, God, that trials don't last forever but that the qualities you build in me do. You are truly good to me. Amen.

EVER LISTENING

The Lord will hear when I call to Him.
Psalm 4:3 HCSB

In the silence of the night when your household lies quietly resting, sometimes difficult thoughts will prevail in your mind. Perhaps you've been careful not to voice your concerns with others because you didn't want to worry them. But in that desolate moment you are alone with your struggles, and you wish someone could share them and comfort you.

In peace I will both lie down and sleep, for You, Lord, alone make me dwell in safety and confident trust.
Psalm 4:8 AMP

God hears you. He is with you, with his ear always bent toward you, waiting for you to invite him into your situation.

You don't have to go on feeling alone. Call out to him and tell him your concerns. Let him comfort you. He's always ready to listen.

God, thank you for your comforting presence in my loneliest hours and for always hearing my prayers. Truly, you are good and loving. Amen.

WHATEVER HE WANTS

*Even if it isn't what we want to do. We will obey
the LORD so that all will go well for us.*
JEREMIAH 42:6 CEV

*Listen to and obey My
voice, and I will be
your God and you
will be My people;
and walk in the
whole way that I
command you, that
it may be well
with you.*

JEREMIAH 7:23 AMP

You never go wrong when you commit your way to God. He is always faithful to lead you in the very best way. And he promises that if you obey him he will protect you and cause you to prosper.

Sometimes his instructions will seem counterintuitive—very different from what you expected. And it will take real courage and faith to obey him because his instructions will not make sense from your standpoint. However, you can always be confident that God has excellent reasons for his commands—your protection and your prosperity. Take heart and commit to being faithful and obeying God today. Assuredly, you'll be glad.

*Dear God, sometimes it is hard to obey, but I trust you to lead me
well. Thank you that all of your commands are good. Amen.*

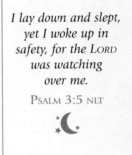

GOD'S NIGHT WATCH

I will lie down and sleep in peace, for you alone,
O LORD, make me dwell in safety.
PSALM 4:8 NIV

Agood night's sleep is one of those small blessings that are often taken for granted until you lose it, tossing fitfully, unable to relax your guard. Peaceful sleep? David could appreciate it more than the average person could. He was a man who slept in caves while on the run from a king with murderous intent. Yet even in the

I lay down and slept, yet I woke up in safety, for the LORD was watching over me.

PSALM 3:5 NLT

midst of life-threatening danger, his heart was at peace because he knew that God alone made him dwell in safety.

No deadbolt or bar at the window can replace the serenity that comes from trusting God for your security. Because of his night watch over you, you can crawl into bed and sleep the deep slumber of a child, comforted by the knowledge that God is guarding you body and soul.

I know, dear Lord, that you guide me and that you provide for me.
Thank you for meeting my needs and for blessing my deeds. Amen.

NO WAY BUT UP

*Amazement seized them all, and they glorified
God and were filled with awe, saying, "We have
seen extraordinary things today."*
LUKE 5:26 ESV

*At once the man got
up in front of them all,
took the bed he had
been lying on,
and went home,
praising God.*

LUKE 5:25 GNT

The four men heard that Jesus could do miracles, and a miracle was just what their paraplegic friend needed to be healed and to walk again. They carried him to where Jesus was staying.

Unfortunately, there were too many people for them to enter the house, and there was only one way for them to go—*up*. They transported their friend to Jesus by way of the roof, and they saw him miraculously healed because of their faith. You know people who are hurting as well. When you help them look up to Jesus, you see extraordinary things happen in their lives.

Today you'll meet people who really need Jesus. Show them the way up.

*Dear God, I know that you love my hurting
friends. Help me to show them how extraordinarily
healing it is to look up. Amen.*

30

PREPARED FOR HIS PRESENCE

By Your abundant lovingkindness I will enter
Your house, at Your holy temple I will
bow in reverence for You.
PSALM 5:7 NASB

When traveling to another nation, diplomats, business-persons, and missionaries often must engage in extensive study of the culture they're visiting. The kiss on the cheek that is common in Venezuela would be impolite in Singapore, where the head is considered sacred. Consequently, travelers must train themselves to show respect to the people they're meeting.

Each morning you listen to my prayer, as I bring my requests to you and wait for your reply.
PSALM 5:3 CEV

The wonderful thing about God is that he himself prepares you to meet with him. He instructs you concerning the habits that please him and cleanses you from those that don't. Whatever is needed for you to come into God's presence, he provides. Don't be shy. God loves you unconditionally, so enjoy his company.

God, thank you that I don't have to be nervous in your presence. You want the real me, and that makes me love you even more. Amen.

A SERVANT FIRST

He came to serve, not to be served.
MARK 10:45 MSG

You have one Teacher, the Christ. The greatest among you will be your servant.

MATTHEW 23:10–11 NIV

Some people decline to follow God because they are afraid that he will be an insatiable taskmaster. That is far different from how God has revealed himself in the Bible and throughout history. In fact, the greatest example of a humble servant is Jesus.

True, God asks for obedience. Yet he does so in order to free you to enjoy his blessings. He serves you by providing the peaceful, joyful, and fulfilling life you desire.

He will not answer the cries of your heart with fleeting remedies. He grows you in holiness and love so that you can experience the abundant life to the deepest degree.

Dear God, thank you for this abundant life. May I daily imitate you and humbly take part of your work in the world. Amen.

A MANTLE OF LOVE

Let all those who take refuge and put their trust in You
rejoice; let them ever sing and shout for joy, because
You make a covering over them and defend them.
PSALM 5:11 AMP

It has been speculated that intelligent people want to be perceived as physically attractive and that good-looking people want to be seen as clever. Yet what most people truly desire is to be accepted and loved.

You bless the godly,
O LORD; you surround
them with your
shield of love.
PSALM 5:12 NLT

That's exactly what you are when you take refuge in God. As you spend time with him, he envelops you in his majesty and grace, and his splendor shines through you. You are good-looking to him, and you are not only smart but also wise. Not only are you accepted and loved, you also become joyful and loving.

Therefore, instead of worrying about whether you are good-looking or smart enough, rejoice that you're clothed in God's mantle of love. Because that, friend, is what makes you truly exceptional.

God, thank you for covering me with the mantle of your love.
I love and praise you with all my heart. Amen.

A LETTER OF RECOMMENDATION

*You are a letter of Christ, cared for by us, written not
with ink but with the Spirit of the living God.*
2 CORINTHIANS 3:3 NASB

*If you listen to constructive criticism,
you will be at home
among the wise.*

PROVERBS 15:31 NLT

In Paul's time, false teachers forged letters of recommendation in order to establish their authority. Yet Paul declared that he needed no such letters, because whenever he taught about Jesus, changed human hearts confirmed God's approval and authority.

God enables you to teach others about Jesus. Though theological training is useful, it is not as important as having a vibrant, living relationship with God, where his Spirit permanently writes on your heart.

You have his truth engraved within you. In fact, you are a letter of Christ. This morning, rejoice that it is a letter that many will be blessed in reading.

*God, thank you for teaching me deep within
my heart by your spirit. May many read the
letter you have written in me. Amen.*

A SURE RESCUE

*O Lord, deliver my life; save me for the sake
of Your steadfast love and mercy.*
PSALM 6:4 AMP

Perhaps you've opened this devotional tonight with some important issue pressing on your mind that consumes your energy and creativity. Maybe you've come here wondering two things.

*The LORD has heard
my plea for help;
the LORD accepts
my prayer.*

PSALM 6:9 HCSB

First: Can God help me? Yes, the almighty God who created the universe is certainly able to handle your situation. Second: Will God help me? This question goes to God's love for you—especially if you've messed up in some way. Yet the answer is yes! His love for you is unconditional, which means he'll surely rescue you.

Rest in the confidence that God can work in your situation, though it may not be in the way you expect.

*God, thank you for loving me unconditionally and helping me.
I entrust this situation to you, knowing that your power
will transform my circumstances for good. Amen.*

THE WORDS THAT IMPROVE

An honest answer is like a kiss on the lips.
PROVERBS 24:26 NIV

Let the message about Christ, in all its richness, fill your lives. Teach and counsel each other with all the wisdom he gives. Sing psalms and hymns and spiritual songs to God with thankful hearts.

COLOSSIANS 3:16 NLT

Most people would agree that honesty is the best policy—unless it is honest criticism. That kind of candor is often difficult to take. People respond three ways to criticism. One is to find fault with the messenger. Another is to internalize it so that it destroys their self-esteem.

The third way is to take the criticism to God and ask him to reveal the truth in it. In this way, you allow him to teach you and reveal blind spots in your character that need work.

Today, remember that honesty really is an excellent policy—especially when it is accompanied by God's grace and truth.

Dear God, thank you that honest criticism doesn't have to hurt but that it can truly improve me. Thank you for gently and lovingly teaching me your truth. Amen.

HE HEARS

The Lord has heard the voice of my weeping. The Lord has heard my supplication; the Lord will receive my prayer.
PSALM 6:8–9 NKJV

At times you may confide in people, and although they appear to be paying attention, they may not really grasp what you're telling them. They do not comprehend the depth of your emotions or the seriousness of your situation. Even if they can empathize with you, they will be unable to offer you genuine, lasting relief.

O Lord, rescue my soul; save me because of Your lovingkindness.

PSALM 6:4 NASB

Yet when you call out to God, he truly hears you—even the words you don't say. He understands the pain you feel and is committed to giving you the most effective help with whatever you're facing. Have you taken your troubles to others, only to be let down? Then turn your concerns over to God. He's always glad to listen and has promised never to fail you. Trust him.

God, thank you for hearing my prayers—even the wordless ones that come from my heart. Truly, you are my most wonderful confidant, and I praise you. Amen.

RECEIVING THE MESSAGE

The LORD God gives me the right words to encourage the weary.
Each morning he awakens me eager to learn his teaching.
ISAIAH 50:4 CEV

Who among you fears the LORD and obeys the voice of his servant? Let him who walks in darkness and has no light trust in the name of the LORD and rely on his God.

ISAIAH 50:10 ESV

This morning, God is calling you to learn from him. He whispers that he loves you and that you can trust him. He tells you that when you think there is no help for you, he will rescue you.

He encourages you to be strong because he vindicates you and never lets you be dishonored. He says that his wisdom, power, and love have worked together to provide good plans for your life.

He also wants you to know that he has comforted you in order to prepare you to encourage others. His words can give life and hope to the weary, if only you will receive and share them.

Dear God, I do receive your words today. Thank you
for such profound promises. Help me to share
them with whoever needs them. Amen.

THE FAIR JUDGE

Awake, my God; decree justice.
PSALM 7:6 NIV

In King Saul's court, many people were jealous that David would succeed Saul as ruler of Israel. So they made trouble for David—telling Saul that David wanted to kill him. This, of course, was a lie. David cried out to God to reveal the truth.

Judge me, O LORD, according to my righteousness and according to the integrity that is in me. Oh, let the evil of the wicked come to an end, and may you establish the righteous.
PSALM 7:8–9 ESV

When people concoct falsehoods about you, sometimes the worst part is that you can't defend yourself. Their cruel fabrications endanger your reputation, relationships, and even your future. Yet you don't have to avenge yourself—God will come to your defense as he did for David. Be patient and honor God. Soon enough, you'll see his justice done and your false accusers exposed.

Thank you, God, for seeing the truth and making it known. It may take some time, but you're a fair Judge, and justice will be done. Amen.

KNOWING HIM IS ETERNAL

This is eternal life, that they know you the only true God, and Jesus Christ whom you have sent.
JOHN 17:3 ESV

Build yourselves up in your most holy faith; pray in the Holy Spirit; keep yourselves in the love of God, waiting for the mercy of our Lord Jesus Christ that leads to eternal life.
JUDE 1:20–21 ESV

There will be times in your life when your only source of comfort will be God. It will be through worship, prayer, and Bible study that you gain the energy, wisdom, and hope to make it through the day.

This is not a trial, this is the goal—to need no earthly encouragement because God has become everything to you. Your comfort, peace, and joy all come from God. It is during these times that God replaces your earthly nature with a love and longing for the eternal.

Rejoice. God is preparing you for eternal life by changing your perspective and helping you to know him better.

I thank you, God, that learning about you today is about loving you in countless tomorrows. I love you and praise your wonderful name. Amen.

WAITING FOR JUSTICE

Judge me and show that I am honest and innocent.
You know every heart and mind, and you always do right.
PSALM 7:8–9 CEV

It can be truly disheartening when others advance because of the lies they have told about you. That is what happened to David. Those who were jealous of his success accused him of treason. With his life in danger and no way to defend himself, David turned to the only One he could truly count on: God. David was confident that the Lord would defend him and prove his innocence.

You, God, are my shield, the protector of everyone whose heart is right.
PSALM 7:10 CEV

Are you powerless to counteract the false charges of others? Are their allegations endangering your future? Do not fear. Just as God defended David, he will protect you as well. Therefore, continue to honor God in every aspect of your life, and be patient. His justice is coming, and soon everyone will know the truth.

God, thank you for seeing my innocence and for
defending me. However long it takes, I trust you
to bring justice out of this situation. Amen.

ASKING FOR HELP

*Appoint some competent leaders who respect
God and are trustworthy and honest.*
EXODUS 18:21 CEV

*These judges can
handle the ordinary
cases and bring the
more difficult ones to
you. . . . You won't be
under nearly as much
stress, and everyone
else will return home
feeling satisfied.*

EXODUS 18:22–23 CEV

Though Moses believed he should mediate the people's disputes, it was just too much for him to handle—the line of aggravated Israelites was endless. His father-in-law gave him this excellent advice: Find capable people to share the responsibilities—people who could do the job if something happened to him.

You don't have to handle everything by yourself either. In fact, it is not only acceptable for you to get help, but it is also part of God's plan for training others to do his work. In this way you relieve your own burden while blessing someone else with a ministry.

Find reliable people to mentor today, and enjoy watching them grow.

*Dear God, help me to be humble enough to
ask for help in my responsibilities so that
others can learn to serve you. Amen.*

GOD OF THE GLORIOUS HEAVENS

O LORD, our Lord, your greatness is seen in all the world!
Your praise reaches up to the heavens.
PSALM 8:1 GNT

Even with all of the technology available to us, we can't count all the stars in the universe or estimate the light and energy that are generated through them. Still, knowing that the sun converts more than 250 million tons of matter into illumination and heat every minute gives us a clue concerning the immensity of what's occurring.

I see the moon and stars, which you created. But why are people important to you? Why do you take care of human beings? You . . . crowned them with glory and honor.
PSALM 8:3–5 NCV

☽

Yet even the centillions of stars that exist together pale in comparison to the splendor of God. And he wants to show his glory to others through you. Whenever you feel insignificant, consider the radiant heavenly bodies. As his best creation, you reflect God even more brightly.

God, truly you are more brilliant and beautiful than all the stars in the universe! May my life reflect your glory and draw others to you. Amen.

OF DISCIPLINES AND VICTORIES

If anyone competes as an athlete, he does not win the prize unless he competes according to the rules.

2 TIMOTHY 2:5 NASB

I press on toward the goal for the prize of the upward call of God in Christ Jesus.

PHILIPPIANS 3:14 NASB

Just as determination and physical discipline go hand in hand for athletes, so faith and a spiritually consistent life work together for you who believe in God.

Athletes train their bodies daily and observe the rules because victory is their goal. Without the goal, there is no reason to train. Without training, they will not achieve their goal.

Like the athlete, you exercise your spiritual muscles through prayer, Bible study, and obedience to God. These disciplines make your faith in God's promises stronger and bring you closer to the prize of knowing God. They work together to bring you the victory.

Dear God, starting today, help me to have a consistent spiritual life that builds strong faith—and the strong faith that motivates a godly life. Amen.

WHY SHOULD HE CARE?

When I look at the night sky and see the work of your fingers—
the moon and the stars you set in place—what are . . .
human beings that you should care for them?
PSALM 8:3–4 NLT

Sometimes it is surprising to discover how deeply and sincerely you are loved. Perhaps you even find others' devotion difficult to accept because you are accustomed to thinking of yourself as unlovable or unworthy.

> *O LORD, our Lord, how majestic is Your name in all the earth, who have displayed Your splendor above the heavens!*
>
> PSALM 8:1 NASB

This may be especially true when considering God's perfect, unconditional love. After all, he is majestic and holy—capable of creating the world and everything in it. If you have ever wondered why God loves you, then realize you are pondering the wrong question. God's nature is love, and he created you for the glorious purpose of expressing his wonderful, unlimited care for you. Therefore, accept it!

My God, thank you so much for loving me unconditionally!
Help me to accept the reality of your love with
all my heart, soul, mind, and strength. Amen.

LIVING IN THE LIGHT

Christim will give you light.
EPHESIANS 5:14 NKJV

[You are] light in the Lord. Walk as children of light— for the fruit of the light [results] in all goodness, righteousness, and truth.

EPHESIANS 5:8–9 HCSB

As the sun rises this morning, it is easy to see why light is a blessing—it is essential for sight and growing things. Yet spiritual light is even more amazing because it produces goodness, righteousness, and truth.

Jesus illuminates your life. He sees the good you do in secret and celebrates it with you. His radiance heals the areas of hurt hidden deep within you that prevent you from growing. And he brightens your way with hope whenever the road ahead seems dark.

Jesus is your light. And as he illuminates your life, he kindles your goodness, grows you in righteousness, and lights your way with truth.

Dear God, thank you for the beautiful light of Jesus that helps me to grow and to see as you do. My life is hopeful and bright because of you. Amen.

HIS NAME IS TRUSTWORTHY

Those who know your name put their trust in you, for you,
O LORD, have not forsaken those who seek you.
PSALM 9:10 ESV

You may be wondering what it means when you're reading the Bible and you see the word LORD in all capitals. This was the way translators signified that God's name had been used in the original text.

In Hebrew, God's name is transliterated *Yahweh*, which means "I AM." He is the living God, who is as faithful and loving today as he was to all generations before—and as he'll con-

I will give thanks to the LORD with my whole heart; I will recount all of your wonderful deeds. I will be glad and exult in you; I will sing praise to your name, O Most High.
PSALM 9:1–2 ESV

☾

tinue to be for all eternity. That is why you can trust God. He is unchanging. The psalmists saw God's faithfulness proven daily, and you can as well. Call upon his name. You'll certainly find that he's completely trustworthy.

My God, the great I AM, I thank you for being utterly dependable and reliable, faithful and trustworthy. May your name always be praised. Amen.

THE FABRIC OF THE EVERLASTING

From everlasting to everlasting the LORD's
love is with those who fear him.
PSALM 103:17 NIV

As God's chosen people,
holy and dearly loved,
clothe yourselves with
compassion, kindness,
humility, gentleness
and patience.

COLOSSIANS 3:12 NIV

Wrap yourself in this beautiful promise today—God's love is always, constantly, and ceaselessly with you. His love adorns you with salvation, protection, guidance, and provision. It shrouds you from your cold, piercing fears. Nothing can reach you, except that which is allowed by his covering grace.

Though you may lay his love aside and get far away from him in your own heart, he remains close by.

He weaves himself intimately into your life so that nothing can separate his eternal cords from your earthly cloth. Joyfully wear the love of God forever.

Dear God, how great and steadfast is
your love. Dress me in it this morning,
and my heart will sing your praises forever. Amen.

DECEPTIVE FEELINGS

O LORD, why do you stand so far away?
Why do you hide when I am in trouble?
PSALM 10:1 NLT

The circumstances that trouble you may suggest that God has abandoned you. Yet the truth is, he will never leave you or forsake you. It may seem as if God is ignoring your prayers and tears, but he takes special care of each one. You may even cry out, "My God, why don't you help me?" However, he is working all things out for your good even when you cannot see it.

Lord, surely you see these cruel and evil things. People in trouble look to you for help. You are the one who helps the orphans.

PSALM 10:14 NCV

✦☾✦

At times your feelings will tempt you to doubt God, which is why you must always cling to the promises he gives you in his Word. Never allow your emotions to cloud the truth of God's unfailing love. The fact is, he is with you and will never fail you. Therefore, rejoice in his holy name.

God, I praise you for sticking by me—even when my heart begins to wander. Please forgive me for doubting you. Help me to trust you more. Amen.

IT WAS VERY GOOD

God looked over everything he had made;
it was so good, so very good!
GENESIS 1:31 MSG

God planned for us to do good things and to live as he has always wanted us to live. That's why he sent Christ to make us what we are.

EPHESIANS 2:10 CEV

God is at work in you. The fact that you awoke this morning with a desire for a word from him demonstrates his activity. In opening his word and praying, you welcomed him into your life to continue forming you into a good, useful instrument.

He is constantly drawing and teaching you—making you ready for good works that are uniquely suited to you. Though you may feel useless or unworthy, he sees what pleases him—what he deems as very, very good.

He is readying you for great endeavors. Rejoice that God is proud of you and has deemed you worthy of being his choice instrument for important assignments to come.

Dear God, thank you for working in my life
and for doing good things in me and through me.
May I truly be a useful instrument. Amen.

DISTINCT AND BEAUTIFUL

Arise, O LORD! O God, lift up Your hand!
Do not forget the humble.
PSALM 10:12 NKJV

Back in the days when mothers routinely sewed their children's clothes, dressmaking was a big event, especially when the dresses were cut from a particularly beautiful piece of cloth. A girl would watch eagerly as her mother's fingers transformed the fabric into a brand-new dress.

The LORD is King forever and ever; nations have perished from His land. O LORD, You have heard the desire of the humble; You will strengthen their heart, You will incline Your ear.
PSALM 10:16–17 NASB

The excitement faded when a girl realized her sisters' dresses were going to be made from the same cloth and from the same pattern as well. Then the mother would add distinctive touches—a lace collar, a scalloped edge, or a looping rickrack design. The dresses were masterpieces—unique and beautiful for each girl.

Dear God, keep my eyes on Jesus, who refused to turn stones into bread, jump from great heights, or take over the rule of earthly kingdoms. Amen.

THE DELIGHT OF CREATING

The LORD made the heavens and everything
in them by his word.
PSALM 33:6 CEV

*Delight yourself also
in the Lord, and He
will give you the
desires and secret
petitions of your heart.*

PSALM 37:4 AMP

God takes joy in creating. He loves inventing worlds of delight for you.

First, he plants a desire in you—a seed that he lovingly nurtures. Undoubtedly, some special hope comes to mind. You know that it originated with him because it is impossible to achieve without him. You know that when it is accomplished, he will receive all the glory and praise.

Then, he creates conditions for that hope to mature and blossom. He delights in growing it into something that is beyond what you could imagine. And he loves to see your joyous face when you finally grasp the delightful things he created just for you.

Dear God, you are my joy. Just as you created the
world by your word, I know you are powerfully
inventing good things for me. Amen.

WHO QUALIFIES?

LORD, you know the hopes of the helpless.
Surely you will listen to their cries and comfort them.
PSALM 10:17 NLT

When the giant Goliath challenged Israel to send out its mightiest warrior for a duel, no one imagined that it would be David who'd do the job. The youngest, weakest, and least impressive of his brothers, David was a mere shepherd boy—completely unskilled in the issues of war. Nonetheless, God was with him, and Goliath was defeated.

You take notice of trouble and suffering and are always ready to help. The helpless commit themselves to you; you have always helped the needy.

PSALM 10:14 GNT

You may believe that only the wealthy, strong, or brave qualify for God's help. However, God aids whoever calls upon him, honors him, and entrusts themselves to his care.

No matter what you face, trust God to make you victorious. Commit to doing his will, and watch every obstacle crumble before you.

God, thank you that your only requirement for me is that I be willing to obey you. I praise you that when I'm weak, you're strong. Amen.

53

THE NAME OF JOY

*You are to name Him Jesus, because He
will save His people from their sins.*
MATTHEW 1:21 HCSB

*We can rejoice in our
wonderful new rela-
tionship with God—
all because of what
our Lord Jesus Christ
has done for us
in making us
friends of God.*

ROMANS 5:11 NLT

Many people believe that the phrase "God helps them that help themselves" is in the Bible. However, it was actually written by Benjamin Franklin. The truth is that there are issues in which you cannot help yourself. There are hurts you do not know how to heal, mistakes you need forgiveness for, and obstacles to knowing God that you are unable to overcome by yourself.

God brings you joy because he prevails over *all* those things. Your victory is not about how hard you try, but about how he loves and helps you. God has done extraordinary things for you—even providing the way for you to know God. His is the name of joy—say it today with gladness.

*Dear God, your name makes me rejoice. Thank you for doing
everything necessary so that I can enjoy you forever. Amen.*

TRUE STABILITY

The Lord is in his holy temple;
the Lord is on his heavenly throne.
PSALM 11:4 NIV

Your life can change in an instant—you get a bad doctor's report or are the victim of a crime; you lose a job or, worse, a loved one. In that horrible moment you experience something that leaves you reeling in pain and confusion. Perhaps your sense of stability is seriously damaged.

The Lord always does right and wants justice done. Everyone who does right will see his face.

PSALM 11:7 CEV

When your world is shaken, turn to the One who is completely unwavering. No matter what's happened to you, God is still on the throne, and he's able to help and comfort you. So don't look any further—embrace the only security that will never fail. God will surely keep you stable and strong. Trust him.

God, I'm so glad that no matter what happens,
you are my stability and strength. Your love gives
me hope when everything else fails. Amen.

IN HIS HANDS

The king's heart is like channels of water in the hand
of the LORD; He turns it wherever He wishes.
PROVERBS 21:1 NASB

I will raise up Cyrus
in my righteousness:
I will make all his
ways straight. He will
rebuild my city and set
my exiles free.

ISAIAH 45:13 NIV

When the Israelites went into captivity, God promised that it would not last forever. He assured them that they would someday return to their homeland.

God eventually moved King Cyrus's heart to send them back to Jerusalem and give them the resources needed to rebuild the city. God's ability to help you is limitless. All things concerning your situation—including the hearts of people in authority over you—are in his hand. You may not be able to influence the people who could change your circumstances, but God certainly can and will.

Take peace this morning knowing that he is directing your situation like a watercourse and is helping you mightily.

Dear God, thank you that the hearts of the people who
could help me are in your hands. The ways you
help me are truly limitless. Amen.

THE COMING RESCUE

*"Because of the oppression of the weak and the groaning
of the needy, I will now arise," says the LORD. "I will
protect them from those who malign them."*
PSALM 12:5 NIV

When David faced Goliath, he was merely a boy and was unfamiliar with the sword. One might imagine that David was afraid to face the massive giant. After all, everyone else in Israel was. Yet instead of being frightened by Goliath's threats, David remembered the faithfulness of God, and he trusted the Lord to rescue him.

*The words of the
LORD are pure words,
like silver refined in a
furnace on the ground,
purified seven times.*
PSALM 12:6 ESV

Are you on your own to face a challenge that is too enormous to handle? Are the negative comments of others filling you with fear and discouragement? Call out to God, and obey whatever he tells you. Just as he rescued David by empowering him to slay Goliath, he will give you triumph over your trial if you will trust him. So do not fear. Your deliverance is coming. Watch for it.

*God, no challenge is too difficult for you! Thank you for
giving me hope in this trial. I know I am never alone
or defeated as long as you're with me. Amen.*

NONE OTHER BESIDE HIM

To you it was shown, that you might realize and
have personal knowledge that the Lord is God;
there is no other besides Him.
DEUTERONOMY 4:35 AMP

The LORD brought us out
of Egypt with a strong
hand and . . . signs and
wonders. He led us to this
place and gave us this
land, a land flowing
with milk and honey.

DEUTERONOMY 26:8–9
HCSB

As Israel prepared to claim the Promised Land, God reminded them of the great miracles he had done to rescue them from Egypt. No obstacle impeded him—not Pharaoh's army, not the Red Sea, or not even the lack of food and water in the wilderness. God did it all so that Israel would acknowledge him as God and have confidence in him.

God sometimes gives you obstacles as well—to build your trust in his love and power. Today, acknowledge that he is God and there is no other worthy source of help beside him. Go to him with your troubles, and be confident that he will care for you.

Dear God, you did wondrous things for Israel, and you've done
amazing things for me. Truly, you are worthy of praise. Amen.

WORDS

*The words of the LORD are pure words, like silver
tried in a furnace of earth, purified seven times.*
PSALM 12:6 NKJV

It's often been said that words cannot injure like a rock or a stick could, but the truth is that sometimes they wound you in a manner that's far more dangerous. While physical abrasions heal, abrasions made by words can pierce the heart and fester. Years after you've forgotten they were said, abrasive words can cripple you.

*The LORD replies,
"I have seen violence
done to the helpless,
and I have heard the
groans of the poor.
Now I will rise up to
rescue them, as they
have longed for
me to do."*

PSALM 12:5 NLT

God knows they're there, and he looks upon you with compassion. He sends his Word to root out the wounding words and restore you. Other people may hurt you with their words, but God never will. Today trust him and allow his Word to do its uplifting work.

*Heal me, God, from the wounding words of others. I thank you that
your Word is pure, powerful, and always trustworthy. Amen.*

AS SOON AS YOU PRAYED

God thinks highly of you, and at the very moment you started praying, I was sent to give you the answer.
DANIEL 9:23 CEV

God answered their prayers because they trusted him.
1 CHRONICLES 5:20 MSG

Often it is in the early morning hours when you are reminded of your most cherished, private prayers. The thought flickers in your mind, *Is today the day that God answers me? Will I see my deepest longing fulfilled?*

God's response to you is the same as the angel reported to Daniel—at the very moment you started praying, he began to answer.

You may see God's answer today, but be encouraged even if you don't. Be assured that God has heard your prayer and has sent his mighty power and provision in response to it. His help is on the way. Trust him—his answers are always right.

Dear God, thank you so much for answering my prayer. Though I may not see your provision today, I praise you that it is definitely coming. Amen.

WAITING FOR AN ANSWER

Please listen, LORD God, and answer my prayers.
Make my eyes sparkle again.
PSALM 13:3 CEV

As you know, there are consequences to waiting. When you ask God about something important and he doesn't answer right away, you'll not only struggle with your own doubts, but you may have to address the questions of others. They will want to know what your course of action will be and why you're allowing opportunities to pass by. You may not have any answers.

I trust your love,
and I feel like
celebrating because
you rescued me.
You have been good to
me, LORD, and I will
sing about you.
PSALM 13:5–6 CEV

In those times, it'll be difficult to keep waiting—but do it anyway. Allowing God to answer will strengthen your faith. Be patient, friend. God will undoubtedly answer you in a way that will bring that sparkle back to your eyes. Count on it.

God, waiting is extremely difficult, but I will trust you.
I know that you will never let me down and
that your promises are sure. Amen.

A LONG MARCH

Shout, for the LORD has given you the city!
JOSHUA 6:16 NKJV

Their strength and weapons were not what won the land and gave them victory! You loved them and fought with your powerful arm and your shining glory.

PSALM 44:3 CEV

The Israelites were instructed to march once around Jericho for six days—and seven times around on the seventh day. Finally they were to shout, and the city's walls would fall.

The weary Israelites were probably dubious about the instructions. However, they obeyed God and shouted out in faith—confident that he had already conquered Jericho. God has given you Jerichos as well—strongholds that you've wanted to conquer. You trust God's promises, but you're exhausted from such a long march.

This morning, you must shout. Claim success and loudly proclaim that God has fulfilled his pledge. Express your faith that the march is nearly done—and that triumph is already yours.

*Dear God, it has been a long, tiring march,
but I shout out in praise that you've already won.
Thank you for the coming success. Amen.*

NOT NATURAL . . . SUPERNATURAL

There is no one who does good.
PSALM 14:1 NASB

Have you ever wondered if something within you fights against honoring God? If so, you are right. It is contrary to human nature to submit to him. People's natural inclinations can only lead to destruction; there is nothing inherently good about them.

> *The LORD looks down from heaven on the sons of men to see if there are any who understand, any who seek God.*
> PSALM 14:2 NIV

When you begin to seek God, it is not by natural means; rather, he draws you *supernaturally* by his Spirit. In fact, when you believe in him to save you, he gives you his Holy Spirit to guide, teach, and transform you. It is then that you can obey him, that you can truly do good.

Through the power of God's Spirit, you can choose to honor him. Therefore, embrace the supernatural life and enjoy his extraordinary blessings. Because what he offers you is truly out of this world.

God, thank you for drawing me to you by your Spirit.
Teach me the difference between your direction and
my natural desires so I can always honor you. Amen.

HIS TREASURE

*Rejoice with me, because I have found
my sheep which was lost.*
LUKE 15:6 AMP

*Where your treasure
is, there will your
heart be also.*

LUKE 12:34 AMP

The tender words of the Shepherd paint a beautiful picture of seeking out and finding a lost lamb, one he cares for and loves.

God seeks you out as well. Not only for salvation—though that is the most important reason—but to care for you.

He searches the areas of your life where you are distant from him—the areas of pain that you fear showing him—so he can protect you from danger and heal your wounds.

When you feel lost, afraid, or alone, God is right there for you. And he rejoices when you return to him, because you are his treasure—truly valuable and loved.

This morning, praise God that he is your treasure as well.

*Dear God, this morning I thank you for treasuring me.
I cherish you and commit myself to discovering
just how priceless you are. Amen.*

THE SEEKERS

*From heaven the Lord looks down to see if
anyone is wise enough to search for him.*
Psalm 14:2 CEV

What do you think God is looking for when he peers down from heaven? Why do you suppose God would bother to look away from the glorious beauty of his celestial home?

> *God is with those
> who obey him.*
> Psalm 14:5 GNT

Some may believe that his intention is to catch us doing something we shouldn't, but that's not the case. Rather, what God is observing is something very precious to him—he's watching for people who are looking for him. He's searching for seekers who know that there's more to this life than the affairs of this world.

Are you seeking God? He's looking down from heaven at you. He loves the fact that you want to know him.

*God, I want to love you with all my heart.
Thank you for all the ways you make yourself
known to me. Amen.*

OF GOD OR MEN?

*You are not setting your mind on
God's interests, but man's.*
MATTHEW 16:23 NASB

*There you shall be
rescued; there the
LORD will redeem you.
. . . But they do not
know the thoughts of
the LORD; they do not
understand his plan.*

MICAH 4:10, 12 ESV

It is difficult to watch people you love choose courses that are fraught with challenges or experience a very painful trial. Sometimes you will not understand what God is doing in them, and you will want to safeguard them from experiencing distress.

God may have an important purpose for their circumstances that you are not aware of.

It is okay when you do not comprehend what God is doing, but it is not acceptable to hinder him. Today, do not shield your loved ones from trials. Rather, pray for and support them.

*Dear God, I pray for my hurting loved ones. Thank you
for doing important things in their lives. Please
show me how to encourage them. Amen.*

WORTHY OF HIS HOUSE

Lord, who may abide in Your tent?
Who may dwell on Your holy hill?
PSALM 15:1 NASB

Who is fit for heaven? What does it take to be close to God? Psalm 15 says that you must be blameless, virtuous, and truthful, and never speak badly of others. You must never accept money that comes from taking advantage of others, you must keep your oaths, and you must never do any wrong.

Whoever does these things will always be secure.
PSALM 15:5 GNT

Does this sound unfeasible? In a sense, it's supposed to be. Your failings were meant to show you that it's impossible for people to make themselves fit for heaven. You must depend on Jesus to make you worthy of his house. He makes you completely fit. Believe in him.

God, thank you for preparing me to live in heaven with you. Thank you for making the impossible possible for me. Amen.

HUMBLY ACCEPTING HIS TEACHING

I will instruct you and teach you in the way you should go.
PSALM 32:8 ESV

I pay careful attention as you lead me, and I follow closely. As soon as you command, I do what you say.

PSALM 119:59–60 CEV

It is truly marvelous when God answers your prayers and fulfills the promises you've waited so long for. Though you know that everything is possible with God, his work is transformed from an intellectual fact to a deep peace within you. Faith fills your heart.

God is teaching you. You realize that he was guiding you when the path seemed strange; he was working when you couldn't see his hand.

God teaches you as much when he fulfills his promise as while you're waiting. This morning, accept his direction. When you look back, you'll see how he adjusted your path and how today's obedience was integral to tomorrow's blessings.

Dear God, I look forward to following your instruction today. Thank you for guiding me in the way I should go. Amen.

BLESSINGS AHEAD

*LORD, You are my portion and my cup
[of blessing]; You hold my future.*
PSALM 16:5 HCSB

Caught in traffic and feeling the anxiety of the things you have to accomplish today, the only thing ahead seems to be the unblinking red taillights of the car in front of you. You're stopped—stuck—with responsibilities behind you and more before you.

I will always look to you, as you stand beside me and protect me from fear.
PSALM 16:8 CEV

Friend, this situation is frustrating because you cannot see any relief or reward in the future, but don't make the mistake of thinking that things will never change. God is going to bless your hard work and faithfulness.

Go to God for comfort and draw your strength from him. Be patient and keep watch. Soon enough, the light will turn green on all of your blessings.

*God, thank you for holding my future and planning
wonderful blessings ahead. Even though I cannot
see them, I trust that you'll provide them. Amen.*

CHOOSING THE INFLUENCE

The Law of the LORD makes them happy,
and they think about it day and night.
PSALM 1:2 CEV

They are like trees growing beside a stream, trees that produce fruit in season and always have leaves. Those people succeed in everything they do.

PSALM 1:3 CEV

What influences you? From where do you receive information? Psalm 1 draws an interesting distinction between people who chase after temporary things and those who look to God.

It may seem appropriate to study the newest techniques or listen to the latest guru to help you accomplish your goals. However, though some of their strategies may have some value, they will not have the enduring results that God promises.

Meditate on the Bible and drink in the principles that nourish your soul and help you find success. Your accomplishments will not be based on earthly things that pass away, but on a lasting foundation that is eternal.

Dear God, I choose you as my influence and meditate on the Bible. Thank you for accomplishing wonderful, eternal things through me. Amen.

COMFORT IN GOD

I have set the LORD always before me: because he is at my right hand, I shall not be moved.
PSALM 16:8 KJV

You live with a daily onslaught of tragic news from around the world and close to home—sad images from the television, heartbreaking stories from a dear friend. These hard realities can rob you of your joy and replace it with fear.

You must constantly bolster your hope in the eternal love and protection of God, who guides you always. His power touches your heart, mind, and soul. This mystery of God's daily work in your life is beyond your ability to understand. It is the great mystery of life that you are, as a child of God and a tabernacle of his Spirit, mighty and invincible. You can lay your fears to rest. You can give God your cares and burdens and place your trust completely in him.

You have turned for me my mourning into dancing; You have put off my sackcloth and clothed me with gladness, To the end that my glory may sing praise to You and not be silent.
PSALM 30:11–12 NKJV

God, all I have and all I am come from you. I place myself wholly in your will and know you will care for me and quiet my fears. Amen.

BY HIS SPIRIT

"Not by might nor by power, but by my Spirit,"
says the Lord Almighty.
ZECHARIAH 4:6 NIV

I'm filled with God's power, filled with God's Spirit of justice and strength.

MICAH 3:8 MSG

As you awoke this morning, what was on your mind? Was it the challenge you will face today? Are there problems you need to confront—issues that are too massive for you to handle?

God knows everything that concerns you today. And though you may not be able to conquer the difficulties on your own, God strengthens and enables you to face them by his Spirit.

You don't have to rely on your own strength and wisdom; God provides his boundless resources to you. No matter what is ahead today, take heart. You will be amazed by what you can accomplish when your work is empowered by God's Spirit.

Dear God, thank you that the things ahead today are conquerable by your Spirit. Thank you for giving me your strength and wisdom. Amen.

A TIME FOR REST

With all my heart, I will celebrate,
and I can safely rest.
PSALM 16:9 CEV

Rest is a variety of activities that includes loafing, goofing off, hanging out, wandering around, sauntering, and killing time. Rest is that restorative time where you play, leaving obligations and responsibilities on your desk for a while. You just let things happen. You go for undirected walks in your imaginations where you are like a small child, ready for the next adventure to turn up.

> *You let me rest in fields of green grass. You lead me to streams of peaceful water, and you refresh my life.*
> PSALM 23:2–3 CEV

For a while you can let go of your cares and skip along behind God. Who knows what will happen? You can wear a different pair of spectacles that let you see things as if they were new. You can be like a butterfly on a summer day. Doing nothing can revive a waning spirit, and it's best done in the security and comfort of God's love.

God, teach me to let myself rest in your love and care,
releasing every burden to you. Amen.

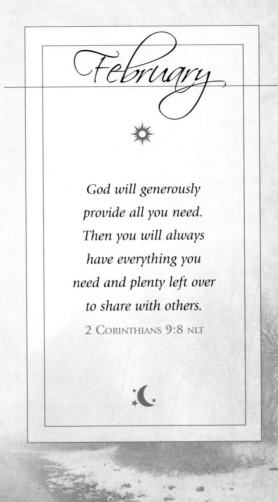

February

*God will generously
provide all you need.
Then you will always
have everything you
need and plenty left over
to share with others.*

2 CORINTHIANS 9:8 NLT

A BETTER PERSPECTIVE

*Love each other as brothers and sisters and
honor others more than you do yourself.*
ROMANS 12:10 CEV

Are there people in your life with whom you have a conflict? Do you have expectations of how they will react to you when you see them?

Whether those expectations are positive or negative, your responsibility is to love those people and honor them above yourself.

The apostle Paul did so by trying to understand other people's points of view. He knew if he could see from their perspective, he could better represent Christ to them.

*I entered their world
and tried to experience
things from their point
of view. I've become
just about every sort
of servant there is in
my attempts to lead
those I meet into a
God-saved life.*

1 CORINTHIANS 9:22
MSG

Expect the best of those people when you see them today, and give them the benefit of the doubt. Not only will you have a better perspective about them, you will better represent Christ.

*Dear God, help me to see things from other people's perspective so
that I can truly represent you well when I see them today. Amen.*

THE PATH OF LIFE

You have shown me the path to life, and you make me glad by being near to me. Sitting at your right side, I will always be joyful.
PSALM 16:11 CEV

There's a big difference between those who make promises and those who actually keep them. There are many who guarantee that their product or belief system will bring you happiness in this life. Unfortunately, their solutions are only temporary. They disregard that your nature is eternal and fail to give you real contentment.

My heart is glad and my glory rejoices; my flesh also will dwell securely. For You will not abandon my soul.
PSALM 16:9–10 NASB

But God not only gives you joy in this life, he's actively preparing you for eternity. You can trust him to show you the truly wonderful path of your future.

God keeps his promises forever and knows what will bring real peace and joy to your soul. Follow him. You'll find the way lined with unending blessings.

God, I confess that I've sought temporary fixes for the hunger of my soul. Thank you for showing me the joyous path of everlasting life. Amen.

PAUL, A PRISONER

I, Paul, am a prisoner for the sake of Christ.
PHILEMON 1:1 MSG

We continually remember before our God and Father your work produced by faith, your labor prompted by love, and your endurance inspired by hope in our Lord Jesus Christ.

1 THESSALONIANS 1:3 NIV

Paul had been telling people about Jesus. This angered the religious leaders, and they had him arrested. Undoubtedly, those who had been blessed by his ministry were heartbroken. What a shame that this great man had been imprisoned—prevented from doing God's work.

Or was he? Paul did not waste the time God had given him as a prisoner. He wrote letters to encourage the churches. And those letters—now a vital, irreplaceable part of the New Testament—have encouraged churches and taught Christians throughout the ages.

Paul's work was more meaningful than even he could have imagined. Remember that the next time you feel locked away. God has an eternal purpose for putting you where you are.

Dear God, this morning I thank you that in every real and symbolic prison, you are still working out your wonderful will. Amen.

EXONERATED

May my vindication come from you;
may your eyes see what is right.
PSALM 17:2 NIV

Whether they're being intentionally destructive or just foolish, some people can make terrible decisions. Unfortunately, their choices can seriously harm your character, and you know that if you continue to associate with them, you'll be dishonoring God.

Your love is wonderful. By your power you save those who trust you from their enemies.
PSALM 17:7 NCV

When you're in such a situation, your only acceptable course of action will be to walk away. Of course, you'll wonder if the opposition you'll face is worth it. Friend, just remember that your first responsibility is to God. If he shows you that leaving is the right thing to do, you have no reason to fear. God will make the justice of your choice known in due time.

God, I'm scared, but I want to honor you. Please protect me and vindicate me. Please show me what I should do. Amen.

WHOLEHEARTED WORK

Whatever you do, do your work heartily,
as for the Lord rather than for men.
COLOSSIANS 3:23 NASB

I would rather be a doorkeeper in the house of my God than dwell in the tents of wickedness. . . . No good thing will He withhold from those who walk uprightly.

PSALM 84:10–11 NKJV

God allows situations in your work and life that will make no sense to your dreams—aspirations that you thought had come from him. Nevertheless, God instructs you to carry on as if working for him, rather than dwelling on your circumstances. That is because it is through those situations that he becomes your central focus, and you learn to cling to him above all other things—including your ambitions.

Today, take heart that as long as you serve God, you are doing exactly as you are supposed to. Even if you lack work, he has assignments for you to accomplish. Someday soon, he will restore your dreams in a powerful way.

Dear God, thank you for my situation—even though it is confusing to me. I will work wholeheartedly for you. Please bless the work of my hands. Amen.

SWEET VINDICATION

*Show Your marvelous lovingkindness by Your right hand,
O You who save those who trust in You from
those who rise up against them.*

PSALM 17:7 NKJV

Whenever you serve God, there will be those who do not understand your devotion to him and may even oppose what he has commanded you to do. Their heated words and antagonism may be discouraging, but be strong. Continue to do what is right—honoring the Lord.

You have tested my heart; You have visited by night; You have tried me and found nothing [evil].

PSALM 17:3 HCSB

As hard as they try, no one can prevent God from fulfilling his purpose for you. His loving character will shine through you in a manner that they will not be able to deny. Therefore, pray that your adversaries will accept the freedom that God offers. Then, whether or not they decide to follow him, you will have succeeded in doing what is right and keeping your heart clean. That is all the vindication you really need.

*God, I do pray for those who oppose your work in
the world. Help them to accept the truth of your love,
and help me always to honor you. Amen.*

A COURAGEOUS LIFE

*I . . . hope that I will in no way be ashamed, but will
have sufficient courage so that now as
always Christ will be exalted.*

PHILIPPIANS 1:20 NIV

*Live in a way that
brings honor to the
Good News of Christ
. . . standing strong
with one purpose, that
you work together as
one for the faith of
the Good News.*

PHILIPPIANS 1:27 NCV

Sometimes you will have an immense longing for heaven. To be free of suffering, fear, illness, debt, heartbreak, and stress would be just . . . well, heavenly.

This was Paul's condition in prison. His greatest joy was thinking about being with Jesus in heaven—free from persecution and pain. Yet until God called him home, he was determined to live in a manner that honored Christ.

It takes courage to live as a Christian—to face challenges by redirecting your focus from your weaknesses to God's strength. Yet that is what you have been called to do. And you can do it. You can live courageously today. And God will certainly be exalted in you.

*Dear God, I want to live in a way that honors you. Give me
the courage to look past my problems to your power. Amen.*

FINDING FAVOR WITH GOD

Keep me as the apple of Your eye;
hide me under the shadow of Your wings.
PSALM 17:8 NKJV

Parents try never to have favorites among their children. With the birth of each child comes a love tailor-made just for him or her. The biblical David, however, unabashedly assumed he was the apple of God's eye. He assumed he was a favored son. From that place of special favor, he asked for God's protection. In intimate language, he depicted a mother hen covering her hatchlings—whenever startled, the chicks run toward their mother, and she lifts a protective wing to hide them.

Please, LORD, save us;
please, LORD, give us
success. God bless the
one who comes in the
name of the LORD. We
bless all of you from
the Temple of the LORD.
PSALM 118:25–26 NCV

You, too, can be a favored child. He lifts a spreading wing to cover you with warmth and safety, and you can take refuge in his protection. Being a favored son or daughter entitles you to the bounty of God's goodness and grace.

Dear God, you affirm me in many ways. Your power
upholds me and your love enfolds me. You say yes
to me even when I say no to myself. Amen.

THE DEFENDER SEES

Nothing is concealed that will not be revealed,
or kept secret that will not become known.
MATTHEW 10:26 AMP

Wake up! Come and defend me! My God and Lord, fight for me! LORD my God, defend me with your justice. Don't let them laugh at me.

PSALM 35:23–24 NCV

You will occasionally find yourself in situations in which you cannot defend yourself. You may be required to remain quiet in the face of others saying erroneous things about you. Or perhaps you will face the consequences of another's decisions; though you know the folly of their actions, you are not in a position to question what they are doing.

This morning, take heart. Remember that God knows everything about your situation and that he is in control. Be confident that he will defend you when you can't speak up for yourself and that he will bring the truth to light. He knows the good you've done and will not let you down.

Dear God, thank you for caring about me.
You are my great defender, and I know that you
will bring the truth to light. Amen.

HEAVEN

*When I awake in heaven, I will be fully
satisfied, for I will see you face to face.*
PSALM 17:15 TLB

Y ou use the word *heaven* to refer
to the joyous fulfillment of the
purpose of your life—union with
God. Certainly life offers you many
fleeting foretastes of heaven, yet your
present life is truly only preparation
for the ultimate reward God has
for you. All the pain, care, and
imperfections of life will fall away.
The restless yearning that goads and
prods you will be gone at last. You and your loved ones will
be permanently reunited. All your errors will be forgiven. All
distance between you and love will be erased.

*God is good, and
he loves goodness;
the godly shall
see his face.*

PSALM 11:7 TLB

You will have perfect rest and happiness and complete freedom from want and anxiety. Let heaven keep you going as you
allow God's unbreakable promise to lead you through this life
to the joy that is in him.

*God, thank you for heaven and all that it
holds for me and for those I love. Amen.*

85

GROWING CLOSER WITH FORGIVENESS

*Her sins, which are many, have been
forgiven, for she loved much.*
LUKE 7:47 NASB

*O Lord, you are
so good, so ready to
forgive, so full of
unfailing love for all
who ask your aid.*

PSALM 86:5 NLT

Asking for forgiveness required humility, but the sinful woman was well aware of her neediness. She also knew that only Jesus could give her what she most wanted—relief from her guilt. As she wiped his feet with her tears, she received something unexpected—her heart began to overflow with love.

You grow closer to God when you receive his forgiveness. When you allow him to heal your deepest guilt, the freedom he gives produces a great spring of love in you. And that love results in profound worship.

This morning, experience his forgiveness and the wonderful overflow of his love.

*Dear God, please forgive my sin. Thank you for
giving me freedom so that I can grow closer to you
and experience your wonderful love. Amen.*

LOVING GOD

*I love you, LORD; you are my strength. The LORD is my rock,
my fortress, and my savior; my God is my rock,
in whom I find protection.*
PSALM 18:1–2 NLT

God's grandeur inspires awe. His perfect goodness is imponderable. He is so big; you are so small. He is beyond your understanding. How then can you love him? By embracing him and making him part of your daily life

To do that, you must first acknowledge your utter dependence on him. You must remind yourself that his handiwork is everywhere and in everything, and that he is greater than the most marvelous thing you can imagine. You must wake up to the truth that you are important because he made you, he loves you, he protects you, and he preserves you. He is your strength.

*Let all those who seek
You rejoice and be
glad in You: Let such
as love Your salvation
say continually, "The
LORD be magnified!"*

PSALM 40:16 NKJV

*God, help me to end each day by whispering an amen to
you as I go to sleep and to wake up each morning
with a hallelujah in my heart. Amen.*

PRACTICE AND PERFECTION

*If we love each other, God lives in us, and his love
is brought to full expression in us.*
1 JOHN 4:12 NLT

*May the Lord make
your love for each
other and for everyone
else grow by leaps
and bounds.*

1 THESSALONIANS 3:12
CEV

Love is a gift from God that must be used in order to be useful. The more you love others, the more your capacity to love will grow. The more you sacrifice for others, the more deeply you will care for all people.

You also have the wonderful promise that if you love others, God—the source of love—lives in you. The more you practice his unfailing love, the more his presence is perfected in you.

The blessing of love is twofold. Love others, and not only will your love grow, but God—the spring from which all love flows—will show himself more powerfully within you. Love is a dynamic force. Love reaches out to others and is God's energy in action.

*Dear God, thank you for your loving presence.
Help me practice being loving toward others so that
your love is fully expressed through me. Amen.*

WHEN YOU PRAY

My cry to him reached his ears. Then the earth reeled and rocked;
the foundations also of the mountains trembled and quaked.
PSALM 18:6–7 ESV

David was thankful. As he recalled the many times God had delivered him from dangerous foes, he could not help but testify about the Lord's unfailing faithfulness. Whatever the situation, no matter how dire the trial, God *always* answered his prayers.

He took me to a safe place. Because he delights in me, he saved me.

PSALM 18:19 NCV

However, you may wonder what happens when *you* pray. Does God respond to you as he did David? Yes, he does. He moves heaven and earth to answer anyone who calls to him with faith and sincerity. Although his reply may not be what you expect, he never fails to do what is in your best interest and what will ultimately fulfill his purpose for you. Therefore, call out to the Lord with whatever concerns you. David found him exceedingly faithful, and there is no doubt you will too.

God, thank you for hearing my prayers and for answering
me as you did King David. Truly, you are faithful,
loving, and worthy of all my praise. Amen.

WHAT GROWS FROM YOUR TEARS

He who goes out weeping, bearing the seed for sowing, shall come home with shouts of joy, bringing his sheaves with him.
PSALM 126:6 ESV

Our mouths filled with laughter, and our tongues with singing. Then they said among the nations, The Lord has done great things for them.

PSALM 126:2 AMP

Sometimes the tears just flow. Burdens get so heavy and decisions so difficult that your natural response is to weep.

God knows the tears you have cried, and he honors every one of them by transforming them into seeds of hope. He produces a harvest of virtues within you—righteousness, humility, faith, and perseverance all grow from your weeping.

Rejoice that your tears are not in vain. God cultivates each glistening drop and transforms it into a blessing. When you see what God has done in you and how he has worked in your situation, you will also have a harvest of truly unshakable joy.

Dear God, I praise you that one day I will shout with joy over the harvest of virtues you have produced from my tears. Amen.

A PERSONAL PASSAGE

*He reached down from on high and took hold
of me; he drew me out of deep waters.*
PSALM 18:16 NIV

Each life is a uniquely personal passage, a journey through time. As you travel through difficult places, you need not give in to hopelessness. God is able to bring you safely to your destination when you place your trust in him.

You will show me the way of life, granting me the joy of your presence and the pleasures of living with you forever.

PSALM 16:11 NLT

God is the Author of each journey. He knows the way through every dark and frightening valley. He knows the safest path along each high and treacherous mountain trail. God knows where the cool, refreshing waters flow and where you can find the provisions to meet each of your needs. He shares the weight of the burden you carry and causes you to lie down and rest in lush green meadows. He gives you hope and courage as you walk with him, step by step, one day at a time.

God, as I face the challenges of my personal journey through life, I am thankful for your presence that guides and protects me. Amen.

EXALT HIM

Honor and majesty surround him;
strength and joy fill his dwelling.
1 CHRONICLES 16:27 NLT

Make a joyful noise to the Lord, all you lands! Serve the Lord with gladness! Come before His presence with singing!

PSALM 100:1–2 AMP

God is exalted above all of creation. He is the King of kings —the mighty sovereign of everything that exists. He is the Lord of lords—the able protector and provider for all he surveys.

He deserves your praise. His goodness and love are like a never-ending spring quenching your thirst. His holiness and wisdom bring joy to your heart. There is nothing too difficult for your God— and no good thing he would withhold from you.

Exalt God today with your praise, and call to him whenever you are overwhelmed. He can overcome any problem you have, and he thoroughly delights in your songs of trust.

My God and my King, you are beautiful in my sight. I praise you for your holiness and strength. Thank you for loving me. Amen.

HEMMED IN, SET FREE

He brought me out to a wide-open place;
He rescued me because He delighted in me.
PSALM 18:19 HCSB

Some days you'll wonder how you got to where you are—completely entangled in the strong cords of duty and difficulty. You've been following God, and you can't understand why he'd allow the weight of your burdens to crush you in such a way. You feel that if another problem comes to you, you'll break.

The LORD rewarded me according to my righteousness; according to the cleanness of my hands He has recompensed me.

PSALM 18:20 NKJV

Don't despair, friend. God hemmed you in for a reason. He's bringing you into a place of freedom, but first he must teach you to trust him for today.

Stop worrying about the future and focus on honoring God with the task that's in front of you. He loves you and will set you free.

God, I thank you for teaching me to trust you during this difficult time. Help me to honor you in all that I do. Amen.

A HEAVENLY ACCORD

God . . . sent Christ to make peace between himself and us, and he has given us the work of making peace between himself and others.
2 CORINTHIANS 5:18 CEV

> *God was in Christ, offering peace and forgiveness to the people of this world. And he has given us the work of sharing his message about peace.*
>
> 2 CORINTHIANS 5:19 CEV
>
> ☀

An important truth is that *God accepts you.*

His acceptance began in heaven with his desire to have a relationship with you. He provided the way to have that relationship through Jesus, and the communication that keeps the relationship healthy through his Holy Spirit. God made it possible for you to be united with him in peace.

Tell people. Today, tell others of how God has done wondrous things to show how he accepts you—and them too. It is a heavenly accord they will want to be in on.

Dear God, thank you for making peace between us. I look forward to sharing that peace with others today. Amen.

TAKING YOU HIGHER UP

He makes me like a deer that does not stumble;
he helps me stand on the steep mountains.
PSALM 18:33 NCV

There are certain things that you can learn only by doing them. No amount of explanation of geological formations can prepare a young deer or goat for getting up to the apex of a mountain. Rather, the deer or goat must strengthen its muscles by actually climbing.

You have also given me the shield of Your salvation, and Your right hand upholds me; and Your gentleness makes me great.

PSALM 18:35 NASB

Likewise, your faith can only grow in the midst of the doubts and unknowns of your circumstances. You exercise your trust in God, and he strengthens your spiritual muscles so that you can reach higher and achieve more with him.

When you follow God, life is a wonderful adventure. So get ready for the climb, friend. The view is truly worth it.

God, thank you for training me for the heights
through my circumstances. I know that with you
I'll achieve all I've been created for. Amen.

A UNIQUE PEACE

I give you peace, the kind of peace that only I can give. It isn't like the peace that this world can give. So don't be worried or afraid.
JOHN 14:27 CEV

The LORD will give strength to His people; The LORD will bless His people with peace.

PSALM 29:11 NKJV

Peace, by the world's standard, is defined by absence of conflict and achieved by abundance of strength. It is easy to assume that you should only go to God when you are strong or on your best behavior.

You don't have to be tough or without troubles in order to have peace. God gives you peace when you feel tired and weak—even when you've failed. That is because it is when you are vulnerable that you are truly receptive to him.

God gives you perfect, unfaltering peace through the protective power of the Holy Spirit. This morning, rest calmly in the strength of God.

Dear God, thank you for the unique peace you give to those who trust in you. I will not be afraid knowing you protect me. Amen.

THE BUILDER OF GREATNESS

Your gentleness has made me great.
PSALM 18:35 NKJV

God uses each challenge you experience to mold you into a person of significance and excellence. This does not imply he is making you wealthy or famous by the world's standards; rather, it means he is preparing you to reveal his glory. Perhaps this seems unlikely to you. Maybe you once thought yourself special, but the years have destroyed the dreams that once thrilled your heart. Yet just as God took the shepherd David and made him a king, he can lift you out of your ordinary situation and reveal your wonderful potential, if you will let him.

LORD, You light my lamp; my God illuminates my darkness. With You I can attack a barrier, and with my God I can leap over a wall.
PSALM 18:28–29 HCSB

Will you accept the trials that come as his training and allow him to build greatness in you? It is your choice. So embrace the future that is better than you can imagine.

God, thank you for seeing more in me than I see in myself.
I trust you to use every situation to develop your godly
excellence in me. To you be all the glory. Amen.

ENCOURAGED AND HOPEFUL

*Hope does not disappoint, because the love of God has been
poured out within our hearts through the Holy Spirit.*
ROMANS 5:5 NASB

*Let us rejoice and exult
in our hope of experi-
encing and enjoying
the glory of God.*

ROMANS 5:2 AMP

True hope is hard won. It begins with the daily pressures you face. Through them, you grapple with the truth of God—who he is and what he has promised.

Pressures produce perseverance—the ability to keep going and be patient because you see that God has never let you down. And that perseverance produces character, because your life is not based on daily changes but on God's eternal truth.

That truth produces hope, which does not disappoint because you have seen his goodness.

Through it all you know him and love him more—and that is truly a reason to feel encouraged and hopeful.

*Dear God, today I praise you for pouring out your
love and giving me hope. Even in the daily pressures,
you are doing wonderful things. Amen.*

A STORY TO TELL

The heavens declare the glory of God,
and the sky above proclaims his handiwork.
PSALM 19:1 ESV

All the wonders of the heavens declare the glory of God and proclaim his exquisite handiwork. And guess what? You do too.

When you believe in God, you become a living psalm, a walking demonstration that he exists, he is faithful, and he does all things well. People will experience his presence

Let my words and
my thoughts be
pleasing to you,
LORD, because you
are my mighty rock
and my protector.
PSALM 19:14 CEV

through the words you speak, your attitude, and even your actions toward them. They will realize that the God of grace loves them and wants to illuminate their life with his joy, mercy, and salvation. Is that what you are saying with your life? Are you shining brightly as a light to those who need God's hope? You have a story to tell, so do it well. It may make an eternal difference to those who hear you.

God, I am so inspired to tell others your story. Guide
my words and my heart so that I can honor you and
encourage others to know you as well. Amen.

UNCHANGING HEAVENLY LIGHT

I am GOD—yes, I AM. I haven't changed.
MALACHI 3:6 MSG

Every good gift and every perfect gift is from above, coming down from the Father of lights with whom there is no variation or shadow due to change.

JAMES 1:17 ESV

One of God's wonderful attributes is that he does not change—which is why you can have absolute confidence in him and patiently wait for whatever he has promised you.

God has never misled anyone, and he has never failed to fulfill his promises. Though sometimes he will allow you to wait in order to build your faith, his promise remains sure.

Just as he faithfully gave Abraham, Joseph, and David their heart's desires after they had waited, he will do the same for you. Be patient, and let this truth light your way when it seems dark. God has not changed his mind concerning you—and he never will.

Dear God, this is the light I keep for the dark times—you never change. Thank you for the promises that you are perfecting for me. Amen.

JOY OF THE BRIDEGROOM

The sun comes out like a bridegroom from his bedroom.
It rejoices like an athlete eager to run a race.
PSALM 19:5 NCV

The above verse paints a word-picture of a new day bursting forth into the world with the joy and vigor of a bridegroom fresh from his wedding chamber. The anticipation of a new day is like the joy of an athlete ready to go. In the brightness, you sense God pouring out an unquenchable love.

The LORD God is a sun and shield: the LORD will give grace and glory: no good thing will he withhold from them that walk uprightly. O LORD of hosts, blessed is the man that trusteth in thee.
PSALM 84:11–12 KJV

Each new day bears God's stamp of approval that he sees in his creation. Each new day is delivered to you like a wrapped package that contains the gift of life. The very air you breathe bears witness to his overwhelming kindness toward you. Let every sunrise remind you of the unique opportunity to praise him. Let every race or athletic competition remind you of your praiseworthy God. There will never be another day just like today.

God, thank you for those small daily happenings that make life so spectacular. Help me celebrate the holiness of the common day. Amen.

OUT OF THE DEEP

He reached down from on high and took hold of me;
He pulled me out of deep waters.
PSALM 18:16 HCSB

He brought me out
to a wide-open place;
He rescued me
because He
delighted in me.

PSALM 18:19 HCSB

Difficult days come unexpectedly —as a flood. You cannot plan for them; neither can you prepare for how they affect you. Though outside, unexpected forces may be their cause, they mainly come through the common things of life. The abundance of small, daily problems can inundate your soul.

Even as the waters of adversity rage, remember that God is your great lifeguard and that he is able to rescue you. Turn each problem—each drowning drop of difficulty—over to him this morning. Surely he will lift you out of the overwhelming waters and bring you out to a spacious place where you can breathe.

Dear God, thank you for rescuing me out of
any deep wave of difficulty that comes my
way. I truly delight in you. Amen.

LOVE FOR HIS WORD

The statutes of the LORD are right, rejoicing the heart.
PSALM 19:8 NKJV

Of all the books in the world, none has endured as well or changed as many lives as the Bible. That is because it is God's unique revelation of himself. Through his Word and his Spirit within you, you get to know your Creator, you are able to receive his comfort and direction, and you discover how to live a life that is pleasing to him.

The judgments of the LORD are true; they are completely right. They are worth more than gold, even the purest gold. They are sweeter than honey, even the finest honey. By them your servant is warned. Keeping them brings great reward.
PSALM 19:9–11 NCV

Are you reading the psalms as you are reading this devotional? God wants to give you joy through this wonderful love letter he has inspired for your edification. Embrace this treasure trove of wisdom and allow him to change your life through it. Certainly it is the best book you will ever read.

God, I praise you for your wonderful Word. Create a love for your precepts and promises in me and help me to know you better through it. Amen.

WHEN OTHERS SEEK
YOUR KINDNESS

*Please promise me in the LORD's name that you will
be as kind to my family as I have been to you.*
JOSHUA 2:12 CEV

*Have reverence for
Christ in your hearts,
and honor him as
Lord. Be ready at all
times to answer any-
one who asks you
to explain the hope
you have in you.*

1 PETER 3:15 GNT

As the great army of Israelites advanced across the Promised Land, word spread about the mighty, powerful God who helped them conquer every foe.

Many—understanding that the Israelites served the one true God—pledged their help and allegiance in return for the Israelites' assurance of kindness and safety.

Today, you will meet with people who will see God's power in you. They will realize there is something very special about the God you serve. They may even ask you questions.

Be kind to them and tell them about the great God who has shown you such profound love. They will find safety in him, and will surely appreciate your helpfulness.

*Dear God, may your goodness shine in me so others will see how
wonderful you are and seek your kindness and security. Amen.*

HUMBLY BEFORE HIM

Let the words of my mouth and the meditation of my heart be acceptable in Your sight, O LORD, my strength and my Redeemer.
PSALM 19:14 NKJV

Do you ever feel uncomfortable when talking to God? Does communicating with him intimidate you? You don't have to be afraid of expressing yourself, because God wants you to be honest with him. Still, it's good to be reverent when praying to the One who created you. How do you do that? You ask God to show you.

The statutes of the LORD are trustworthy, making wise the simple. The precepts of the LORD are right, giving joy to the heart.
PSALM 19:7–8 NIV

✷☽✷

There's nothing wrong with asking God to help you honor his majesty. Seek his wisdom and instruction. He's certainly able to show you what an honest, worshipful, humble heart looks like. Don't be afraid. God delights in teaching you how to have a deeper relationship with him.

God, I want my words and thoughts to be acceptable to you. Please teach me how to honor you and love you more. Amen.

A WORK OF HIS HANDS

The LORD will fulfill [His purpose] for me.
LORD, Your love is eternal.
PSALM 138:8 HCSB

LORD my God, You have done many things—Your wonderful works and Your plans for us; none can compare with You.
If I were to report and speak [of them], they are more than can be told.

PSALM 40:5 HCSB

☀

This morning, are you pondering what God is doing in your life? You may not know, and that is okay. However, the real question is this: Do you have confidence that God knows where he is leading you?

Your hope should not be based on your understanding of God's purpose for you. Rather, your faith should be firmly grounded in God, who is bringing it about in you. Even if that purpose seems distant, you still trust him to bring you successfully to the destination.

It is his able hand—not yours—that works out his plans. Trust him to do exactly what is needed to bring them to fulfillment.

Dear God, I trust that you are a faithful and able leader. Thank you that my future is a work in your hands. Amen.

A PRAYER FOR YOU

*May he give you the desire of your heart
and make all your plans succeed.*

PSALM 20:4 NIV

Friend, today these words rise up to God on your behalf. As you go, may he answer your prayers and protect you from trouble. May he make you aware of the many amazing ways he's working around you and empowering you—giving you wisdom and creativity—for all of your tasks.

We will shout for joy over your victory and celebrate your triumph by praising our God. May the LORD answer all your requests.

PSALM 20:5 GNT

May God remember all the ways you've served him faithfully. May he give you the desire of your heart and bring success to all your plans.

Today these words rise up to God that you would trust him and commit to obeying him. May all who know you praise God for the magnificent victories he gives you.

*God, thank you for this prayer today, and
for giving me success. May my life bring you
much praise, for you are truly worthy. Amen.*

YOU HAVE YOUR BEING

You are worthy, our Lord and God, to receive glory . . .
for you created all things, and by your will they
were created and have their being.

REVELATION 4:11 NIV

You know me inside and out, you know every bone in my body; You know exactly how I was made, bit by bit, how I was sculpted from nothing into something.

PSALM 139:15 MSG

As you look into the mirror this morning, embrace this wonderful truth: God created everything about you. Your talents, personality, looks—the details that make you unique—were lovingly chosen by God.

This may cause you some astonishment if there are things about yourself that you don't like. However, you are precious to God. Everything he has given you—every facet of who you are—is lovely to him.

He built you with remarkable potential and has made no mistakes in constructing you. As you peer into the mirror, praise him for how he made you. He is truly a wonderful Creator.

Dear God, you really are worthy to receive glory.
Thank you for loving me inside and out, and for
how wonderfully you have created me. Amen.

AUTHENTIC POWER

Some nations boast of their chariots and horses,
but we boast in the name of the LORD our God.
PSALM 20:7 NLT

Imagine being a soldier on the field of battle. The enemy armies of Ammon and Aram are thundering toward you with armaments of war that you've only heard of in stories. There are so many of them and so few of you—how can you possibly hope to triumph? Yet such was one of the many battles David fought and won in God's strength.

I know that the Lord saves His anointed; He will answer him from His holy heaven with the saving strength of His right hand.
PSALM 20:6 AMP

Did you face a battle today in which the resources of your adversary far outpaced your own? Do not fear—God is with you. Their combat assets may create the illusion of power, but nothing can overcome the mighty strength of the Lord. Trust him for your victory.

God, yours is the only authentic power, so I
have nothing to fear. Thank you for bringing
me victory in this situation. Amen.

A HEARING STANCE

The Lord is in His holy temple; let all the earth hush and keep silence before Him.
HABAKKUK 2:20 AMP

It is good that he waits silently for the salvation of the LORD.

LAMENTATIONS 3:26
NASB

This morning, before the daily commotion begins, find a place where you can be very quiet before God. Relinquish to God as an offering the things that fill your mind. Offer yourself as well, and listen.

Picture yourself before God's great throne. Imagine him in his holy temple. Is anything impossible for God?

Let his Spirit speak deeply to your heart. What is he teaching you? Do you need forgiveness? Ask him. Does praise fill your heart? Sing.

Keep silent before him, and fully enjoy the presence of the Lord God. Get yourself into a hearing stance, and he will surely give you the very words of life.

Dear God, I sit before you in quiet and joyful expectation. Truly, you are God. Show yourself in a mighty way through the stillness. Amen.

VICTORY IS HIS GOAL

How the king rejoices in your strength, O LORD!
He shouts with joy because of your victory.
PSALM 21:1 NLT

It's not necessary to understand why God leads you in a certain way—it's only necessary to obey him. Trust him even when he appears to direct you away from your goal.

You have given him his heart's desire and have not withheld the request of his lips.

PSALM 21:2 AMP

This may not seem logical, but there are factors that affect your situation that you simply cannot see. Fortunately, God is well aware of those influences, and he sees the path ahead of you. He knows exactly what you will need to succeed.

So trust him and obey his instruction. Soon enough, all of his seemingly illogical directions will reveal the straightest path to your triumph. And you'll find that your victory was his goal the whole time.

God, thank you for leading me. I trust you even when I don't understand your directions. Thank you that with you, the victory is assured. Amen.

OF YOUR WORD

Let your "Yes" be "Yes," and your "No," "No."
MATTHEW 5:37 NKJV

You'll only hear true and right words from my mouth; not one syllable will be twisted or skewed.

PROVERBS 8:8 MSG

You have heard the sales pitches, slick-talkers, and spin—the exaggerations and downright distortions of the truth. When looking for someone to trust, the search can get disheartening.

When Jesus taught the principle of yes and no, he was talking about being true to your word. When you mean yes, say yes without caveats or lengthy assertions—and then carry out whatever you have committed to do.

You will be a trustworthy person if you simply stand by your word and fulfill the promises you have made. People will believe what you say, not because of fancy words, but because they will know that you don't say it lightly.

Dear God, today help me to be straightforward in my responses and keep my promises so that I will be a trustworthy person. Amen.

OF PRAISE AND POWER

Be exalted, Lord, in Your strength;
we will sing and praise Your power.
PSALM 21:13 AMP

Allow the words to roll from your lips, "Lord, I praise your wonderful power." Say the phrase aloud, "My God, I trust your faultless strength."

You have granted him the desire of his heart and have not withheld the request of his lips. You welcomed him with rich blessings.

PSALM 21:2–3 NIV

Is this exercise of adoration difficult for you tonight? Is there an issue weighing on your heart that prevents you from adoring the Lord? If so, it is even more essential for you to turn your thoughts away from your suffering and to his sufficiency, to replace the pain of your trials with the reality of his triumph.

Worship the Lord who can and will help you. Rejoice and be glad that he is with you and will never fail. It is when you refocus your attention on him that you will see victory as a possibility. That, friend, is the true power of praise.

God, I want to trust you—so I will praise you with
an open heart. I rejoice in your faultless strength and
know your mighty hand will provide the victory. Amen.

GET UNSTUCK AND BELIEVE

I do believe; help my unbelief.
MARK 9:24 NASB

*All things are possible
to him who believes.*

MARK 9:23 NKJV

Have you ever been stuck between belief and unbelief?

It happens when there is no earthly solution to your dilemma and your only hope is that God will help you. Though you believe that God did miracles in ancient Israel, it is different trusting him to relieve your present-day problem. Can he *really* do it?

You are assured that anything is possible if you will just believe.

Just as he has worked powerfully throughout history, God is present and willing to work in your unique situation as well. Today, get unstuck by letting go of your doubts. Trust God to do the impossible for you, and truly believe.

*Dear God, I do believe that you can do the
impossible and that you will help me in my
circumstances. Thank you. Amen.*

A RECORD OF RESCUE

*Our ancestors trusted you. They trusted, and you
rescued them. They cried to you and were saved.
They trusted you and were never disappointed.*
PSALM 22:4–5 GOD'S WORD

Hundreds of prophecies in the Old Testament predicted the coming of the One who would deliver people from their sins. Psalm 22 contains some of the particulars about the Messiah, and almost a thousand years after it was written

*In the midst of the
assembly I will praise
You. You who fear the
LORD, praise Him!*
PSALM 22:22–23 NKJV

those details came true in the person of Jesus Christ. Jesus is not only the Savior; he is also living proof that the Lord keeps *all* of his promises. Although Psalm 22 is a difficult passage to read, it is also a wonderful reminder that all who trust in him are never disappointed.

Therefore, trust the Lord Jesus to save you from your sins and to rescue you in all of your difficult circumstances. You can count on him, because not only is his record the best—it is perfect.

*God, you are utterly astounding! Thank you for saving
me from my sins and rescuing me from my troubles.
Truly you are worthy of all my praise! Amen.*

STEADFAST TRUST

He will have no fear of bad news;
his heart is steadfast, trusting in the LORD.
PSALM 112:7 NIV

Light arises in the darkness for the up-right. . . . His heart is established and steady, he will not be afraid while he waits to see his desire established.
PSALM 112:4, 8 AMP

There is a confidence that goes beyond whatever has happened in the past or what may come to pass in the future. That confidence comes from trusting in God.

Thomas Manton wrote, "If a man would lead a happy life, let him but seek a sure object for his trust, and he shall be safe."

Nothing in this world is certain, but the person who trusts in God is never disappointed. Every obstacle is an opportunity for God to show his power—every difficulty a way to learn from him and know his comfort.

Do not fear what is ahead. Instead, exercise your steadfast trust in God.

Dear God, even in this world of uncertainties, I will trust in you—the unfaltering and sure focus of my hope and affection. Amen.

ENDING IN PRAISE

In the midst of the congregation will I praise You. You who fear (revere and worship) the Lord, praise Him!
PSALM 22:22–23 AMP

Psalm 22 was written about a thousand years before Jesus was born, but it forecasts many things that happened during his trial and crucifixion. It may appear strange that a psalm that envisions such a difficult event would contain such praise as you find in vv. 22–23. Yet it movingly depicts the hopefulness you can have in your most difficult situations.

Our ancestors trusted you, and you rescued them. When they cried out for help, you saved them, and you did not let them down when they depended on you.

PSALM 22:4–5 CEV

Just as Jesus did not stay in the grave but was gloriously resurrected, the dreams that have died for you will come to life again. You can praise God in the midst of your troubles because death isn't final. Rather, joy and life are your ultimate destination.

God, thank you that I can end in praise because of your wondrous work in my life. To you be all honor and glory. Amen.

STRONG IN THE LORD

Let the mighty strength of the Lord make you strong. Put on all the armor that God gives, so you can defend yourself.
EPHESIANS 6:10–11 CEV

The LORD loves what is right and does not abandon his faithful people. He protects them forever.

PSALM 37:28 GNT

God gives you spiritual armor to protect you as you live for him. It is all tied together with the belt of truth, which keeps you safely on the right path.

As you go, the breastplate of righteousness protects your heart from sin, and the helmet of salvation safeguards your mind with God's great promises. The shield of faith deflects the temptations that wound you, and the gospel gives you peace and purpose. Finally, the sword of the Spirit is your defensive weapon, your preparation for whatever comes.

Today, put on God's armor and stand firm in him. Rejoice that you are clothed in his wonderful and mighty strength.

Dear God, thank you for clothing me in your spiritual armor. With your mighty defense, I know I will be strong and stand firm. Amen.

THE SHEPHERD PROVIDES

The LORD is my shepherd;
I have everything I need.
PSALM 23:1 NCV

Think about the shepherd— how he provides for his sheep. How he finds them water without parasites to quench their thirst. How he'll walk miles to lead them to grass that will nourish them and give them strength.

Surely goodness and mercy shall follow me all the days of my life, and I shall dwell in the house of the LORD forever.

PSALM 23:6 ESV

The gentle shepherd knows when his sheep need rest, and he watches over them while they sleep. With him, they don't fear predators, because he's a strong, skilled protector. Neither do they despair when the terrain is too difficult, because they know the shepherd won't fail them.

Today your Good Shepherd is with you—so don't be afraid. Trust his perfect leadership and unfailing love to keep you, and follow him confidently every day of your life.

God, thank you for being my faithful, compassionate, and wise Shepherd. I will follow you and trust your loving provision and protection. Amen.

BETTER THAN SACRIFICE

*To do righteousness and justice is more
acceptable to the LORD than sacrifice.*
PROVERBS 21:3 NKJV

*Loving him with
all passion and
intelligence and
energy, and loving
others as well as you
love yourself. Why,
that's better than all
offerings and sacrifices
put together!*

MARK 12:33 MSG

In the Old Testament, sacrifices were made to cover sins and maintain a right relationship with God. Yet sometimes people who participated in the rituals were not truly obedient or honest with God. Outwardly they did everything they were supposed to, but inwardly they were no different than those who disobeyed God outright.

The important thing to God is not that you go through the motions of religion, but that you truly know him and love him more every day. Be honest with God today, and obey him. Your genuine change of heart will please him far more than any sacrifice you can dream up.

*Dear God, thank you for caring about the condition of my heart
even more than sacrifices. Help me always to do your will. Amen.*

AT PEACE WITH THE WORLD IN GOD

He makes me to lie down in green pastures; He leads me beside the still waters. He restores my soul.
PSALM 23:2–3 NKJV

Trying to live without God is un-imaginably self-defeating. Living without God makes you vulnerable to every sting, swipe, and bludgeon that may come your way. Despite all the intelligence and cunning that God has gifted you

For God alone, O my soul, wait in silence, for my hope is from him.

PSALM 62:5 ESV

with, if you do not rest in God and place all your hope in him, you won't succeed at anything you do. Failure is impossible with God.

Without God in your life, demons of self-doubt can goad you and undermine your best efforts. Anxiety can eat at you and leave you an easy prey for despair and defeat. Fear and trembling accompany you wherever you go. But with God you are safe and secure. You are swathed in a glow of love and peace. You are able to become all he intended you to be.

God, thank you for giving me victory over the world through my relationship with you. No longer will I be victimized by my own weakness, for when I am weak, you are strong. Amen.

LOVING LIVING

What does the LORD require of you? To act justly and to love mercy and to walk humbly with your God.
MICAH 6:8 NIV

Love the LORD your God and always obey all his laws.
DEUTERONOMY 11:1 GNT

You know you can't earn God's love, but how can you live your life in a manner that honors him and shows him you love him? The prophet Micah gives you some guidance.

First, *act justly*. Be a person of integrity and honesty, and love everyone impartially. Second, *love mercy*. Always model God's compassion and grace to others. Third, *walk humbly with your God*. Acknowledge that God's great wisdom is more than sufficient to guide you as you obey him.

This morning, your life will show how much you love God when you act justly, love mercy, and accept his instruction with humility.

Dear God, help me to love you with my life and reflect your righteousness, compassion, and wisdom so that you will be glorified. Amen.

NO FEAR!

Yea, though I walk through the valley of the shadow of death, I will fear no evil: for thou art with me; thy rod and thy staff they comfort me.
PSALM 23:4 KJV

When the line of clothing called No Fear seized the youth market in the mid-1990s, bumper stickers sporting the logo appeared on cars all across the nation. The designer's slogan appealed to its street-savvy customers. *No Fear* represented a gutsy approach to a life lived to the extreme.

Blessed be the Lord— day after day he carries us along. He's our Savior, our God, oh yes! He's God-for-us, he's God-who-saves-us. Lord GOD knows all death's ins and outs.

PSALM 68:19–20 MSG

But God had the meaning of the slogan first. He's always been in the no-fear business, giving you comfort in the midst of your darkest hours and guiding you back to the right path when you lose your footing. Bravado can't measure up to the heart that has learned the true meaning of having no fear.

Dear God, some of my fears are between my ears, but others are real. Help me know the difference. Teach me to respond to real fear in true faith. Amen.

ARE YOU HIS?

By this all people will know that you are My
disciples, if you have love for one another.
JOHN 13:35 HCSB

I give you a new com-
mandment: love one
another. Just as I have
loved you, you must
also love one another.

JOHN 13:34 HCSB

How do you identify a Christian? Most people would describe a person who obeys a whole list of rules—including being a drug-free teetotaler who dislikes off-color jokes and only watches G-rated movies.

However, the most important defining factor for Christians is how they express their love.

This is because when you love God, you obey him out of respect and caring—not out of ritual or fear. And when you love others, you humbly desire what is best for them—not analyze how they could benefit you.

Show that you are a Christian through your love for others today. People will surely know you are one of his.

Dear God, please increase my love for you and for others,
so that people will know that I truly belong to you. Amen.

DIVINE NOURISHMENT

*You serve me a six-course dinner right in front of my enemies.
You revive my drooping head; my cup brims with blessing.*
PSALM 23:5 MSG

Food gives you the energy to keep going. There's no sign more welcome at the end of a long day on the road than RESTAURANT. Turning in, you anticipate the satisfying meal that waits inside. Cool water, maybe with lemon. Fresh garden salad. Hot bread or rolls. Tasty entrée. Two or three veggies. Perhaps a satisfying dessert.

My soul longs, indeed it faints for the courts of the LORD; my heart and my flesh sing for joy to the living God.

PSALM 84:2 NRSV

In the same way, God allows you to fill up from time spent with him. Some days you may only have time for brief snacks—a hurried prayer, a verse you've memorized. But once you settle in for a full-course spiritual meal, you realize what you've been missing and eat heartily.

*Move in me, dear God, that I may see life from your point
of view. May my spirit listen to your Spirit in all things.
Make me each day more aware of your presence. Amen.*

WINNING WITH PRAISE

*Jehoshaphat appointed men to sing to the LORD
and to praise him for the splendor of his holiness.*
2 CHRONICLES 20:21 NIV

Jehoshaphat then led all the men of Judah and Jerusalem back to Jerusalem—an exuberant parade. GOD had given them joyful relief from their enemies!

2 CHRONICLES 20:27 MSG

When Jehoshaphat was confronted with the armies of Ammon and Moab, he knew that his forces were no match for them. Yet he also knew that God had promised to help him. So as God instructed, Jehoshaphat gathered the people together to praise God.

You may think that this was a strange thing for Jehoshaphat to do. Yet God inhabits the praise of his people and gives them victory through it. With Jehoshaphat, God routed the enemy, and he never had to lift a sword.

He will help you too. Lift your voice in praise to him today, and watch as he helps you in a miraculous way.

*Dear God, I praise the splendor of your
holiness and the glory of your grace. Thank you
for helping me in all my battles. Amen.*

IT'S ENOUGH

The earth is the LORD's, and all it contains,
the world, and those who dwell in it.
PSALM 24:1 NASB

When the Philistine army slew thirty thousand of Israel's soldiers and carried away the holy Ark of the Covenant, the Israelites despaired of ever getting it back. The Philistines were far too powerful—and the Israelites too discouraged.

> GOD *is at their side;*
> *with GOD's help*
> *they make it.*
> PSALM 24:5 MSG

Fortunately, God is never without resources. Through a miraculous series of events, God convinced the Philistines to bring the Ark back to Israel.

Tradition holds that David wrote Psalm 24 to honor the Ark's return to Jerusalem. Israel learned firsthand that God had all the resources necessary to help them.

Embrace that message. Whatever your need, God's provision is more than enough to help you. He's in control; trust him to turn everything around for you.

God, thank you for reminding me that you're in control—there's no need or foe I should fear. Thank you for providing for me. Amen.

AN OPPORTUNITY TO BUILD

*When the builders had finished laying the foundation of the temple,
the priests put on their robes and blew trumpets in honor of the LORD.*
EZRA 3:10 CEV

They took turns singing: "The LORD is good! His faithful love for Israel will last forever." Everyone started shouting and praising the LORD because work on the foundation of the temple had begun.

EZRA 3:11 CEV

It had been fifty years since the temple had been destroyed. The Israelites longed to rebuild it, and when King Cyrus of Persia finally gave them the opportunity to do so, they were filled with great joy.

Any dream worth pursuing requires hard work—and sometimes just beginning the work takes a long time. Yet when you finally see God opening the door for you to pursue your aspirations, it will fill you with delight.

Are you waiting for your opportunity to build? Today take joy that you will soon see the foundation laid. God will be with you every step of the way.

Dear God, thank you for being the skilled architect of my dreams, and that my opportunity to build is just ahead. Amen.

THE MESSAGE IN THE GATES

Lift up your heads, O ye gates; and be ye lift up, ye everlasting doors; and the King of glory shall come in.
PSALM 24:7 KJV

Elaborate gates frame the walled city of Jerusalem. The gates still retain a noble look today, thousands of years after their construction. Though you will pass through thousands of gates and doors in your lifetime, you may not have stopped to consider what they signify. Gates and doorways are points of entry as well as points of exit. They allow people and objects to come in and go out. Gates and doorways protect and defend; they include and exclude.

Enter into his gates with thanksgiving, and into his courts with praise: be thankful unto him, and bless his name. For the LORD is good; his mercy is everlasting; and his truth endureth to all generations.
PSALM 100:4–5 KJV

Open the doorway to your heart and let people enter to find welcome and peace.

Dear God, I know that at the heart of every problem is a problem of the heart. Make my heart a pure and welcoming place. Come into my heart now. Amen.

ANTICIPATING A GLORIOUS FUTURE

I consider that the sufferings of this present time are not worth comparing with the glory that is to be revealed to us.
ROMANS 8:18 ESV

If we are God's children, we will receive blessings from God together with Christ. But we must suffer as Christ suffered so that we will have glory as Christ has glory.

ROMANS 8:17 NCV

This is a promise for you to claim today. Your pressures and trials—however difficult they may be—will be like nothing to you when God's glory is revealed.

Hurts, stresses, and frustrations—they all belong to this world. God uses them for good to teach you character, patience, humility, and faith.

Yet the glory belongs solely to God. It is the achievement of his good plan and the splendor of his presence, and he freely shares both with you.

Claim this promise today, and look forward to the great things God will reveal to you. Anticipate the fabulously glorious future.

Dear God, I can endure my present problems because I know that your plan will be fulfilled and that I will see your wonderful glory. Amen.

THE GOD YOU LOVE

Who is this great king? He is the LORD, strong and mighty, the LORD, victorious in battle.
PSALM 24:8 GNT

Do you love God for what he does or because of who he is? Do you pay him lip service to get what you want, or do you worship him because you are truly in awe of his amazing grace?

The earth is the LORD's, and all it contains, the world, and those who dwell in it.

PSALM 24:1 NASB

Like you, God desires to be loved for himself. He desires that you honor him because he is astoundingly imaginative, unwaveringly kind, steadfastly holy, completely powerful, and wise. He also wants to have a deep, abiding relationship with you so you can experience his unconditional love.

So consider: Why do you seek him? Are you looking for someone to cater to your needs? Or have you realized that you are simply not whole without him in your life? Do you praise him for your sake or for his?

God, I want to love you for who you are—even though my motivation is sometimes misplaced. Help me to know you and love you more every day. Amen.

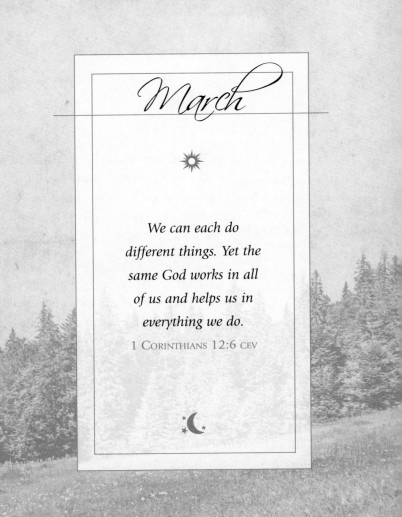

March

We can each do different things. Yet the same God works in all of us and helps us in everything we do.

1 Corinthians 12:6 CEV

SEEING HIS FACE

The LORD look with favor on you and give you peace.
NUMBERS 6:26 HCSB

The Lord bless you and watch, guard, and keep you; the Lord make His face to shine upon and enlighten you and be gracious (kind, merciful, and giving favor) to you.

NUMBERS 6:24–25 AMP

This benediction that God gave as a blessing to the Israelites is given to you this morning. May God bless your day by showing himself to you and giving you a peaceful heart.

His mercy and compassion are cause for praise. His approval and blessing are like a nourishing spring filling you with joy. Though he rules all of heaven and earth, he cares for you, knows your deepest hopes, and gives you tranquillity in the midst of the storms.

This is the heart of your God—shining his light on your life and being gracious to you. So turn your face toward him this morning and praise him.

Dear God, thank you for showing me your beautiful face. I praise you for your peace and goodness—for your comfort, wisdom, grace, and protection. Amen.

WHAT DO I DO?

Make Your ways known to me, Lord; teach me Your paths.
Guide me in Your truth and teach me, for You are the
God of my salvation; I wait for You all day long.
PSALM 25:4–5 HCSB

It is difficult to say, "I don't know what to do" if you are accustomed to being self-sufficient and finding your own way in every situation. When this realization settles in, the anxiety may overwhelm you, especially if others are depending upon you to do what is best. With all options exhausted, where can you turn?

Are there those who respect the Lord? He will point them to the best way. . . . My eyes are always looking to the Lord for help. He will keep me from any traps.

PSALM 25:12, 15 NCV

These circumstances did not happen by chance. God will allow you to reach the end of your resources so you will turn to him and seek his guidance. Instead of thinking that you must have all the answers, pray. Read the Bible. Listen for God's direction. He will certainly show you the very best path to take.

God, it is so hard to give up control. Please forgive me for being so resistant to your direction. Thank you for your gentleness and for helping me through this trial. Amen.

NOTHING AT ALL

I am the LORD, the God of all the peoples of the world. Is anything too hard for me?
JEREMIAH 32:27 NLT

*Ah Lord GOD!
Behold, You have
made the heavens
and the earth by Your
great power and by
Your outstretched
arm! Nothing is too
difficult for You.*

JEREMIAH 32:17 NASB

The situation looked desperate. The Babylonians were poised for attack, and the people of Judah refused to ask God for help. The prophet Jeremiah knew that if the Babylonians carried off all the people, as was their practice, the Promised Land would be lost to God's people for good. God assured Jeremiah that the land was safe because it was in his hands.

Impossible situations are God's specialty. At times, it will seem that if anything can go wrong, it does. But nothing is too difficult for God. You can have patience during times of difficulty knowing that all the obstacles in your path are nothing at all to God.

*Dear God, thank you that impossible situations are
your specialty and that nothing is too hard for
you. I count on your wonderful might. Amen.*

PEOPLE ARE TO BE HELPED, NOT SHUNNED

Good and upright is the Lord; therefore
He teaches sinners in the way.
PSALM 25:8 NKJV

When you were a child, your parents warned you to stay away from "bad" companions who might cause you to stray from the right path. Certainly this was and is good advice for the very young and the easily influenced.

But you learn from Scripture that God loves all his children and wants you to be united with him. You also learn that as a believer you have a responsibility to be a blessing not only to those who are living godly lives but also to those who are not. You are a mirror of God's love in the world; you reflect and pass along the goodness and mercy shown to you. And you practice this commandment most notably when you reach out to people who do not know that God loves them.

Who can understand his errors? Cleanse me from secret faults. Keep back Your servant also from presumptuous sins; Let them not have dominion over me.

PSALM 19:12–13 NKJV

✷☾

God, give me the courage to reach out to those who do not yet know you. Give me the words to speak truth and love into their lives. Amen.

ABSOLUTELY POSSIBLE

Nothing is impossible for God!
LUKE 1:37 CEV

> *The Mighty One has done great things for me, and His name is holy.*
>
> LUKE 1:49 HCSB

It was truly shocking to discover that elderly, barren Elizabeth was pregnant. Yet when young Mary went to visit her, she had even more miraculous news. Mary—a virgin—was going to have a baby too.

Some miracles are not only incredible, but they are also downright beyond belief, almost. Your most wonderful promises from God may seem like utter foolishness to others—not just improbable, but patently impossible. In fact, if it were not for your faith, you wouldn't believe them either.

Don't worry—you are not peculiar. God often does the impossible to show his glory. And just as a virgin can have a baby, God can bring whatever he promised you into being too.

Dear God, I thank you that even inconceivable things are possible with you. Thank you for doing the impossible for me. Amen.

NECESSARY ANALYSIS

*Examine me, God. . . . Make sure I'm fit inside and out so
I never lose sight of your love, but keep in step with you.*
PSALM 26:2–3 MSG

Sometimes you'll be surprised at the temptations you succumb to. In fact, you may be shocked at what you're capable of—especially if you're doing your best to honor God. How can you fight those enticements?

> *I will walk in my integrity; redeem me and be merciful to me. My foot stands in an even place; in the congregations I will bless the LORD.*
>
> PSALM 26:11–12 NKJV

The first step, of course, is to confess what you've done and receive God's forgiveness. Yet there's a second thing you should do— allow God to search you and reveal what makes those temptations appealing to you.

When you invite God's analysis, he can reveal the needs deep within you—those you may not even realize you have—that are causing trouble. Then he can fill those needs in a constructive way, and ultimately save you a lot of heartache.

*God, I do want to honor you. Examine me—reveal the deep
needs within me so that I can love you with my life. Amen.*

HE KNOWS THE WAY

*Whenever you turn to the right or to the left, your ears will hear
this command behind you: "This is the way. Walk in it."*

ISAIAH 30:21 HCSB

*I guide you in the way
of wisdom and lead
you along straight
paths. When you walk,
your steps will not be
hampered; when you
run, you will
not stumble.*

PROVERBS 4:11–12 NIV

Everyone asks the question "What is God's will for me?" at one point or another, especially during decision-making times. People try to be very conscious of God's will because they fear disappointing him and missing his blessings.

God's will is for you to be so close to him that you are confident that he is always leading you. True, the way may sometimes seem confusing or obscure. But God knows the way—the best way—to take you.

Today, listen to God, and he will make his will known to you. Then obey him as he reveals the path. You may find that you are already walking in it.

*Dear God, thank you for teaching me your will.
Help me to be so close to you that I always
know I am doing what you want. Amen.*

STABILITY

*Now I stand on solid ground, and I
will publicly praise the LORD.*
PSALM 26:12 NLT

Where do you go for stability? When your world crumbles around you, where do you turn? Friend, God should not be your last resort.

*Your steadfast love
is before my eyes,
and I walk in
your faithfulness.*

PSALM 26:3 ESV

When chaotic situations occur, only he can steady you with his assurance, teach you wisdom and self-control, and train you to remain faithful. Rather than allowing events to throw you off balance, he shows you how to stay in the center of his will and cling to his unwavering promises.

God is the only One who can truly bring you stability because he is completely consistent and unchanging—he stays steady, though the rest of the world may tremble. Stand on solid ground by setting your feet on the path God has for you. There, you will surely never be shaken.

*God, what would I do without you to cling to? I praise
you for your faultless character that I can always
depend upon. Truly you are wonderful. Amen.*

MORE POWER THAN THAT?

Understand the incredible greatness of God's power for us who believe him. This is the same mighty power that raised Christ from the dead.
EPHESIANS 1:19–20 NLT

God, You are awe-inspiring in Your sanctuaries. The God of Israel gives power and strength to His people. May God be praised!
PSALM 68:35 HCSB

Think about the power that God exerted when Christ was resurrected. That power took on the sin of the world and destroyed it. It took the shackles from death and demolished them. And it forever changed how humanity relates to God.

No small power was exerted there. In fact, the imagination can barely conceive it. Yet, it is the same power that has been given to help you in your every need.

You have not been left alone to fend for yourself. God has given you his great power. Rejoice today that you will never have a problem that requires more power than that.

Dear God, I cannot think of a situation that needs more power than the resurrection. Thank you for making that power available to me. Amen.

KNOWING HIS SECRETS

The secret counsel of the LORD is for those who fear Him, and He reveals His covenant to them.
PSALM 25:14 HCSB

A strange and wonderful thing occurs as you spend time with God—circumstances begin to make sense to you that never did before. Your spirit becomes sensitive to the important details of life, and you can discern how certain situations will turn out.

Show me your ways, O LORD, teach me your paths; guide me in your truth and teach me, for you are God my Savior, and my hope is in you all day long.
PSALM 25:4–5 NIV

This is not about supernatural premonitions. Rather, your heightened perception has to do with understanding God's will for you—seeing his activity in your life with spiritual eyes.

When your gaze is fixed on the Lord, you know where he's taking you, what he's teaching you, and the ways he's transforming your life. So spend time with him every day and allow his wisdom to shed light on your path.

God, I look forward to spending time with you and learning your ways. I love you and want to know you with all my heart. Amen.

EMPOWERING FOR GOOD

*God is working in you, giving you the desire to obey
him and the power to do what pleases him.*

PHILIPPIANS 2:13 NLT

*May our Lord Jesus
Christ Himself and
God our Father, who
has loved us and given
us eternal comfort and
good hope by grace,
comfort and strengthen
your hearts in every
good work and word.*

2 THESSALONIANS
2:16–17 NASB

The desire you have to serve God comes from him. Whether it is because of thankfulness for your salvation, out of a desire for others to know him, or through his call for you to live for him—all of those feelings are evidence of God working in you.

Do not be afraid about how you will serve. Do not question whether you are strong, good-looking, smart, or talented enough to do a good job for him. And do not fret over your faults or weaknesses. He will provide you with everything you need, and he will accomplish amazingly good things through you.

*Dear God, thank you for giving me the desire to serve
you. I praise you for giving me the power
to do whatever you call me to do. Amen.*

THE FORGIVING HEART

*Look on my affliction and my pain,
and forgive all my sins.*
PSALM 25:18 NKJV

Someone once said that forgiveness is not for the forgiven, but for the sake of the forgiver. Forgiving those who have wronged you brings a deeper understanding of the character of God. Forgiveness is the cornerstone of relationship with him. When you hold a grudge, you keep God at a distance. When you let it go, you are restored to him instantly and inner peace returns. He forgets there was ever a rift between you.

Create in me a clean heart, O God. Renew a right spirit within me.
PSALM 51:10 NLT

If you are struggling tonight, you can release your right to be angry and release the desire to pass sentence on the one who hurt you, for no one is beyond God's forgiveness. That's the wonder of his mercy. Follow his example and erase the record of wrongs. It takes courage, but it will free you to experience amazing joy.

*God, help me understand your compassion and mercy.
Help me see others as you see them, and turn my
thoughts and actions toward forgiveness. Amen.*

AN INTERMISSION TO YOUR DREAMS

God has prospered me in the land of my sorrow.
GENESIS 41:52 MSG

The LORD was with him. And whatever he did, the LORD made it succeed.

GENESIS 39:23 ESV

When Joseph was young, God gave him the dream of being a great leader. Yet many difficult things happened that seemed to contradict that vision completely. Undoubtedly, Joseph must have wondered if what he had dreamed was a mistake.

Thankfully, God used those hard things in Joseph's life to prepare him to be Pharaoh's top adviser.

You also will have experiences that seemingly distance you from your dreams. However, if you stick close to God, he will give you success.

Today, take heart that your experiences are not a change of course. Rather, they are simply an intermission to the great dreams God is making real in you.

Dear God, I praise you for working powerfully in the intermissions. Thank you for making the dream real in me. Amen.

GOD'S FIX FOR FEAR

*The L*ORD* is my light and my salvation; whom shall I fear? The
L*ORD* is the strength of my life; of whom shall I be afraid?*
PSALM 27:1 NKJV

Fear is a predator. It crouches in the shadows and stalks its prey, you, waiting for any sign of weakness or vulnerability on your part. When fear strikes, it can ravage your life. It is a fierce and deadly enemy. Fear can rob you of family and relationships, destroy your talent, and wipe out your resources.

> *I praise God for what
> he has promised. I
> trust in God, so why
> should I be afraid?
> What can mere
> mortals do to me?*
>
> PSALM 56:4 NLT

God has given you faith, which is a mighty sword with which to fight the predator fear. Faith protects you from fear's torment and allows you to face each new day with hope and confidence. Faith frees you to tackle the real obstacles in your life rather than to waste your energies dealing with difficulties that might never materialize. Your faith in God gives you the courage to face fear and drive it away.

*Thank you, God, for the gift of faith that brings
me hope and drives fear away. Amen.*

HE CARES FOR YOU

Cast all your anxiety on him because he cares for you.
1 PETER 5:7 NIV

Give your worries to the LORD, and he will take care of you. He will never let good people down.

PSALM 55:22 NCV

You can let go of your fears. In fact, it is imperative that you do because your worries impede you from enjoying the life God has given you.

Today, cast all of your cares—the anxieties, doubts, and all of the things that distract, irritate, and drive you crazy—upon God. Give each one—from the least to the greatest—to God so that he can carry them for you.

Allow him to care for you—everything that concerns or has an effect on you. He loves you greatly, and he will faithfully handle everything better than you could ever hope to. Praise his holy name.

Dear God, it is hard to let go of my fears. Yet I give them to you and trust you to care for me. Amen.

THE MASTER PLAN

Teach me how to live, O LORD.
PSALM 27:11 NLT

An architect carefully creates a master plan for each new building, plotting all the details on paper before the first beam of wood is cut or the first nail is driven into place. The integrity of the structure depends on the architect's skill and the degree to which the builders follow the master plan.

> *I will instruct you and teach you in the way you should go; I will counsel you and watch over you.*
>
> PSALM 32:8 NIV

God has a master plan for your life as well. When you disregard that plan or deviate from it in significant ways, you create an unstable structure that could come crashing down. When that happens, you must cling to hope and turn to God, the divine architect. He is always ready to help you rebuild your life. If it is too late for master plan A, then your faithful God will unfold the blueprint for master plan B.

God, I will look to you as the architect of my life. Help me build wisely, according to your master plan. Amen.

FINDING MERCY

Whoever conceals his transgressions will not prosper, but he who confesses and forsakes them will obtain mercy.
PROVERBS 28:13 ESV

Count yourself lucky, how happy you must be—you get a fresh start, your slate's wiped clean. Count yourself lucky—GOD holds nothing against you and you're holding nothing back from him.
PSALM 32:1–2 MSG

The truth about sin is that you do more harm to yourself when you hide it than when you confess it openly to God. This is because when you conceal it, it creates a destructive cycle within you.

Yet when you confess it, you acknowledge you need God's mercy and strength to help you. God sets you free from the damaging cycle by working on its root cause—removing the fear, bitterness, and corruption that spawned it.

God heals you, loves you, and gives your life significance and success. Confess your sins to him today so that he can teach you real freedom and you can find mercy.

Dear God, I do confess my sin to you. Thank you for your great mercy and for giving me such wonderful freedom. Amen.

DON'T CHARGE AHEAD

Wait for the LORD; be strong, and let your heart take courage; wait for the LORD!
PSALM 27:14 ESV

At times the doors of opportunity don't seem to open fast enough—especially when your need is great. You come to the edge of your wits, strength, and resources; you wonder if there's something else you could do to improve your situation.

I am certain that I will see the LORD's goodness in the land of the living.

PSALM 27:13 HCSB

The great temptation is to disregard God's leadership and forge ahead, creating your own mediocre solutions. However, the doors of God's best blessings can't be forced open.

There are times for stepping out in faith and times for patience—and God will show you what is necessary for your situation. Even so, listen to God, take heart, and trust him. No one can close the doors of blessing God has for you.

God, I will be patient and listen to you—I won't charge ahead. Your timing is perfect, and I thank you that the blessings you have for me are mine forever. Amen.

THE BLESSED BELIEVE TO SEE

Have you believed because you have seen me? Blessed are those who have not seen and yet have believed.
JOHN 20:29 ESV

These are written that you may believe that Jesus is the Christ, the Son of God, and that believing you may have life in His name.

JOHN 20:31 NKJV

Very few had Thomas's opportunity—seeing and touching Jesus on earth after his resurrection. Jesus said you would be especially blessed because you have not seen him, and yet you believe.

This is the essence of faith—not seeing, but always trusting. Jesus overcame sin and gave you a new life. It is not a truth that you can grasp with your hands as Thomas did. You must believe in order to see God. You must have confidence before God can bless your life.

Today, forget your doubts. Believe God and be blessed by how clearly he shows himself to you.

Dear God, I do believe you, and I thank you that one day I will see your face. Amen.

THE SILENT TREATMENT

*O Lord my Rock, be not deaf and silent to me. . . . Hear
the voice of my supplication as I cry to You for help.*
PSALM 28:1–2 AMP

You need answers, so you humble yourself before God's throne and listen. However, there is no response. There is not even the hint of a reply. There is only silence. Repeatedly you pray, wondering why he has not addressed your pleas, searching your soul to see if you have done anything wrong. Your ears strain for a word. Soon your quest is

*The LORD is my
strength and shield. I
trust him with all my
heart. He helps me,
and my heart is filled
with joy. I burst out in
songs of thanksgiving.*
PSALM 28:7 NLT

no longer about getting an answer. You just want to hear his voice. Friend, that is exactly where you need to be.

Has God been quiet lately? He may be waiting until your sole desire is his presence in your life. Keep seeking and loving him. When he does finally answer, it is going to be a very important message, and you will not want to miss it.

*God, please do not let me miss your instruction. Rather,
help me to keep seeking you even when you are silent—
because you mean everything to me. Amen.*

REMEMBER

I remember your wonderful deeds of long ago. They are constantly in my thoughts. I cannot stop thinking about your mighty works.
PSALM 77:11–12 NLT

O God, your ways are holy. Is there any god as mighty as you? You are the God of great wonders! You demonstrate your awesome power among the nations.
PSALM 77:13–14 NLT

This morning, take a moment to remember the wonderful deeds of God. Remember how he showed his mighty power in the Bible and in the lives of the people you love.

Remember how God has revealed himself to you and has worked in your life. Remember how he acted in the past on your behalf and how he orchestrated circumstances just to show you how deeply and intimately he cares about you. Remember the times the Bible gave you peace and God's presence gave you joy.

Remember all these things today so that you can remain faithful to him and so that your hope will remain strong.

Dear God, fill my thoughts with your wonderful deeds and remind me of your works, and I will sing your praise all day long. Amen.

JUST TRUST—REALLY

The LORD is my strength and my shield; in him,
my heart trusts, and I am helped; my heart exults,
and with my song I give thanks to him.
PSALM 28:7 ESV

The psalms are all about trusting in God. That's because they were written by real people who had real emotions about real struggles. When they cried out to the living God, he truly helped them and vindicated their faith in him.

You shouldn't forget that. Though the psalms are beautiful and poetic, they are the authentic feelings and experiences of people just like you. Just

The Lord is their [un-yielding] Strength, and He is the Stronghold of salvation to [me] His anointed. Save Your people . . . nourish and shepherd them and carry them forever.
PSALM 28:8–9 AMP

as the psalmists trusted in God and saw his victorious provision, so can you. Whatever you are facing today—anger, apathy, fear, joy, contentment, or sorrow—there's more than likely a psalm that echoes your emotions. And undoubtedly its conclusion is this: Trust God. The psalmists did, and you should too. Really.

God, thank you for the psalms—the testimonies of people who trusted you and saw your deliverance. Truly you are fully trustworthy. Amen.

A WAY OUT

*When you are tempted, he will show you
a way out so that you can endure.*
1 Corinthians 10:13 nlt

*The Lord knows how
to rescue the godly
from temptation.*

2 Peter 2:9 nasb

You will have temptations today—that is a basic truth of the Christian life. However, just because you have temptations does not mean you will necessarily sin. Just the opposite. Because you have temptations, you have a unique opportunity for success.

The word that Paul used here for *tempted* is also translated as *tested*. These tests can make you stronger if you seek God in them and take the way out he gives you.

This morning, set your heart on God and resolve that you will listen to him when temptation comes your way. He will show you an excellent way out—a way that leads you to victory.

*Dear God, thank you for giving me a way of
escape from my temptations. Help me always
to grow stronger through the tests. Amen.*

THE BASIS FOR YOUR TRUST

Ascribe to the Lord glory and strength. Give to the Lord the glory due to His name; worship the Lord in the beauty of holiness.
PSALM 29:1–2 AMP

You have been encouraged to trust God; but why should you be confident in his care? How can you depend upon someone you have never seen?

The Lord controls the flood. The Lord will be King forever. The LORD gives strength to his people; the LORD blesses his people with peace.
PSALM 29:10–11 NCV

Understand that your faith in God is not to be blind or unsubstantiated. Rather, it should be based on his faultless character. He is all-powerful, completely able to do whatever is necessary to help you. God is all-knowing. His wisdom concerning your situation and how to deliver you is flawless. In addition, he is perfect in his love for you, which means that he will only do what is in your absolute best interest. Trust God to help you. You have great reason for confidence. He is willing and able to bring you the victory.

God, you are so worthy of praise and adoration. I thank you for your faultless character and great help to me. I am truly blessed by your love. Amen.

SLOW TO REACT

You, Lord, are a compassionate and gracious God, slow to anger and abundant in faithful love and truth.
PSALM 86:15 HCSB

People who make fun of wisdom cause trouble in a city, but wise people calm anger down.

PROVERBS 29:8 NCV

Here is a picture of God that should be imitated by believers—he is compassionate, gracious, slow to anger, and abundant in faithful love and truth.

How very different this is from what is recommended by worldly sources. Society suggests that in order to achieve, one must be ruthless—quick to react and make decisions. Yet this is God's will—that you not *react* but that you set yourself to be *proactive*. Be like God in your attitude to others—not making quick judgments, but acting slowly and deliberately with tenderness and self-control. By doing so, you not only bring honor and glory to God, but you also build up the people around you and keep conflict from building.

Dear God, please help me to slow down when reacting toward others so that I may treat them with compassion, love, and truth. Amen.

VOICE-QUAKE

The voice of the LORD is powerful; the voice of the LORD is full of majesty. . . . The voice of the LORD shakes the wilderness.
PSALM 29:4, 8 NKJV

At the sound of his voice, the winds and the waves obey and calm down. At his command, the rains fall or the rivers recede.

He spoke and created day and night; heaven and earth; animals, birds, and fish; flowers, plants, and trees; and man and woman. He opened his mouth, and the stars appeared—and the entire universe with them. When God speaks, all of creation responds and trembles. His word is powerful—it's the foundation for everything that exists. So listen to him and don't be afraid when his voice shakes you. Embrace his message, because he's creating things for you that are better than you can imagine.

Above the floodwaters is GOD's throne from which his power flows, from which he rules the world. GOD makes his people strong. GOD gives his people peace.
PSALM 29:10–11 MSG

God, I know your voice is powerful and wondrous!
I praise you for your wonderful word—let me
hear you clearly today, my God. Amen.

UNCONDITIONAL

Mephibosheth knelt down again and said,
"Why should you care about me?"
2 Samuel 9:8 cev

May your unfailing love rest upon us, O Lord, even as we put our hope in you.

Psalm 33:22 niv

King David wanted to honor his best friend Jonathan, who was killed in battle. He sought out Jonathan's children in order to show them kindness on Jonathan's behalf. The only one living was Mephibosheth—a sad, crippled man.

Fearfully, Mephibosheth expressed his unworthiness before the king. Why would David bother with him? David welcomed him wholeheartedly into his home because of his great love for Jonathan.

Any fears you have regarding God are similarly unfounded. When God looks at you, he never thinks of you as unworthy. Rather, he sees Jesus in you and responds in love.

Today, enter God's presence with confidence and experience his unconditional love.

Dear God, thank you for loving me unconditionally and welcoming me wholeheartedly. Your love is too wonderful for words. Amen.

GOD'S POWER, PRESENCE, AND PEACE

He will give his people strength. He will bless them with peace.
PSALM 29:11 TLB

Consider all the moments you have when you sense God's power, presence, and peace— moments when the clouds part and a sudden, all-prevailing sense of peace washes over you. You know then that you are truly loved by almighty God, and you are filled with gratitude and

The LORD is my light and the one who saves me. I fear no one. The LORD protects my life; I am afraid of no one.

PSALM 27:1 NCV

a new sense of security. It is as if you have suddenly discovered who you really are, and you feel more alive than ever.

These moments become more frequent if you cultivate quality time with God. This requires spiritual discipline and fortitude. The rewards are boundless and will immeasurably enrich your life. Daily prayer, Scripture reading, and meditation on God's attributes will deepen your understanding and make you a ready receptacle for his grace.

God, I don't want to wait until I get to heaven to enjoy your power, your presence, and your peace. Help me receive all that you have for me each day. Amen.

AN ATTITUDE OF LOVE

*Christ sacrificed his life for us. This is why we ought
to live sacrificially for our fellow believers.*
1 JOHN 3:16 MSG

*I led them with cords
of human kindness,
with ties of love; I
lifted the yoke from
their neck and bent
down to feed them.*

HOSEA 11:4 NIV

Novelist and minister Ian Maclaren wrote, "Be kind, everyone you meet is carrying a heavy burden." This is why Jesus treated everyone with such wonderful compassion. He knew that people deal with difficult things that influence how they react. He also knew that people didn't need more burdens—they needed more love. And so he cared for everyone, regardless of how they responded to him.

As you meet people today, take this truth to heart and have an attitude of love. Though you cannot see why people react the way they do, you can be a blessing to them. Even if they cannot reciprocate, they will surely see God in you.

*Dear God, thank you for knowing the burdens I bear.
Help me to love other people as you do. Amen.*

THE HEALING POWER OF GOD

O LORD my God, I cried to you for help,
and you have healed me.
PSALM 30:2 NRSV

Prayer is good medicine. It's a fact, and medical science has finally caught on. Studies show that when you pray regularly and commit your welfare to God, you recover from serious illness and trauma faster than those who have no faith

Come, O Lord, and make me well. In your kindness save me.

PSALM 6:4 TLB

in God. Your outlook on life is more positive; your hope for the future is stronger. And as far as minor illnesses are concerned, you even get fewer colds than those who face life without the advantage of genuine faith.

Prayer and thanksgiving relieve stress, alleviate anxiety, promote positive thinking, and generally foster happiness and contentment. Is it any wonder that such things contribute to your health? When you know that God is in charge of everything and is your guide, you are less likely to take yourself too seriously.

God, faith is so important to every aspect of my life.
Without it, I would be lonely and without hope. Thank
you for being there to hear me when I pray. Amen.

A HOPEFUL EXPECTANCY

The LORD will surely comfort Zion . . . he will make her deserts like Eden, her wastelands like the garden of the LORD.
ISAIAH 51:3 NIV

Those who have been ransomed by the LORD will return. They will enter Jerusalem singing, crowned with everlasting joy. Sorrow and mourning will disappear, and they will be filled with joy and gladness.

ISAIAH 51:11 NLT

Changed from an arid, barren land to a plush paradise. Transformed from a stony terrain to a flourishing botanical wonderland. This is the inheritance of those who believe in God.

Every believer goes through periods of dryness in his or her spiritual life—times of confusion when it is difficult to hear God or perceive that he is still leading. You may even feel that you have stopped growing spiritually.

These times should not wither your trust in him. Rather, they should nourish your hopeful expectancy in the hearty fruitfulness to come. For God will surely comfort you and turn all your deserts into havens of beauty and grace.

Dear God, thank you for comforting me during these dry, confusing times. I praise you that soon I will see renewal and fruitfulness. Amen.

FROM DESPAIR TO DELIGHT

Weeping may endure for a night,
but joy comes in the morning.
PSALM 30:5 AMP

Everything appears more frightening in the dark. The house that's so warm and inviting while sunlight streams through its windows is ominous during a stormy night. As unknown creaks and groans echo through the walls, your place of shelter can feel confining and treacherous. The same is true when there's darkness in your circumstances. The unknown can be fearsome and restrictive, and you long for the light of understanding to shine on your situation.

You changed my sorrow into dancing. You took away my clothes of sadness, and clothed me in happiness. I will sing to you and not be silent. LORD, my God, I will praise you forever.
PSALM 30:11–12 NCV

Don't be discouraged—it's never as bad as it seems. The fresh sunrise will reveal God's insight and provision for your problems. As he illuminates your situation, you'll see that what brought you despair was really an opportunity for delight.

God, I'm counting on you to turn this time of sorrow into a vehicle of joy. Thank you for shedding light on my circumstances. Amen.

GIVING THANKS FOR YOU

I never stop giving thanks for you as I remember you in my prayers.
EPHESIANS 1:16 HCSB

Every time I think of you—and I think of you often!—I thank God for your lives of free and open access to God, given by Jesus.

1 CORINTHIANS 1:4 MSG

✴

Thankful—that is to be your attitude toward others. Believers are challenged to look at their loved ones, friends, co-workers, neighbors, and acquaintances with a spirit of gratefulness.

Know that as you read this meditation this morning someone is giving thanks for you—for God's work in your life and for what you mean to the people around you. You are also called to give thanks for those you know. Even if those people are difficult, you can praise God that he is teaching you through them.

You will be amazed at how much God will bless you—making your love for them and for him grow through your thankfulness.

Dear God, I am thankful for the people around me. Thank you for growing me through them and increasing my love for them. Amen.

TAKING REFUGE IN STRENGTH

Incline your ear to me; rescue me speedily. Be a rock of refuge for me, a strong fortress to save me.
PSALM 31:2 NRSV

Lighthouses are pictures of steadfastness. Battered by hurricane-force gales, pelted by sea spray, and baked by the sun, those stone giants cling year after year to the coastline. They stand sometimes for centuries, and they are fascinating. A favorite with artists and photographers, lighthouses come to mind when you

My honor and salvation come from God. He is my mighty rock and my protection. People, trust God all the time. Tell him all your problems, because God is our protection.
PSALM 62:7–8 NCV

think of words like *refuge, strong,* or *fortress,* words that were used to describe God when David penned the thirty-first psalm.

Lighthouses guide ships to safety by throwing light out into the night, beckoning the captains to shore. In a similar way, you might easily stray into dangerous waters if not for God's light thrown on your path.

Dear God, may I listen for your guidance in the soft whispers and feel it in the gentle nudges of everyday life. Help me follow your light when I know it comes from you. Amen.

167

GOD'S POWERFUL RESOURCES

*Don't be afraid, for those who are with us
outnumber those who are with them.*

2 KINGS 6:16 HCSB

*Defend my cause,
and set me free;
save me, as you
have promised.*

PSALM 119:154 GNT

The king of Aram was angry because the prophet Elisha kept foiling his plans. He sent his forces to capture Elisha.

When Elisha's servant saw what was happening, he was thoroughly frightened. Elisha prayed that the servant's eyes would be opened to what was happening spiritually so that he could see that they were not alone. God's mighty forces protected them.

Today you may feel like Elisha's servant—overwhelmed with the problems that confront you. However, God is on your side, and his powerful resources are encamped around you. Ask him to open your eyes so that you may behold the mighty power he has prepared for your defense.

*Dear God, help me to see your active defense on my behalf.
Thank you for being on my side. I never need to fear. Amen.*

HE UNDERSTANDS YOUR HURT

*I will be glad and rejoice in your love, for you saw
my affliction and knew the anguish of my soul.*
PSALM 31:7 NIV

Do you find it difficult to explain everything you're feeling about your circumstances, your disappointments, and the dreams that have taken far too long to materialize? Truly, who could put words to all the emotions that rise up within you?

I will praise you, LORD, for showing great kindness when I was like a city under attack. I was terrified. . . . But you answered my prayer when I shouted for help.

PSALM 31:21–22 CEV

☾

Yet there is One who understands every bit of your anguish. Jesus came to earth to experience what you're feeling and to understand your inner struggles. Because of his perfect wisdom concerning you, Jesus knows exactly how to restore your heart and comfort your soul. So don't be afraid that no one understands what you're going through. Jesus does. Today turn to him and allow him to heal your wounded heart with his love.

*God, thank you for understanding me and healing me with
your love. I'm so thankful that you comprehend the
things for which there are no words. Amen.*

SEEK AND PURSUE

Seek peace and pursue it.
1 PETER 3:11 NKJV

Agree and have concern and love for each other. You should also be kind and humble. Don't be hateful and insult people. . . . Treat everyone with kindness. You are God's chosen ones, and he will bless you.

1 PETER 3:8–9 CEV

It is the image of a runner eagerly and steadfastly racing toward the finish line. This is how the apostle Peter described the important pursuit of peace. Peace cannot be achieved passively. Rather, it is an aspiration you must strive for and be proactive about.

First, you must care about others and be earnestly concerned about their well-being. Then you must do your best not to create or give in to conflicts—as long as they do not compromise your core values. Finally, when conflicts do arise, you must deal with them swiftly and constructively.

Invest yourself in the pursuit of peace. You will be greatly pleased at the returns you receive.

Dear God, peace is a difficult thing to achieve, but I set myself to pursue it—to your honor and glory. Amen.

RISING TO THE CHALLENGE

All who trust the LORD, be cheerful and strong.
PSALM 31:24 CEV

A stony peak rises in the distance—cold and formidable against the early morning sky. To the casual observer, it would seem to be an unforgiving fortress, off limits to any human. Then a climber is spotted scaling the face of the peak, inching upward—one toehold, one handhold at a time.

Yes, he alone is my Rock, my rescuer, defense and fortress. Why then should I be tense with fear when troubles come?

PSALM 62:2 TLB

When you look ahead and see nothing but cold, stony, uninviting peaks crowding the landscape of your life, you must not lose heart. God has promised to help you tackle every challenge, and he will give you hope and encouragement to continue upward one toehold and one handhold at a time. God will hold you steady as you make your way to the summit. He will restore your hope as you gaze down into the lush valley on the other side.

God, when my future seems to be filled with stony peaks, I will place my hope in your strength and faithfulness. Amen.

171

TO SOAR AS EAGLES

They shall lift their wings and mount up
[close to God] as eagles [mount up to the sun].
ISAIAH 40:31 AMP

The LORD . . . does
not become tired or
need to rest. No one
can understand how
great his wisdom is.
He gives strength to
those who are tired
and more power to
those who are weak.

ISAIAH 40:28–29 NCV

✸

They say that eagles in flight take no concern for obstacles below. How wonderful it would be to forget all earthly constraints and challenges and soar high above—carried effortlessly by air currents and refreshing breezes.

There are mornings when you will wake up tired. You will feel how truly earthbound you are and come to the conclusion that your gravity-defying goals are too lofty to hope for.

Take heart today that God never grows tired or weary. He promises to renew your strength when you wait upon him. And like the powerful, majestic eagle, he will lift you high above the obstacles of earth—and you will soar.

Dear God, thank you for helping me to soar
like an eagle. I will not think of the obstacles but
will praise your wonderful strength. Amen.

A COMPLETE FORGIVENESS

Happy is the person whose sins are forgiven,
whose wrongs are pardoned.
PSALM 32:1 NCV

Nobody has to tell you what the worst things you've done are. They burn in your heart, destroying your joy—always condemning you and tainting the good things you do. Just when you really feel loved by God, an awful thought destroys your peace. *How can God accept me when I've been so wayward?*

I acknowledged my sin to You, and my iniquity I did not hide; I said, "I will confess my transgressions to the LORD"; and You forgave the guilt of my sin.

PSALM 32:5 NASB

✦☽

Friend, when God forgives you, he does so completely—he makes you absolutely clean. You never have to remember those sins again. He certainly doesn't.

So confess your sins once and for all, and whenever thoughts of your past plague you, think about God's perfect forgiveness. Rejoice that when he looks at you, he sees a person he truly loves.

God, I praise you for not holding my past against me.
I rejoice that you forgive me! Thank you for loving
me and making me new. Amen.

LORD, I KNOW YOU WILL

Be still in the presence of the LORD,
and wait patiently for him to act.
PSALM 37:7 NLT

Put your hope in the LORD. Travel steadily along his path. He will honor you by giving you the land.

PSALM 37:34 NLT

God is waiting for you to get quiet before him—to cast aside your worries and truly seek the tranquillity of his presence. He is God—the almighty and wonderful, your powerful defender and loving friend. He is the Lord who makes you whole and gives you the desires of your heart.

He is waiting for your heart to be calm—for you to realize that nothing in heaven or on earth can stop him from doing good things on your behalf. He is waiting for you—by your silence and quiet trust—to express your confidence that he will do as he promised.

Today, be still before him. And know him.

Dear God, silence is a challenge. Help my spirit to be calm and quiet before you so that I may know you and trust you more. Amen.

GOOD-BYE TO GUILT

I confessed my sins and told them all to you. I said, "I'll tell the Lord each one of my sins." Then you forgave me and took away my guilt.
PSALM 32:5 CEV

There are those who believe that humanity is inherently flawed, and in a sense, they are right. Sin corrupts from within, and people are powerless to break its influence over them. Thankfully, you are not without hope. Though you cannot help yourself, you know the

You are my hiding place; You shall preserve me from trouble; You shall surround me with songs of deliverance.
PSALM 32:7 NKJV

☽

One who erases your guilt and releases you from its bondage. The problem you have is letting go. You somehow convince yourself that the wickedness within you is more than Christ can handle. However, that simply is not true.

Friend, if you are seeking freedom from the destructive power of sin, there is only one way to find it—and that's through Jesus Christ. Stop trying to earn what he has offered you freely. Instead, embrace the good he wants to do in and through you and say good-bye to your guilt.

God, thank you for forgiving me of my sins. You have released me from my guilt and given me a clean heart. I praise your holy and powerful name! Amen.

BEFORE AND BEHIND

The LORD will go before you, and the God of Israel will be your rear guard.
ISAIAH 52:12 ESV

May the LORD bless you from Zion, so that you will see the prosperity of Jerusalem all the days of your life.
PSALM 128:5 HCSB

There are two intrinsic factors that will shape how you carry out your day today—the past and the future. Your history will influence your attitudes and beliefs, reactions and fears. Your future will be instrumental in how you plan and will be based upon your goals and hopes.

God is fully with you today and always—timelessly guarding and guiding your path. He brings good out of the experiences in your yesterdays that have shaped you, and prepares you for what will happen in your tomorrows.

God goes behind you—protecting you; and before you—pointing you in the right direction. Rejoice that as you follow him, he fully safeguards your days.

Dear God, thank you for being with me in my yesterdays and in my tomorrows. I praise you for blessing all the days of my life. Amen.

HIDDEN IN THE SECRET PLACE

Thou art my hiding place; thou shalt preserve me from trouble;
thou shalt compass me about with songs of deliverance.
PSALM 32:7 KJV

A secret childhood hiding place can be so vivid in your memory that at times it flashes back in Technicolor. Perhaps your hiding place was the broad branch of a tree where you could perch unseen thanks to the cover of a thousand green leaves. Or perhaps it was a shallow cave cut into the side of a slope or a small glade hidden behind

Rescue me from my enemies, LORD; I come to You for protection. Teach me to do Your will, for You are my God. May Your gracious Spirit lead me on level ground.
PSALM 143:9–10 HCSB

a willow tree that formed a leafy curtain. You felt safe in your secret place—wonderfully alone, yet not fearful. You could go there anytime you wanted to.

Years later, God still hides you in the secret place of his protection. Though God's secret place is not tangible with leafy borders, your spirit recognizes at once how real this wonderful hiding place is. And you are at peace.

Even when I can't see you, O God, I know you are there because you have always been there. I cannot remember a time you were not present in my life, and I thank you for that. Amen.

AN EASY YOKE

Take My yoke upon you and learn from Me, for I am gentle and lowly in heart, and you will find rest for your souls.
MATTHEW 11:29 NKJV

Are you tired? Worn out? Burned out on religion? Come to me. Get away with me and you'll recover your life. I'll show you how to take a real rest.

MATTHEW 11:28 MSG

Your relationship with God is not meant to enslave you but to set you free. The yoke, which was used for plowing, was useless if it was too heavy. Yet a good yoke harnessed the power of the oxen in order to accomplish more.

That is why God does not burden you or wear you out with a strict religious regimen. Rather, he offers you a life-giving relationship so that together with him you can accomplish more.

This morning, God offers you his sweet assurance that he will give you rest for your soul. So go to him, learn from him, and find the yoke that fits best of all.

Dear God, thank you for removing the burden of religion and for giving me rest. I am honored to be yoked together with you. Amen.

AN OUTPOURING OF BEAUTY

Sing for joy in the LORD, O you righteous ones;
praise is becoming to the upright.
PSALM 33:1 NASB

Would you consider yourself beautiful? Every culture has its standards for attractiveness, yet there are character attributes that are seen as universally lovely in every society. A woman who is loving, joyful, peaceful, patient, kind, good, faithful, gentle, and self-controlled is regarded as exquisite all over the world. That is because these are

Sing to Him a new song; play skillfully [on the strings] with a loud and joyful sound. For the word of the Lord is right; and all His work is done in faithfulness.

PSALM 33:3–4 AMP

☾

traits created in you by God's Holy Spirit. They flow from you effortlessly when you live your life in obedience and adoration to him.

Would you like to be considered truly lovely? Then remember that you are most attractive when you are praising him and letting his beauty shine through you. Moreover, when his radiance covers you, you are stunning no matter where you go.

God, thank you for making me radiant with your beauty!
May adoration and praise flow from my life so all will
worship you and give you the glory. Amen.

EVEN GREATER

*If you have faith in me, you will do the same things
that I am doing. You will do even greater things.*
JOHN 14:12 CEV

*When you become
fruitful disciples of
mine, my Father will
be honored.*

JOHN 15:8 CEV

Are you humbled by the thought that you could do greater things than Jesus could? What could be greater than being raised from the dead and providing eternal life for all of humanity?

Yet, the meaning here is not about bigger miracles—it is about honoring God. Jesus' purpose was to provide the way to God so that others could know him. Now that he has provided the way, you can know God, and he can shine through you.

Jesus saw the potential you have to bring glory to God. Today, emulate his example by telling others of how great a gift it is to honor him with your life.

*Dear God, thank you for the great purpose of
introducing others to you. I am honored to live for
you and to give you all the glory. Amen.*

UNBREAKABLE

The LORD's plans stand firm forever;
his intentions can never be shaken.
PSALM 33:11 NLT

God has spoken concerning an issue that's very important to you, and he's given you a promise that resonates deep within your soul. You know it's from him because his Word confirms it and his deep peace fills you when you pray.

Yet lately you've seen obstacles arise that appear to completely block your way from getting to the goal. You may be tempted to doubt—but don't.

Sing a new song of praise to him; play skillfully on the harp, and sing with joy. For the word of the LORD holds true, and we can trust everythng he does.

PSALM 33:3–4 NLT

No impediment can hinder God's wonderful plans for you. Just as God faithfully fulfilled his covenant to bring the Israelites into the Promised Land, he will carry out his pledge to you as well. Count on it—God's word to you will never be broken.

God, thank you that your promises to me are completely unbreakable and that the obstacles before me are nothing to you. I praise your powerful name! Amen.

UNFAILING COMPASSION

*[Because of] the LORD's faithful love we do
not perish, for His mercies never end.*
LAMENTATIONS 3:22 HCSB

*Deep in my heart I
say, "The LORD is all I
need; I can depend on
him!" The LORD is
kind to everyone who
trusts and obeys him.*

LAMENTATIONS 3:24–25
CEV

✸

You are not done—your hope has not come to an end. That is what Jeremiah meant when he wrote that because of God's love you would not perish.

Because God's goodness, kindness, and faithfulness have no end, you can eagerly expect that he again will make all things bright and hopeful.

Just as his mercy is renewed every morning, so also can your dreams have innumerable new beginnings.

Give thanks to God for his unfailing compassion that gives you a fresh start this morning. Whatever happened yesterday is washed clean and transformed by God's abundant love for you. Today you will experience how truly great his faithfulness is.

*Dear God, I do thank you for your wonderful, unfailing compassion.
Thank you for bringing new beginnings to all of my dreams. Amen.*

FAITH, HOPE, AND LOVE

Yes, Lord, let your constant love surround us,
for our hopes are in you alone.
PSALM 33:22 TLB

The spiritual strength that God gives you is founded on the wonder-working triad of faith, hope, and love. Your Lord shows you how you are to behave with others by actively demonstrating these three virtues through his own unblemished behavior toward you.

Be of good courage, and he shall strengthen your heart, all ye that hope in the LORD.

PSALM 31:24 KJV

If you take God at his word, your ordinary day-to-day life should be a reflection or an acting-out of his promises to you. Your relationships with others should be an energetic, vital mirror image of the trustworthy, loving, and merciful God you have come to know. It really is as simple as one, two, three. Faith, hope, love. You must strive for faith, hope, and love in all your dealings, whether with others or with yourself, if you want to be fully pleasing to God.

God, I want to build my life upon the principles of faith, hope, and love. Guide me and keep me on the right path. Amen.

WHAT COUNTS

The Lord does not see as man sees; for man looks at the outward appearance, but the Lord looks at the heart.
1 Samuel 16:7 nkjv

Serve Him with a whole heart and a willing mind, for the Lord searches every heart and understands the intention of every thought. If you seek Him, He will be found by you.

1 Chronicles 28:9 hcsb

Who would be Israel's new king? Samuel knew it was to be one of Jesse's sons. But which one? As the men filed past him, God told Samuel to keep looking.

Finally, Jesse's youngest son, David, came in from tending sheep, and God directed Samuel to set him apart as king. Though he was handsome and brave, God's reason for choosing David was his heart—the love David had for God and his great faith.

That is what counts for you as well. God chooses you—not because of your looks or strength, but because you love God and are willing to serve him faithfully.

Dear God, thank you that what matters most to you is my heart. Help me to love you more so that I may please you. Amen

FEAR NOT

I sought the LORD, and he answered me
and delivered me from all my fears.
PSALM 34:4 ESV

W hy are you afraid? What anxieties keep you awake at night, wondering what terrible news tomorrow will bring? Fear is a very destructive emotion; it can make everything in your life fall apart.

Those who look to him for help will be radiant with joy; no shadow of shame will darken their faces.

PSALM 34:5 NLT

That is why God not only frees you from your difficulties, but from the power of fear as well. How does he do so? First John 4:18 explains, "God's perfect love drives out fear" (NCV). He teaches you that anything that enters your life must first pass through his loving hand. If he allows a difficult situation to affect you, then he will most certainly use it for your good.

Therefore, do not be afraid. When you lie awake troubled by anxieties, turn your thoughts to his perfect love and allow him to calm your heart.

God, thank you for protecting me and teaching me courage through your wonderful love. Truly, with you, I have absolutely no reason to fear. Amen.

HE WILL REMEMBER

The Lord your God will have mercy—he won't destroy you or desert you. The Lord will remember his promise.

DEUTERONOMY 4:31 CEV

He has made His wonders to be remembered; the Lord is gracious and compassionate. . . . He will remember His covenant forever. He has made known to His people the power of His works.

PSALM 111:4–6 NASB

The Israelites stood on the brink of claiming the Promised Land. God encouraged them by vowing to remember his covenant. The challenge of conquering the land was intimidating, and yet they knew that with God empowering them, they would succeed.

As you come to the edge of the promise God has given to you, you may be overwhelmed with the work ahead or the things that remain unknown. But God brought you to this point, and he will not forget what he promised you. You will succeed.

Today, praise him that he remembers the promise and will be with you every step of the way to achieving it.

Dear God, this is intimidating, and I thank you for remembering your promise to me. I know that with your help I will succeed. Amen.

YOU'RE GLOWING!

*They looked to Him and were radiant; their faces
shall never blush for shame or be confused.*
PSALM 34:5 AMP

When Moses returned from meeting with God on Mount Sinai, his face shone so brightly that it astonished the Israelites. Such was the result of being in God's presence— God's brilliance lingered on Moses' countenance.

*My soul will boast in
the LORD; let the
afflicted hear and
rejoice. Glorify the
LORD with me;
let us exalt his
name together.*
PSALM 34:2–3 NIV

Though your time with God may be somewhat different than Moses,' the lasting effect will nevertheless be the same: God's glory will show through you. You may not notice any difference when looking in the mirror, but others will see the glow of his likeness in your spirit and character.

Every time you meet with God, it'll affect you in a positive way. So spend time with him often and let the beauty of his radiance shine through you.

*God, you bring such light to my life! Thank you for shining through
me. I pray that others will see your glory and love you. Amen.*

FROM FEW TO MANY

You were faithful with a few things, I will put you in charge of many things; enter into the joy of your master.
MATTHEW 25:21 NASB

To those who use well what they are given, even more will be given, and they will have an abundance.

MATTHEW 25:29 NLT

What are your talents? What gifts do you possess? All people have things that they do well. That includes you. You have many special abilities that you could use to glorify God.

The interesting thing about your gift is that as you use them—you gain more. That is because God rewards faithfulness. When he sees that you are a good manager of what he has given to you, he expands your abilities and your opportunities for success.

Today, make a list of what you do well and pray about how God wants you to serve him. He will find you faithful, and you will share his joy.

Dear God, I want to be faithful and honor you with my abilities. Please show me how you would like me to serve you. Amen.

WINGS OF MERCY

O taste and see that the LORD is good:
blessed is the man that trusteth in him.
PSALM 34:8 KJV

High above the treetops, a black-winged hawk soars majestically. The bird's swoops and glides appear effortless as it moves along on the late afternoon breezes. It seems to fear nothing above or below as it sails back and forth, up and down, soaking up the last lingering rays of the sun. Its awesome grace is breathtaking.

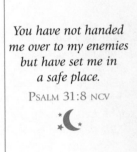

You have not handed me over to my enemies but have set me in a safe place.
PSALM 31:8 NCV

In the midst of difficult times, it's tempting to look up at the hawk and wish that you, too, could sail along on gentle breezes, high above your painful circumstances. During those seasons when your strength seems almost gone, be assured that God is beside you, ready to sweep you up onto his mighty wings of mercy and grace. There you find rest, comfort, and healing for your broken hearts and wounded spirits.

God, when my life seems unbearably painful, I will place
my hope in you. I will forsake my own failing strength
and rest on your wings of mercy. Amen.

SEEING TO BELIEVE?

*Take your finger and examine my hands.
. . . Don't be unbelieving. Believe.*
JOHN 20:27 MSG

Through Christ you have come to trust in God. And you have placed your faith and hope in God because he raised Christ from the dead and gave him great glory.

1 PETER 1:21 NLT

Thomas's sorrow was so great that he could not believe what the other disciples were saying. After all, he had seen Jesus on the cross. With his own eyes he watched Jesus breathe his last breath. How could the others say he was raised from the grave?

God understands that at times it is difficult for your heart to recover from what your eyes have seen. Yet he still calls you to believe.

This message is especially for you this morning, because your heart needs to take hold of what has been hidden from your eyes. Believe God and rejoice that his power goes beyond anything that you've ever seen.

Dear God, I do believe, even though I cannot see. Thank you for working in the unseen and always giving me hope. Amen.

DENYING THE DRAMA QUEEN WITHIN

Do you want to live and enjoy a long life? Then don't say cruel things and don't tell lies. Do good instead of evil and try to live at peace.
PSALM 34:12–14 CEV

During the trial, your friends urge, "Go ahead, get it out of your system." So you do. You allow the emotions to pour forth. You spout things you do not really mean, and you blow your troubles out of proportion.

You feel better for a moment. Then the feelings come back stronger than ever, and they are even more painful and harder to shake off. You have allowed your emotions to run amok. Now you are trapped by the drama you have created. That is why whenever something difficult comes into your life, you must seek God's understanding about it. Express yourself to him and allow his wisdom to guide you. Although it is the less dramatic route, the path will lead you to peace.

> *The LORD is close to the brokenhearted, and he saves those whose spirits have been crushed. People who do what is right may have many problems, but the Lord will solve them all.*
> PSALM 34:18–19 NCV

God, I do not need drama in my life—I need your peace. Please forgive me for spouting off. Help me to deal with my emotions in a way that honors you. Amen.

BECAUSE HE IS

*I am the Lord your God; so consecrate yourselves
and be holy, for I am holy.*
LEVITICUS 11:44 AMP

*To the one who comes
near me, I will show
myself holy; before
all the people, I
will show my glory.*

LEVITICUS 10:3 MSG

Hippocrates said, "Things that are holy are revealed only to men who are holy." True, God himself made you holy through Jesus. Yet your forgiven inward condition should be demonstrated through your outward activities. And the more you imitate God's holiness, the better you will know him.

The word *holy* means "to be set apart." You have been set apart for God—to both imitate and represent him. As you faithfully do so, he is able to teach you more deeply, empower you more mightily, and shine through you more brightly.

Be holy today because he is, and he will reveal himself in a more profound way than ever before.

*Dear God, I do want to know you more and be holy because you
are holy. Thank you for revealing yourself to me. Amen.*

GOD'S ANSWER IS ON THE WAY

The righteous cry out, and the LORD hears,
and delivers them out of all their troubles.
PSALM 34:17 NKJV

Camping out deep in the woods, you notice that night falls quickly and thickly. The darkness wraps everything in its blanket of black, making a flashlight the camper's best friend in an emergency. The camper's watch snags on the foliage, snapping from his wrist, so he retraces his steps with the light beamed out in front of him, illuminating the ground. He hears rustling in the bushes and shines the flashlight in that direction, making light circles, searching for the source.

Rise up! Be our help, And redeem us for the sake of your lovingkindness.
PSALM 44:26 NASB

In a similar way, your heart beams out into the darkness, calling to God when you're troubled or simply in need of an answer. He promises that when you search for him, you will find him. Often what you find is that his answer is already on the way.

Dear God, I stand on tiptoe as I wait for your answer to my prayers.
When I hear from you, it will be more than worth the wait. Amen.

LAWFUL VERSUS HELPFUL

All things are lawful for me,
but all things are not helpful.
1 CORINTHIANS 6:12 NKJV

People should think of us as servants of Christ, the ones God has trusted with his secrets. Now in this way those who are trusted with something valuable must show they are worthy of that trust.

1 CORINTHIANS 4:1–2
NCV

How do you balance the freedom you have in Christ and the proper conduct for a Christian? Aren't Christians able to live as they please, knowing they've been set free from the sinful nature?

Though it is true that God has forgiven you of your sins and that sin no longer has power over you, you should still avoid it. This is for the simple reason that certain actions not only hinder your growing relationship with God, but may also impede others from seeking him. Those actions may be lawful for you, but they aren't helpful to anyone. Today, practice only those activities that are helpful to your growing relationship with God.

Dear God, I want to live a life that is worthy of you. Please help me to choose only those activities that honor you. Amen.

194

WHEN YOU'D LEAST EXPECT HIM

The LORD is near to the brokenhearted and saves those who are crushed in spirit.
PSALM 34:18 NASB

Like most people, you may not seek God's presence when you are feeling low. Beat down, undermined, or simply exhausted, you may question your worth and judge yourself useless to him.

The LORD's people may suffer a lot, but he will always bring them safely through.
PSALM 34:19 CEV

Thankfully, God knows that this is precisely when you need him the most, and he rushes in to comfort you. Though it's when you'd least expect anyone to be interested in you, God is near when you're crushed and brokenhearted. And it's when you're most vulnerable and powerless that he can be strong for you and others can see him working through you.

So tonight let God comfort you. His mercy will heal your heart, and others will see his compassion.

God, thank you for loving and comforting me when I feel worthless and vulnerable. May others see your powerful love and seek you in return. Amen.

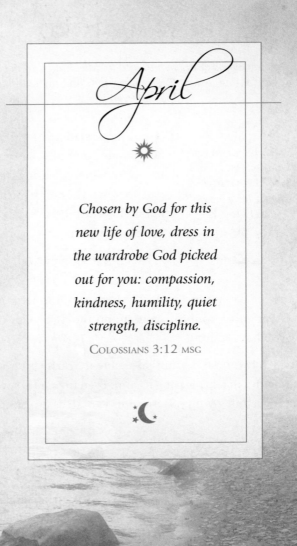

April

*Chosen by God for this
new life of love, dress in
the wardrobe God picked
out for you: compassion,
kindness, humility, quiet
strength, discipline.*

COLOSSIANS 3:12 MSG

SHOW ME, LORD

*May the words of my mouth and the meditation of my heart
be pleasing to you, O Lord, my rock and my redeemer.*
PSALM 19:14 NLT

*Teach me to do your
will, for you are my
God! Let your good
Spirit lead me on
level ground!*

PSALM 143:10 ESV

In every relationship, there is a certain amount of guesswork involved when pleasing the other person. You never completely know how to best satisfy his or her expectations.

This is not so with God. You never have to guess what is pleasing to God because he communicates his desires to your innermost being. His Spirit either confirms you are on the right path or shows how you have strayed.

The God who saves you is also able to teach you how to live in a manner that is pleasing to him. Even now he is speaking to your Spirit and giving you the ability to do as he asks.

*Dear God, thank you for teaching me what you
want and for giving me the ability to do it.
May my life always please you. Amen.*

EXCHANGING TRIALS FOR GLORY

My whole being will exclaim,
"Who is like you, O Lord?"
PSALM 35:10 NIV

If you are strong or gifted enough to accomplish a task, what room is there for God to work? If you can personally guarantee a successful conclusion to the assignment you face, what need is there for faith?

Those who want the best for me, let them have the last word—a glad shout!—and say, over and over and over, "God is great—everything works together for good for his servant."

PSALM 35:27 MSG

That is why God will challenge you beyond what you can handle. It is only when you cannot manage your circumstances that you acknowledge God's hand. Any success you achieve is from God. Of course, no one likes to relinquish control, but that is what it takes to see his astounding work in your life. Are you committed to following him no matter what it takes? Are you willing to encounter trials in exchange for experiencing his glory? When you are, you will truly get to know him, and that is definitely worth it.

God, I want to know you, but I am afraid of losing control.
Teach me to respond to situations in a way that honors
you and helps me grow in your love. Amen.

YOUR BEST

*Love bears all things, believes all things, hopes
all things, endures all things.*
1 Corinthians 13:7 esv

*Let whoever is wise
pay attention to these
things and consider
the Lord's acts of
faithful love.*

Psalm 107:43 hcsb

Love bears all things. As Jesus faithfully bears your weaknesses, so faithfully bear his strength in helping others.

Believes all things. As Jesus believes your life is worth sacrificing his, so believe that proclaiming his good news of salvation is worth investing yours.

Hopes all things. As Jesus hopes that you will willingly reflect his image, so maintain the hope that anything that comes into your life works toward that end.

Endures all things. As Jesus endured the cross to provide you eternal life, so obediently endure in this life in order to give him the glory. Just as Jesus has given you his best, so freely give him yours.

*Dear God, I know your love never fails. Help me
to give my best by bearing, believing, hoping,
and enduring all things in your love. Amen.*

THEIR OPINIONS WON'T STICK

Rouse yourself, O Lord, and defend me;
rise up, my God, and plead my cause.
PSALM 35:23 GNT

It's just not fair. You help someone, but he or she denigrates you in return. You conscientiously do excellent work for someone, but then that someone blames you for problems that aren't your fault. The godly love you've attempted to express has resulted in your disparagement and discouragement.

May those who delight in my vindication shout for joy and gladness; may they always say, "The LORD be exalted, who delights in the well-being of his servant."
PSALM 35:27 NIV

Does anyone realize the injustice of it all? Yes, God does. He sees everything you do and knows you're motivated by your love for him. Though the people you tried to assist have snubbed you, God won't allow their false claims against you to remain.

Their opinions won't stick—so honor him and forgive them. Others will surely see his love flowing through you and will respect you even more.

God, it is difficult to forgive my detractors, but I will. Thank you for defending and loving me. It's an honor to serve you. Amen.

SEEING YOUR JOY COMPLETE

On that day they offered great sacrifices and rejoiced
because God had given them great joy.
NEHEMIAH 12:43 HCSB

Our God didn't aban-
don us. He has put
us in the good graces
of the kings of Persia
and given us the heart
to build The Temple
of our God, restore its
ruins, and construct a
defensive wall in Judah
and Jerusalem.

EZRA 9:9 MSG

When the wall of Jerusalem had been rebuilt, the Israelites did not congratulate themselves for fortifying the city. Though they all had worked very hard and had sacrificed a great deal, they realized that they had only played a small part. Their accomplishment would never have been possible apart from God's help and provision. Imitate their example today and praise God for the victories and achievements he has helped you to attain. God empowered you and paved the way for your success.

You will find that your joy is more abundant and complete when you acknowledge the God who loved you and helped you bring your accomplishments into being.

Dear God, thank you so much for making my goals
realities. It is because of you that I have success,
and I praise your wonderful name. Amen.

THE PRICELESS SHADOW

How precious is Your steadfast love, O God! The children of men take refuge and put their trust under the shadow of Your wings.
PSALM 36:7 AMP

Success is invigorating to experience—especially when your dreams are coming true and you soar to new heights. Even so, you need protection when you're achieving your goals, lest you become conceited about your abilities.

Your lovingkindness, O LORD, extends to the heavens, Your faithfulness reaches to the skies. Your righteousness is like the mountains . . . O LORD, You preserve man.
PSALM 36:5–6 NASB

Thankfully, God's sheltering wing is your protection against arrogance. Under his glorious wing, you remember that he lifted you to the pinnacle and that you're accountable to him for your actions. Were you to fall from such an elevation due to your pride, you'd be crushed. But God keeps you humble and safe. With him you know that even if you fall you'll rise again. Surely he's worthy of adoration for the provision of his protective wing.

God, thank you for giving me success and protecting me as my dreams become reality. Truly, you are worthy of all honor, glory, and praise! Amen.

A MERRY FACE

*A twinkle in the eye means joy in the heart,
and good news makes you feel fit as a fiddle.*
PROVERBS 15:30 MSG

*It is good to praise you,
LORD. . . . It is good to
tell of your love in the
morning and of your
loyalty at night. . . .
LORD, you have made
me happy by what
you have done.*

PSALM 92:1–2, 4 NCV

When you are a person of praise, everyone knows it. It shows in your words and actions. It even shows in your countenance.

Praise expresses your confidence that God is with you—no matter what comes. It helps you remember the faithful love of God that sustains you and the profound wisdom of God that guides you. And it changes your focus from your limited understanding to the wonderful strength and power of God.

God becomes the light of your eyes and the good news of your heart. Praise God today, and people will know by your merry face that you have been in his presence.

*Dear God, the thought of you puts a smile on
my face. I praise you for your goodness and might—
your love, wisdom, and power. Amen.*

THE LORD RENEWS AND REFRESHES YOUR LIFE

With You is the fountain of life; in Your light we see light.
PSALM 36:9 NKJV

As the psalm says, God is the fountain of life, and by his light you see light. He is the source of all good things, and it is your privilege to go to him for nurturing and encouragement, day after day. Your regeneration in God is a life-long affair.

I will never forget thy precepts: For with them thou hast quickened me.

PSALM 119:93 KJV

God is the light by which you see the world and yourself. God is the light through which you understand your reason for being. God is the author of your existence, the creator of your ability to see his light. His light discloses to you the drama of all that he has created. Stay close to his light. If you stray from his light, your world will be plunged into darkness. His light will enable you to fulfill the purpose for which you were created.

God, help me stay close to you, returning day after day for strength and refreshment of your love and care. Amen.

SECURITY IN HIS WORD

Say the word, and my servant will be healed.
LUKE 7:7 NKJV

When Jesus heard this, he was amazed. Turning to the crowd that was following him, he said, "I tell you, this is the greatest faith I have found anywhere."

LUKE 7:9 NCV

The centurion knew that Jesus was true to his word. That is why he did not ask Jesus to go all the way to his house when his servant was sick. If Jesus said so, the servant would be healed. And sure enough, the servant was well from that very moment.

Does that rule hold for you? When God speaks to you through prayer or the Bible, do you take him at his word?

You have security in the Bible—it is absolutely true—and what God says will certainly be accomplished. Today, believe wholeheartedly so that, like the centurion, you will be commended for your faith.

Dear God, the Bible is wonderful, and I believe it is true. Help me to cling to the certainty of the Bible. Amen.

DELIGHTING AND REQUITING

Delight yourself in the LORD, and he will
give you the desires of your heart.
PSALM 37:4 ESV

There is a desire that germinates in your heart—like a rare, sacred flower it grows and fills you with joy and purpose. God has planted it in you. You made him your focus and delight, and he's given you this special yearning in your soul.

Wait for the LORD,
and keep His way,
and He will exalt you.
PSALM 37:34 NASB

Yet perhaps you're wondering when this sweet promise will bloom—when you will see its wondrous petals of blessing unfold. The days come and go, yet you have no sign of it blossoming.

Friend, the God who sows this hope in you will reap a glad harvest in due time. Just keep enjoying him. Soon enough, the desires of your heart will flourish and you'll rejoice in him anew.

God, you truly are my delight. Thank you for the
continued assurance that you will keep your promises
to me. I praise your precious name. Amen.

MAKING PEACE

Do your best to live at peace with everyone.
ROMANS 12:18 CEV

The Scriptures say . . . "If your enemies are hungry, feed them. If they are thirsty, give them something to drink. In doing this, you will heap burning coals of shame on their heads." Don't let evil conquer you, but conquer evil by doing good.

ROMANS 12:19–21 NLT

There may be people in your life that—no matter how accommodating and nice you are—will not return your friendship. It can be frustrating. You want to have peace, but they prefer conflict.

If you respond in anger, there will never be harmony between you. However, when you continue to treat them with kindness, eventually you prevail over whatever feelings they have against you. You don't have to surrender your principles—you must simply assert them with gentleness and wisdom.

The only way to sway your rivals is to pray for them and be kind. You will find that as you were busy making peace, you were also making a friend.

Dear God, please show me how to be kind to those who are abrasive. Thank you for helping me overcome their evil with good. Amen.

ALREADY DONE

*Commit your way to the Lord, trust also
in Him, and He will do it.*
PSALM 37:5 NASB

God anointed David to be ruler of Israel years before David ever occupied the throne. To David, the time provided numerous opportunities for questions and doubts. Often, David wondered if he'd live to be king and just had to trust that God would fulfill his promise.

*Be still and rest in
the Lord; wait for
Him and patiently
lean yourself
upon Him.*

PSALM 37:7 AMP

Yet to God, this was purely a training period—there was no question he'd keep his pledge. God was simply preparing David to honor him in all the affairs of state.

The point is, what you perceive as a long time of doubtful unknowns has a purpose to God. His promise to you is already accomplished. So make the most of this waiting time by knowing him better.

*God, thank you for putting the times of waiting into perspective. I praise
you that all you've planned for me is already accomplished. Amen.*

BIG OBSTACLES

[Caleb said,] "Let's go and take the land. I know we can do it!"
NUMBERS 13:30 CEV

Do not be afraid of the people of the land, because we will swallow them up. Their protection is gone, but the LORD is with us. Do not be afraid of them.

NUMBERS 14:9 NIV

The people were like giants—or so reported ten of the spies who scoped out the land promised to them by God. Though they were so very close to receiving the desire of their hearts—a land of their own—they were so intimidated by the obstacles that they wanted to give up. However, Joshua and Caleb knew that with God's help, no obstacle could stop them.

Take this to heart today: No obstacle is too big for you when God is with you. Obstacles are object lessons for your faith—they cannot prevent what God has promised you.

Go today and claim the land that God has promised you. You can do it.

Dear God, with your help, I can do it. I thank you, my God, that no obstacle is ever too big for you to fulfill your promises. Amen.

TRAVELING MERCIES

When a person's steps follow the LORD, God is pleased with his ways.
If he stumbles, he will not fall, because the LORD holds his hand.
PSALM 37:23–24 NCV

Guide horses on group trail rides are seldom picked for their beauty. Instead, the rancher chooses horses that are surefooted. The horses you find most beautiful are known for their refined breeding and high spirits. But the plodding, surefooted breeds have a high reputation of dependability on the trail or in a harness. Their work ethic is unmatched.

Thou hast also given me the shield of thy salvation: and thy right hand hath holden me up, and thy gentleness hath made me great. Thou hast enlarged my steps under me, that my feet did not slip.
PSALM 18:35–36 KJV

Life's journey is fraught with unexpected twists and turns, and the risk of stumbling is high. No doubt the psalmist knew this, but he had the boldness to pen words that comfort you centuries later. When God holds you by the hand, a stumble doesn't result in a fall. With his supporting arm, you catch your footing and continue surefooted along the trail.

Thank you, God, for my roots that sink deep into your promises.
Keep me building always on rock, never on sand. Make
me secure as I surrender to you. Amen.

BELIEVE GOD

The Scripture was fulfilled which says, "Abraham believed God, and it was accounted to him for righteousness." And he was called the friend of God.

JAMES 2:23 NKJV

Abraham's faith and deeds worked together. He proved that his faith was real by what he did.

JAMES 2:22 CEV

Your life and how you conduct yourself hinge on whether or not you believe God. Take Abraham for example. He willingly did all God asked him to do because he wholeheartedly trusted God. And God called him a friend. That is why people are still encouraged by Abraham's story today—because of his great faith and how God blessed him and the world through it.

Every day you have the same choice as Abraham—believe God and do as he says or not. You can make an extraordinary difference in the world if you will just trust him and step out in faith.

Will you believe God and be his friend?

Dear God, I want to have great faith and be your friend. I'll follow you, believing that you know the best path for my life. Amen.

WHEN CLOUDS COME

I am old now; I have lived a long time, but I have never seen good people abandoned by the LORD or their children begging for food.
PSALM 37:25 GNT

A mother and her son stood before a statue of Christ with outstretched arms reaching downward in an act of blessing. It was beautiful to the little boy. The sun shone brightly around it, and the blue sky made a serene backdrop. Suddenly clouds moved in, and no one could see the statue. This upset the little boy. He clutched his mother's hand and gasped a loud sigh. "Mommy, what happened to him? Where did he go?" His mother smiled and spoke warmly to her son, "Oh, honey, he's still there. He never goes away."

I have relied on you all my life; you have protected me since the day I was born. I will always praise you.
PSALM 71:6 GNT

☽

God's presence is not predicated on your awareness of it. No amount of inattention on your part erases the company God keeps with you.

Dear God, thank you for paying attention to me even when I don't pay attention to you. Your faithfulness gives me a great and wonderful peace. Amen.

GLORIOUS PROVISION

*My God will supply all your needs according to
His riches in glory in Christ Jesus.*
PHILIPPIANS 4:19 HCSB

*You are rich in
everything—in faith,
in speaking, in knowl-
edge, in truly wanting
to help, and in the
love you learned from
us. In the same way,
be strong also in the
grace of giving.*

2 CORINTHIANS 8:7 NCV

✴

Paul had experienced it—God's glorious provision. He had seen God's help in a powerful way through the very church in Philippi to which he lovingly penned this letter. They had been very generous with him, and he assured the church that God was going to bless them because of it.

This is a wonderful promise for you to claim today. As you are generous with others, you never have to fear being short in resources for your own needs. On the contrary—you open yourself up to God's glorious supply.

Rejoice and freely share with others today. You will certainly receive the great provision God has reserved just for you.

*Dear God, thank you that as I give to others
I don't need to fear for my own needs. I praise
you for your wonderful provision. Amen.*

THE GIFT OF GIVING

*He is ever merciful, and lends; and
his descendants are blessed.*
PSALM 37:26 NKJV

Giving generously from the heart is extremely satisfying for many reasons, but the most important reason is that it glorifies God. When you give freely, you are acknowledging the abundant, unreserved generosity he has poured out on you, his children. Everything you have, *everything*, is a gift of God—the clothes on your back, the food on your table, the roof over your head, the color of your eyes, the size of your feet.

You are the Fountain of life; our light is from your light. Pour out your unfailing love on those who know you! Never stop giving your blessings to those who long to do your will.
PSALM 36:9–10 TLB

There are many ways to give to others and to give back to God. Money is often the first thing that comes to mind; but the gift of time often may be an even greater sacrifice. No matter how you choose to give, you can be sure that God is pleased and will pour out his grace on you in return.

*God, open my heart and open my hands to
share all you have given me. Amen.*

SEASONS OF BLESSINGS

He did good by giving you rains from heaven and fruitful seasons, satisfying your hearts with food and gladness.
ACTS 14:17 ESV

The LORD will open up his heavenly storehouse so that the skies send rain on your land at the right time, and he will bless everything you do.

DEUTERONOMY 28:12 NCV

✹

Throughout Israel's history, the success or failure of Israel hinged on two short rainy seasons. Everything depended on the precipitation. If it rained well, there would be plenty of crops. If it did not, there would be famine and devastation.

It was easy for them to look at the cloudless sky and fear that the dry days would continue. Perhaps this morning it is the same in your life. It feels like nothing is going to change—that the rains of abundance will not pour forth for you.

Just as God faithfully sent the rain for fruitful seasons, trust him to send you showers of blessings that will satisfy you and gladden your heart.

Dear God, thank you for sending your showers of blessings at just the right time. You are truly good to me. Amen.

WORDS OF THE WISE

The godly offer good counsel;
they teach right from wrong.
PSALM 37:30 NLT

When you are hurting, a friend's timely counsel can be a precious gift. Yet how can you discern if what he is telling you is godly and wise—or if it is foolish and destructive?

Look at those who are honest and good, for a wonderful future awaits those who love peace.

PSALM 37:37 NLT

First, his words must line up with God's Word, never contradicting the principles of Scripture. Second, his instruction should direct you to the Lord and encourage you to honor him completely. Third, whether he is offering you comfort or correction, he should not be fishing for a certain response. Rather, he must be honest, compassionate, and tactful so you can grow in your faith. Sometimes it will be obvious that a friend's advice is straight from God, but when it is not, turn his words over to God in prayer. He will certainly show you whether it is worthwhile counsel or not.

God, please help me discern whether the advice I receive
and give is godly and wise. I want to honor you, Lord,
especially in the counsel I give to others. Amen.

A BIG GOD

Powerful is your arm! Strong is your hand!
Your right hand is lifted high in glorious strength.
PSALM 89:13 NLT

The God who made the world and everything in it is the Lord of heaven and earth and does not live in temples built by hands.

ACTS 17:24 NIV

Someone asked the movie director John Huston what was the toughest subject he ever had to work with in making a motion picture. He said it was the Bible stories, especially the creation scene and the flood scene in the movie *The Bible*. "I had a terrible time making them," he said. "I really don't know how God managed it." God managed it because he is almighty. God is supreme and sovereign over all of life.

God's sovereignty over all of life means your life is divinely ordained and profoundly significant. God has written his will and way for you into your very being. Your response to what God wants is of major importance and foremost consequence. God made you special and important. He gave you what it takes.

I fall at your feet, O God, overcome by your might and majesty. You are the greatest! Amen.

HE SEES THROUGH THE ACT

Lord, all my desire is before You; and my sighing is not hidden from You.

PSALM 38:9 AMP

We've all done it. Someone asks, "How are you?" and our automatic answer is, "Fine." Unfortunately, that's not always true. It's just easier—and safer.

It's intimidating to be real with people. They may get offended. They could criticize you or make you feel guilty. They could even use your confessions against you.

Lord, don't leave me; my God, don't go away. Quickly come and help me, my Lord and Savior.

PSALM 38:21–22 NCV

The thing is, you can't hide your emotions and troubles from God. He sees the un-sugarcoated truth of your heart and still accepts you, which means you don't have to fear communicating openly with him. You may put on an act with others, but you shouldn't with God. He knows—and will always love—the real you. Be honest with him.

God, thank you for being compassionate and loving me completely—even the parts that I'm ashamed of. Help me to be truthful with you in all things. Amen.

WITH YOU TO THE END

*I'll be with you as you do this, day after day
after day, right up to the end of the age.*
MATTHEW 28:20 MSG

*I will ask the Father
to send you the Holy
Spirit who will help
you and always be with
you. The Spirit will
show you what is true.*

JOHN 14:16–17 CEV

This was the comforting promise Jesus gave to the disciples when he sent them out to tell the good news of salvation. Through the Holy Spirit, Jesus would help them wherever they went.

This is God's promise to you as well. He knows that life can get lonely—especially when you deal with personal issues that are difficult to share with others. Yet you are never alone. God is right there for you—always caring for the deep issues of your heart.

This morning, pray to your constant friend and allow him to fill you with his comfort. He loves you and is with you to the end.

*Dear God, thank you for being with me in the
issues I can't share with others. Thank you
for never leaving me alone. Amen.*

TODAY IS THE GOOD DAY

Lord, remind me how brief my time on earth will be. Remind me that my days are numbered—how fleeting my life is.
PSALM 39:4 NLT

The calm sea produces a sudden tsunami. The clear, brilliant skies fill with the smoke of an unexpected explosion. The body that appears fit is imperceptibly racked with disease.

These unanticipated calamities shock your soul, but they also infuse you with valuable wisdom: You must appreciate your loved ones today, for you may not have tomorrow.

"My entire lifetime is just a moment to you; at best, each of us is but a breath." . . . And so, Lord, where do I put my hope? My only hope is in you.
PSALM 39:5, 7 NLT

Friend, no matter what your hopes are for the future, don't wait to start living until you achieve them. Make the most of every moment and care for those around you. Today is the good day, so honor God by living it out fully. Worship God, love your family, and make it the best day of your life.

God, I thank you for every moment of my life. Help me to not worry about tomorrow but focus on honoring you now. Amen.

GENTLE REMINDER

Be completely humble and gentle; be patient,
bearing with one another in love.
EPHESIANS 4:2 NIV

Follow my example,
as I follow the
example of Christ.
1 CORINTHIANS 11:1 NIV

As a Christian, you have the most glorious privilege of being an example of Christ to everyone around you. You best do so by being humble, gentle, patient, and loving— just as God has been with you.

Think of what that means for you today. You have the opportunity to remind others that God loves them dearly. And they will be attracted to him because of the qualities he shows through you.

Will you live as a worthy representative of God today— inviting him to be humble, patient, and loving through you —so that others can see God's true nature? Will you be his gentle reminder?

Dear God, I want to be a good and worthy
example of your gentleness, humility, patience,
and love. Work through me today. Amen.

THE SOURCE OF HOPE

Now, Lord, what wait I for? my hope is in thee.
PSALM 39:7 KJV

The song of the robin, the majesty of snow-covered mountain peaks, the lustrous beauty of a spring flower, and the predictable movement of the stars in the night sky are but a few of the wonders that point you to God, the source of all hope. They are reminders that no

Shout with joy to the LORD, all the earth! Worship the LORD with gladness. Come before him, singing with joy.

PSALM 100:1–2 NLT

circumstance—poverty, pain, sickness, loss, disappointment, grief, even the prospect of your own death—can steal your hope when it is safely anchored in God.

God is the author of all hope, and he will never leave your side as you walk through the dark, confusing, lonely, and painful places in your life. He will replace your clouds of despair with the brilliant, penetrating light of his everlasting love. He will fill your heart with peace and your mind with wisdom and understanding.

Thank you, God, for a voice with which to sing your praises with my whole heart. Amen.

THE ONE WHO DEFENDS YOU

*I saw heaven opened, and behold, a white horse, and
He who sat on it is called Faithful and True.*
REVELATION 19:11 NASB

*Great and amazing are
your deeds, O Lord God
the Almighty! Just and
true are your ways, O
King of the nations!
Who will not fear,
O Lord, and glorify
your name?*

REVELATION 15:3–4 ESV

Your defender is the gentle Lamb of God who takes away the sin of the world, but he is also the mighty warrior who defeats evil and administers justice. Though his powerful hand is worrisome for the enemy, he is always tender toward you.

Standing in the opened heaven, he surveys all that happens from an elevated perspective and takes in the complete picture of your life and struggles. A brilliant strategist and tactician, Jesus is devoted to you, his beloved, and honorably fulfills his promises.

Trust him—the one who defends you is faithful and true. He does everything in his power to help you, and it is *always* enough.

*Dear God, you are faithful and true, my great defender.
I praise you for your mighty and gentle hand that
helps me today and every day. Amen.*

A PATTERN OF PATIENCE

*I waited patiently for the Lord; he inclined
to me and heard my cry.*
PSALM 40:1 NRSV

Tulips and daffodils, in all the brilliant colors of spring, hide throughout the long winter in tight little shells deep beneath the surface of the soil. You barely know they exist as the wind blows and the cold holds you in its grip. But with the first warming breeze of spring, you notice green shoots bursting through the surface of the soil. Soon waving everywhere are the red, pink, and yellow flags that represent God's faithful promise that summer, winter, springtime, and harvest will continue on the earth, and in your life, each at its appointed time.

You made me suffer a lot, but you will bring me back from this deep pit and give me new life. You will make me truly great and take my sorrow away.
PSALM 71:20–21 CEV

You must be patient and cling to your hope in God. In his perfect time, the ambassadors of spring will burst forth in your life once more, fulfilling the promise of God's faithfulness.

*God, thank you for the promise of springtime in my life.
I will wait patiently through the difficult seasons
and hope earnestly in your faithfulness. Amen.*

INDELIBLY ENGRAVED

*I would not forget you! See, I have written
your name on the palms of my hands.*
ISAIAH 49:15–16 NLT

*You will know I am
the LORD. Anyone
who trusts in me will
not be disappointed.*

ISAIAH 49:23 NCV

The Israelites used the practice during the time of Isaiah. In order to show their love or commitment to some important person or place, the people would permanently mark their hands.

It is the sign God gives to you—engraving your name as a commitment to love and care for you. There is no way he could ever forget you.

In fact, God's thoughts are always turned toward you. So if you are feeling far from him this morning, remember his loving hands indelibly marked with your name. Then turn to him and allow him to engrave his name and comfort on your heart.

*Dear God, thank you that my name is on your hands for
all of eternity. You are most definitely written
on my heart. Amen.*

WHAT A MESS!

He lifted me out of the . . . mire; he set my feet
on a rock and gave me a firm place to stand.
PSALM 40:2 NIV

You've probably heard that old cowboy proverb: "If you find yourself in a hole, stop digging." It reflects the principle that if you've created problems for yourself through your mode of operation, you must alter your methods to get out of trouble.

He put a new song in my mouth, a song of praise to our God. Many will see and fear, and put their trust in the LORD.

PSALM 40:3 ESV

Friend, if you're constantly getting into messes, you have to change your conduct in order to get the results you want. The good news is that God wants to teach you a new way to do things that'll satisfy your soul.

Submit to God's instructions, and he'll show you his path out of your predicament. He'll transform the way you think and give you a firm place to stand.

God, thank you for getting me out of my hole and onto your rock!
Thank you for transforming my mind and the way I operate. Amen.

GOD WILL DELIVER YOU

The king said to Daniel, May your God,
Whom you are serving continually, deliver you!
DANIEL 6:16 AMP

God rescues and saves people and does mighty miracles in heaven and on earth. He is the one who saved Daniel from the power of the lions.

DANIEL 6:27 NCV

Daniel was guilty of praying to God—in direct conflict with the Persian decree that people should pray to no one except the king. So Daniel was sentenced to the lions' den—certain death.

Yet when morning came, Daniel had not been devoured. God had shut the mouths of the lions.

It seems an amazing story, but it is consistent with the character of God. When others punish you for being faithful to him, he does astounding things to help you—even saving you from the jaws of lions.

Serve him faithfully today, and do not fear what others will do. Your God will certainly deliver you in a marvelous way.

Dear God, you really do amaze me. Thank you that I can serve you faithfully with the assurance of your help and protection. Amen.

LIFE AS HIS VESSEL

He put a new song in my mouth, a song of praise to our God. Many people will see this and worship him. Then they will trust the Lord.

PSALM 40:3 NCV

It is generally easier to believe the negative things people say about you rather than the positive. *Ugly. Stupid. Disgraceful. Worthless.* These words make lasting wounds on your heart, and it is difficult to overcome them.

> *Let all who seek you rejoice and be glad because of you. Let those who love your salvation continually say, "The LORD is great!"*
>
> PSALM 40:16
> GOD'S WORD

Yet remember, it is not what the vessel is made of that gives it value but what it contains. When you believe in God, he fills you, and your life becomes a vessel of praise to him. You have been completely changed. You no longer have any reason to feel shame, because God has provided you with a new identity based on his beauty, wisdom, holiness, and worth. Friend, you have been emptied of your indignities and filled with God's glory. Let him shine through you so others can trust him as well.

God, you have changed me from inside out, and I praise your name! Thank you for giving me such hope, worth, beauty, wisdom, and holiness. Amen.

WITHOUT FAULT

To him who is able to keep you from falling and to present you before his glorious presence without fault and with great joy.

JUDE 1:24 NIV

He has reconciled you by His physical body through His death, to present you holy, faultless, and blameless before Him—if indeed you remain grounded and steadfast in the faith.

COLOSSIANS 1:22–23
HCSB

Spotless. Flawless. Holy. Without blemish. Beautiful. These are all words that describe you because of what Jesus has done.

It is often easier to believe the negative things people say than to keep a steady heart knowing that Christ has taken away your failings. Yet before you catalog your faults this morning, call this to mind—you are wonderfully created, beautifully forgiven, and flawless in God's sight.

Whatever others may say, whatever the world may prescribe, whatever you have been raised to believe—God looks at you with great joy. Praise him today for transforming you and bringing you into his presence without fault.

Dear God, thank you for accepting me completely without fault and with joy. To you be all the honor, glory, power, and praise. Amen.

A DECISION TO TRUST

Blessed is the man who makes the LORD his trust, who does not look to the proud, to those who turn aside to false gods.

PSALM 40:4 NIV

Learning to swim is daunting. You'll probably never forget how it felt to squint across the pool before filling your lungs with that last deep breath. Three strokes later, your hesitant paddling ended in frantic sputtering when water started

In You, O LORD, I put my trust; let me never be ashamed; deliver me in Your righteousness.

PSALM 31:1 NKJV

☾

closing over your head. At the same moment, strong arms caught you from beneath and lifted you back up to the surface. Dad or Mom had been there all along.

A heart of trust is one of life's sweet but hard-won gifts. The discovery that God is always there, ready to lift you up when you start to sink, replaces fear with courage and timidity with boldness. Along with that courage and boldness comes the strength to face whatever life throws at you—even when it requires a long, scary swim to the other side.

Dear God, I am a child in your arms. Thank you for holding me in your loving embrace. I depend on your provision and protection. Amen.

ENDORSEMENTS

*This is My beloved Son, with whom I
am well-pleased; listen to Him!*
MATTHEW 17:5 NASB

*Obviously, I'm not try-
ing to win the approval
of people, but of God.
If pleasing people were
my goal, I would not
be Christ's servant.*

GALATIANS 1:10 NLT

People respond to endorsements—they add credibility. So when Peter saw Jesus transfigured and conversing with Moses and Elijah, it was no wonder that he wanted others to see it too. Surely those two giants of the faith could convince others that Jesus was truly the Messiah.

Yet the only endorsement Jesus required was from God himself. This is true for you as well. Though it is nice to have affirmation from others, you do not have to earn everyone's support, especially when the only one you really need to please is God.

Today, seek to have God's approval. After all, his is the only endorsement that really counts.

Dear God, I want to be pleasing to you. Help me not to seek earthly endorsements but to live a life that gives you glory and joy. Amen.

BETTER THAN YOU CAN IMAGINE

You have multiplied, O LORD my God, your wondrous deeds and your thoughts toward us; none can compare with you! I will proclaim and tell of them, yet they are more than can be told.
PSALM 40:5 ESV

What would you like to be doing in ten years? Perhaps you have a picture in mind of what the perfect future looks like. Interestingly, many people who achieve all their goals find that their success was not as satisfying as they thought it would be.

I did not hide Your righteousness in my heart; I spoke about Your faithfulness and salvation; I did not conceal Your constant love and truth from the great assembly.
PSALM 40:10 HCSB

Yet there are also those who've forgotten their own plans in order to pursue God. As David testified in Psalm 40, they discover a life full of purpose and love—abundant in hope and wonder.

Friend, you can imagine great things, but God's plans for you are infinitely better than all of them. So pursue and obey him. He'll grant your heart's deepest desires and never disappoint you.

God, I thank you that your plans for me are far better than anything I can envision. I'm excited about the great things you will do. Amen.

EXPRESSING IT TO HIM

Let all that I am praise the LORD; with my whole heart,
I will praise his holy name.
PSALM 103:1 NLT

The LORD is my
strength and song,
and He has become
my salvation; He is my
God, and I will praise
Him; my father's God,
and I will exalt Him.

EXODUS 15:2 NKJV

☀

Have you ever been so filled with wonder at the love and goodness of God that you burst out in praise to him? The Israelites did. They saw God take an impossible situation and turn it into a victory.

The powerful Egyptian army had pursued the Israelites and had trapped them at the Red Sea. The situation seemed hopeless. God not only provided a way out, but he also made sure that the Egyptians would never bother the Israelites again.

It is fitting to express gratefulness to God. Look for ways God is turning the impossible into a victory for you today, and thank him with all of your heart.

Dear God, thank you for working as powerfully today as you did for
the Israelites. I praise you with thankfulness and joy. Amen.

DELIGHT IN HIS WILL

I delight to do Your will, O my God,
and Your law is within my heart.
PSALM 40:8 NKJV

Be delighted with the Lord. Then he will give you all your heart's desires. Commit everything you do to the Lord. Trust him to help you do it, and he will.

PSALM 37:4–5 TLB

You mark the arrival of a new year through the simple task of hanging a fresh calendar on the wall. Flipping through the calendar, you may pause to scan the pages of the months ahead and wonder what they hold in store for you. Will March bring a surprise blessing? Will you have an unexpected opportunity in July? Will there be a disappointment in September? What will happen between now and when December rolls around again?

Though you anticipate the future, and sometimes worry about it, God is the one who sets your course and imprints each day with the events that become your life. A heart committed to God can leave the passing of time in his hands and trust that he will fill in the blanks of the calendar with perfect order.

Dear God, no matter the circumstances, when I am in your will I am in a large place. I fix my mind and heart now on doing your will. Amen.

REAL LOVE PREFERS TRUTH

If you really love me . . .
GENESIS 20:13 CEV

Your love is ever before me, and I walk continually in your truth.

PSALM 26:3 NIV

Have you ever been asked by a loved one to exaggerate your accomplishments or qualities in order to impress their colleagues or friends? It can be heartbreaking, because it can feel as if they do not accept you as you are.

However, you should never have to pretend in order to prove your love to another person. You do not have to act like someone different in order to be lovable. Real love always prefers the truth.

God loves you and accepts you just as you are. This morning, rejoice that he brings out the best in you—who you were truly created to be—and that you never have to hide yourself from him.

Dear God, thank you that real love is about truth, and that you love me just as I am. Truly, you are good. Amen.

A PROMISE FOR THE MERCIFUL

How blessed is he who considers the helpless;
the LORD will deliver him in a day of trouble.
PSALM 41:1 NASB

You resemble God's character when you show love and mercy to someone who is in need. God takes note each time you allow him to shine through you—every instance when you have compassion on others who cannot help themselves or who have mistreated you because of their own inner pain.

You will help me, because I do what is right; you will keep me in your presence forever. Praise the LORD, the God of Israel! Praise him now and forever! Amen!
PSALM 41:12–13 GNT

Though it's easier to pass them by, and though it's often inconvenient and uncomfortable to relate to people you don't associate with or agree with, still, that's when you are doing his work in the most poignant way. Remember that you harvest what you plant. So make it your goal to show mercy wherever you go, being sure that you'll find it when you're in need.

God, thank you for this wonderful promise. Please reveal opportunities for me to express mercy today, and help me to show others your love and compassion. Amen.

AGAIN I SAY REJOICE!

Rejoice in the Lord always. Again I will say, rejoice!
PHILIPPIANS 4:4 NKJV

Let all who take refuge in you rejoice; let them ever sing for joy, and spread your protection over them, that those who love your name may exult in you.

PSALM 5:11 ESV

Paul knew the amazing power of praise. He remembered being in the Philippian prison with Silas, his co-worker. Beaten and in chains, they sang hymns to God, knowing that their joy came from him and not from their circumstances. It was then that the doors of the prison flew open and they were freed.

That is why Paul knew that these words would be meaningful to the Philippians. They had seen it firsthand.

They are meaningful for you as well. Whatever your difficult situation—it does not control you. Your joy comes from God. So rejoice. Soon he will fling open the doors of your situation and set you free as well.

Dear God, I rejoice. My joy comes from you, and I praise you with gladness. Amen.

I CAN GET TRUE SATISFACTION

As a deer longs for a stream of cool water,
so I long for you, O God.
PSALM 42:1 GNT

A deer's need for water is never completely gone. Though it may drink and be satisfied for a while, soon enough its body will demand more.

My soul thirsts for God, for the living God. When can I go and meet with God?

PSALM 42:2 NIV

You have similar requirements, though not just for physical sustenance such as food and water. You need love, acceptance, and purpose. Most of all, your soul must have God.

It's true that you can attempt to fill those needs with other things—relationships, wealth, activities, etc.—but they'll never truly fulfill you. They only mask your true yearning and make you hungrier. Deep inside, you long for God—and you can have as much of him as your heart can handle. So don't go thirsty. Drink him in and satisfy your soul.

God, I've been filling my soul with other things,
but I realize that I really only yearn for you. Please
satisfy my hunger with your presence. Amen.

HE IS YOUR JOY

*Shout his praise with joy! For great is the Holy
One of Israel who lives among you.*
ISAIAH 12:6 NLT

*Praise the LORD in
song, for He has done
excellent things; let this
be known throughout
the earth.*

ISAIAH 12:5 NASB

God does not dwell on your mistakes. Rather, he faithfully turns away from anger in order to comfort and heal you. You are his joy.

He saves you from traps and schemes. Always trustworthy, he chases away all of your fears. He is your protector, defender, redeemer, savior, and friend. You are his joy.

He satisfies the deepest hungers of your soul. He teaches your heart with wisdom and nourishes your soul with his presence. You are his joy. So praise God today, for his goodness and might. Thank him that all your great blessings have come from his hand. Express your loving thoughts toward him—because he is *your* joy.

*Dear God, you are my joy. I praise you for
loving and protecting me. I glorify your name
for your goodness to all your people. Amen.*

YOUR SOUL'S TRUE YEARNING

My soul thirsts for God, for the living God.
When shall I come and appear before God?
PSALM 42:2 NKJV

You cannot seem to fill that uneasy longing within. You go shopping, but it doesn't help. You eat something delicious, but that does not satisfy you. You try socializing more to fill the emptiness, but that doesn't do it either. Your soul requires spiritual growth and refreshment. You need God. You need God more than you need food, clothing, sunshine, or shelter. God satisfies your yearning for purpose, worth, and eternity, teaching you his insight and inspiring you with his presence.

The LORD will send His faithful love by day; His song will be with me in the night —a prayer to the God of my life.

PSALM 42:8 HCSB

Neither the spoon nor the credit card can help you, but prayer and reading his Word can. So do not ignore this crucial need. Your thirst is for God. Drink and be filled.

God, thank you for satisfying the deep needs of my soul—for inspiring me with your purpose and refreshing me with your presence. You truly fill me with joy. Amen.

STREAMS OF TRANQUILLITY

If anyone thirsts, let him come to Me and drink.
JOHN 7:37 NKJV

Rivers of living water will brim and spill out of the depths of anyone who believes in me this way, just as the Scripture says.

JOHN 7:38 MSG

The soul often strives in vain after those things it cannot attain and which it cannot fulfill. Yet once your soul drinks of God, there is an endless supply of him to satisfy you. You never have to fear lack because God's Spirit is constantly ready to fill you with as much of God as you are able to receive.

Instead of the turmoil of running after fruitless earthly things, your soul finds rest and tranquillity because it is filled to overflowing with the peace of God's Spirit. If you thirst today, drink deeply from the limitless stream of living water that will truly satisfy your soul.

Dear God, I am thirsty for you. Fill me to overflowing and give me peace today so that I may bring you glory. Amen.

GOOD TIMES PAST

My heart is breaking as I remember how it used to be:
I walked among the crowds of worshipers, leading
a great procession to the house of God.
PSALM 42:4 NLT

Can you think of a time when your relationship with God felt deeper and more meaningful? Maybe you remember when your faith was new and his presence seemed to permeate your every activity. Alternatively, perhaps you recall an encounter with him that powerfully transformed your life.

Why are you down in the dumps, dear soul? Why are you crying the blues? Fix my eyes on God—soon I'll be praising again. He puts a smile on my face. He's my God.
PSALM 42:5 MSG

Yet understand, your relationship with God is not just about what happened yesterday, but it is about how you love and obey him now. Keep your eyes fixed on him always, and you will experience a more intimate relationship than you ever thought possible.

God, I want our relationship to be healthy and flourish.
Help me to seek you daily so our intimacy can grow
deeper all the days of my life. Amen.

PRAY BELIEVING

Whatever you ask for in prayer, believe (trust and be confident) that it is granted to you, and you will [get it].
MARK 11:24 AMP

If you have faith in God and don't doubt, you can tell this mountain to get up and jump into the sea, and it will.

MARK 11:23 CEV

This morning, what is the main thing you pray for—the desire that you most hope to receive?

It may seem far away and impossible. However, when you pray with faith, you acknowledge that God can solve any dilemma and that you fully trust him to help you.

As he answers, you follow his instructions with a humble spirit of hope. If your request is God's will, he will faithfully provide it. If it is not, he will change your desires to something vastly better.

Pray expectantly, knowing that God loves to answer you. His response may not happen immediately, but be certain that he is moving mountains for you.

Dear God, I praise you for answering my prayers. I believe that you will either grant my request or provide something infinitely better. Amen.

A NEW WAY OF THINKING

*Why art thou cast down, O my soul? And why art
thou disquieted in me? hope thou in God: for I shall
yet praise him for the help of his countenance.*
PSALM 42:5 KJV

Thoughts of failure, loss, and hopelessness can invade your mind, chasing, tormenting, and even destroying you. You run from these thoughts, only to find that they are nipping at your heels. You try to hide, only to realize that they are behind you, stalking you.

*Keep me as the apple
of the eye, hide me
under the shadow of
thy wings.*

PSALM 17:8 KJV

When angry, bitter thoughts leave you running for your life, God offers sanctuary and shelter. With one wave of his mighty hand, he chases away the brutal thoughts, and, one by one, he replaces them with thoughts of kindness, goodness, gentleness, and faith. Love transforms your mind, and hope restores your heart. He promises that even though you may hear the wild beasts growling in the distance, they can never again harm you as long as you dwell in the shelter of his loving arms.

*God, I thank you for restoring hope to my heart and peace
to my mind. You are my Savior and my God. Amen.*

A NEW THING

I am doing a new thing; now it springs forth, do you not perceive it? I will make a way in the wilderness.
ISAIAH 43:19 ESV

Praise God, the Father of our Lord Jesus Christ. God is so good, and by raising Jesus from death, he has given us new life and a hope that lives on.

1 PETER 1:3 CEV

Some days your heart will cry out for good news—some indication that you can be optimistic about the future. When God spoke the words to Isaiah, he was telling the prophet to look for the hope ahead. He says the same to you today.

The good news for you is that no matter what is going on in your life, God has the power, wisdom, and love to help you. He is doing something new today—whether you see it or not—providing new opportunities for you and endless possibilities. Giving you hope.

God is making a way in the wilderness for you. Look for it with a glad and hopeful heart.

Dear God, thank you for providing new opportunities and for giving me hope. I praise you for all the good things you are doing. Amen.

DAY AND NIGHT

The LORD will send His faithful love by day; His song will be with me in the night—a prayer to the God of my life.
PSALM 42:8 HCSB

You can't predict when you'll need to be comforted—and neither can your loved ones. You want to talk, but they're unavailable. Perhaps it's because they're not home or it's just too late to call. Maybe they're facing deep struggles of their own. Whatever the case, they can't help you. Where can you turn?

Why am I so sad? Why am I so troubled? I will put my hope in God, and once again I will praise him, my savior and my God.

PSALM 42:11 GNT

Day or night, you can always talk to God. Although your confidants may get tired or lack the ability to console you, God never will.

No matter your situation, you can always pray. In fact, God invites you to communicate with him at all times. He wants to be a constant, loving presence in your life—so call upon him frequently.

God, you know the troubles in my soul. Speak peace to me, my God, and help me always turn to you in my time of need. Amen.

MUTUAL ENCOURAGEMENT

*We may be mutually strengthened and encouraged
and comforted by each other's faith.*
ROMANS 1:12 AMP

*I am yearning to see
you, that I may impart
and share with you
some spiritual gift
to strengthen and
establish you.*

ROMANS 1:11 AMP

Paul was pleased that the Romans were growing in the faith—especially in a culture so opposed to Christianity. He had not met the people of the Roman church, but that did not take away from his concern for them. He knew they would benefit from his teaching and that he would gain by knowing them.

This is the wonderful nature of the church. Its members exist for mutual encouragement. Believers can strengthen each other during difficult times with their various gifts.

You can be a blessing to other believers. Be willing to use your gifts so that others will be encouraged.

*Dear God, thank you that believers can encourage each
other. Please use my gifts today to strengthen, establish,
and comfort others—and bring you glory. Amen.*

HIS WAY IS THE HIGHWAY

Send out your light and your truth; let them guide me. Let them lead me to your holy mountain, to the place where you live.
PSALM 43:3 NLT

It's not about coming up with ways to serve God—what pleases him is that you obey him. He doesn't want a relationship with you based on regulations. Rather, he expects its foundation to be love.

Though it's easier to follow a set of spiritual rules, that's not what God has called you to.

I will worship at your altar because you make me joyful. You are my God, and I will praise you. Yes, I will praise you as I play my harp.

PSALM 43:4 CEV

That's why sometimes when you're doing everything "right," God sets you on a darkened path—he's showing you how to rely upon him completely.

God would rather have a healthy, authentic relationship with you than watch you observe some sacred ritual. His way is higher than mere religion, so follow him. He'll teach you to really love him.

God, I praise you for valuing relationships over regulations and love over rituals. Teach me to love you more every day, my wonderful Lord. Amen.

EVEN UNDER SIEGE

Blessed be the Lord! For He has shown me His marvelous loving favor when I was beset as in a besieged city.
PSALM 31:21 AMP

> *Be of good courage, and He shall strengthen your heart, all you who hope in the LORD.*
> PSALM 31:24 NKJV

These are the difficult places—where the soul feels stifled and confined. You cannot find true safety there, but neither can you leave because to do so would expose you to more danger.

There is only one place to turn, and that is to your God. It is even in the times when you feel under siege that God's loving favor comforts you and makes you brave. That is when his voice is most powerful and encouraging, and his presence is most dear.

Are you besieged today? Then think of yourself closed in with God, and receive all the tender favor he desires to show you.

Dear God, you are powerful, kind, and good. Protect me on my way so that I might find my true safety and freedom in you. Amen.

LEARNING TO LOVE HIM

I will go to the altar of God, to God my exceeding joy;
and upon the lyre I shall praise You, O God, my God.

PSALM 43:4 NASB

The student who studies to play an instrument with a mediocre teacher will take on the mentor's shortcomings. It is only through the patient training of a skilled maestro that the student is able to discover the true art of the instrument.

Send your light and your truth. Let them guide me. Let them bring me to your holy mountain and to your dwelling place.

PSALM 43:3
GOD'S WORD

☽

The same is true for love. Sometimes people are negatively influenced by those who first love them, and their devotion to God falls short. The wonderful thing about God is that he gladly teaches people how to love him. Did you have a flawed example of love when you were growing up? Do not despair. The great Maestro will show you the excellent way to express love and to be loved in return.

God, you are the great Maestro of my heart. Teach me to love as you do, unconditionally, sacrificially, with joy and trust. To you be all the glory. Amen.

THE AMAZING GIVER

*Your Father knows what you
need before you ask Him.*
MATTHEW 6:8 NASB

*Praise be to God, who
has not rejected my
prayer or withheld
his love from me!*

PSALM 66:20 NIV

☀

How intimately he knows you—how amazing is his attention to every detail of your life. Your loving God knows the longings of your soul before you even ask.

Then why pray? you may wonder. Why persistently present your dearest requests before his throne?

Because it is in those times of prayer that *you* know *him*. He is not only hearing your request, but he is also inviting you to experience a close, profound relationship with him.

This morning as you pray, do not just go to God with an extensive list of requests. Go to him for his sake—the best gift of all. You will find how truly amazing he is.

*Dear God, when I think of what my soul really longs for,
it is you. Thank you for knowing my needs and
for filling them so faithfully. Amen.*

PRAYER IN A DRY SEASON

*Why are you in despair, O my soul? And why
are you disturbed within me? Hope in God.*

PSALM 43:5 NASB

Occasionally you may experience spiritual dry spells, which can be precipitated by the loss of a loved one, a personal defeat, or any number of adverse circum-stances. During those uncomfortable, barren times, it often becomes difficult to pray. God may seem like a vague idea to you rather than a living reality.

*Give ear to my prayer,
O God, and do not
hide Yourself from
my supplication. Attend to me, and hear
me; I am restless in
my complaint, and
moan noisily.*

PSALM 55:1–2 NKJV

This is not an unusual occurrence. Many heroes of the faith experienced loss of direction and had their faith tested. Even David was afflicted by depressions brought on by treachery, betrayal, adversaries, and his own sins. Persist in prayer. Faith and vitality will return. God does not forsake you.

*God, I know there will be times when my faith is tested and I
cannot feel you as near as I do right now. When those times come,
I know that you will never leave me or forsake me. Amen.*

I WILL SEE HIS GOODNESS

Yet I am confident I will see the LORD's goodness
while I am here in the land of the living.
PSALM 27:13 NLT

Surely your goodness
and love will be with
me all my life.

PSALM 23:6 NCV

You can make it through today. Though your schedule may be full, though issues you face are difficult, and though you may not see the obstacles ahead—you can know for sure that you are going to be all right.

Why? Because God's goodness is with you, and he wants you to have joy. He will comfort you during the difficult moments, and he will strengthen you for whatever challenges come your way today.

No matter what today holds, God is with you—to love you and help you through it. Put your confidence in him and take notice of all the ways he shows you his goodness.

Dear God, I am confident that I will see your
goodness today. Thank you for showing me
your goodness in every situation. Amen.

BRAGGING RIGHTS

Not by their own sword did they win the land . . . but your right hand and your arm, and the light of your face, for you delighted in them.
PSALM 44:3 ESV

It's a trap to believe that the past was "the best of times." You boastfully reminisce about achieving a certain goal, having a special relationship, or experiencing some smashing victory—and lament that your golden era is gone forever.

I don't trust my bow to help me, and my sword can't save me. You saved us from our foes. . . . We will praise God every day; we will praise your name forever.
PSALM 44:6–8 NCV

Such a view is usually centered on personal triumphs that were always destined to fade. Instead, your focus should be on God, who doesn't grow weaker in you. Rather, God will work more powerfully through you as you walk with him daily.

Friend, stop bragging about "the good ol' days" and look forward to your magnificent future with God. Your best days are ahead, so praise the One who gives you everlasting life.

God, please help me to let go of the past. Sometimes it's hard to be optimistic about the future, but I know I can trust you. Amen.

HIS GOOD NAME

You, O GOD my Lord, deal on my behalf for your name's sake;
because your steadfast love is good, deliver me!
PSALM 109:21 ESV

I will praise you forever for what you have done; in your name I will hope, for your name is good. I will praise you in the presence of your saints.

PSALM 52:9 NIV

God instructed Moses to teach the Israelites his name—*I Am Who I Am.*

However, the Hebrew language is different from modern languages because it does not indicate a sense of time. His name could just as easily be translated *I Am Who I Have Been* or *I Will Forever Be Who I Am Now.*

God is consistent and holy. Because his name indicates his character, you can trust him to help you as he has always helped those who love him.

Therefore, take heart today with the assurance that the God who so faithfully provided for Moses will provide for you today.

Dear God, I take comfort that your name indicates a consistent, faithful character. I know that those who have trusted in you have never been disappointed. Amen.

ALL YOU REALLY NEED

Not in my bow do I trust, nor can my sword save me. But you
have saved us. . . . In God we have boasted continually,
and we will give thanks to your name forever.
PSALM 44:6–8 ESV

King Jehoshaphat of Judah realized that his nation did not stand a chance against the invading armies of Ammon, Moab, and Mount Seir. So he prayed, asking the Lord for instruction.

It wasn't their power that gave them victory. But it was your great power and strength. You were with them because you loved them.

PSALM 44:3 NCV

God's direction to him went against all conventional wisdom. Instead of fighting the enemy with swords and bows, the people of Judah were to worship the Lord with singing. So they did. They praised him as their enemies advanced. And miraculously, he won their battle for them. Are you facing a challenge that seems overwhelming to you today? Seek God's guidance. His instructions may not make sense, but obey him anyway, doing exactly as he says. He will surely triumph in this battle for you, and he will teach you that he is all you really need.

God, I have been fretting because I do not have the resources for the challenge I face today. Thank you for showing me that all I need is to obey you. Amen.

May

*God speaks in
different ways, and
we don't always
recognize his voice.*

JOB 33:14 CEV

THE GENTLE SHEPHERD

The LORD is my shepherd.
PSALM 23:1 NKJV

They will lie down in pleasant places and feed in the lush pastures of the hills. I myself will tend my sheep and give them a place to lie down in peace, says the Sovereign LORD.

EZEKIEL 34:14–15 NLT

God is the kind of good and gentle shepherd with which a flock will undoubtedly thrive. He knows his sheep—he provides for and nurtures them with knowledge and understanding. He guides them past any dangers to places of rest.

He defends them with his skill and robust strength, gladly giving his life rather than seeing one fall to a foe. Gently and mercifully he attends to each one from birth to death, assuring that each one has a good life and receives joyful rewards.

Truly, this gentle shepherd is good. He is *your* shepherd—your God. Claim him as your own, for surely, with him, you shall never want.

Dear God, you are my gentle shepherd. Today, I thank you that your goodness and mercy are with me all the days of my life. Amen.

TAKING HOLD OF GRACE

Grace is poured into thy lips: therefore
God hath blessed thee for ever.
PSALM 45:2 KJV

God's grace is abundantly evident in the world around you. The rosy blush of the sunrise as it bursts above the horizon reminds you that the sparkling dawn of a brand-new day is replacing the long dark night. The resplendent spectrum of the rainbow reminds you that

O sing to the LORD a new song, for he has done marvelous things. His right hand and his holy arm have gotten him victory.

PSALM 98:1 NRSV

the sun is busy chasing away the rain clouds. The whimsical laugh of a child at play reminds you that you, too, are a child—God's child.

God's grace is evident in his creation, and it is God's gift to help you through the difficult times that life can bring your way. God's grace is the visible evidence of his everlasting love. Even when it appears that sorrow and grief threaten your joy, God offers his grace to you and you experience the hope of his promise.

God, when my heart is heavy with sorrow, your grace lifts me up and gives me a new song to sing. Amen.

HIS WILL BE DONE

Father, if You are willing, remove this cup from Me;
yet not My will, but [always] Yours be done.
LUKE 22:42 AMP

The world and every-thing in it that people desire is passing away; but those who do the will of God live forever.

1 JOHN 2:17 GNT

It is a simple refrain as you begin your day—*Lord, your will be done.* It was the humble attitude of heart and willingness to obey that Jesus exhibited as he opened the way to God for every person.

You are called to the same, agreeing with God in good times and bad because only he can make you truly happy. You count his plans more wonderful, more profoundly satisfying, and infinitely wiser than your own.

Make this your song today—*Lord, your will be done.* It will fill your life with such a beautiful melody of gentleness and grace that both you and those around you will be eternally changed.

Dear God, whether it is difficult or easy—I want to do as you ask. I know that above all, your plans are best. Amen.

HOW HE SEES YOU

The king is enthralled by your beauty;
honor him, for he is your lord.
PSALM 45:11 NIV

God is not looking at a magazine cover—he's gazing at you and he likes what he sees. He perceives a heart longing to know and obey him, a mind seeking his truth, and lips offering sincere praises. He observes a soul cleansed by his forgiveness, hands that do his will, and a soul that increasingly bears his image. Every day he sees you, his beloved, filled with potential—needing his grace, yearning for his presence, and learning his ways. And he is completely enthralled with you.

> *God himself has blessed you forever. . . . In your majesty, ride out to victory, defending truth, humility, and justice. Go forth to perform awe-inspiring deeds!*
> PSALM 45:2, 4 NLT

Friend, God loves you deeply and finds you absolutely beautiful. So gaze back into his adoring face, and realize that your splendor is really a reflection of his.

Lord God, how wonderful to be seen by you this way!
Fill my eyes with your magnificent face and
my heart with your wonderful love. Amen.

PURELY THE TRUTH

God never tells a lie! So, at the proper time, God our Savior gave this message and told me to announce what he had said.

TITUS 1:2–3 CEV

God is not like people, who lie; he is not a human who changes his mind. Whatever he promises, he does; he speaks, and it is done.

NUMBERS 23:19 GNT

You can only put your trust in something that is completely true—and the Bible has proven absolutely faithful throughout history.

Certainly, there are things that have yet to be seen—such as the second coming of Christ and what life will be like in heaven. Nevertheless, you can know that everything you see is evidence for all you have not yet seen.

God does not lie. He cannot mislead you. His holiness absolutely prevents it. What he communicates to you about your life, the world, and eternity is unquestionably true.

You can count on God to be honest—so trust him today with whatever comes.

Dear God, I praise you for telling the truth— and being the truth. I trust you to lead me because you are absolutely honest and faithful. Amen.

THOUGH THE WORLD FALLS APART

God is . . . always ready to help in times of trouble. So we will not fear when earthquakes come and the mountains crumble into the sea.
PSALM 46:1–2 NLT

As human beings, we tend to describe our security in terms of the earthly things that make us feel safe. Our family, friends, home, job, church, community, and national resources usually comprise our core infrastructure of protection. But what happens when those things tremble—or worse, tumble? What can we depend on when everything is suddenly taken from us?

Though its waters roar and foam and the mountains quake with their surging. . . . God is within her, she will not fall; God will help her at break of day.
PSALM 46:3, 5 NIV

You've read enough of this devotional to know that the answer is God—but is that truth ingrained deeply within your heart? This world was not meant to last. The earth shakes, houses collapse, and businesses fail—they're all temporary. Only God remains trustworthy and steadfast forever. He's the only sure foundation for your security.

God, please help me to base all my confidence in your love and unshakable security. Thank you for sustaining and protecting me. Amen.

A SECURE HOLD

This hope we have as an anchor of the soul,
both sure and steadfast.
HEBREWS 6:19 NKJV

Christ has entered, not into holy places made with hands, which are copies of the true things, but into heaven itself, now to appear in the presence of God on our behalf.

HEBREWS 9:24 ESV

An anchor holds a ship in place even when waves, winds, and currents try to move it. In the same way, Jesus holds you securely to the Father, even though life, trials, and cultural tides may buffet you.

Jesus is the constant connection between you and the Father—always representing you to him, and helping you to understand what he is doing. He is the perfect minister to your soul because he provides unbroken communication between you and your Creator.

Jesus never waivers—even when everything around you is sinking. Therefore, take this hope as an anchor for your soul today. Jesus has a secure hold on you. And because of him, you have smooth sailing with God.

Dear God, thank you that you are my sure anchor and that I don't have to drown in my circumstances. I praise you. Amen.

ASSURED IN HIS PRESENCE

God is in that city, and so it will not be shaken.
God will help her at dawn.
PSALM 46:5 NCV

Assyrian soldiers were known for their ruthless obliteration of any nation that dared resist their progress. When the invading army drew near to Jerusalem, King Hezekiah had a tough choice to make. Should he surrender unconditionally to the Assyrians in the hope of saving his people? Or should he trust God to deliver them? In a leap of faith,

> *God is our Refuge and Strength [mighty and impenetrable to temptation], a very present and well-proved help in trouble.*
>
> PSALM 46:1 AMP

Hezekiah chose the Lord. Psalm 46 is thought by some to be the song of triumph written when God honored Hezekiah's faithfulness and delivered Jerusalem.

Has God been leading you to make a very difficult decision? Like Jerusalem, you will not fall as long as you trust in God and obey him. So take the leap of faith and be confident that he will lead you victoriously.

> *O God, you know the struggle I am having with this decision. Yet I will have faith and do as you say. Please protect me, and lead me to victory. Amen.*

SO THAT IT GO WELL

Do what is right and good in the sight of the LORD,
that it may be well with you.
DEUTERONOMY 6:18 NKJV

The LORD our God commanded us to obey all these decrees and to fear him so he can continue to bless us and preserve our lives, as he has done to this day.

DEUTERONOMY 6:24 NLT

The purpose of obedience is twofold. Though you never have to obey God to earn his love—that is always given freely—you obey him because he is, in fact, God. He is your Lord, and it is good to express your thanks to him by doing as he says.

There is a second purpose for obedience. As you follow God, he positions you perfectly to receive the deepest desires of your heart. He blesses you—and no one knows how to give you joy like God does.

Obedience is not only about thankfulness but also about doing what is best for your life. Therefore, today, obey him gladly —and everything will go well for you.

Dear God, obedience is difficult at times. Please help me to obey so that I may show my thankfulness and fully receive your great blessings. Amen.

SEEKING HIM THROUGH THE QUIETNESS

Be still, and know that I am God.
PSALM 46:10 NKJV

We fill our world with noise. If it's not the television or radio, it's the blare of activities or our own anxious thoughts. We expect to connect with God through the tumult, but are we really listening to him?

When your world is in an uproar, your best plan is to step away from the commotion and listen to him. He speaks words of peace to your soul and strength to your life.

The Lord of hosts is with us; the God of Jacob is our Refuge (our High Tower and Stronghold). Selah [pause, and calmly think of that]!

PSALM 46:11 AMP

Your life is too hectic to keep going without taking a few minutes to seek him in the quietness. Stand in his presence and know that God is with you. His voice is the best sound you'll hear all day.

God, being still doesn't come naturally to me. Please help me to get quiet and really hear you. Thank you for speaking to me. Amen.

REMEMBERING THE DRY GROUND

As soon as the feet of the priests who were carrying the Ark touched the water at the river's edge, the water above that point began backing up.
JOSHUA 3:15–16 NLT

The LORD your God caused the water to stop flowing until you finished crossing it, just as the LORD did to the Red Sea. . . . The LORD did this so all people would know he has great power.

JOSHUA 4:23–24 NCV

God commanded the priests to carry the ark into the Jordan's rushing floodwaters. As their feet touched the river's edge, the waters piled up.

To Joshua and Caleb—who had been present forty years earlier—this was remarkably similar to when God parted the Red Sea and helped them escape from Egypt. The memory of that dry ground between the two walls of water gave them the courage to go forward. When God asks you to step out in faith, he often brings some memory of past faithfulness to help you. As you face challenges today, remember how God has parted the waters for you—and trust him to lead safely.

Dear God, you have always helped me. Help me to step out in faith by reminding me of how trustworthy you have been in the past. Amen.

YOUR THANKFULNESS AND PRAISE TO GOD

Clap your hands, all you peoples; shout to God with loud songs of joy. For the Lord, the Most High, is awesome, a great king over all the earth.
PSALM 47:1–2 NRSV

It's easy to forget to be grateful, to let daily worries distract you from the abundance that is yours. Mortgage payments, troublesome children, a looming deadline, a broken water heater, a headache, even a burned pizza or a fallen cake can interfere with your appreciation

Your great love reaches to the skies, your truth to the heavens. God, you are supreme above the skies. Let your glory be over all the earth.
PSALM 108:4–5 NCV

for the blessings you have been given. Inconveniences will pass, but God's blessings and love will keep showering down on you.

Open all your prayers with the praise and thanksgiving that are God's due. When you wake in the morning and before you fall asleep at night, make praise and thanksgiving your first and last thoughts. For whatever your circumstances may be, God has in fact given you the gift of abundant life in the here and now and the promise of life everlasting in the future.

Lord, I am rich in love and comfort, and my heart is full to the brim. I praise you and thank you for all you have given me. Amen.

SUCH LOVE

God so greatly loved and dearly prized the world that He [even] gave up His only begotten (unique) Son.
JOHN 3:16 AMP

He had always loved those in the world who were his own, and he loved them to the very end.

JOHN 13:1 GNT

From birth, Nicodemus was raised as a Pharisee—living in obedience to the law. Every day he said the prayers and performed the rituals that would keep him right before God. It was a tedious life.

Nicodemus learned that God wanted more than just obedience to laws and regulations—God wanted a genuine relationship based on love. You may think that in order to know God, you have to do certain things. Yet Jesus has already done everything necessary for you to be close to God. His love never binds you unmercifully to regulations or rituals. His love sets you free so you can love him in return.

Dear God, I love you. Thank you for doing so much to have a genuine love relationship with me. You are truly wonderful. Amen.

GLORY TO THE KING

God is King of all the earth,
so sing a song of praise to him.
PSALM 47:7 NCV

Today just think about God—how he is creative and powerful, wise, holy, and completely faithful. Consider God's works—how he's helped his people throughout history. Through his power, the Red Sea parted for the Israelites, the walls of Jericho crumbled, David slew Goliath, and Jesus was raised from the dead.

God ascends amid shouts of joy, the LORD, amid the sound of trumpets. Sing praise to God, sing praise; sing praise to our King, sing praise!
PSALM 47:5–6 HCSB

Meditate on his character—how all he does is because of his unconditional love for you. He is mighty and good, virtuous and trustworthy, wise and compassionate. Think about God and voice your praise to him aloud. He is the magnificent king of glory who has plans for you that are better than you can imagine. Certainly he deserves your adoration.

Sweetest, most wonderful God, truly you merit my worship.
How good you are and how deep your love—may the
whole world rejoice at your name! Amen.

NO FEAR IN LOVE

*There is no fear in love; instead,
perfect love drives out fear.*
1 JOHN 4:18 HCSB

*We can confidently say,
"The Lord is my helper;
I will not fear; what
can man do to me?"*

HEBREWS 13:6 ESV

The apostle John knew the security of Jesus' love firsthand. He had seen his worst fears confirmed at the crucifixion but utterly defeated at the resurrection.

Years later, John daily experienced persecution. Yet he affirmed that as long as he had Jesus' love, there was no reason to be afraid. Fear, after all, is based in punishment. And how could anyone truly hurt him as long as the resurrected Jesus protected him? Who could possibly stand against the God who had overcome death?

When you belong to God, you never have to fear. He is stronger than any foe you could face, and his perfect love will always protect you.

*Dear God, thank you for protecting me with your
wonderful love and your mighty power. Truly,
I have no reason to fear. Amen.*

ETERNITY IN YOUR HEART

As we have heard, so have we seen in the city of the LORD of hosts, in the city of our God; God will establish it forever.

PSALM 48:8 NKJV

Does it ever feel as if you simply do not belong in this world? As if you are longing for something beyond what exists here? You are not imagining things, and you are certainly not alone.

This God, our God forever and ever—He will lead us eternally.

PSALM 48:14 HCSB

Hebrews 11:13, 16 explains that faithful people throughout the ages have "agreed that they were only strangers and foreigners on this earth.... They were looking forward to a better home in heaven" (CEV).

You see, when you believe in God, he awakens the desire for eternity in you. Each time you sense that you are out of place here, it is because he's further along in the process of transforming you to live in heaven forever. Whenever you feel that your heart is somewhere else—that is okay. Just remember, friend, you are not home yet.

God, thank you for preparing me for heaven. I may not understand it all, but I praise you for establishing a wonderful home for me with you forever. Amen.

A SPRING OF STRENGTH

The joy of the LORD is your strength.
NEHEMIAH 8:10 NASB

All the people went away to eat, to drink, to send portions and to celebrate a great festival, because they understood the words which had been made known to them.

NEHEMIAH 8:12 NASB

Ezra read from the Book of the Law—the record of God's past faithfulness. Though the people were humbled by the stories, they were inspired to celebrate the wonderful God they served. God's joy is in his interaction with you and all those who have loved him throughout history. Scripture tells of his faithfulness and forgiveness—how he gladly provided for his people and delighted in helping them.

Studying the Bible and discovering how he has acted in others' lives will be a spring of encouragement and gladness for you. This morning, celebrate the great gift you have been given in the Bible, and take strength from reading about his joy.

Dear God, I praise you for your wonderful interaction with people recorded in Scripture. It gives me great strength knowing that I am your joy. Amen.

MAKING A SANCTUARY FOR THE SPIRIT

Our God, here in your temple we think about your love.
PSALM 48:9 CEV

Some people find that designating a specific time and creating a particular place to meet with God helps them bring more focus and consistency to their quiet time. It is good advice. Some people like to set aside time in the morning. But any time of the day or night will work just fine. Where you meet

> *I wake up early in the morning and cry out. I hope in your word. I stay awake all night so I can think about your promises.*
>
> PSALM 119:147–148 NCV

with God each day is also a matter of personal choice. It can be anywhere, inside or outside, if it is quiet, peaceful, and conducive to reflection and meditation.

Although you pray throughout the day, and even are instructed to pray "constantly," having a little retreat from the world's cares is a great boost for your prayer life. A retreat can bring the full attention of your heart and mind to God.

God, thank you for meeting me whenever I come before you. Let me leave the world behind as I bask in the wonder of your love for me. Amen.

DISCOURAGED?

Why are you cast down, O my soul, and why are you in turmoil within me? Hope in God.
PSALM 42:11 ESV

Why must I go about mourning . . . ? Send forth your light and your truth, let them guide me; let them bring me to your holy mountain, to the place where you dwell.

PSALM 43:2–3 NIV

Every morning, you have an option. You can choose either to be discouraged or to hope. This is an especially difficult choice if you have not slept well, are sick, or face a busy day full of challenges. It is a decision that remains in your power.

You can govern your attitude—especially when meditating on the God who can turn everything around for you. Your circumstances need not dictate your mood. You will find that when you choose your attitude, you will be better able to affect how your day turns out.

Are you discouraged this morning? Put your hope in God. He will certainly bless your soul.

Dear God, with you the choice is easy. Help me to center my hope on you so that I will have a good attitude today. Amen.

FOREVER GOD

This is God, our God forever and ever.
He will guide us forever.
PSALM 48:14 ESV

God exists. Before there was time, God was there. He's as infinitely past as he is eternally future. If that's a difficult concept for you to grasp, you're in good company. We as human beings are linear thinkers—we understand things in terms of beginnings and endings. How is it that God was never born? What does it mean that he'll never die?

We heard about it, then we saw it with our eyes—in GOD's city of Angel Armies, in the city our God set on firm foundations, firm forever. We pondered your love-in-action, God.
PSALM 48:8–9 MSG

Yet God is more than all of that. He's above how we function—beyond the constraints of hours, days, and years.

That's why God's wisdom regarding your life can be trusted. He knows everything concerning your past and all about your future. His perspective will never fail you. Listen to him.

God, my mind cannot comprehend you, but my heart trusts you. Thank you for your perfect perspective. I'm glad my future is in your hands. Amen.

PEACE THROUGH FAITH

Your faith has made you well; go in peace.
LUKE 8:48 NASB

Only God gives inward peace, and I depend on him.

PSALM 62:5 CEV

She had tried everything—but nothing could rid her of the infirmity she had endured for over a decade. When she heard that Jesus was close by, she went to see him. She knew that if she could just touch the remarkable man of God she would be healed.

Many people crowded in on Jesus that day, but only that woman touched him with her faith. Because of that, Jesus' power was released, and the woman received peace from her illness.

Believing is the key to peace. Today, reach out to God in faith and hold on to him. He will give you rest from whatever troubles your soul.

Dear God, you know what hurts my heart. I truly believe that you can help me. Thank you for your lovely peace. Amen.

RICHES OF KNOWING

*My mouth shall speak wisdom; and the meditation
of my heart shall be understanding.*

PSALM 49:3 AMP

Investments come in all shapes and sizes, but they generally share one goal: to produce wealth. Unfortunately, they also have one end in common: They don't last forever. Thankfully, there is a type of asset that doesn't rust or fade—that others cannot steal or manipulate. Instead, it is eternal because it's an investment in the kingdom of God.

Man, despite his riches, does not endure. . . . But God will redeem my life from the grave; he will surely take me to himself.

PSALM 49:12, 15 NIV

Every moment you spend in God's presence—praying to him, worshiping him, knowing him, studying his Word, and obeying him—you're becoming rich in treasure that's everlasting. True wisdom and wealth are found in seeking God and understanding his ways. So invest yourself in knowing and serving God. A life based on him will never be misspent.

*God, I want to be a wise investor. Grant me the riches of knowing
you more deeply during my times in your presence. Amen.*

BLESSED IS THE BELIEVER

*You are blessed because you believed that
the Lord would do what he said.*
LUKE 1:45 NLT

*My soul magnifies the
Lord, and my spirit has
rejoiced in God my
Savior. For He has
regarded the lowly state
of His maidservant;
for behold, henceforth
all generations will
call me blessed.*

LUKE 1:46–48 NKJV

There is so much peace in simply believing and just knowing that God will do as he said.

Even at her young age, Mary understood that. Perhaps that is the reason God chose to bless her with being the mother of the Messiah—because her faith was so strong.

Certainly, it is not always easy to simply rest in God's promises. Your mind will strive to think of every obstacle that could impede you. When you believe—really fully trust—that God will do as he says, you will experience a deep, abiding peace that will truly bless you. You will know his presence and power in a way that will amaze everyone.

*Dear God, I want to have Mary's faith,
the kind that believes the impossible. Thank you
for blessing and strengthening my faith. Amen.*

THE BALM OF THANKSGIVING

*Bring your thanks to God as a sacrifice, and keep your
vows to the Most High. Call on me in times of trouble.
I will rescue you, and you will honor me.*
PSALM 50:14–15 GOD'S WORD

The Bible encourages you to give thanks to God in every situation, even in the circumstances that are difficult. This shows your willingness to have faith in him even in the most trying areas of your life. Yet perhaps as you are expressing your gratefulness, you find that there

*Giving thanks is a
sacrifice that truly
honors me. If you
keep to my path, I
will reveal to you the
salvation of God.*

PSALM 50:23 NLT

are experiences and troubles that you just cannot trust him with. The wounds are too deep and the sacrifice too painful.

Friend, God understands. Yet he does not ask for gratitude for his sake. He does it to make you whole. When you praise him, it exposes the hidden injuries of your heart to his healing touch. Thank him, even when it is a sacrifice. You can truly be grateful for his loving restoration.

*My God, you know how difficult this is for me. This area
is so painful. Yet I will trust your loving touch. Thank
you for healing me, my precious Lord. Amen.*

IN THE STILLNESS

The LORD of hosts is with us.
The God of Jacob is our refuge.
PSALM 46:11 NKJV

God is our shelter and strength, always ready to help in times of trouble. So we will not be afraid, even if the earth is shaken and mountains fall into the ocean depths.

PSALM 46:1–2 GNT

The hurly-burly pace of your life can leave you tired and discouraged if you have no oasis of rest. That is why a relationship with God is so poignant.

He is the great well of peace and strength from which you can always draw. You must drop your concerns at his feet and abandon your right to worry about them.

Be still before him and relax. He can handle all of it.

It is in the stillness of your heart that God's power protects you in times of turmoil. And it is in that quietness that you will have the patience and endurance for everything that comes your way today.

Dear God, before the day gets going, help me to be still before you. Fill me with your peace and strength and I will praise your name. Amen.

GOD DISPELS CONFUSION AND DOUBT

Call on me when you are in trouble,
and I will rescue you, and you will give me glory.
PSALM 50:15 NLT

You have probably experienced the disruption and confusion of moving to a new home, with all your possessions packed and transported from the order and familiarity of your old home to the unfamiliar chaos of your new one. It can be disorienting and stressful to have to

O send out thy light and thy truth: let them lead me; let them bring me unto thy holy hill, and to thy tabernacles.

PSALM 43:3 KJV

search for the items necessary to the conduct of your life. If only you had a map showing where everything was packed away.

God has provided a map for your life. His commandments and teachings give you the meaning and clarity you need to live peacefully and productively. If you are momentarily confused or doubtful, you can call on him. He will help you find what you need to carry on. God is right there, waiting for an invitation to step in and set things right.

God, when I experience times of confusion and doubt, help me
remember that you are there waiting to comfort and guide me. Amen.

285

A GOOD CROP

These are the ones who, having heard the word with an honest and good heart, hold on to it and by enduring, bear fruit.
LUKE 8:15 HCSB

The rest of the seeds fell on good ground where they grew and produced a hundred times as many seeds.

LUKE 8:8 CEV

There was a farmer who went out to plant seed. However, birds and wind took some seed away; and thorns and stones choked even more seed. Yet there was also good seed that properly took root and grew.

Jesus explained that the seed is the word of God—and if it finds a fertile place in your heart, it produces a wonderful result.

No harvest grows up overnight—every good fruit has its time. This is why it is important for you to be patient with the effect the Bible has on your life. You may not be able to see it grow, but it is certainly producing a good crop in you.

Dear God, thank you that if I remain consistent with studying the Bible, you will produce wonderful things in me. Please help me to be patient. Amen.

GIFTS OF GRATEFULNESS

He who sacrifices thank offerings honors me, and he prepares
the way so that I may show him the salvation of God.
PSALM 50:23 NIV

God doesn't need your thanks, praise, or adoration. He doesn't need an ego boost or validation. Rather, God asks you to express your gratefulness because of what it means to your own soul

It's in those moments of thanksgiving when you realize that he's the source of all your blessings—and that they're not given because of your

I am God Most High!
The only sacrifice I
want is for you to be
thankful and to keep
your word. Pray to me
in time of trouble. I
will rescue you, and
you will honor me.
PSALM 50:14–15 CEV

worthiness, but because of his love for you. As your words echo back into your ears that God is the great Provider, his power fills you, and your heart is transformed.

So sing out your gratefulness to God. Thank him for his goodness to you. Undoubtedly, the one who'll be most blessed is you.

God, there's so much to thank you for: my life and
family, provisions and blessings. But most important,
thank you, God, for loving me. Amen.

IMPACTING THE WORLD

*You obey the law of Christ when you offer
each other a helping hand.*
GALATIANS 6:2 CEV

*Through love you
should serve
one another.*
GALATIANS 5:13 AMP

Sometimes it may seem as if you are not making a meaningful impact. Your daily routine feels unimportant—especially with everything happening in the world. You wonder if you could do more with the life God has given you.

D. L. Moody wrote, "He does the most for God's great world who does the best in his own little world."

All around you are people who could be wonderfully affected by your help and kindness. God asks you to have an impact on the world by loving them as he loves them.

The most meaningful work you can do is to care for the people around you. Will you do it?

*Dear God, show me someone to help today.
Thank you that I can truly have an impact on the world
by loving people the way you love them. Amen.*

PURPOSE THROUGH FORGIVENESS

Wash away all my guilt and make me clean again. . . . Then I will teach
your ways to those who do wrong, and sinners will turn back to you.
PSALM 51:2, 13 NCV

If you have ever asked God to forgive your sin, then you know how much relief it brings. You were no longer oppressed by the stress and guilt they caused you. You were transformed into a new creation with a clean, peaceful heart and you regained your hopefulness for a

Save me from
bloodguilt, O God,
the God who saves
me, and my tongue
will sing of your
righteousness.

PSALM 51:14 NIV

bright future. Undoubtedly, such a wonderful liberation made you feel like celebrating. Hopefully you are not enjoying your liberty alone.

People need hope—they are longing to find the same forgiveness you have been given. Tell others about God's forgiveness and salvation so they, too, can be liberated. Share the message with everyone you know.

God, I praise you for your astounding forgiveness. Help me
to tell others about your salvation so that they can enjoy
the same freedom that you have given to me. Amen.

THE FACE OF FORGIVENESS

If now I have found favor in your sight, then take my present from my hand, for I see your face as one sees the face of God.
GENESIS 33:10 NASB

When people sin, you should forgive and comfort them, so they won't give up in despair. You should make them sure of your love for them.

2 CORINTHIANS 2:7–8 CEV

Jacob had feared this meeting for years. He knew he had treated his brother, Esau, badly—stealing his blessing and tricking him into forfeiting his birthright. Esau had every right to detest him.

Yet when Esau saw Jacob, he ran to him—hugged and kissed him. To Jacob, knowing that Esau forgave him was like seeing the face of God.

Is there someone in your life whom you need to forgive? No doubt, it is difficult to do. God can give you the grace to embrace and pardon that person. In doing so, you set both of you free from the past. Undoubtedly, God will shine through your forgiving face.

Dear God, this is tough, but I know that I will feel better after I forgive. May this person see your face shining through me. Amen.

ADMITTING HE'S RIGHT

Against you, you only, have I sinned and done what is evil in your sight, so that you may be justified in your words and blameless in your judgment.
PSALM 51:4 ESV

One of the most difficult aspects of having a relationship with God is realizing that he knows what's best for you. That's why he will point out destructive habits or mistakes in your life and invite you to agree with him that you have a problem. He doesn't want you to feel ashamed about it; rather, he wants you to get better.

You are kind, God! Please have pity on me. You are always merciful! Please wipe away my sins. Wash me clean from all of my sin and guilt.
PSALM 51:1–2 CEV

Friend, you need to admit to God that you're struggling with your situation before he will start the process of healing you. Then God will unearth the causes of your troubles and restore you—he'll make you feel clean and new. So do it— admit he's right. You'll be glad you embraced the healing that sets you free.

God, this is difficult, but I trust you and admit you're right. I praise you for being compassionate as you reveal my sins and heal me. Amen.

THE SACRED AND THE SIFTING

*Satan has asked for you, that he may sift you as wheat. But
I have prayed for you, that your faith should not fail.*

LUKE 22:31–32 NKJV

*Holy Father, keep them
safe by the power of
your name, the name
you gave me, so that
they will be one, just
as you and I are one.*

JOHN 17:11 NCV

Sifting—the shaking of wheat until
it separates. You know what it is
like—to be strained to the point that
everything falls apart.

Though it is not strange that
you are sifted, it is amazing who is
praying for you. Your intercessor is
Jesus, who defends you and walks
with you daily. Can you imagine the power and insightfulness
of Jesus' prayers?

It is in the sifting that you experience the sacred because you
receive Jesus' very thoughts concerning you. And so, instead of
shaking apart you become one with him.

Today, remember that God the Son is praying for you. Then
your faith will not fail, but it will remain strong and hopeful
in him.

*Dear Jesus, thank you for praying for me. I know I can make it through
anything with you as my defender and constant friend. Amen.*

READY TO RENEW

Wipe out all that I have done wrong. Create a clean heart in me, O God, and renew a faithful spirit within me.

PSALM 51:9–10 GOD'S WORD

Psalm 51 records David's repentance for committing adultery with Bathsheba and murdering her husband. It is the profoundly moving prayer of a man devastated by the depth of his sin. Yet in the midst of his despair, he clung to the love and grace of God and refused to let go.

Restore the joy of your salvation to me, and provide me with a spirit of willing obedience. . . . O God, you do not despise a broken and sorrowful heart.

PSALM 51:12, 17
GOD'S WORD

Perhaps you have been shocked at the temptations that have seized your own heart. You may have even fallen in sin, and your spirit is as broken as David's was. Remember, friend, just as God forgave and restored David, he will forgive and restore you if you will confess your sin and repent. Do not lose hope. Rather, cling to God. Trust him, and he will not only cleanse your heart, but he will renew your spirit as well.

God, thank you for forgiving my sin and renewing my relationship with you. I cling to your love and rejoice in your wonderful mercy. Amen.

OF SILVER AND GOLD

I will bring the third part through the fire, and will refine them as silver is refined and will test them as gold is tested.
ZECHARIAH 13:9 AMP

The LORD their God will save them on that day as the flock of His people; for they are like jewels in a crown, sparkling over His land.

ZECHARIAH 9:16 HCSB

To make gold and silver fit for use, they must be put to the fire. This process serves to both remove their impurities and make the precious metals malleable.

God prepares you and makes you ready for service in much the same way. In the heat and pressure of everyday life, God burns away all the things that hinder you from serving him, and he molds you into someone who truly shines with his love.

Has God turned up the heat in your life today? Take heart—he sees something truly valuable and beautiful in you, and he has allowed the fire for the refining of your soul.

Dear God, thank you for valuing me so greatly.
Please help me to endure the heat in my life
so I can truly shine for you. Amen.

WHAT HE ACCEPTS

*The sacrifices of God are a broken spirit; a broken
and a contrite heart, O God, You will not despise.*
PSALM 51:17 NASB

God will never kick you when you're down. He won't look at you when you're feeling tired and unworthy and say, "What's the matter with you? Try harder!"

God isn't looking for impressive feats of showmanship from you; rather, he's looking at the attitude of your heart. He has compassion for you when you've failed, and he treats your wounded spirit with love.

Create in me a clean heart, O God. Renew a loyal spirit within me. . . . Restore to me the joy of your salvation, and make me willing to obey you.

PSALM 51:10, 12 NLT

God accepts you, friend, just as you are. Don't ever fear that you're not good enough for him, because that's not what God is interested in. He just wants you to be eager to obey him and willing to trust him more. Because then you're truly a person he can work with.

*God, thank you for accepting me and handling
my broken heart with kindness. I am eager to
obey and willing to trust you. Amen.*

SO REAL TO ME

*I admit I once lived by rumors of you; now I have it
all firsthand—from my own eyes and ears!*
JOB 42:5 MSG

*I will see him for
myself, and I long
for that moment.*

JOB 19:27 CEV

The book of Job is full of theories and theologies. The questions abound. Why do good people suffer? Is God punishing Job for some wrong action? Shouldn't people who trust in God prosper?

God's desire is not for you to form hypotheses about him. Rather, God wants you to trust him—and it is only when you allow yourself to be vulnerable that you can experience him fully.

After all of his suffering, Job was able to say that God was real to him, more personal than he could have imagined. And it filled him with joy.

Today, set your heart on really knowing God instead of just knowing *about* him.

*Dear God, I want to know you. Help me to be vulnerable
with you so that I can experience you
fully in every situation. Amen.*

GOD'S LOVE MAKES YOU WEALTHY

See the one who would not take refuge in God, but trusted in abundant riches, and sought refuge in wealth!
PSALM 52:7 NRSV

You are constantly bombarded with the message that you should want more, buy more, have more. Doing so will bring you happiness, you are told. Potential acquisitions are depicted not only as desirable but essential. You are encouraged to acquire a bigger house and a finer car. You are urged to use your credit cards as you fill those houses to the brim with purchases you often neither really want nor need.

They that trust in their wealth, and boast themselves in the multitude of their riches; none of them can by any means redeem his brother, nor give to God a ransom for him.
PSALM 49:6–7 KJV

Ultimately "things" can never really satisfy you. As soon as you have acquired a certain possession, the novelty begins to wear off, and you begin to yearn for something else. Start now to live a life in which God is the center. His love is the wealth you truly want, and only in him will you find peace.

God, help me to remember that "things" cannot satisfy the deep longing in my heart that can only be filled by you. Amen.

AN EXCELLENT GUIDE

He leads the humble in what is right,
and the humble He teaches His way.
PSALM 25:9 AMP

Lead me by your truth
and teach me, for you
are the God who saves
me. All day long I put
my hope in you.

PSALM 25:5 NLT

If you desire to be taught this morning—you are willing to accept God's counsel and acknowledge it as superior to your own—then you fulfill the requirements for him to lead you. As chaplain Thomas Goodwin wrote, "The Lord will teach the humble his secrets, he will not teach proud scholars."

God speaks to your listening soul, showing you his ways step by step. He leads you in an adventure of discovery and understanding, and he sets a purposeful course that brings him glory and you satisfaction.

It is good that you have humbled yourself to God this morning. Listen to him, and he will share his excellent secrets with you.

Dear God, I want your counsel and acknowledge
that your wisdom is far greater than my own.
Teach me your magnificent ways. Amen.

HOW TO THRIVE

I am like a green olive tree in the house of God;
I trust in the mercy of God forever and ever.
PSALM 52:8 NKJV

Have you received an assignment that's less than thrilling? Are you discouraged because it seems beneath your expertise and training? Then you're thinking about the wrong thing. Instead of focusing on the negative aspects of the task, consider these questions: "Why has this duty come to me? Why does it require my attention?"

I will praise You forever for what You have done. In the presence of Your faithful people, I will put my hope in Your name, for it is good.

PSALM 52:9 HCSB

Perhaps you've received it to model godly character to someone else, or because you must learn some humility. Possibly, the task is more important than you realize, or maybe it's God's provision for your bills. Whatever the reason, it's an opportunity for excellence. So don't be discouraged. Rather, honor God with your assignment. No doubt, you'll be glad you did.

God, please help my attitude. I don't know your purpose for this task, but I'll do my best to honor you and thrive in it. Amen.

A FLAWLESS RECORD

Not a word failed of any good thing which the LORD
had spoken to the house of Israel. All came to pass.
JOSHUA 21:45 NKJV

It is the LORD your
God who fights for you,
just as he promised
you. Be very careful,
therefore, to love the
LORD your God.

JOSHUA 23:10–11 ESV

God promised childless centenarian Abraham that his offspring would be as numerous as the stars. He guaranteed that they would have a land of their own—but only after a four-hundred-year captivity in Egypt. And he assured Moses that he would lead those two million plus descendants of Abraham out of Egypt and back to the land they were pledged.

Standing in that Promised Land, Abraham's descendants knew that God had faithfully kept *all* those vows and more.

Throughout Israel's history, God pledged some really amazing things—and he delivered *every one*. His record on promise keeping is flawless. Therefore, whatever he has assured you of is no problem whatsoever. Trust him.

Dear God, truly you have done astounding things. I praise you that
not one word of your promises has ever failed. Amen.

WHEN THINGS SEEM UNFAIR, REMEMBER

I will always thank God for what he has done;
I will praise his good name when his people meet.
PSALM 52:9 CEV

Before David ever took the throne of Israel, he had many heartbreaking experiences. At one point, he ran from King Saul and asked for help from the priests of Nob. Although the priests did not know Saul was pursuing David, the king put them to death for aiding his enemy.

I am like a flourishing olive tree in the house of God; I trust in God's faithful love forever and ever.

PSALM 52:8 HCSB

You can imagine how David felt when he heard what had transpired. Psalm 52 records his thoughts. It was so unfair—why would God allow it? Yet remember, even when life does not seem fair, God is still in control. Are you experiencing circumstances that seem completely counter to what God promised you? Hope in the Lord, because he will work everything out for your good in time.

God, thank you for helping me. When things seem unfair,
I will trust you—remaining confident that you will transform
this situation for my good and your glory. Amen.

A FAITHFUL BRIDGE BUILDER

It was necessary for him to be made in every respect like us . . . so that he could be our merciful and faithful High Priest before God.
HEBREWS 2:17 NLT

In bringing many sons to glory, it was fitting that God, for whom and through whom everything exists, should make the author of their salvation perfect through suffering.

HEBREWS 2:10 NIV

How can a God who is limitless in power, wisdom, and love understand what it is like to live in your world? Though he created it, does he know how frustrating and frightening it can be? Though he knows the thoughts and heart of every person, can he understand how raw emotions feel? Can he know human pain or the fear of facing death?

The answer is *yes*, because Jesus came to connect the expanse between you and God. The bridge he builds between God and your humanity is also the path for you to know God. Jesus completely understands both, and he serves as the perfect mediator. He is wonderful, isn't he?

Dear God, it is hard to understand all you have done for me, but I am so thankful that you understand me perfectly. Amen.

WHO IS WISE?

God looks down from heaven on the human race to see if there is one who is wise and who seeks God.
PSALM 53:2 HCSB

When reading Psalms, perhaps you've noticed that Psalm 53 is very similar to Psalm 14. Why, then, would it be included in the Bible? British minister Charles Spurgeon explains, "[God's Word] never repeats itself needlessly, there is good cause for the second copy of this Psalm."

God restores the fortunes of his people.
PSALM 53:6 ESV

The truth is that sometimes—even though we trust God—we fail to seek him. We forget the many times he's helped us. That's why we need this psalm repeated—to remind us to look to him continually.

To be truly wise is to seek God in every situation. Do you have some need today? Seek him. He's always ready to extend his aid and loves it when you ask.

*God, thank you for always being ready to help me.
Please increase my wisdom by continually
reminding me to seek you. Amen.*

AN INNER PREPARATION

*Get your minds ready for action, being self-disciplined,
and set your hope completely on the grace to be brought
to you at the revelation of Jesus Christ*
1 PETER 1:13 HCSB

*You are receiving the
goal of your faith, the
salvation of your souls.*

1 PETER 1:9 HCSB

I t is difficult to be disciplined when there is no goal ahead. Yet you have a wonderful goal—a great and high calling.

Peter taught that before his time, the prophets looked forward to Messiah's coming. They searched out all of the details regarding the Messiah so that they would be ready for him.

Now that Jesus has come and has provided salvation, you are to follow their example—studying his life and allowing God's Spirit to prepare you for when you see him.

Whether it is in heaven or by his second coming here on earth, get yourself ready to greet God today by being disciplined in learning about him.

*Dear God, how wonderful that I get to see you.
Help me to be disciplined so that I'll be prepared
when I meet you face-to-face. Amen.*

THEY ARE NOT SO STRONG

You have rescued me from all my troubles,
and I have seen my enemies defeated.
PSALM 54:7 GNT

As David and his weary men fled from King Saul's relentless forces, they came to the Desert of Ziph, hoping they could hide and get some rest. Unfortunately, the people there were Saul's allies, and they divulged David's covert location. Saul's soldiers closed in on David, and all seemed lost.

God is my helper; the Lord is with those who uphold my life.

PSALM 54:4 NKJV

Whenever difficulties close in on you, you may feel as David did—defenseless, drained, and discouraged. Everything will seem to be working toward your defeat.

Yet you must understand that God showed himself stronger than Saul's army—they were forced to abandon their pursuit of David. No matter how tough your problems are, they're never as mighty as God is. Trust and obey him—you'll surely see your troubles defeated.

God, I praise you that you're always mightier than my problems.
Thank you for helping me and for leading me to victory. Amen.

WITH YOUR HEAD HELD HIGH

*I have set you free; now walk
with your heads held high.*
LEVITICUS 26:13 CEV

*I will look on you
with favor and
make you fruitful.*

LEVITICUS 26:9 NIV

This morning, you have been set free. You are no longer a captive. You have been released from wrongdoing, fear, and guilt.

Is that how you are living?

God has freed you in order to inspire the highest within you. Certainly, there are guidelines in that—but they do not oppress or hurt your spirit. Rather, they are the kind of disciplines that Olympic hopefuls have—those that stretch you to be your very best and help you reach your greatest aspirations.

You have been released to be the finest you possible. Therefore, go with your head held high, knowing that God is with you and he has set you free.

*Dear God, thank you for setting me free. I will
live with my head held high—being the best
me I can be for your glory. Amen.*

REST FOR THE WEARY

*Oh that I had wings like a dove! for then
would I fly away, and be at rest.*
PSALM 55:6 KJV

You have probably experienced the sensation of flying in a dream, floating high above the crowd, and reveled in it. To be like the birds, you think, and just fly away when the world presses in too closely; to experience the heady joy of unrestricted movement. You long

He renews my strength. He guides me along right paths, bringing honor to his name.

PSALM 23:3 NLT

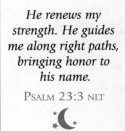

to have "wings like a dove," but most of the time you feel more like a chicken, flapping miserably around in the barnyard, unable to get off the ground for sustained flight.

When you are bone-weary and eager to fly away, God can give you rest and sustain you. In that place of physical, emotional, and spiritual exhaustion, a divine paradox emerges. When you are weak, he becomes strong in you. Your very weakness is a tool that magnifies his glory.

*Show me, dear God, that while there is no music in a rest,
there is the making of music in it. When I rest in you, I am
close to your power, which becomes my strength for life. Amen.*

A GOOD FUTURE

"I know the plans I have for you," declares the LORD . . .
"plans to give you hope and a future."
JEREMIAH 29:11 NIV

"Don't let your eyes fill with tears. You will be rewarded for your work!" says the LORD. . . . "There is hope for you in the future."
JEREMIAH 31:16–17 NCV

It wasn't in the midst of a peaceful time that God spoke these words to Jeremiah—it was as the nation of Judah faced a seventy-year captivity in Babylon. Yet God faithfully fulfilled his promise to bring them back to their homeland and to give them a good future.

Though unfortunate things will happen in your life, God is with you, and his plans for you are filled with hope. You don't have to fear the future, or worry that you'll be stuck in your situation forever.

God used those years to teach Judah to trust him. He is teaching you too. Believe him. He is faithful to help you with whatever happens today.

Thank you, God, for giving me a wonderful future and for teaching me to trust you more. I look forward to your excellent plans. Amen.

HE DOESN'T TIRE

*Morning, noon, and night you hear
my concerns and my complaints.*
PSALM 55:17 CEV

There are circumstances that will consume every bit of your energy. They're real and pressing, all-consuming and painful. No matter what you do, your situation is in the forefront of your mind. You simply can't shake it.

As for me, I will call upon God, and the LORD shall save me.

PSALM 55:16 NKJV

Your loved ones may be supportive, but you cannot expect them to comfort you every time the anxieties surface or the tears begin to flow. They get weary and so do you.

It's in those times that you must draw upon God's comfort, strength, and wisdom. Others will let you down, but God never will. So call upon his unflagging love morning, noon, and night—whenever you need him. He is always ready to help you.

*God, I praise you for being my tireless Comforter,
Provider, and Friend. Thank you, God, for
hearing me whenever I call to you. Amen.*

LIKE THE EAGLE

*He was like an eagle hovering over its nest, overshadowing
its young, then spreading its wings, lifting them
into the air, teaching them to fly.*

DEUTERONOMY 32:11 MSG

*He will cover you with
His pinions, and under
His wings shall you
trust and find refuge;
His truth and His
faithfulness are a
shield and a buckler.*

PSALM 91:4 AMP

It has been observed that an eagle will slowly hold back from feeding its chicks in order to get them to fly. The adult will appeal to its hungry children with tasty morsels so that as the parent swoops up into the sky, the eaglets will catch the updraft and take flight.

God works in much the same way. He allows there to be some hunger in your life so that you will step out and seek him. As you step out in faith to follow him, he bears you up on his wings of faithfulness and love, and teaches you to soar.

*Mighty God, thank you for teaching me to fly.
Thank you that even the needs in my life are your
wonderful way of instructing me. Amen.*

SHIFTING THE PILE

Pile your troubles on GOD's shoulders—he'll carry your load, he'll help you out. He'll never let good people topple into ruin.
PSALM 55:22 MSG

You should always make your loved ones a priority in your life. Yet you must also understand that sometimes God will use circumstances to prevent you from helping them when they're struggling.

Evening and morning and at noon I will pray, and cry aloud, and He shall hear my voice. He has redeemed my soul in peace.

PSALM 55:17–18 NKJV

Whether it's because of distance, health, responsibilities, or even relational barriers, God may have allowed the separation to keep you from interfering in what he's teaching them. You may want to shoulder a burden that only he can carry for them. Or perhaps he is refining their character through their troubles.

Whatever the case, you must shift your worries about them to God. Always remember that he's able to care for them better than you are. Just keep praying, and let him work.

God, it's rough seeing loved ones making bad decisions or suffering, but I trust you to work in them. I pray they'll depend on you. Amen.

NO EYE HAS SEEN

No eye has seen, no ear has heard, no mind has conceived what God has prepared for those who love him.
1 CORINTHIANS 2:9 NIV

You did awesome things beyond our highest expectations. And oh, how the mountains quaked!

ISAIAH 64:3 NLT

Your imagination is capable of great things, but it is no match for God's imagination. Your thoughts may reach high, but God's good plans for you are infinitely higher.

Whatever it is you dream about, it may seem marvelous—quite certain to make you happy. Yet God wants to increase your wonder and joy by creating something extraordinary. God wants you to be so amazed at what he does that any memory of hardship fades away and you spontaneously praise him.

Today, therefore, do not fret about what your eyes haven't seen. Rather, thank him for it—knowing that what is ahead is sure to be out of this world.

Dear God, what amazing things have you prepared for me? I will praise you today knowing that it is better than anything I could possibly imagine. Amen.

WHEN FEAR COMES CHARGING IN

When I get really afraid I come to you in trust.
PSALM 56:3 MSG

Fear is a powerful, unreasonable emotion. It influences how you think and react, and it even affects your physical well-being. Fear will stop you from reaching your potential or from allowing your loved ones to be all they can be. You know God is directing you in a certain way, but you refuse to step out in faith because of your apprehensions.

In God, whose word I praise, in God I have put my trust; I shall not be afraid. What can mere man do to me?

PSALM 56:4 NASB

Understand that your fear is based on an expectation of punishment—you believe it's inevitable that only bad things will happen. Instead, you must focus on God's character. God is all-powerful, all knowing, and completely loving. So obey him—he'll only lead you in what's best for you. With God, you never have to be afraid.

God, fear is a powerful influence in my life. Help me to obey you in faith and trust you whenever my anxieties come charging in. Amen.

THEN I AM STRONG

For Christ's sake, I delight in weaknesses, in insults, in hardships, in persecutions, in difficulties. For when I am weak, then I am strong.
2 CORINTHIANS 12:10 NIV

If I must boast, I would rather boast about the things that show how weak I am. God, the Father of our Lord Jesus, who is worthy of eternal praise, knows I am not lying.

2 CORINTHIANS
11:30–31 NLT

You know your weaknesses— and perhaps you regret them. However, they are the very areas through which God can perform miraculously.

Conversely, when you have exceptional talents and assets, you can fall into the trap of thinking you do not need God.

Though he can work through you when you acknowledge you need him, it is a different story when you believe you can accomplish everything by yourself. Then he must teach you that his good plans are achieved only through his power.

So don't worry about your weaknesses today. They are wonderful opportunities for God to show you his glory.

Dear God, I praise you for my weaknesses. Thank you for achieving your great plans and showing me your glory through them. Amen.

IN THE PROPER PERSPECTIVE

*By [the help of] God I will praise His word; on God I
lean, rely, and confidently put my trust; I will not fear.
What can man, who is flesh, do to me?*
PSALM 56:4 AMP

Sometimes the negative words of others can be devastating. Because of them, you struggle with thoughts of doubt, fear, or condemnation. However, the psalmist learned how to put the words of others in the proper perspective, and you can too.

You know how troubled I am; you have kept a record of my tears. . . . You have rescued me from death and kept me from defeat. And so I walk in the presence of God, in the light that shines on the living.

PSALM 56:8, 13 GNT

When you believe in Jesus Christ as your Savior, you gain a fresh sense of unshakable hope and peace. The connection you have with him empowers you to stand firm against the most deceptive thought or attack. You discover how to say as the psalmist did, "I will not fear!" because you know that your Lord defends you no matter what others may say. Therefore, open your heart and mind to Jesus' personal love and care for you. You will not be disappointed.

God, thank you for providing the hope I need to get through every situation. I will find hope and peace in your word. Amen.

WRITE IT DOWN

*Then the LORD replied: "Write down the revelation
and make it plain on tablets."*
HABAKKUK 2:2 NIV

*Write the things which
you have seen, and the
things which are, and
the things which will
take place after
these things.*

REVELATION 1:19 NASB

Journaling is a wonderfully encouraging activity. As you pray and read the Bible, you record your concerns, what you learn, and how God answers you. It becomes a record of your communication with him.

There is something about seeing his words to you formed on paper that somehow makes them more real—more possible. You document God's personal promises to you, and the certainty of them gives you peace. And if you ever begin to doubt, you can always go back and read them again.

This morning, write down what you learn during your time alone with God. He will certainly bless you through it.

*Dear God, help me to write down what you want me
to remember. Thank you for making your promises
real to me through the written word. Amen.*

TEARS IN A BOTTLE

Thou tellest my wanderings: put thou my tears into thy bottle: are they not in thy book?
PSALM 56:8 KJV

The verse above paints a word picture that is at once hard to believe and awe-inspiring. Like a woman who saves a rare perfume in a bottle, God stores your tears in his bottle and records them in his book. The divine bookkeeper chronicles every twist and turn you take down the path of life.

LORD, my Rock, I call out to you for help. Do not be deaf to me. If you are silent, I will be like those in the grave. Hear the sound of my prayer, when I cry out to you for help. I raise my hands toward your Most Holy Place.

PSALM 28:1–2 NCV

When David wrote this psalm, he was running for his life from King Saul's men. His cry to the Lord did not fall on deaf ears; God heard him. His tears were not wasted; God knew and cared about them. Your tears won't be wasted either. Though you may not be in mortal danger, it's a comfort to know that God notes your every teardrop, just as he notices when one tiny sparrow falls from a tree.

Cushion me, dear God, when I am anxious. I know you can clear the darkest sky and bring day to night. Amen.

317

NOT BECAUSE OF YOUR MERIT

*He did it out of sheer love, keeping the
promise he made to your ancestors.*

DEUTERONOMY 7:8 MSG

*GOD, your God, chose
you out of all the
people on Earth for
himself as a cherished,
personal treasure. GOD
wasn't attracted to you
and didn't choose you
because you were big
and important.*

DEUTERONOMY 7:6–7
MSG

God was forthright with the people of Israel. He did not choose them because of any merit of their own. He chose them because he loved them and had made a covenant with their ancestors.

It is a humbling thing to be accepted by God because of his great love for you. Yet it should also give you peace. Because you did not earn it, you cannot lose it. Because his love is unconditional, there is nothing you can do to mess it up. It is not by your strength, beauty, brilliance, or talent that you gain God's acceptance. He just loves you for who you are. Today, love him back.

*Dear God, I do love you back. Thank you for
the peace and joy that comes from your
marvelous, unconditional love. Amen.*

YOUR PROTECTED PURPOSE

I will cry out to God Most High,
to God who performs all things for me.
PSALM 57:2 NKJV

You'll come to places that seem like abrupt ends to your dreams. Every door will appear closed, and you may even have to accept responsibilities that seem completely incompatible with the promises God has given you. Before you begin to think *It's all over*, remember that only this portion of your journey has concluded.

Be gracious to me, God, be gracious to me, for I take refuge in You. I will seek refuge in the shadow of Your wings until danger passes.

PSALM 57:1 HCSB

Don't despair. God is developing your character and strengthening your faith. The purpose for your life is so important that God himself protects it for you—you don't have to fear that it's been lost or ruined forever. So no matter how long it takes, obey and follow God without wavering. Despite the detours, he'll unfailingly lead you to your purpose.

God, thank you for protecting my future and for leading
me to your purpose for my life. Help me to follow
you obediently and without wavering. Amen.

A PROMISE PROVEN TRUE

*The Holy Spirit had shown him that he would
see the Messiah of God before he died.*
LUKE 2:26 MSG

*Simeon . . . took the
child in his arms and
praised God, saying,
"Sovereign Lord, now
let your servant die
in peace, as you have
promised. I have seen
your salvation."*

LUKE 2:28–30 NLT

Everyone wanted to see the great deliverer that God had promised to send. Yet Simeon had God's special assurance that he would meet him.

As time went by, perhaps Simeon wondered if he had heard God correctly—would he live long enough to meet the deliverer? However, he obediently went to the temple whenever God moved him. And on one very special day, the promise was proven true—Simeon met Jesus.

You may have a promise that has been long in coming. You wonder whether you heard God—or just the loud longings of your heart. Today, be obedient to God, and you likewise will see his promises to you proven true.

*Dear God, thank you that all your promises
to me are true. Help me to be patient until
you faithfully fulfill them. Amen.*

FOR HIS GLORY

Be exalted, O God, above the highest heavens!
May your glory shine over all the earth.
PSALM 57:5 NLT

There will be times when it is hard to contain the love you feel for God. Sunshine warms your face, a gentle breeze blows softly, and suddenly you are reminded of all the times you have experienced his blessings. They are more than you can number.

I cry out to God Most High, to God who fulfills his purpose for me.

PSALM 57:2 ESV

He sustains you when trouble comes. He moves quickly to lift you up whenever you fall and cry out to him. He protects you as you drive along busy thoroughfares. When you wonder if he is listening to the prayers of your heart, he shows up in some miraculous way, letting you know that he hears every word. He is God, and the earth is full of his glory. He also is the Lord who loves you with an everlasting love. So trust him, because he is truly faithful.

I bow down before you, God. I am in awe of your
greatness and in wonder of your infinite love.
Thank you for your ceaseless grace. Amen.

June

*More than anything
else, put God's work first
and do what he wants.
Then the other things
will be yours as well.*

<small>MATTHEW 6:33 CEV</small>

FULLY ASSURED

*Faith is the assurance of things hoped for,
the conviction of things not seen.*
HEBREWS 11:1 NASB

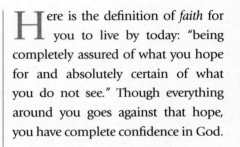

*May the Lord direct
your hearts into
[realizing and
showing] the love
of God and into the
steadfastness and
patience of Christ.*

2 THESSALONIANS 3:5

AMP

Here is the definition of *faith* for you to live by today: "being completely assured of what you hope for and absolutely certain of what you do not see." Though everything around you goes against that hope, you have complete confidence in God.

You believe that God can do the impossible. Perhaps the lingering question is this: *Will he?* Does God love you enough to help you?

The answer is absolutely yes. Even though God has shown his love for you in Christ, you still must accept his love by faith, fully assured that he will not fail you. Therefore, have strong faith today in the wonderful God who loves you.

*Dear God, not only do I believe you exist and
can do anything, but also I completely trust
that you love me enough to help me. Amen.*

JUSTICE SERVED

The godly will rejoice when they see injustice avenged.
PSALM 58:10 NLT

Does it ever seem as if the unrighteous get away with their terrible schemes, while you are always caught no matter what mistake you make?

People will say, "There really are rewards for doing what is right. There really is a God who judges the world."

PSALM 58:11 NCV

The truth is, no one really gets away with anything. Sin has many consequences, and God holds each person accountable for his or her actions. However, he does not want you dwelling on how and when he will move against the unjust. Rather, he calls you to be mindful of his ability to deal with every situation. He is in control, and in his perfect timing every wrong will be addressed.

He also wants you to pray for those who are trapped in sin—because it is only when they know him that they will be able to escape from its terrible grasp.

God, teach me to pray for those who do not know you and to act wisely as I live my life for you. I praise you for righting every wrong. Amen.

THE LEAST AND HIM

*Whatever you did for one of the least of these
brothers of Mine, you did for Me.*
MATTHEW 25:40 HCSB

*I was naked and you
clothed me, I was sick
and you visited me, I
was in prison and
you came to me.*

MATTHEW 25:36 ESV

It is extraordinary to realize how closely Jesus relates to the neediest people. His association is so intimate and sincere that you are promised that whatever good you do for them, you do for him.

This is because Jesus could look into people's lives and thoroughly know their deepest needs, whether those needs were for food and shelter or for healing and forgiveness. Perhaps it is because his empathy is so profound that he so greatly appreciates your service on their behalf.

When you compassionately see a person's need, you are not only acting *for* Jesus, but you are also acting *like* Jesus. You relate out of mercy and react just as he would.

*Dear God, thank you for your mercy to me.
Help me to meet others' needs with your sincere
compassion and profound sympathy. Amen.*

NOT IN VAIN

Everyone will say, "It's true! Good people are rewarded.
God does rule the earth with justice."
PSALM 58:11 CEV

Serving God isn't easy. You'll encounter trouble from the strangest places. You'll try to help people, and others will criticize what you're doing. You'll work long years trying to make a difference, but you won't see the outcome you expected.

Good people will be glad when they see him get even.

PSALM 58:10 NCV

Yes, serving God is difficult. But it is wholeheartedly worth it. You see, there's a great reward for those who do God's work on earth. Not only is God pleased while you're obeying him, but you'll see the fruit of your labor in heaven.

All the love you pour out will generate unimaginably wonderful results in God's kingdom. So have faith and keep serving him. You'll never find a better return for your work.

God, keep me strong as I serve you. Remind me that
it's not about seeking others' approval or earthly
rewards, but about glorifying you. Amen.

A BEAUTIFUL MESSAGE

How beautiful on the mountains are the feet of the messenger who brings good news, the good news of peace and salvation.
ISAIAH 52:7 NLT

Your watchmen lift up their voices; together they sing for joy; for they shall see eye to eye the return of the Lord to Zion.

ISAIAH 52:8 AMP

People need hope. They try to find it in many things, but the only real and lasting hope is in God. That is why it is wonderful to be his representative.

Most people have a distorted perception of God, either as a controlling taskmaster or an impersonal being that does not bother to intervene. Yet you know who he really is—the God who gives joy and eternal life.

Today, tell others the beautiful message of the God of hope so that they can experience his peace and salvation as well. You will find their gratitude is utterly overwhelming when they finally meet and embrace the God they've longed to know.

Dear God, I praise you for your beautiful message. Help me to repeat it to those who need hope so they may know you as well. Amen.

WATCHING

I will keep watch for You, my strength,
because God is my stronghold.
PSALM 59:9 HCSB

When learning to draw, you're taught a new way to see—you observe light, shadow, perspective, and depth in order to make your portraits realistic. The same concept is true in your spiritual life. You may be very good at assessing your earthly landscape, but if you fail to notice what's happening spiritually, you're only getting half the picture. That's why you must watch for God's activity.

You have been my refuge, a place of safety when I am in distress. O my Strength, to you I sing praises . . . the God who shows me unfailing love.
PSALM 59:16–17 NLT

Friend, what you see with your physical eyes is temporary, but what you perceive God doing in your spirit is eternal. So ask God to open your spiritual eyes to his supernatural work. When you learn to observe his ways, you'll undoubtedly view life a lot more clearly.

God, please open my spiritual eyes so that I can see
your wonderful, eternal ways. I'll keep watch for you,
my God, because you are my strength. Amen.

SETTING THE STANDARD

In everything set them an example by doing what is good.
TITUS 2:7 NIV

Give special emphasis to these matters, so that those who believe in God may be concerned with giving their time to doing good deeds, which are good and useful for everyone.

TITUS 3:8 GNT

The churches on the island of Crete badly needed leaders. Interestingly, when the apostle Paul wrote to help them, he did not require that potential teachers have an impressive scope of knowledge. Rather, he advised that what was truly essential was that they be people of good character.

Though knowledge is important, you teach others most by your example. It is crucial that others observe how the godly life is lived out rather than just to talk about it.

Today, teach those around you by being self-controlled, having integrity, and being eager to do good. People will see the standard you set and will be attracted to the God you serve.

Dear God, help me to do good and to have good character, self-control, and integrity and so that others will be drawn to you. Amen.

330

YOUR NOT-SO-SECRET WEAPON

With God's help we will do mighty things.
PSALM 60:12 NLT

At first glance, a task may seem too great for you. You try to make a schedule, but confusion and fear set in. Before you know it, you feel tempted to run. However, deep within your heart, God is saying, "Stay where you are. Trust me. I'll help you."

Use your powerful arm and give us victory. Then the people you love will be safe.

PSALM 60:5 CEV

God's desire is to guide you at every turn in life, and he has promised to lead you past places of difficulty and extreme pressure in order to prove his faithfulness. You never have to be afraid, because he promises to provide all you need.

Are you facing an overwhelming challenge today? Have faith in the One who has all you need to achieve the victory. He will not fail you; rather, he will lead you to triumph—so trust him.

God, there are times when I feel overwhelmed by the circumstances of life, but I know you have promised to do mighty things in and through me when I trust you. Amen.

BRINGING OUT THE BEST

Iron sharpens iron, and one man sharpens another.
PROVERBS 27:17 HCSB

I am a friend to all who fear You, to those who keep Your precepts.

PSALM 119:63 HCSB

A knife is sharpened by whetting it with another piece of iron—generally with a parallel movement. However, if you set the knife contrary to the other metal—striking edge to edge—you will dull, damage, or even break the blade.

The principle is the same for your relationships. If your companions are living contrary to God, they can hurt your relationship with him. However, if your closest friends are on a parallel course in knowing God, you will sharpen and bring out the best in each other.

Do your dearest friends hone your relationship with God or turn you away from him? Today, seek buddies who will encourage you to be your best for God.

Dear God, help me to find friends that will help me grow in you—and to be a friend to those who need you. Amen.

HIS BANNER OVER YOU

*You planted a flag to rally your people,
an unfurled flag to look to for courage.*
PSALM 60:4 MSG

Though he'd successfully conquered many of the surrounding territories, King David was not prepared for this military tactic. As he fought the Arameans in the north, the Edomites executed a surprise attack from the south.

*With God we will
gain the victory.*
PSALM 60:12 NIV

Of course, David was humble about his triumphs—always attributing them to God's banner of protection. So God rewarded him with victories over both armies.

You'll certainly face times of success when unexpected problems sneak up from behind and stun you. That's why David instructs you to look to God's banner for your courage. When God is your strength and focus, you cannot fail. Victory comes from God—so keep your eyes on him. He'll certainly honor you for it.

*God, I look up to your banner—my focus on your
unfailing character. You are always my protection and
hope. Thank you for leading me to triumph! Amen.*

KEEP WATCH WITH ME

My soul is exceedingly sorrowful, even to death.
Stay here and watch with Me.
MATTHEW 26:38 NKJV

They came to a place named Gethsemane; and [Jesus] said to His disciples, "Sit here until I have prayed."

MARK 14:32 NASB

Jesus experienced agonizing sorrow in the Garden of Gethsemane. His disciples could neither understand nor share it with him. Jesus asked them to stay nearby because their presence and prayers were comfort to him.

It is hard to know what to say to a loved one who is suffering. You know his heart is breaking, and you want to help. Yet what can you do?

You can express your love for him by just being near. Your presence comforts him and shows him he is not alone—even if you cannot share his burden.

Today, don't fall asleep on your loved ones. Keep watch with them during their time of need.

Dear God, you know exactly what my loved ones need. I will sit with them and pray— please make me a comfort to them. Amen.

SEEKING AND YEARNING FOR GOD

Hear my cry, O God; listen to my prayer. From the end of the earth I call to you, when my heart is faint.
PSALM 61:1–2 NRSV

Until you place your life fully in God's hands, you will never quiet the anxious thoughts that can cry out from within and leave you feeling unhappy and defeated. You can search frantically for happiness, success, and fulfillment. You can flail about and wonder why you are never satisfied, why you are always restless. You may wonder why new acquisitions merely whet your desire for more.

I cry to God Most High, to God who fulfills his purpose for me.

PSALM 57:2 NRSV

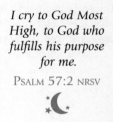

What you are yearning for and trying to find has been there all the time. God alone can satisfy your desperate longings. Without him, even the sources of human happiness, such as children, family, homes, fond possessions, dreams and ambitions, invite stress and agitation because you know one day you will lose them. Only when you make God the center of your life will you find true fulfillment.

God, as I look to you, fill my life to overflowing with your peace and joy. Keep me always in the palm of your hand. Amen.

SEASONED WITH GRACE

Let your speech always be gracious, seasoned with salt, so that you may know how you ought to answer each person.
COLOSSIANS 4:6 ESV

The right words will be there. The Holy Spirit will give you the right words when the time comes.

LUKE 12:12 MSG

✹

Salt is useful for many reasons. Not only does it make food tasty, but it also acts as a preservative and purifier. The same is true when grace is applied to your speech.

God does amazing things to your words. He prepares them to be appetizing to the person listening. He makes them preservative—giving them lasting beneficial value. And he purifies them—assuring that they will be safely received.

You never know when something you say will touch a person's heart. However, when your speech has been seasoned with God's grace, you know that your words will be a feast for the hearer.

Dear God, thank you for making my words appetizing, preservative, and pure by your grace. I pray that they will bring you glory. Amen.

A SOLID PLACE TO STAND

From the end of the earth I will cry to You, when my heart is overwhelmed; lead me to the rock that is higher than I.

PSALM 61:2 NKJV

At times you may lose your perspective about a situation because it is so overwhelming and earth-shattering. Perhaps you have done something that cannot be fixed, and the realization of your mistake is taking you on a downward spiral of disappointment. God knows your heart, and he is willing to come to your aid.

You have been a refuge for me, a strong tower in the face of the enemy. I will live in Your tent forever and take refuge under the shelter of Your wings.

PSALM 61:3–4 HCSB

On several occasions, David's confidence was shaken by his enemies, but the Lord repeatedly sustained him and gave him the victory. No matter what happened, he learned that God was with him, and that reality gave him peace.

Is your world being shaken by a tremendous challenge? Experiencing God's presence provided David with the stability and strength he needed to continue, and the same can be true for you. Therefore, plant your hope firmly in him.

God, please help me to sense your presence and rest in your care. Thank you for giving me a solid place to stand though the world around me quakes. Amen.

BOUND BY LOVE AND FAITHFULNESS

Let love and faithfulness never leave you. . . . Then you will win favor and a good name in the sight of God and man.
PROVERBS 3:3–4 NIV

Loving-kindness and mercy, loyalty and faithfulness, shall be to those who devise good.

PROVERBS 14:22 AMP

Two things are given for you to write upon your heart this morning—*love* and *faithfulness*. If you embrace them with your whole being, they will define your character and course.

Show your love by being kind and compassionate to others, and by trusting and worshiping your God. Prove your faithfulness by exercising integrity and being honest in all of your dealings—fully obedient and loyal to God's word and will.

You have been promised that if you are bound by love and faithfulness you will be respected by others and blessed by God. Truly a wonderful way to spend your day, indeed.

Dear God, bind love and faithfulness to me. Make them permeate my character and future so that I will, indeed, win favor with you and others. Amen.

A HERITAGE OF FAITH

*You, O God, have heard my vows; You have given
me the heritage of those who fear Your name.*

PSALM 61:5 NKJV

Hopefully you're trusting in God for your struggles today. One wonderful way to strengthen your confidence in him is to consider the people who've served God before you.

Whether your parents and grandparents knew God or not, you have a heritage of faith to encourage you.

From the end of the earth I call to you when my heart is faint. Lead me to the rock that is higher than I, for you have been my refuge.

PSALM 61:2–3 ESV

Throughout the Bible are histories that'll fill you with awe at the power and faithfulness of God. Yet you'll also observe what others have trusted God for—things beyond human imagination—and how they were rewarded. You're not alone in your relationship with God. From Genesis to Revelation you will find outstanding examples of overcoming faith and answered prayer. Ours is a heritage to be proud of.

*God, thank you that the Bible was written for my
encouragement and is a record of your faithfulness throughout
history. You are worthy of great praise! Amen.*

HIS STEADFAST LOVE

The earth is full of the steadfast love of the Lord.
PSALM 33:5 ESV

The Lord watches over those who obey him, those who trust in his constant love. . . . We put our hope in the Lord; he is our protector and our help.

PSALM 33:18, 20 GNT

Because of the Lord's unwavering love for you, this morning brings a brand-new sunrise—unlike any that has ever been before. It lights a world brimming with creative ways that God shows himself to you.

From the early hues of the sky to the birds that fly in it—he has painted them for you. From the bounty of the ocean to the harvest of the field, he tirelessly brings them forth to show you his unfailing provision.

He does not grow fatigued of watching over and protecting you. He never grows weary of your prayers. Rather, his enduring joy is showing you his steadfast love through all the wonders of creation.

Dear God, of all the wonders of this world, you are more wonderful than they all are. Thank you for your unwavering love. Amen.

WAITING FOR GOD'S TIMING

Truly my soul silently waits for God;
from Him comes my salvation.
PSALM 62:1 NKJV

No amount of worrying can make things happen, let alone make them happen the way you want. Oswald Chambers, in his classic *My Utmost for His Highest*, wrote, "When God brings a time of waiting, and appears to be unresponsive, don't fill it with busyness, just wait. . . . If you have the slightest doubt, then he is not guiding."

> *I waited patiently for God to help me; then he listened and heard my cry. He lifted me out of the pit of despair, out from the bog and the mire, and set my feet on a hard, firm path, and steadied me as I walked along.*
>
> PSALM 40:1–2 TLB

The story of Abraham and Sarah shows the futility of imposing your own timing on a divine promise. Tired of waiting for a son, Sarah took matters into her own hands. God's timetable will deliver an Isaac when the time is right.

Slow me down, God, when I am in a hurry and you are not.
Help me walk with you, not ahead of you. Teach me to
plant the seed and leave the harvest to you. Amen.

MANDATORY BARRIERS

Why aren't you in awe before me? Yes, me, who made the shorelines to contain the ocean waters.
JEREMIAH 5:22 MSG

The boundary lines have fallen for me in pleasant places; indeed, I have a beautiful inheritance.

PSALM 16:6 HCSB

Can you imagine if there were no shorelines to contain the oceans or rivers? If you have ever experienced a flood, you know the devastation that rushing waters can cause. Can you imagine how difficult life would be if the tides were not at least somewhat predictable?

Throughout the natural world there are barriers that separate land, sea, sky, and space, barriers that keep the world working and in order. God provides you with boundaries as well, principles that help you remain safe, happy, and free from disaster.

God gives you his decrees to protect you. Approach him in awe today, therefore, and thank him for keeping your world in working order.

Dear God, you truly amaze me. Even if I don't understand your principles, I know you work through them to protect me from danger. Amen.

RESTORATIVE HOPE

I find rest in God; only he gives me hope.
PSALM 62:5 NCV

Have you gotten to the point that you feel you can't continue? Sometimes this is because of legitimately strenuous tasks. But more often than not, this happens when you handle your responsibilities in your own strength. You keep working and pushing—feeling that if you fail, everything will fall apart. You trust yourself for success rather than God, and it's wearing you out.

> *On God rests my salvation and my glory; my mighty rock, my refuge is God. Trust in him at all times, O people; pour out your heart before him; God is a refuge for us.*
> PSALM 62:7–8 ESV

Friend, you need to rest and trust that God will reenergize and inspire you. He'll show you how to work smarter—instead of harder—and accomplish everything in his strength. So take a break and let him restore you. He'll fill you with his wisdom and empower you for all your tasks.

God, it's hard to let go because there's so much to do. Help me to trust you, and please multiply my times of rest. Amen.

SEEING THE POWER OF GOD

Truly this was God's Son!
MATTHEW 27:54 AMP

He was shown with great power to be the Son of God by being raised from death.

ROMANS 1:4 GNT

Had he been an ordinary man, his lifeless, bleeding body on the cross may have inspired grief and perhaps disgust—but certainly not awe. Yet when the centurion looked up at Jesus, he spontaneously uttered the words *Truly this was God's Son!*

That is because what he saw was the unleashing of God's amazing, majestic power. The moment Jesus died, there was a rock-shattering earthquake—the mighty force that had been restrained in his body was finally released to defeat death and give eternal life.

The centurion saw the power of God, and so can you today. Allow it to be released in your life, for truly he is God's Son.

Dear God, I can't even begin to imagine the remarkable power you hold. Thank you for expending it for my good and your glory. Amen.

344

UNTIL YOUR SOUL IS SATISFIED

O God, you are my God, and I long for you. My whole being desires you; like a dry, worn-out, and waterless land, my soul is thirsty for you.
PSALM 63:1 GNT

Responsibilities and struggles can drain your energy and emotions. You wonder how any good can come from what you are experiencing. But it can. Problems are a natural part of life. Without much warning, stress can build, and before

You satisfy me more than the richest feast. I will praise you with songs of joy.
PSALM 63:5 NLT

you know it, you are crying out for help. However, instead of cowering in fear, the psalmist used his trying situation as an opportunity to express his deep commitment to God.

Can you? Have you found shelter in the Lord's presence and fulfillment in his love? Then praise him for satisfying your hungry, weary soul, and express your trust that he will work everything out for your good.

God, thank you for inviting me to experience your wonderful love. I long to know you better and experience your encouraging, satisfying presence. Amen.

HEARING YOUR HEART

We do not know what to pray for as we ought, but the Spirit himself intercedes for us with groanings too deep for words.
ROMANS 8:26 ESV

The Father who knows all hearts knows what the Spirit is saying, for the Spirit pleads for us believers in harmony with God's own will.

ROMANS 8:27 NLT

To say that words are not sufficient to express everything that is inside of you is an amazing understatement. Could you shout it out, you would exhaust your vocal cords before you ever got close to finishing. All of the frustrations and sorrows, of the hopes and dreams—they are so profound and full of emotion that mere words fall hopelessly short of conveying them.

Yet God wants to hear your heart, so he sends his Spirit to examine you—your conscious and subconscious, your innermost thoughts and feelings. And God's Spirit beautifully communicates in his glorious words what is so difficult for you to express.

Dear God, thank you that your Spirit communicates the deep things within me. Thank you that whenever I pray, you really hear me. Amen.

A BANQUET FOR YOUR SPIRIT

My soul will feast and be satisfied,
and I will sing glad songs of praise to you.
PSALM 63:5 GNT

Is there a need inside you that just can't be satisfied? It can't be filled by food, possessions, or entertainment. You've tried it all, and it's all failed.

It may be that the part that's calling out to be fed is your soul. There is within each person an appetite for God that can only be satisfied in his presence. Whether in prayer, worship, Bible study, or service, your soul must be nourished by God. Perhaps you don't really believe this, so here's a challenge for you: The next time you feel that longing, allow your soul to be filled by God. Undoubtedly, you'll find that he was what your spirit was seeking all along.

I have looked upon you in the sanctuary, beholding your power and glory. Because your steadfast love is better than life, my lips will praise you.
PSALM 63:2–3 ESV

God, you say that those who hunger for righteousness will be satisfied and blessed. Fill my emptiness, God. Only you can fill my heart with joy. Amen.

BEFORE YOU KNEW

God demonstrates His own love toward us, in that
while we were yet sinners, Christ died for us.
ROMANS 5:8 NASB

I trust in your love. My
heart is happy because
you saved me.

PSALM 13:5 NCV

You don't have to earn God's love. He gives it to you freely. You may sometimes feel as if you need to do something to keep in good standing with him—making a promise or doing some good work— but you don't.

He loved you before you knew he existed. In fact, he loved you before *you* existed.

God demonstrated his love for you in a powerful way through the death and resurrection of Jesus. Two thousand years ago, before you knew you needed his love, he was providing it for you.

If you feel lonely or unworthy today, you can cling to this wonderful truth. He loves you. Praise his wonderful name.

My God, thank you for loving me even before I knew how
much I needed your love. You really are wonderful. Amen.

SLEEPLESS

I remember you while I'm lying in bed;
I think about you through the night.
PSALM 63:6 NCV

The clock is ticking louder than usual. The bed doesn't feel right either. You toss and turn, trying to get comfortable. Eventually you realize that your maddening thoughts are making you restless.

You have been my help, and in the shadow of your wings I will sing for joy. My soul clings to you; your right hand upholds me.

PSALM 63:7–8 ESV

Your mind is on, and you can't stop what's rushing through it—worry after worry bombards you without respite. You try to think of something else, but the anxieties come back more obtrusive than before. When you're sleepless, friend, turn your thoughts to God and think about all he's done for you. Pray to him, and give him all your concerns. Make your wakefulness into a worshipful time with him. He'll surely calm your soul and lead you into true rest.

God, only you can bring tranquillity to my barrage
of thoughts. Bring rest to my sleepless soul. I know
that I'm safe within your loving care. Amen.

FROM WAILING TO DANCING

You have turned my mourning into joyful dancing. You have taken away my clothes of mourning and clothed me with joy.
PSALM 30:11 NLT

Sing to the LORD, you saints of his; praise his holy name. For his anger lasts only a moment, but his favor lasts a lifetime; weeping may remain for a night, but rejoicing comes in the morning.

PSALM 30:4–5 NIV

Last night you may have had issues that weighed your heart down with sorrow. Yet this morning, God is working to bring you joy.

Mourning and dancing—two responses that are staggeringly different. But God easily alters circumstances that seem hopeless into great reasons for rejoicing. As quickly as God turns night into day, he can change your situation. He can transform your sorrow into jubilation and your cries of pain into hoots of happiness.

What is it that looks dark to you at this moment? Fear not. In just a little while you will be praising him for shining his light on your life and turning your wailing into dancing.

Oh, God—let it be so. You know why I cry, and what would make me dance. May your wonderful, transforming favor shine on me. Amen.

PRAYER BANISHES WORRY AND FEAR

Hear my voice, O God, in my meditation;
Preserve my life from fear of the enemy.
PSALM 64:1 NKJV

Worry and fear are the bane of human existence. Any number of events or circumstances can trigger them to cripple or incapacitate you. Worry and fear strike when you feel far from God. They rise up and crash over you when you are not paying attention to what is important in life—your relationship with God. That's when you need to stay focused.

I cry out to God Most High, to the God who does everything for me. He sends help from heaven and saves me. He punishes those who chase me. God sends me his love and truth.
PSALM 57:2–3 NCV

The more you pray, the closer you draw to God and the better you know him. His presence and power surround you, dissolving your worries and fears. You can cope with whatever comes along because you know you are shored up and strengthened. You are a recipient of his bountiful grace.

God, I know that you will banish my fears as I put my trust in you and walk with you in prayer. Amen.

ABOVE THE ARK

From above the mercy seat, from between the two cherubim that are upon the ark of the Testimony, I will speak intimately with you.
EXODUS 25:22 AMP

Here I am in the place of worship, eyes open, drinking in your strength and glory. In your generous love I am really living at last! My lips brim praises like fountains.

PSALM 63:2–3 MSG

Deep within the temple—in the Most Holy Place—was a beautifully decorated chest called the ark of the Testimony, where God would meet with the high priest.

Interestingly, the word for *ark* in Hebrew means "coffin." Meditate upon that striking picture and poignant principle—God's glory appeared above a coffin.

God's power always rushes in where all hope seems lost. It triumphed over the grave when Jesus was resurrected, and it does wonders for you as well. Whatever dreams have died for you—whatever seems irreparably lost—God will show you his glory above it. Meet with him today, and offer him your lifeless dreams. He will speak intimately with you and give you great hope.

Dear God, thank you for bringing life back to my dreams. I praise you for your astounding power and glory that always give me hope. Amen.

HIS HEALING ARROWS

Both the inward thought and the heart of man are deep.
But God shall shoot at them with an arrow.

PSALM 64:6–7 NKJV

Have you ever gotten up in the morning and remembered some deed done to you as if it just happened? You try to shake off the memory, but you walk around all day feeling as though you're under a cloud of anger. And then you can't sleep.

> *Then all men will fear,*
> *and they will declare*
> *the work of God, and*
> *will consider what*
> *He has done.*
>
> PSALM 64:9 NASB

God does not want your bitterness to rob you of the power and joy he has for you. That is why he will target it like a bowman with an arrow, so that you will deal with the issue consuming your thoughts, energy, and emotions.

It is easy to cling to feelings of unforgiveness, anger, or resentment, but God calls you to do the opposite—to forgive and move beyond the hurt. When you let go of past sorrows, you are free to accept the blessings he has for you.

God, I am in awe of your awesome love. Thank you
for revealing my old wounds and healing me of
their pain. Truly you are wonderful! Amen.

PERFECT PEACE

You keep him in perfect peace whose mind is stayed on you,
because he trusts in you. Trust in the LORD forever.
ISAIAH 26:3–4 ESV

He has done
everything well!
MARK 7:37 HCSB

Have you ever tried to help someone with a task, only to be told that you were doing it wrong? You were doing your best, yet because it was not the way the other person would do it, it wasn't "right."

People often treat God the same way. He has an amazing plan for each of us, yet we still try to wrestle the control from him. He provides his best for us, yet we question and complain because he isn't doing it our way.

Don't miss God's wonderful peace today by choosing your own plans over his. He will give perfect peace to you when you trust him and how he does things.

Dear God, please forgive me for choosing my plans
over yours and complaining. Thank you for your
perfect plans and perfect peace. Amen.

NO CONTEST

Then everyone will be afraid; they will proclaim the mighty acts of God and realize all the amazing things he does.
PSALM 64:9 NLT

It's all about getting ahead. You must prove yourself to be the best—whether it's through your intellect, beauty, wealth, or skills People are naturally disposed to comparing themselves to others—to competing and seeking prominence at whatever they consider their strength.

The righteous shall be glad in the LORD, and trust in Him. And all the upright in heart shall glory.

PSALM 64:10 NKJV

But you don't have to put yourself through such a useless and destructive exercise. God loves you just the way you are. He's given you unique talents that he's going to work through, so you don't have to contend against other people—you can work with them. Friend, don't compete. When God is working through you, you're already the best you can be. You're already a winner, so be gracious and act like it.

God, I want to feel special. Help me to realize that how I compete isn't what makes me unique, successful, and loved. You make me unique, successful, and loved. Amen.

WHY IT HAPPENED

This happened so the power of God could be seen in him.
JOHN 9:3 NLT

> *God, order up your power; show the mighty power you have used for us before.*
>
> PSALM 68:28 NCV

It was the same question every time: *Who did wrong?* If the man had been born blind, then someone's mistake must have caused it. Yet Jesus set the disciples straight. It happened so that God's power could be shown.

You may be wondering today why something is happening to you. Though you have prayed, the problem continues. You may even wonder, *What did I do to deserve this?* This has not happened because of some wrong you have done. Rather, it is because God wants to show his power in you. As with the blind man, he will open your eyes to his mighty power and you will see God.

Dear God, I look forward to seeing your power in this situation. Thank you that this is so your glory will be shown. Amen.

THE PRIVILEGE OF HIS PRESENCE

*How happy is the one You choose and
bring near to live in Your courts!*
PSALM 65:4 HCSB

God will challenge you to do many wonderful things in this life—he will encourage you to launch out in faith with the tasks he calls you to do. But there is something that brings an even greater degree of satisfaction than anything you can experience on a human level, and that is time spent in quiet devotion

You answer us in amazing ways, God our Savior. People everywhere on the earth and beyond the sea trust you.

PSALM 65:5–6 NCV

to him. Though your life may seem too full to take time to be alone with him, consider this: He is never too busy to be with you. His one consuming desire is for you to know him. When you begin to do this, even the smallest of activities will take on new meaning.

So spend time with him, and enjoy the awesome privilege of being in his presence. Surely it will be the best time you have had all day!

*God, for far too long, I have dismissed your efforts
to touch my heart. Please open my life up to you
so I may experience all you have for me. Amen.*

AN ANSWER IS COMING

*In the morning, O LORD, you hear my voice; in the morning
I lay my requests before you and wait in expectation.*
PSALM 5:3 NIV

*I will listen [with
expectancy] to what
God the Lord will say,
for He will speak
peace to His people.*

PSALM 85:8 AMP

There is such a sweetness and benefit to seeking God in the morning. By starting your day with the Bible and prayer, you open yourself to a conversation with him throughout the day.

It is important to go to God with more than requests and longings. Go to him with a hearing heart. How often do you go to God with the simple intent of listening?

Certainly, there are things you have been asking him about. And his answer is coming to you—that is sure. This morning, listen quietly to your God and wait in expectation for his wondrous reply. His answer is coming—so don't miss it.

*Dear God, thank you for hearing me. I want to
hear you. Speak straight to my heart, O Lord.
I wait in eager expectation. Amen.*

CREATOR AND SUSTAINER

*God of our salvation, the hope of all the ends of the
earth and of the distant seas; You establish the
mountains by Your power, robed with strength.*
PSALM 65:5–6 HCSB

Have you ever wondered why God created the earth—laying its foundation with such ingenuity and care? Have you considered why he'd fill it with such a variety of birds, animals, and fish? Why he'd create mountains and valleys, rivers and seas? Why there would be such different seasons and climates, colors and foliage?

*You care for the land
and water it; you
enrich it abundantly.
The streams of God
are filled with water
to provide the people
with grain, for so you
have ordained it.*

PSALM 65:9 NIV

✶🌙✶

Friend, God did it for you. God filled the world with wonder and sustenance not only to feed your stomach, but also to nourish your imagination and soul.

So praise your magnificent Creator and Sustainer, who has constructed this amazing world. Surely, the One who's done all this is mighty and is able to care for all of your needs.

*God, you are astounding and majestic—your creation inspires
my soul. Thank you, God, for filling the world with such
imaginative creatures and beautiful landscapes. Amen.*

WRESTLING WITH TIME

How long, O Lord?
Psalm 13:1 NKJV

*Look on me and
answer, O Lord
my God. Give light
to my eyes.*

Psalm 13:3 NIV

This morning, are you crying out, *How long, O Lord?* Most things are endurable as long as you know you will soon have relief. Yet when you have no idea when or if your circumstance will have a resolution, it can be discouraging.

You are not only dealing with your situation, but you are also wrestling with the uncertainties of time. Everything could change in a minute or endure interminably.

Be patient. Your God hears you and is the master of both time and your situation. Though you do not know how long it will last, he does. And your waiting will not last one second longer than is necessary.

*Dear God, my time is in your hands—and I trust you.
It is hard to wait, but it is worth it knowing
that you are handcrafting my future. Amen.*

NATURE: GOD'S HERALD

What a rich harvest your goodness provides!
Wherever you go there is plenty.
PSALM 65:11 GNT

Young schoolchildren often take nature walks with brown paper bags in hand. As they set out on the trail, a teacher instructs them to bring back as many intriguing bits of nature as they can find: an acorn, a brightly colored leaf, a pine needle, a flower bud, an empty cocoon, an interesting pebble, a piece of bark.

He covers the heavens with clouds, sends down the showers, and makes the green grass grow in mountain pastures. He feeds the wild animals, and the young ravens cry to him for food.
PSALM 147:8–9 TLB

As adults you may not venture outdoors with a bag in hand, but like children you can stop and marvel at God's fingerprint on the world around you. You see it everywhere, from a flower to the watercolor of a sunset. You also see God's artistic expression in his crowning achievement in creation: one another.

Thank you for the world, dear God, a mighty volume wherein you declare yourself. I see your signature everywhere on the garments of what you have made. Amen.

SEARCHABLE SECRETS

Call to Me and I will answer you and show you great and mighty things, fenced in and hidden, which you do not know.
JEREMIAH 33:3 AMP

It is the LORD who gives wisdom; from him come knowledge and understanding.

PROVERBS 2:6 GNT

The mind cannot even begin to conceive all that God knows concerning the construction of the world and everything in it. He says that if you call to him, he will show you.

Amazingly, as you spend time with God, he starts awakening you to things you never even thought to think about. He gives you insights into yourself and other people that are unfathomable without his guidance and teaching.

He also reveals himself to you—the greatest and most wonderful of all knowledge.

Call upon the Lord today, and listen intently to his answer. Surely he will show you great secrets that you will love to know.

Dear God, I listen intently to all you have to share with me. Please teach me all the mighty hidden things I do not know. Amen.

IMPOSSIBILITIES

Take a good look at God's wonders—they'll take your breath away. He converted sea to dry land; travelers crossed the river on foot. Now isn't that cause for a song?
PSALM 66:5–6 MSG

The night the storm broke out on the Sea of Galilee, the wind picked up without warning. Then the waves began to swell, and a hard rain beat down. Fear consumed the disciples' minds and hearts.

Yet their anxiety was unfounded, because Jesus was with them. When their cries woke him, Jesus commanded the wind and the waves to be still. The same is true for you whenever you experience overwhelming storms of life. God is with you. He will provide the protection you need to get through every trial.

Bless our God, you peoples! And make the voice of His praise to be heard, who keeps our soul among the living, and does not allow our feet to be moved. For You, O God, have tested us; You have refined us as silver is refined.
PSALM 66:8–10 NKJV

Words cannot express my love for you, God. You are my refuge, and I am overwhelmed by your greatness and humbled by your love for me. Amen.

OPENHEARTED

Always be generous, open purse and hands, give to your neighbors in trouble, your poor and hurting neighbors.
DEUTERONOMY 15:11 MSG

Give to them freely and unselfishly, and the LORD will bless you in everything you do.

DEUTERONOMY 15:10

GNT

As the Israelites settled into the Promised Land, God instructed them to do something quite shocking. At the end of every seven years, they were to cancel all debts.

Also during that seventh year, they were to put down their tools and relax. It was to be a year of rest from both toil and obligations. Why? Because God wanted the Israelites to understand that everything they had came from him. And so, knowing his openheartedness toward them, they should likewise be benevolent with others.

God is a giving God, and he wants his people to be generous as well. Today, be openhearted with those who are in need around you.

Dear God, I know that everything I have comes from you. Help me to see others' needs so that I can be as generous as you would. Amen.

SURE FOOTING

*Let everyone bless God and sing his praises; for he holds
our lives in his hands, and he holds our feet to the path.*

PSALM 66:8–9 TLB

So steep and treacherous are the paths along the walls of the Grand Canyon that those who wish to traverse them rarely set out on foot. They depend on remarkable animals with hoofs designed to hug the narrow, dusty paths and bodies proportioned for maximum strength, endurance, and balance.

> *He will command his angels concerning you to guard you in all your ways; they will lift you up in their hands, so that you will not strike your foot against a stone.*
>
> PSALM 91:11–12 NIV

In the course of your life, many of you will encounter certain mountain paths that are simply too difficult to attempt alone. But when you set out on those trails, you can depend on God to keep you from falling. He will provide the assistance you need.

*Faithful God, when I must follow a steep and treacherous path
on my journey through life, I will place my hope and trust in your
promise to help me reach my destination safely. Amen.*

GOD IS NEAR

Your GOD is present among you, a strong Warrior there
to save you. Happy to have you back, he'll calm you
with his love and delight you with his songs.
ZEPHANIAH 3:17 MSG

One of His disciples,
whom Jesus loved
[whom He esteemed
and delighted in], was
reclining [next to Him]
on Jesus' bosom.

JOHN 13:23 AMP

When you separate yourself from impediments and interruptions, you can feel the closeness of God. When you shut the door on the demands on your attention and time, it is possible to know the peace God brings through his presence.

A guide was directing visitors through a large city in his country, speaking to them in hesitant and halting English. As they went down one of the busiest streets in the city, he said to them in an urgent tone, "Stick on me." In moments of sacred quiet, you can get so close to God that your heart sticks to his. When you separate yourself from what comes next on the list of things to do, you can move God to the top of the list of places to be.

When I quiet my soul, O God, you are nearer than breathing—
closer to me than I am to myself. Amen.

PERSONAL MEMORIALS

Come and hear, all you who fear God,
and I will tell what he has done for me.
PSALM 66:16 NRSV

The art of storytelling, no doubt, dates back to the Garden of Eden, and for good reason. Most people enjoy the pleasure factor of a good story, and you probably do as well. You enjoy the purpose—and the memories—that you find in stories. Through oral histories you learn what went before you, and through them you pass on what has happened in your own life stories so that time will not erase your experiences.

Parents will tell their children what you have done. They will retell your mighty acts, wonderful majesty, and glory. And I will think about your miracles. They will tell about the amazing things you do, and I will tell how great you are.
PSALM 145:4–6 NCV

Personal memorials commemorate your blessings. When you "tell of what he has done," you are twice blessed: in seeing the joy it brings to others and in the reliving of your story.

Praise you, God, for the story you write in my life,
the story of how you save me because you love me.
Thank you for the good news of this story. Amen.

A SPECIFIC SALUTATION

This, then, is how you should pray: "Our Father in heaven:
May your holy name be honored; may your Kingdom come;
may your will be done on earth as it is in heaven."
MATTHEW 6:9–10 GNT

God! Let people thank
and enjoy you. Let all
people thank and
enjoy you.
PSALM 67:3 MSG

The disciples saw Jesus often on bended knee and, one day, asked him to teach them how to pray. He taught them that the first thing to do is to address God directly, to be specific in salutation, to know what God means, and to call him what he is.

Prayer acknowledges the personal nature of your relationship to God. God is a friend with whom you share, and in whom you confide. Through prayer, you speak to God and God speaks to you. The strength of your prayer comes from the intensity of your bond with God.

When you talk to God, you talk to someone you know well and with whom you have a deep and close relationship.

Dear God of heaven and earth, I am first to
you and you are foremost to me. Amen.

CHOICES

If I had been cozy with evil,
the Lord would never have listened.
PSALM 66:18 MSG

Whenever you make a choice, you declare what's important to you and progress in a definite direction. This is because you've elected either to honor God or to serve something else.

Let the whole world bless our God and loudly sing his praises. Our lives are in his hands, and he keeps our feet from stumbling.

PSALM 66:8–9 NLT

What about the mundane choices? Does it matter where you eat lunch or what you wear to work? In such cases, it's always best to ask yourself, *Is there anything about my selection that God would object to? Are there any godly principles that would help me pick a better alternative?*

Often, it's not the major decisions that change the course of your life, but the little ones you make daily. So honor God with all your choices—his way will always be your best option.

God, teach me the principles that will help me make the best choices, and help me to honor you in all my decisions—even the mundane ones. Amen.

SIT IN SILENCE

*For God alone my soul waits in silence, from him comes
my salvation. He alone is my rock and my salvation,
my fortress; I shall never be shaken.*
PSALM 62:1–2 NRSV

*When the Lamb broke
open the seventh seal,
there was silence in
heaven for about half
an hour. Then I saw
the seven angels who
stand before God,
and they were given
seven trumpets.*

REVELATION 8:1–2 GNT

Silence is golden when you desire God's presence. It closes down the racket made by urgent schedule and full agenda. With those noises dismissed, you have a clear channel. Silence enables you to hear with your heart as God speaks from his.

Sitting in silence in a quiet place gives God a chance to bless you. In the only one of Phillips Brooks's hymns to survive the test of time, "O Little Town of Bethlehem," a line in the third stanza reads, "How silently, how silently, the wondrous gift is given!" As you wait and watch in silence, God touches you with the blessing of his presence. Silence beckons you into intimacy with God. God's best gift, the gift of himself, is often given in silence.

*Silently I wait for you, O God, in the quiet depths
of my open and expectant heart. Amen.*

ANSWERED PRAYERS

Praise God, who did not ignore my prayer
or hold back his love from me.
PSALM 66:20 NCV

Silence can seem to be loud and intimidating when you are waiting for an answer to your prayers. In the nighttime of the soul, God's silence thunders down at you, rattling your confidence and leaving you wondering if he has abandoned you.

The LORD has heard my cry for help; the LORD will answer my prayer.

PSALM 6:9 NCV

At those times when God is silent, you must place your hope in two mighty truths: the truth of God's sovereignty and the truth of his faithfulness. God answers all your prayers, but always in his own time and in his own way. When you place your hope in him, you will not be disappointed—even when the answer that comes is not what you expected. You are wise to trust him and wait patiently. It is in these times that your faith is tested, strengthened, and established.

God, when I do not hear your voice, help me to rest in your constant love as I wait for your answer to my prayer. Amen.

GOD IS EVERYWHERE

I look behind me and you're there, then up ahead and you're there, too—your reassuring presence, coming and going.
PSALM 139:5 MSG

You supported me because of my integrity and set me in Your presence forever.

PSALM 41:12 HCSB

Everywhere you are, God is. God is there in all the directions you take, no matter which way you choose to go. God is there in all the conditions of life, whatever their nature or intensity. God, who loves you enough to make you as special as you are, does not leave you alone at any time. God is at your side day to day and step by step.

You can think God isn't around, but that doesn't mean he isn't. You can mark God absent, if that's what you conclude, but you will be making the wrong notation in the roll book. You might feel that God has abandoned you, but he hasn't done anything of the kind. God would never do that to you.

Dear God, thank you for surrounding me all the time with who you are. Amen.

TIME FOR THE HARVEST

Then the earth will yield its harvests,
and God, our God, will richly bless us.
PSALM 67:6 NLT

Any farmer who plants seeds in the ground and then returns the following day expecting to see a full-grown crop is quite foolish. Unfortunately, many of us assume our prayers will produce results in much the same way. We ask God for the deepest desires of our heart, and then we become frustrated when our prayers aren't answered immediately.

May God be gracious to us and bless us; look on us with favor . . . so that Your way may be known on earth, Your salvation among all nations.

PSALM 67:1–2 HCSB

Though we want instantaneous results, God doesn't operate that way. Rather, he gives his best blessings time to mature—to become satisfying to your soul. He also prepares you to receive them.

Friend, God's timing is perfect, so keep praying and be patient. Your harvest of blessing will surely bloom when the time is right.

God, help me to be patient and not lose heart as I wait for your promises to develop. Thank you for always giving me your best. Amen.

LISTEN TO YOUR HEART

Our soul waits for the LORD; He is our help and our shield. For our heart shall rejoice in Him, because we have trusted in His holy name.
PSALM 33:20–21 NKJV

You have put gladness in my heart, more than when their grain and new wine abound.

PSALM 4:7 NASB

God's favorite dwelling place is in your heart. He lives and speaks to you there. He tells you how special you are to him. In your heart, you know the truth about how much you mean to God.

In your heart, you have a powerful interaction with God. From there you can talk with God confidently about his will for you. From there you can speak clearly about your needs and can focus directly on the one who supplies your needs. Your heart is the holy place where you and God meet. Your heart is where you can bask in God's presence and hear his words of love and wisdom. Listen to your heart.

Dear God, I am glad that you dwell in my heart. Amen.

TO ALL PEOPLE

*God blesses us so people all over
the earth will fear him.*
PSALM 67:7 NCV

Whether you realize it or not, showing up at church on Sunday is not the only way to express your love for God. Your life is a living testimony to others. Through your words and actions, you reflect your core beliefs, desires, faith, and fears.

When you care for another person freely rather than out of obligation, you are expressing God's love. When

*Our God, be kind
and bless us! Be
pleased and smile.
Then everyone on
earth will learn to
follow you, and all
nations will see your
power to save us.*

PSALM 67:1–2 CEV

you tell someone about the reason for the hope you have, you honor God. Do you view those around you as he views them—with love, respect, and compassion? Do you share your blessings with them so that they will know the Savior? God knows your heart and how you choose to live each day. Therefore, honor him with everything you say and do so that others may know him and be saved.

*My greatest desire, God, is for others to see you in and through my
life. Help me to share your love with everyone I meet. Amen.*

CLOSE THE DOOR

*When you pray, you should go into your room and close the door
and pray to your Father who cannot be seen. Your Father
can see what is done in secret, and he will reward you.*
MATTHEW 6:6 NCV

*Call to me and I will
answer you. I'll tell
you marvelous and
wondrous things that
you could never figure
out on your own.*

JEREMIAH 33:3 MSG

In the time of Jesus, every Jewish house had a place for private devotion. It was a location where the door could be closed on distractions and interruptions. Such a place was often a small room built on a flat roof, and people went there to draw close to God. Sometimes it was a modest space raised a story above the rest of the house where people retired to nourish their souls in the reality and certainty of God.

You have such a place. It is wherever you can go to be with God in a way you are unable to do anywhere else. As you go to that place, you are excited about what will happen. You know your time there with God will be rich and fruitful.

*Dear God, help me shut out anything that would
take your place in my mind and heart. Amen.*

ISOLATED NO MORE

*A father to the fatherless, a defender of widows, is God
in his holy dwelling. God sets the lonely in families.*
PSALM 68:5–6 NIV

There were none more helpless in ancient society than the widows and orphans. The laws often left those who lost loved ones without much recourse or hope. So God took care of them—he became their Provider and Defender.

The God of Israel is He who gives strength and power to His people. Blessed be God!
PSALM 68:35 NKJV

God knows that when you're alone, the world can be a difficult place—but you don't have to continue feeling lonely, isolated, or helpless. God loves you and invites you to be part of his family. He gives you people to love, who'll love you in return.

So continue to know God and embrace others who belong to his family. As you give of yourself, your loneliness will melt away and your joy will surely grow.

God, thank you for your love and for inviting me to be part of your family. I praise you for being my Provider and Defender. Amen.

ALWAYS AVAILABLE

*This is the confidence we have in approaching God: that
if we ask anything according to his will, he hears us.*
1 JOHN 5:14 NIV

*You will call upon me
and come and pray
to me, and I will
hear you.*

JEREMIAH 29:12 ESV

You will never get a busy signal on God's prayer line. The circuits of heaven are never jammed. You can have an audience with God at a stated time in a holy place or you can talk to him on the run to the next thing in your life. You can get through to God anytime you want.

Ready and constant access to God is your birthright. By being always available, God shows how much you mean to him. You can count on God's focused attention because you count so much to God. God honors who you are to him by listening to everything you have to say. You can talk to God because you know he listens to you. His ears are always outstretched in your direction.

*I am most grateful, dear God, for your listening heart
of love, forgiveness, and renewal. Amen.*

WEIGHTY CHALLENGES

Blessed be the Lord, who daily bears our burden.
PSALM 68:19 NASB

Loads get heavier the longer you carry them. This is true of both physical weight and emotional responsibilities. The more time you contend with them, the more fatigued you become.

Summon your might, O God. Display your power, O God, as you have in the past.

PSALM 68:28 NLT

You may believe that you've gotten accustomed to your burdens—that you can handle them—but they're still draining you. You know that because of how difficult it is for you to deal with new challenges. When you stop having joy, it's obvious you're not managing your problems successfully.

Friend, you don't have to be self-sufficient. God is happy to carry your burdens. He'll be your unfailing strength and will use the weight to help you grow. Trust him with your concerns.

God, I'm not quite sure how to give my burdens to you—please show me how. I truly want to trust you with them. Amen.

SPEAK WITH YOUR FRIEND

*The Lord spoke to Moses face to face
as a man speaks with his friend.*
EXODUS 33:11 NCV

*Servants don't know
what their master is
doing, and so I don't
speak to you as my
servants. I speak to
you as my friends,
and I have told you
everything that my
Father has told me.*

JOHN 15:15 CEV

Prayer is relational. It is talking to someone you know. There are no strangers in the prayer room. When speaking to God in prayer, you can have the same kind of experience with God that Moses had—face to face. You can be friend with friend.

With God as your friend in prayer, you are never too hurt to look back and you are never too scared to look ahead. With God as your friend in prayer, you can look within yourself and celebrate who you are and who you are becoming. You can feel close enough to God to open yourself up and let him come in. When you go to God in prayer, you are in the presence of one you know and one who knows you.

*Thank you, dear God, for being a friend closer and dearer
than any other friend is. You are my very best friend. Amen.*

SHH, LISTEN

*O rider in the heavens, the ancient heavens; listen,
he sends out his voice, his mighty voice.*
PSALM 68:33 NRSV

Of the five senses given to you, listening may be the one most poorly used. Yet it is the key to real communication with others. Often when you ask questions, you may already have formulated the answers you expect. When you engage in conversation, you may often have preconceived ideas of

They speak without a sound or word; their voice is never heard. Yet their message has gone throughout the earth, and their words to all the world.

PSALM 19:3–4 NLT

what you are going to hear. Conditioned by habit or limited thinking, your expectations may drown out what is new and interesting.

If you are to respond with your best self to the world, you have to dust off your hearing skills and turn up the volume. You have to pay attention to the pauses between words, the sighs, the tones of voice coming your way. You have to let the sounds of life get through to you.

*God, open my ears to hear the sounds around me—
the sounds that wake me to the beauty and
grandeur of your wonderful world. Amen.*

381

PEACE AT THE CENTER

*The peace that Christ gives is to guide you in the
decisions you make; for it is to this peace that
God has called you together in the one body.*
COLOSSIANS 3:15 GNT

*You will experience
God's peace, which
exceeds anything we
can understand. His
peace will guard your
hearts and minds as
you live in Christ Jesus.*

PHILIPPIANS 4:7 NLT

Peace in your heart makes your life beautiful and wonderful. It is the peace God gives when you draw close to him to receive his love and blessing. This peace counters the turbulence you have elsewhere in your life. It brings the stability of knowing you belong to God and the security of knowing he is with you always.

God's peace comes when you know how much God loves you, how far he goes to forgive you, how many ways he sustains you, and how many generous life opportunities he offers you. God's peace will guide you in the way you should go. God puts the calm of his presence and the peace of his love at the center of your life.

*Dear God, when I know you in my heart,
I have peace in my life. Amen.*

PAUSING FOR POWER

*You are awesome, O God, in your sanctuary; the God
of Israel gives power and strength to his people.*
PSALM 68:35 NIV

Tragedy and loss can leave you feeling powerless, like a single flower that the wind whips and breaks. You may feel that you no longer have control over the circumstances of your life, and you may feel hopeless and alone. In the midst of those difficult times, you may feel that God is far away.

> *I can lie down and go to sleep, and I will wake up again, because the LORD gives me strength.*
>
> PSALM 3:5 NCV

But God promises that he will always be with you. Even when anger and grief cause you to lose a sense of his presence, he is closer than the beating of your own heart. He assures you that no tragedy can separate you from his amazing love. And he allows you to draw from his power to take responsibility for your life again, to see past your heartache, and to find hope and healing in his presence.

*Gracious God, thank you for loving me, even in the midst
of my anger and grief, and thank you for giving me
the power and strength to live again. Amen.*

July

*The things we see now
are here today, gone
tomorrow. But the things
we can't see now will
last forever.*

2 Corinthians 4:18 msg

NOT A WORD

Everyone kept quiet and listened as Barnabas and Paul
told how God had given them the power to work
a lot of miracles and wonders for the Gentiles.

ACTS 15:12 CEV

The LORD was not in the wind; and after the wind an earthquake, but the LORD was not in the earthquake; and after the earthquake a fire, but the LORD was not in the fire; and after the fire a sound of sheer silence.

1 KINGS 19:11–12 NRSV

Silence invites God into your heart and ignites you with a passion for his closeness. It takes down the bars that the world's busyness and noise put on your soul and opens the door where God stands waiting to enter. Silence is a direct path to God's presence. Many of the wonderful gifts that come from God are given in silence.

When Elijah left a cave and went to a mountain to hear from God, he listened intently for the divine voice in blustery wind, trembling earthquake, and blistering fire. He heard from God, but not in any of that. God chose to speak to Elijah in absolute silence. Silence is a condition in which God makes himself known to you.

Dear God, fade my words into silence. Give me the gift of quiet. Then I will hear you better. Amen.

GOD'S VICTORY OVER SELF-DEFEAT

My sins, O God, are not hidden from you;
you know how foolish I have been.
PSALM 69:5 GNT

When you become aware of your potential to stray from God's love, you may feel shocked and even disappointed. Temptations can entangle you, and sin can settle deep within your heart—preventing you from enjoying a close relationship with God. It is easy to spot the signs of spiritual compromise in your life— you justify the sin and temptation,

> *O God, in the great-ness of Your loving-kindness, answer me with Your saving truth. . . . The humble have seen it and are glad; you who seek God, let your heart revive.*
> PSALM 69:13, 32 NASB

feel that you need to rush about rather than rest in God's presence, and give God and others a list of excuses about why your devotion is off course.

Nothing is more important than your relationship with him. In addition, when you lay aside your sin and go to him with a heart of devotion, you will notice a difference. Your life will be marked by peace and joy.

God, I know my tendency to self-destruct through sin and moral com-promise. Please keep me from straying in my love toward you. Amen.

YOU CAN COUNT ON IT

My Presence will go with you,
and I will give you rest.
EXODUS 33:14 NIV

Fear not [there is nothing to fear], for I am with you; do not look around you in terror and be dismayed, for I am your God.

ISAIAH 41:10 AMP

You can count on God's presence in your quiet moments. Time after time in Holy Scripture, God promises he will be present when you intentionally draw aside to meet him. God's presence is everywhere in the stories of the Bible. God makes the promise of his presence, and he keeps that promise. You can stand on the promise of God's presence to be with you.

God will make himself known to you as a living and bright reality. He will be at your side and will abide there in love and grace. He will move into your heart to embrace your life and guide your way. God is present to your needs. God promises to take up daily residence in your heart.

Dear God of this present moment, thank you
for being right where I am. Amen.

THE PART THAT COMES ALIVE

*You who seek God, inquiring for and requiring Him
[as your first need], let your hearts revive and live!*
PSALM 69:32 AMP

There are hidden treasure troves within you—wonderful gold mines of potential that you may not even know about. God created them within you, and he's the only one who can access them. They can only be cultivated and utilized by spending time with him.

As for me, I will pray to you, LORD; answer me, God, at a time you choose. Answer me because of your great love, because you keep your promise to save.

PSALM 69:13 GNT

You undoubtedly have many talents, but there's even more within you—aptitudes that are inspired and empowered solely by God's Spirit. He makes those hidden abilities come alive and fills you with meaning and purpose through them.

So discover the abundant life God created you for—spend time with him and allow him to make you into all you can be. You'll discover that there's more to you than you thought.

*Thank you, God, for giving me such wonderful gifts
and seeing all the potential in me. I praise you for
helping me experience your abundant life. Amen.*

MORE THAN HIS SHARE

Come to Me, all you who labor and are heavy-laden and overburdened, and I will cause you to rest. [I will ease and relieve and refresh your souls.]
MATTHEW 11:28 AMP

Return, O my soul, to your rest, for the LORD has dealt bountifully with you.

PSALM 116:7 NRSV

✸

Whatever burden you have to carry, God will shoulder the better part of it. God will take the greater portion of your struggle on himself. He will bear the extra weight and move with you to resolution.

Imagine holding a glass of water and wondering how much it weighs. You don't know, but the longer you hold it, the more it seems to weigh. Hold it for a minute, and it's okay. But hold it for ten minutes, and your arm begins to ache. Hold it for an hour, and you might have to call an ambulance. But if you take the glass of water to a table and set it down there, everything is okay again. God will take your load on his back and give you rest.

*Dear God, you lift my burdens with your love.
Thank you for helping me so much. Amen.*

WHAT TO PRAY

May all who seek you rejoice and be glad in you! May those who love your salvation say evermore, "God is great!"
PSALM 70:4 ESV

You may struggle with how to pray for others especially if they're facing challenging circumstances. You want God's will to be accomplished, because you know that ultimately it'll be best for them. Yet you don't want them to experience hardship. What do you do?

> *I am afflicted and needy; hurry to me, God. You are my help and my deliverer; LORD, do not delay.*
>
> PSALM 70:5 HCSB

Pray that whatever God's plan is for them, they'll trust him more through it, and they'll find joy and strength in him and seek him daily. Pray they'll know for certain that he's great, loving, and wise.

Whatever your loved ones are facing, your best prayer for them is that they'd know him better. May all who seek him rejoice and say evermore that God is truly good.

God, I do pray that my loved ones would know you better and trust you more today—no matter what their circumstances. Truly, you are wonderful! Amen.

BUILDING BACK

*Whoever there is among you of all His people, may his God
be with him! Let him go up to Jerusalem which is
in Judah and rebuild the house of the Lord.*
Ezra 1:3 nasb

*Do good to Zion in
your good pleasure;
build up the walls
of Jerusalem.*

Psalm 51:18 esv

When you have disappointments and setbacks in your
life, remember that such experiences
provide a good foundation on which
to regroup and rebuild. God honors
that foundation with his spirit of
renewal and his gift of strength.

When you call on God, receive his support, and accept his
help, a failure may turn out to be one of the best things that
ever happens to you. It provides an opportunity to know who
God is and what he can do. It introduces you to abilities, capacities, and aptitudes you didn't know you had. It lets you
know how powerful your partnership with God is. Failure put
in the hands of God is the first step to something better. It is the
ingredient that gives flavor to future success.

*Dear God, grant me the courage to follow as
you lead me from failure to success. Amen.*

I NEED YOU RIGHT NOW!

*I am poor and needy; make haste to me, O God! You are
my help and my deliverer; O LORD, do not delay.*

PSALM 70:5 NKJV

Have you ever noticed that sometimes when you try your hardest to make something work, it turns out wrong? These are often the times when God allows you to face difficulty in order to teach you to trust him more deeply.

> *Let all who love your
> saving way say over
> and over, "God is
> mighty!"*
>
> PSALM 70:4 MSG

By spending time with him in prayer—listing your concerns, desires, and needs—you are telling him that you need him. Nothing touches his heart more profoundly than hearing your sincere prayer: "Father God, I can't do this on my own. I need you." Such humility immediately stirs his compassion.

Friend, always remember that you can reach your goals by keeping your heart set on him. So call to him. He is certainly ready to respond and will send the wisdom you need for success.

*God, I know there are times when I rush ahead of you.
I'm sorry. I confess my need and ask you to step into my
situation so I will have your infinite support. Amen.*

SOMETHING ON THE WAY

*Peter said, "I don't have any silver or gold! But I will give
you what I do have. In the name of Jesus Christ
from Nazareth, get up and start walking."*
ACTS 3:6 CEV

*On the following
day they came to
Caesarea. Cornelius
was waiting for
them and had called
together his relatives
and close friends.*

ACTS 10:24 NCV

As you draw close to God, you sense something new in the air. You feel the breath of God's Spirit coming toward where you are.

In a painting of the blind man at Jericho by the French master Nicolas Poussin, you can sense the expectancy of the one kneeling before Jesus for healing. His left hand is outstretched, palms open toward Jesus. His right hand is raised and extended in anticipation. The right leg of the blind man is posed to take the first step into a new day of light and wholeness. He has come to Jesus, fully expecting to see. Dawn arrives, and you are standing on the edge of new possibilities. You have absolute assurance that something special is on the way.

*When I realize who you are and what you can do,
dear God, my expectations are always high. Amen.*

HOPE'S REWARD

O Lord, you alone are my hope. I've trusted you,
O LORD, from childhood.
PSALM 71:5 NLT

On the heels of World War II, Peter Marshall, the celebrated United States Senate chaplain during the 1940s, offered a famous prayer called "Bifocals of Faith." Before the statesmen of his day, he prayed, "God, give us the faith to believe in the ultimate triumph of righteousness, no matter how dark

I find rest in God;
only he gives me
hope. He is my rock
and my salvation.
He is my defender; I
will not be defeated.
PSALM 62:5–6 NCV

and uncertain are the skies of today. We pray for the bifocals of faith—that see the despair and the need of the hour but also see, further on, the patience of our God working out his plan in the world he has made."

Hope springs from a heart that trusts in God. Without hope, your life would quickly turn bleak. But with this virtue in your heart, every dark cloud has a silver lining.

Dear God, I see more with my heart than with my eyes.
Through faith, I see your love, encouragement,
and purpose. Thank you for what I see. Amen.

A SPONGE IN THE OCEAN

God is actually not far from any one of us; as someone has said,
"In him we live and move and exist."
ACTS 17:27–28 GNT

The LORD looks at the world from his throne in heaven, and he watches us all.

PSALM 33:13–14 CEV

Attempting to communicate the extent and scope of God to people standing on an Athens hill, Paul gathered up the sentiment of ancient poets and spoke of living and moving and existing in God. All of life, he said, is within God. There is no other context.

When you were a child, you may have thought God existed in space. It is truer, however, that space is in God. Everything is in God. God holds all creation in his palm. God holds the whole world and everything in it. That includes you. As a sponge is in the ocean, you are in God. Your truest and most authentic dwelling place is in God. It is inside the love and providence of God that you live, move, and exist.

Dear God, thank you for including everyone
in the reach of your embracing love. Amen.

LOOKING UP TO YOU

I am an example to many people,
because you are my strong protection.
PSALM 71:7 NCV

Parents often laugh about the way their small children pick up phrases they hear around the house—which are often repeated at inopportune times. Yet children are innocent and just want to be like their mom or dad.

You shall increase my greatness, and comfort me on every side.
PSALM 71:21 NKJV

You, on the other hand, are not a child any longer, but still pick up habits—good and bad—from friends, co-workers, and others. However, God has commanded that you set his Word as your standard for living, obeying anything he commands you to do.

Friend, just as the Lord expects you to set a godly pattern for your loved ones, he also wants you to follow his holy example. Therefore, look to him and imitate his honorable character, because surely his ways will protect you forever.

God, forgive me for the times I have compromised my
testimony of your love. I know what is right, and I ask
that you help me to live in step with your truth. Amen.

SOME REMINDERS

*You must build this Tabernacle and its furnishings
exactly according to the pattern I will show you.*
EXODUS 25:9 NLT

*I will meet the people
of Israel there, and
the Tabernacle will
be sanctified by my
glorious presence.*
EXODUS 29:43 NLT

When God wanted his people to know he was with them, he chose to occupy a tent as the meeting place. In fact, it was called the tent of meeting. It was the place where God and his people got together. Inside the tent was an ark of specific dimensions and decoration that represented God's glory. The imagery reminded the people that God was with them

You need reminders of the presence of God in the place where you meet God. Have an open Bible as a reminder that God speaks to you. Light a votive candle to symbolize your continuing prayer. Place a cross prominently to indicate how much God loves you. A symbol is a reminder of something much greater than it is. It points you to God.

*Dear God, as I consider holy symbols of your presence,
may I know you intimately and joyfully. Amen.*

STAYING STEADY THROUGH TOUGH TIMES

As for me, I will always have hope; I will praise you more and more.
PSALM 71:14 NIV

The tendrils of ivy climb the sides of the brick structure until they cover every square inch. Ivy stems are strong, hearty, and almost unbreakable, and they grip the surface so tightly that only the most determined effort can dislodge them. Ivy is capable of weathering the extremes of both heat and cold without withering and falling away.

Happy is he that hath the God of Jacob for his help, whose hope is in the LORD his God.

PSALM 146:5 KJV

When you place your hope in God, you are clinging to him in the same tenacious way that ivy clings to brick and mortar. When the sun is warm and the rain is gentle, you grow strong and hearty, reaching and moving as you strengthen your grip on God's never-failing love. Then when the strong winds blow and the rain beats at you, you know that you can hang on. You cannot be moved.

Mighty God, help me to cling to you as ivy clings to the brick. Amen.

SEE THE LIGHT

*Jesus once again addressed them: "I am the world's Light.
No one who follows me stumbles around in the
darkness. I provide plenty of light to live in."*
JOHN 8:12 MSG

*The people who walked
in darkness have seen
a great light. For those
who lived in a land of
deep shadows—light!
sunbursts of light!*

ISAIAH 9:2 MSG

The first thing Harlan does in his prayer place is to light a candle. He begins each time of meditation this way. Harlan wants to symbolize that he experiences the presence of God as light. He begins his meeting with God focused on the illumination God provides. He believes God's light is strong enough to eliminate any darkness he might be experiencing.

Light is God's nature. That is why in the Jewish tabernacle there burned a perpetual lamp, a light that never went out. It was there to remind people of the ever-present light of God. The more they let that light into their lives, the less darkness there would be. Nothing eliminates the darkness of the world like the light of God.

*Dear God, your love for me lights up my life.
I praise your holy name. Amen.*

WHY, GOD?

*You have allowed me to suffer much hardship, but you will restore
me to life again and lift me up from the depths of the earth.*
PSALM 71:20 NLT

We ask it as a rhetorical question because we don't really expect God to answer. "Why, God?" we call out—voicing more frustration and confusion over our hurt than real inquiry.

Yet realize that God has permitted your hardship for a reason—it isn't random, and God isn't being unkind. Though God doesn't *cause* all of your troubles, he *allows* them so you'll trust him more and discover his abundant life. God uses everything that comes into your life for good. So when you cry out to him for wisdom, expect him to answer. And even if he doesn't give you understanding immediately, be confident that he has an important reason for all he allows.

*God, your justice
reaches to the skies. You
have done great things;
God, there is no one like
you. . . . You will make
me greater than ever,
and you will comfort
me again.*

PSALM 71:19, 21 NCV

*God, thank you for using everything for good in
my life—even what I'm facing now. It gives
me hope for the days to come. Amen.*

401

BACK TO YOU

Remember that the person who plants few seeds will have a small crop; the one who plants many seeds will have a large crop.
2 CORINTHIANS 9:6 GNT

Bring the full tithes into the storehouse, that there may be food in my house. And thereby put me to the test, says the LORD of hosts, if I will not open the windows of heaven for you and pour down for you a blessing until there is no more need.

MALACHI 3:10 ESV

When you give to God's people, God gives himself to you. The more the early church gave to those in need, the greater the blessings it received. When they gave to others, God gave to them.

Many years ago, a limousine pulled up to where a beggar sat. A well-dressed and obviously rich man in the limousine asked the beggar to share his rice with him. The beggar was taken aback by the request and very grudgingly gave the man three pieces of rice. That night, the beggar discovered three sparkling pieces of gold in his bowl. Shaking his head, he lamented, "If I had only given more." You release the flow of God's blessings to you by letting the blessings you have go through you.

Dear God, I receive every time I give.
Your blessings know the way to me. Amen.

GREAT PEOPLE, GREAT RESPONSIBILITIES

*God, give the king your good judgment
and the king's son your goodness.*
PSALM 72:1 NCV

Friend, if you want to be truly great, you must start now by being honorable with all of your obligations. Practice the standards that God instructs in his Word—even for the smallest tasks—and he'll give you wisdom and success in the challenges ahead.

Let him be honest and fair with all your people, especially the poor. Let peace and justice rule every mountain and hill. Let the king defend the poor, rescue the homeless.

PSALM 72:2–4 CEV

Because the more you rise in reputation and power, the more complicated your responsibilities and decisions will be. But if you're guided by godly principles, the right course of action will be clear.

You'll be entrusted with more as you show that you've been faithful with the duties you've been given. So honor God right where you are. People will see you're reliable and will reward you with their trust.

God, teach me to obey your principles so that I can do my work wisely and honorably. May my life glorify you in everything I do. Amen.

REMEMBER OTHERS

I will certainly not sin against the LORD
by ending my prayers for you.
1 SAMUEL 12:23 NLT

> *He is able also to*
> *save forever those who*
> *draw near to God*
> *through Him, since*
> *He always lives to*
> *make intercession*
> *for them.*
>
> HEBREWS 7:25 NASB

Talk to God about other people. Talk to him about who is physically sick and the form of that sickness. Tell God who is under emotional stress and the cause of their anxiety. Tell God about the people you know who are financially strung out, unable to take care of their families as they want to. Tell God who is experiencing a shattered dream and can't seem to get up off the floor.

Talking to God and telling him about others is to intercede on their behalf. "Intercession," said Andrew Murray in his book *A Ministry of Intercession*, "is the most perfect form of prayer." Lift the names and conditions of others to God. Let God know what they need.

Dear God, I bring the needs of others to you
in faith, confidence, and obedience. Amen.

404

IT ISN'T FAIR!

I had nearly lost confidence; my faith was almost gone because I was jealous of the proud when I saw that things go well for the wicked.

PSALM 73:2–3 GNT

There are times when life seems unjust and you have to find a way to deal with what you have experienced. People can do and say things that are reckless and cruel. However, whenever you feel ignored or rejected, you have an important choice to make. Either you can become bitter or you can

In heaven I have only you, and on this earth you are all I want. My body and mind may fail, but you are my strength and my choice forever.

PSALM 73:25–26 CEV

become better. You can stew in your anger or move on with the knowledge of God's personal love for you.

God's priceless comfort can soften the impact of others' thoughtless words and deeds. So keep your eyes on him. Listen for his voice of encouragement and be willing to forgive those who have hurt you. This is what Jesus did—he forgave because he knew those who accused him did not know the truth.

God, thank you for understanding my hurts and my feelings. Help me to do the same for others when they act without reason or care. Amen.

GOD GUIDES YOU

He scatters His bright clouds. And they swirl about, being turned by His guidance, that they may do whatever He commands them.
JOB 37:11–12 NKJV

You're my cave to hide in, my cliff to climb. Be my safe leader, be my true mountain guide.

PSALM 31:3 MSG

Guidance is high on the list of what God likes to do for you. He likes to get you on the road, acquaint you with its twists and turns, warn you of soft shoulders and slippery surfaces, and put map and itinerary on your lap so you can reach your destination and fulfill your destiny. God gives you directions to follow. God points the way for you that he knows so well.

The Bible is filled with stories of divine guidance. Abraham was guided to a new land, Moses was guided back to it, Jesus was directed into the wilderness, and Paul was led to Macedonia to take the gospel to Europe. Nothing has changed. Your story is one of God's instruction and direction. God leads you each day.

Thank you, dear God, for knowing the way I should go and for showing it to me one step at a time. Amen.

AN ETERNAL PERSPECTIVE

You will keep on guiding me all my life with your wisdom and counsel, and afterwards receive me into the glories of heaven!
PSALM 73:24 TLB

High up in the Rockies, down-hill skiing is treacherous if a skier diverts from the trail onto unmarked terrain. For this reason, occasional signs are posted to warn extreme skiers not to venture beyond the marked zones. Skiers who ignore the signs risk their lives unnecessarily just to experience a thrill ride that may cross pits or rocks hidden by blankets of snow.

Give me understanding, that I may observe Your law and keep it with all my heart. Make me walk in the path of Your commandments, for I delight in it.
PSALM 119:34–35 NASB

Signposts, warning lights, and directional guides were created to keep you safe. God, too, designed a system to ensure your safety. He promises to guide you through life, offering his wisdom and divine counsel. You have the choice to follow those guidelines or to ignore them.

Thank you, God, for your wings under which I am protected from what threatens me and by which I am taken to where you want me to be. Amen.

IN THE MORNING

I tell you the truth, whoever believes has eternal life.
JOHN 6:47 NCV

I write this to you who believe in (adhere to, trust in, and rely on) the name of the Son of God [in the peculiar services and blessings conferred by Him on men], so that you may know [with settled and absolute knowledge] that you [already] have life, yes, eternal life.

1 JOHN 5:13 AMP

Getting close to God and staying there gives you a sense of eternal destiny. Your time of prayer and moments of reflection have about them an eternal dimension. God speaks to you of forever. He assures you of a life that never ends.

A man who was known for his deep faith found out he had a serious disease and would not live long. He sat down and wrote a letter to his best friend. He told his friend, "I learned today of my impending death. Before you read this, I may already be in heaven. Don't bother to write; I'll see you in the morning." You are assured of a home in heaven where you will live with God forever.

*Dear God, thank you for giving me a
life that will never end. Amen.*

408

GIVING OUT

*My flesh and my heart may fail, but God is the
strength of my heart and my portion forever.*
PSALM 73:26 ESV

No matter how you add it up, there's no way your resources will stretch any more. You've done all you can, and you're exhausted.

Like a traveler in the desert with an empty canteen, you're out of options. You can't go on in these conditions, and any hope of finding an oasis of relief has dissipated like a mirage.

The only thing left is to throw yourself onto the mercy of God. Good—

*It is good for me to
draw near to God;
I have put my trust
in the Lord God and
made Him my refuge,
that I may tell of all
Your works.*

PSALM 73:28 AMP

now he can work. As long as you can accomplish something in your own strength, you'll always doubt whether your deliverance was from God or if you achieved it yourself. Your resources have failed, but his haven't. Trust him to help you.

*God, I praise you for your mercy. I don't know how you'll help me,
but I'm thankful that you will. I'm so glad you're in control. Amen.*

YOU ARE A PEARL

God has not given us a spirit of fear,
but of power and of love and of a sound mind.
2 TIMOTHY 1:7 NKJV

The kingdom of heaven is like a merchant in search of fine pearls, who, on finding one pearl of great value, went and sold all that he had and bought it.

MATTHEW 13:45–46 ESV

An oyster embeds itself in the mire of the ocean floor. A pearl grows slowly and gradually within the mucous of the inside of the oyster's shell. This hardly seems an appropriate setting for something as beautiful as a pearl. Think of the lovely pearls you have seen; they shine and sparkle despite their early environment.

No matter what kind of bad situation your life may be in, God sees beyond that. He sees you as the valuable and worthy person you really are. God goes beyond your assessment and that of others to his own appraisal of your merit and significance. God sees the pearl. God looks beyond where you and others watch. He always sees something special in you.

Dear God, I am grateful that you look far
enough in me to see what is there. Amen.

THE GREAT ARCHITECT

*The day is Yours, also the night; You established the moon
and the sun. You set all the boundaries of the earth.*
PSALM 74:16–17 HCSB

With the changing political climate of our world, it would be easy to wonder if God is in control. The answer is yes. The One who established the boundaries for the land and sea, and set the moon and stars in their places, watches over you.

*God my king is
from ancient times,
performing saving
acts on the earth.*

PSALM 74:12 HCSB

When life appears to be spiraling out of control, you can be assured that God is not affected. Sudden changes do not surprise or move him—he remains the same yesterday, today, and forever. When problems come, your first reaction may be one of anxiety. But God is sovereign, and he challenges you to recall the times he has kept you safe, protected your heart, and provided for every need you have. Always remember, nothing is too difficult for him to handle. No, friend—nothing at all.

*God, I want a glimpse of your greatness. Whether changes
occur in my life or on the world stage, I will watch for
your sovereign hand and trust you always. Amen.*

YOU ARE LOVED

I give you a new commandment, that you love one another.
Just as I have loved you, you also should love one another.
JOHN 13:34 NRSV

I will heal their waywardness and love them freely, for my anger has turned away from them.

HOSEA 14:4 NIV

One afternoon, several teenagers were playing basketball in a backyard. A dispute broke out, and the youth whose backyard it was grabbed the ball and roughly ordered the others to leave.

Then he saw his mother looking out the back window. She had heard and seen everything. He slumped in to where his mother stood at the sink. "Mom, I'm sorry I acted like that," he said. She took his hands and said, "I didn't like what you did at all, and you certainly know better than to act that way." Then she hugged him and said, "I love you." He knew his mother loved him. There was no doubt about that. There is nothing like someone loving you no matter what you have done.

Dear God, thank you for those you send who
love me no matter what I do. Amen.

TIMING IS EVERYTHING

You say, "I choose the appointed time;
it is I who judge uprightly."
PSALM 75:2 NIV

Have you ever been the right person in the right place at the right time? When it happens it's quite unexpected. All your circumstances align in a way that's unimaginable, and you realize that something greater than yourself must be controlling every element of your situation. Your experiences have all prepared you for this in a way that you couldn't have anticipated.

We thank you, God, we thank you—your Name is our favorite word; your mighty works are all we talk about.

PSALM 75:1 MSG

That's how God works, friend. He works in a way that when everything's done, there's no other explanation for the outcome other than his perfect timing. So don't worry about the things you have to wait for—just obey God with confidence. Because when the right moment comes, you'll certainly be ready.

God, I don't know why I've waited so long, but I
praise you that when the right moment comes,
I'll know it was your perfect provision. Amen.

PRAYER GETS IT DONE

From now on, whatever you request along the lines of who I am and what I am doing, I'll do it. That's how the Father will be seen for who he is in the Son. I mean it.

JOHN 14:13 MSG

Do not worry about anything, but in everything by prayer and supplication with thanksgiving let your requests be made known to God.

PHILIPPIANS 4:6 NRSV

Prayer is practical. It gets things done. People would ask Charles Spurgeon to explain his phenomenal power as a preacher, and he would reply in an economy of words, "My people pray for me." To light a fire of effectiveness in your life, kneel in prayer. Dwight L. Moody said, "Every great movement of the kingdom can be traced to one kneeling figure."

Prayer is an *up* look that profoundly changes the outlook. It is a fountain from which you drink wisdom for the day and find strength for the way. Its water nourishes your mind to purpose and your will to power. Through prayer, you put yourself in God's hands to be held in love and sent forth in power.

Dear God, through the gift of your power in my life, I can get it done. Amen.

THE SOURCE OF SUCCESS

Not from the east nor from the west nor from the south come promotion and lifting up. But God is the Judge! He puts down one and lifts up another.
PSALM 75:6–7 AMP

God waits for the perfect time to work. Up until the moment you see him in action, you may fear he's forgotten the situations that weigh so heavily on your heart. However, be assured that he knows exactly what he is doing—and success is forthcoming.

God says, "I will break the strength of the wicked, but I will increase the power of the godly."
PSALM 75:10 NLT

In time, you will see how he has been working in the unseen. However, his instruction to you right now is a simple command to be steadfast and true to him. In other words, do not forfeit your faith. Even though you do not see the evidence of his hand at work, he is wholeheartedly committed to honoring his promises to you. God has a plan, and at the right moment, you will see it unfold. He will work all things together for your good in due time.

God, forgive me for the times I forget that you are omniscient and aware of all that is taking place. I know you will accomplish your will. Amen.

SAY AMEN

No matter how many promises God has made, they are "Yes" in Christ.
And so through him the "Amen" is spoken by us to the glory of God.
2 CORINTHIANS 1:20 NIV

Grow in the grace and knowledge of our Lord and Savior Jesus Christ. To him be the glory both now and to the day of eternity. Amen.

2 PETER 3:18 ESV

Have you been in a church service when someone in the congregation says "amen" when the pastor says something? The pastor makes another point, the person again says "amen." The person agrees with what the pastor has said, and he gives voice to his agreement. Sometimes a pastor will encourage the congregation to participate: "Say amen."

Say amen to God's claim on your life and his call in your life. Agree with who God says you are. Be in accord with what God wants you to do. Be enthusiastic in your agreement. Say amen to God's purpose and plan for you. Say amen to who you are, and to the gifts of God's grace you have.

Dear God, I agree with both your short-term and long-range plans for me. Amen.

WHOM TO PLEASE?

You . . . are to be feared [with awe and reverence]!
PSALM 76:7 AMP

Generally, people are either leaders or followers. Those who serve like to give of themselves, but are often pulled in a hundred directions—trying to please everyone. Those who lead can be inspirational to others, but they sometimes become too self-important.

Make vows to the LORD your God and fulfill them; let all who are around Him bring gifts to Him who is to be feared.

PSALM 76:11 NASB

For both these groups, it's exceedingly important to remember whom they're trying to please—the only One truly worthy of their honor and praise. For leaders, they must remember that God is the ultimate authority. Those who follow must serve out of obedience, rather than a desire to be accepted.

Friend, whether you're a leader or a follower, God is the only One you'll ever need to please. So honor him with all you do.

God, I want to be a delight to you. Please forgive me for the times when I lose focus. Help me to honor you and bless others. Amen.

HEAD OVER HEELS IN LOVE

Jesus answered: Love the Lord your God with all your heart, soul, and mind. This is the first and most important commandment.
MATTHEW 22:37–38 CEV

No eye has seen, nor ear heard, nor the human heart conceived, what God has prepared for those who love him.

1 CORINTHIANS 2:9 NRSV

You love God because of his infinite goodness in your life. You love God because he is your Father and you are his child. You love him because he created you and has a meaningful plan for your life. You love God because he first loved you.

Legend has it that a wealthy merchant heard a great deal about Paul. The merchant went to Rome to visit Paul in prison. Timothy arranged it, and the man spent several hours with Paul. Outside the cell, as he was leaving, the man asked Timothy, "What's the secret of this man's power?" Timothy smiled and said, "Paul is in love." When you know how much you mean to God, you fall head over heels in love with God.

*Dear God, you mean everything in the world to me.
I love you more than I can say. Amen.*

THINK ABOUT IT

I will think about each one of your mighty deeds.
PSALM 77:12 CEV

You wouldn't willingly drink water that had toxins in it; you'd find clean water to relieve your thirst. You probably wouldn't eat food that was poisoned either. Rather, you'd wrestle with your hunger until you found wholesome sustenance.

I will remember the LORD's works; yes, I will remember Your ancient wonders.

PSALM 77:11 HCSB

Is the same true of your mind? Perhaps you supply your brain with negative, chewed-over thoughts of hurt. Or maybe boredom—a sign your intellect is starved—causes you to dine on whatever junk comes along. Unfortunately, these diets aren't beneficial at all.

Friend, be careful what you feed your mind—consume only what's good, healthy, and holy. Nourish your understanding with God's Word. It's the only cuisine that'll truly satisfy your mental hunger.

God, please cleanse me of the rubbish in my thoughts. Help me to feed on your Word so I'll be healthy in my body, mind, and soul. Amen.

LITTLE THINGS

God has made everything beautiful for its own time.
ECCLESIASTES 3:11 NLT

Well done, good and faithful servant; you were faithful over a few things, I will make you ruler over many things.

MATTHEW 25:21 NKJV

A woman asked a famous Bible teacher a question that had long been on her mind. She said, "Do you think we ought to pray about the little things in everyday life?" The renowned teacher responded immediately. "Can you think of anything in your life that is unimportant to God?" She couldn't think of a thing.

No problem you have is too small for your prayers to God. No difficulty you experience is too minor to talk to God about. He invites you to tell him about the small occurrences. God has an open ear for you and your life. When you talk to God, don't leave anything out. God is interested in everything in your life. It is all vitally important to him. Nothing is too small.

Dear God, I am comforted by your concern for all the happenings and issues of my life. Amen.

WITH HISTORY AS A GUIDE

You are the God who works wonders; you have made known your might among the peoples.
PSALM 77:14 ESV

The Bible is full of stories of faith—of people trapped in terrible situations who subsequently triumphed because of the Lord. Perhaps like them, you are facing a problem that seems overwhelming. No one understands the way you feel, and the more you try to explain your circumstances, the more you are misunderstood.

I will remember your great deeds, Lord; I will recall the wonders you did in the past. I will think about all that you have done; I will meditate on all your mighty acts.
PSALM 77:11–12 GNT

Yet God knows exactly what you are facing, and he understands your fears. When you feel as though there is no place to turn, he provides a way of escape. Just as he helped the saints throughout history, he can help you. He is just as powerful, faithful, and wise today as when he delivered them.

God, it is easy to trust you in times of sunshine, but help me to have faith in the storm by reminding me of your faithful works throughout the ages. Amen.

GET IN TUNE

*I have given you this as an example, so that you should
do [in your turn] what I have done to you.*
JOHN 13:15 AMP

*My friends, I want you
to follow my example
and learn from others
who closely follow the
example we set for you.*

PHILIPPIANS 3:17 CEV

A man who lived alone had a cello he played for his own enjoyment. He played his cello when he was happy to celebrate the good things in his life. He played it when he was distressed to express his sadness and gloom. Sometimes he played his cello for no obvious reason at all.

Every now and then, his cello got out of tune. When it did, he called a friend at a radio station and asked him to broadcast the true and precise tone of A. By that authentic tone, he tuned his cello and was ready to play again. Jesus is the tone by which you can tune your life. Get your pitch from him every day.

*Dear God, thank you that Jesus walks before
me so I can know which way to go. Amen.*

YOUR LEGACY

We will tell the next generation about the LORD's power and his great deeds and the wonderful things he has done.
PSALM 78:4 GNT

People often ponder what they'll accomplish in the future. Yet sometimes it's good to ask: When I pass away, what story will be told? Will I be remembered for wisdom and mercy—or manipulation and self-centeredness? Will I leave a lasting legacy—or will my endeavors fade like the fog? As you contemplate stepping into eternity, you'll think about what's truly important. No one ever plans to waste his or her life, but it'll happen if you fail to set priorities.

He instructed our ancestors to teach his laws to their children. . . . In this way they also will put their trust in God and not forget what he has done, but always obey his commandments.

PSALM 78:5, 7 GNT

Consider what you will leave behind for those you love. Will your life testify to the eternal love of God—or the temporary things of this world? Your story is still being told, so choose wisely.

God, I want to leave a lasting legacy of love for you. Please direct my steps so that you'll always be glorified in my life. Amen.

SOLITUDE STRENGTHENS

After he had dismissed them, he went up on a mountainside by himself to pray. When evening came, he was there alone.
MATTHEW 14:23 NIV

When evening came, the boat was out on the sea, and he was alone on the land.

MARK 6:47 NRSV

Solitude can increase your capacity for experiencing the presence of God. "Without solitude," Henri Nouwen said, "it is virtually impossible to live a spiritual life." Solitude expresses the beauty, meaning, and glory of being alone with God. Jesus understood this. The world had waited thousands of years for him to come, and one of the first things he did was to announce that he wanted forty days off to be alone with the Father.

Solitude makes you aware of whether you are living from the outside in or from the inside out. When you listen to your heart in rich moments of solitude, you are drawn to significant activity. Solitude enriches your spiritual resources. It is purposeful and productive.

Dear God, in my solitude I am alone with you, your grace, and your wisdom. Amen.

ANSWERS FROM UNEXPECTED PLACES

God made water flow from rocks he split open in the desert,
and his people drank freely, as though from a lake.
PSALM 78:15 CEV

Here is one of the most exciting things about God: He does not always answer your prayers the same way. Just when you think you understand how he will solve a problem, he takes a different route This is why having faith is so important.

They remembered that
God was their rock,
that the Most High
was their defender.

PSALM 78:35
GOD'S WORD

Always make sure that whatever you are doing is in line with the principles of his Word, but also allow him to be God—submit to him whenever he reshapes your plans even when you do not comprehend why he is leading you in a certain way. Never try to box him in with your expectations. You will find that when you think you know all there is to know about him, he will do something far better than you could have ever imagined. That is when you are truly blessed.

God, I love the way you surprise me with your goodness.
Help me to always remain hopeful—anticipating
your answers from unexpected places. Amen.

A GREAT INVESTMENT

Be steadfast, immovable, always abounding in the work of the Lord, knowing that your toil is not in vain in the Lord.
1 CORINTHIANS 15:58 NASB

The eyes of the LORD move to and fro throughout the earth that He may strongly support those whose heart is completely His.

2 CHRONICLES 16:9
NASB

The greatest investment you can make is to give who you are and what you have to God. You will make no wiser investment than to commit your strengths and resources to God. The psychiatrist Paul Tournier understood the return on this investment when he said it is commitment that "creates a person."

Not only does commitment enhance and enrich who you are as a person, but it also nourishes and actualizes God's will in the world. Your commitment gets God's work done. It lets people know how much God loves them. It inspires them to love God back and to serve him in every way they can. Commitment is an investment in your gifts and in God's power.

Dear God, keep me focused on my responsibilities, obligations, and commitments. Amen.

HUMAN NATURE

Their hearts were not really loyal to God. . . . Still God was merciful. . . . He remembered that they were only human, like a wind that blows and does not come back.
PSALM 78:37–39 NCV

Even when you are unfaithful, God never stops loving you. He loves you with an enduring love that is both infinite and unconditional. You cannot do anything to derail His love for you.

Sin harms your fellowship with him because it produces feelings of guilt and shame and causes you to wonder if he still cares for you. Yet understand, although he will not approve of sin, he will never withhold his love from

God led his people out of Egypt and guided them in the desert like a flock of sheep. He led them safely along, and they were not afraid, but their enemies drowned in the sea.
PSALM 78:52–53 CEV

you—he still offers it freely. So how do you handle the times when your human nature tempts you to yield to sin? The best course of action is to ask God to teach you more about his love. Because when you understand how great his love for you is, you will never want to drift in your devotion to him.

God, I want to honor you. Thank you for not holding my past against me. Thank you for forgiving me, loving me, and making me new. Amen.

UP TO YOU

I heard the voice of the Lord, saying, Whom shall I send?
And who will go for Us? Then said I, Here am I; send me.
ISAIAH 6:8 AMP

Commit to the LORD
whatever you do, and
your plans will succeed.

PROVERBS 16:3 NIV

God causes wonderful and significant things to happen in your life. He blesses and gifts you in many ways. Then it is up to you to respond to what God has done. God's touch on your life wakes you to obligation, responsibility, and commitment. God moves in you, and then you move out and on for God.

When an alarm clock goes off in the morning, it wakes you up. But that's as much as an alarm clock can do. It cannot drag you out of bed. Getting up is your responsibility. God touches your heart with presence and call. It is then up to you to respond in faith and dedication. God acts in your life, and he waits for the response of your obedience and trust.

Dear God, help me to take whatever is given
and make it large for you. Amen.

AN EYE ON THE GUIDE

He led them on safely and in confident trust, so that they feared not; but the sea overwhelmed their enemies.

PSALM 78:53 AMP

When God brought the Israelites out of Egypt, he led them with a pillar of cloud by day and a tower of fire by night. These shielded the Israelites from their enemies and reminded the people of God's powerful presence with them.

> *[God] led His own people forth like sheep and guided them [with a shepherd's care] like a flock in the wilderness.*
>
> PSALM 78:52 AMP

Looking to God is an important principle that can keep you from becoming disheartened. As long as you maintain your focus on God, you'll be safe and confident. Yet take your eyes off of God, and you'll be overwhelmed by the troubles surrounding you.

Friend, whatever you are facing today, take no heed of the impossibilities. Keep your gaze fixed solely on God. He'll lead you safely through if you'll just believe in him.

God, thank you for helping me with my troubles today. They overwhelm me, but I am comforted by your strength and loving presence. Amen.

HAVEN AND HARBOR

If you are about to place your gift on the altar and remember that someone is angry with you. . . . Make peace with that person.
MATTHEW 5:23–24 CEV

The next day, when they had come down from the mountain, . . . a great multitude met Him. Suddenly a man from the multitude cried out, saying, "Teacher, I implore You, look on my son, for he is my only child."

LUKE 9:37–38 NKJV

Your inside time with God has outside implications. Prayer is both a haven in which you rest and a harbor from which you sail. One time, Jesus and three of his disciples had a glorious spiritual experience on top of a mountain. Much to the disciples' dismay, Jesus made them get off the mountain to go down and help a sick boy in the valley.

God uses your close times with him to equip you for service in the world. Prayer sensitizes you and helps you recognize where you are needed. It opens doors in your mind and heart and will lead you to others. Prayer enlarges your heart and makes it big enough to hold those who need you most.

Dear God, may I listen closely to you so I will have something to say to others. Amen.

LINGERING LIABILITIES

Do not punish us for the sins of our ancestors.
Have mercy on us now; we have lost all hope.
PSALM 79:8 GNT

Even the best families can have destructive cycles. These are habits, beliefs, and ways of thinking that hinder you from becoming all that God created you to be. In a sense, they are liabilities that are passed down through the generations because they are never taken to the One who can heal them.

Help us, O God of our salvation, for the glory of Your name; and deliver us, and provide atonement for our sins, for Your name's sake!

PSALM 79:9 NKJV

☾

Yet you can break the destructive cycle because God will teach you a different way to live—he'll have mercy on you and give you the strength and hope you need.

So don't be impeded by the mistakes or deficiencies of your ancestors, and don't let those liabilities linger any longer. Let God make you part of his family—healthy, holy, and free.

God, you know the failings of my family and how those failings have affected me. Heal me and teach me to live in a manner worthy of your name. Amen.

SECURITY SYSTEM

The name of the Lord is a strong tower; the [consistently] righteous man [upright and in right standing with God] runs into it and is safe.
PROVERBS 18:10 AMP

I have set the LORD always before me. Because he is at my right hand, I will not be shaken.

PSALM 16:8 NIV

The greatest security system in the world is God. With him by your side, you have confidence that things will be okay. With God beside you, you can handle whatever pops up. God accompanies you with the power of his competence, and you take comfort in this knowledge. You can't go anywhere that God doesn't go along with you.

Security in God is like having an electric fence built around your property to keep out harmful intrusions. It is like an alarm system that goes off when you need to be alerted to danger and risk. It is like having someone with a badge of authority go with you everywhere. God's presence is a security system that helps you smell the smoke and avoid the fire.

No matter what I go through, O God, you go through it with me. Where I am, you are. Amen.

LIGHT IN THE DARK PLACES

*O God of hosts, restore us and cause
Your face to shine upon us, and we will be saved.*
PSALM 80:7 NASB

What is it that you don't want anyone to know about? It'll immediately spring to mind because shame is powerful that way. It convinces you to hide in self-defeating ways.

Friend, whatever you conceal with darkness will control you. You'll guard it fiercely because it's painful and embarrassing; and when anyone

*We shall not turn back
from You; revive us,
and we will call upon
Your name. O LORD
God of hosts, restore
us; cause Your face to
shine upon us, and we
will be saved.*

PSALM 80:18–19 NASB

gets close to discovering your defect, you'll get combative. Your anger is based on the fear that you'll be exposed—and it's destroying you.

It's scary to invite God's light into your deepest secrets—but it's the only way that you'll be free. So don't let the darkness imprison you. Confess your failings to God, and allow him to lead you into the light.

*God, forgive my sins and bring light to my darkest secrets.
Heal me, my God, and set me free. Thank you for helping me. Amen.*

433

JUST AS YOU ARE

*Behold, now is "the acceptable time," behold,
now is "the day of salvation."*
2 CORINTHIANS 6:2 NASB

It is now time for you to wake up from your sleep, because our salvation is nearer now than when we first believed.

ROMANS 13:11 NCV

Charlotte Elliott, artist, singer, and composer, was a vivacious young woman. But when this talented and spirited woman was just thirty years old, a devastating illness made her an invalid. She became depressed and listless. She gave up every activity, turned away from all creativity.

One day Caesar Milan, a well-known evangelist, visited her. Understanding Charlotte's situation, he told her she must come to God right then just as she was. Charlotte Elliott responded to what Caesar Milan said and instantly placed her faith and illness in God's hands. She experienced tranquillity and bliss that day that lasted the rest of her life. To express the joy of her coming to God, Charlotte Elliott wrote the great hymn "Just As I Am."

*Dear God, I come to you right now, just as I am.
You accept, receive, and love me. Amen.*

BY THE LIGHT OF HIS FACE

We shall not turn back from you; give us life, and we will
call upon your name! Restore us, O LORD God of hosts!
Let your face shine, that we may be saved!
PSALM 80:18–19 ESV

About Jesus, John 1:4–5 (NLT) reports, "His life brought light to everyone. The light shines in the darkness, and the darkness can never extinguish it." The light of God's love and salvation can never be quenched.

> *O Shepherd of Israel . . . You who dwell between the cherubim, shine forth!*
> PSALM 80:1 NKJV

When you are lonely, draw near to the Lord and he will brighten your day. When sorrow tries to settle in around you and tempt you to feel discouraged, lost, or forgotten, read his Word and ask him to illuminate your life. He will do it—he will speak to your heart and remind you that you are not alone.

When you encounter emotional clouds or rain, take a moment to ask God to light your way with his everlasting hope. He always answers the prayers of His children.

God, illuminate my life with your unquenchable love
and hope. I praise you that all fear and darkness flees
when your light shines on my heart. Amen.

WHAT FAITH IS

Through [Christ] you believe in God, who raised him from the dead and glorified him, and so your faith and hope are in God.
1 PETER 1:21 NIV

> *To have faith is to be sure of the things we hope for, to be certain of the things we cannot see.*
>
> HEBREWS 11:1 GNT

Faith is a relationship between God and you. Faith aligns you with God and brings you close to each other.

Faith is a *connector* that hooks and binds you and God together. It makes you and God concurrent in purpose and aim. Faith is a *conductor* that takes your petitions to God and carries his power to you. It makes possible conversation and communication between you and God. Faith is a *conveyor* that brings God to you and brings you to God. Through faith, you and God are brought into each other's presence. In that presence, you can take God at the word he speaks to you. Faith opens the eyes of your soul to the quality of your relationship with God.

Dear God, it is by hope that I long for your presence and by faith that I come into it. Amen.

REAPING THE JOY

Sing for joy to God, our strength;
shout out loud to the God of Jacob.
PSALM 81:1 NCV

A trip to the beach on a hot summer day is a ticket to leisure for most folks. Giant waves that would scare most swimmers produce a thrill for good surfers, who glide along the waves rather than be pounded by them. In the same way, author Jim Reimann observed that "the things you try to avoid and fight against . . . are the very things that produce abundant joy in you."

Remember me, O LORD, when you show favor to your people, come to my aid when you save them, that I may enjoy the prosperity of your chosen ones, that I may share in the joy of your nation and join your inheritance in giving praise.
PSALM 106:4–5 NIV

True joy is not built on passing things; rather, true joy is built on the unchangeable love of God. Events you face are powerless to separate you from God's love.

Dear God, I believe joy is the most infallible sign of your presence in my life. It is the banner I fly when you live in my heart. Amen.

AN OPEN DOOR

I assure you, most solemnly I tell you,
that I Myself am the Door for the sheep.
JOHN 10:7 AMP

Listen! I am standing at the door, knocking; if you hear my voice and open the door, I will come in to you and eat with you, and you with me.

REVELATION 3:20 NRSV

In the construction of the usual wooden door there are four panels separated by a long upright center board and a shorter horizontal board. These two boards form the pattern of a cross. This long utilized plan for making doors came from a carpenters' guild in England in the Middle Ages. The artisans in that guild worked the sign of the cross into every door they made. It is no surprise that the motto of this particular carpenters' guild was the words Jesus spoke to the people in Jerusalem: "I am the Door."

As a carpenter and craftsman, Jesus understood the importance of doors. He knew that doors give people access. Jesus is the door through which you enter God's will and are at home there.

Dear God, as I seek your presence in my life,
may I maintain an open-door policy. Amen.

OPEN UP!

I am the LORD your God, who brought you out of the land of Egypt; open your mouth wide, and I will fill it.

PSALM 81:10 NKJV

Psalm 81 was written in celebration of Israel's miraculous deliverance from Egypt. It's a reminder that God's powerful provision is always available for his people—but we must obey him.

You may be tempted to disregard God and handle your serious situation on your own. Just remember that whenever the people of Israel did that, they got into progressively worse

I lifted the burden from your shoulder and took the heavy basket from your hands. When you were in trouble, I rescued you, and from the thunderclouds, I answered your prayers.

PSALM 81:6–7 CEV

trouble. It was only when they trusted God that they entered the Promised Land. What needs do you have? Friend, don't handle them on your own. God will help you and provide for you if you'll be humble enough to admit you need him. Therefore, open up to God—he has exactly what you need.

God, I'm so used to handling things on my own. Yet I'm open to your provision and love. Please teach me how to obey you. Amen.

GROW SLOWLY

Some seeds fell in good soil, and the plants sprouted, grew, and bore grain: some had thirty grains, others sixty, and others one hundred.
MARK 4:8 GNT

I will drive them out before you little by little, until you become fruitful and take possession of the land.
EXODUS 23:30 NASB

Don't be in a hurry with spiritual life. Slow down and let God have his way with you. It takes time to be deep, rich, and full. That which grows slowly becomes strong. It perseveres and endures, from bud to blossom to fruit.

It takes time to know when, where, and how God speaks. In your life with God, take the time to hear what God is saying to you, where he wants you to be, and what he wants you to do. Take the time to understand how God makes his will known. Spiritual growth is a process that occurs little by little, step by step. God is a long-range planner. It takes time to get to where God wants you to be.

Dear God, by your plan and power I grow toward the goals you set for me. Amen.

HIS VERY BEST

Oh that My people would listen to Me. . . . I would feed you with the finest of the wheat, and with honey from the rock I would satisfy you.
PSALM 81:13, 16 NASB

Many people spend a great deal of time and money trying to find a way to feel safe, secure, happy, and peaceful. However, nothing you do apart from Jesus Christ has the ability to satisfy all of your needs and desires.

I took the world off your shoulders, freed you from a life of hard labor. You called to me in your pain; I got you out of a bad place. I answered you from where the thunder hides.
PSALM 81:6–7 MSG

Large sums of money can vanish. People can walk away. Positions of power and fame can end in disgrace. Nothing this world has to offer can ensure future success or security. The one thing you can bank on is this: When God tells you he will satisfy you with the finest of wheat, he will give you his very best.

God withholds nothing from you. All that you need you will have, and you will never lack for anything.

At times it is hard to imagine how you will meet all my needs, but, God, you always do—and your provision is always perfect! Amen.

HELP GOD GROW YOU

I planted, Apollos watered, but God gave the growth.
1 CORINTHIANS 3:6 NRSV

Jesus said, "My Father has never stopped working, and that is why I keep on working."

JOHN 5:17 CEV

God needs help in growing your spiritual life. Paul and Apollos understood this. They knew that they planted and watered but God gave the growth. What they put in the ground, God brought forth from the ground. What they nurtured, God flourished.

When speaking of spiritual growth, the images of acorn and oak are often used. It is certainly true that small acorns become large oak trees. You, however, unlike acorns, can choose to enable or to inhibit your growth. You enable it by the choices you make, the goals you set, and the self-discipline you practice. Determined intentionality is a key to growing your spiritual life. Knowing God is like mining for gold. You have to do some digging.

Dear God, whatever I can do to deepen my life in you is a great and rich blessing. Amen.

THE UNFORGOTTEN

Be fair to the poor and to orphans.
Defend the helpless and everyone in need.
PSALM 82:3 CEV

If I were gone, would anyone notice? Even if you've never thought those words, you can understand the sentiment behind them. Sometimes people feel so powerless and insignificant that they wonder if anyone cares for them at all.

Rescue the weak and needy; deliver them out of the hand of the wicked.

PSALM 82:4 NASB

God does not forget them, and neither should you. In fact, God may be calling you to be his representative of love and support to them.

Who do you know that needs a friend? Rather than forget about them, find out what you can do to better their situation. Sometimes your listening ear, willing heart, and prayers can encourage a person more than you realize. Because of you, they'll know that God hasn't forgotten them.

God, is there someone you want me to help today?
Please bring them to my mind and show me
how to love them as you would. Amen.

KNOWING WHOM TO THANK

That night the secret was revealed to Daniel in a vision. Then Daniel praised the God of heaven. He said, "Praise the name of God forever and ever, for he has all wisdom and power."
DANIEL 2:19–20 NLT

Every good gift and every perfect gift is from above, and comes down from the Father of lights, with whom there is no variation or shadow of turning.

JAMES 1:17 NKJV

Time spent with God is praise time for God's good gifts. Raise your praise to the God of your blessings, benefits, and bounty. Alone with God, take the opportunity to tell how much what he does on your behalf means to you. Take what's in your heart, put it on your lips, and tell God how great he is in your life.

The magic words you learned as a child, *Thank you*, are just as important in your relationship with God as they are in your relationships with other people. When you give thanks to God, you acknowledge what wonderful gifts he has given you.

The most significant prayer you will ever pray is just two words long: "Thank you."

Dear God, I praise you for all the good things you give me. Amen.

TALK TO ME!

O God, do not keep silent; do not be still, do not be quiet!
PSALM 83:1 GNT

Why is it that at times God appears to be altogether quiet? Even though you are seeking him wholeheartedly, why does it seem like he's gone completely silent?

They will know that you are the LORD, that only you are God Most High over all the earth

PSALM 83:18 NCV

Friend, you desire to hear God, and that's wonderful. However, there are times when his silence will do more to grow your faith than anything else will do. That's because you must continue to do as he instructed and exercise your trust without any outside encouragement.

It's difficult, but you can depend on his trustworthy character and lean on his truth, love, and grace. Take heart—he's still working on your behalf. And when you see how much he's done for you, it'll speak volumes to your soul.

God, even if I can't hear you, I trust you. Thank you for your faultless character and for continuing to work on my behalf. Amen.

ON YOUR SIDE

If anyone sins, we have an Advocate with the Father,
Jesus Christ the righteous.
1 JOHN 2:1 NASB

Make glad the soul of Your servant, for to You, O Lord, I lift up my soul. For You, Lord, are good, and ready to forgive, and abundant in lovingkindness to all who call upon You.

PSALM 86:4–5 NASB

When the Bible says God is your advocate, that means that God is on your side. His love for you is so great that he always comes out in favor of you. God puts his big mark of love and encouragement next to your name every time. You can count on God's backing and advocacy.

God's belief in you is your assurance and stability throughout the ups and downs of your days. Knowing God is on your side, you can tackle each challenge with confidence and can persevere toward your goals. God's love for you and faith in you is a support system on which you can depend no matter what happens. Wherever you go today, God is at your side and on your side.

Dear God, thank you for thinking I am special. May
I think as much of myself as you think of me. Amen.

YOUR TRUSTWORTHY GOD

*May they know that You alone—whose name is Yahweh—
are the Most High over all the earth.*
PSALM 83:18 HCSB

There will be times when you cannot speak or defend yourself. Perhaps you are even given a chance to tell your side of the story, but it is as if the Holy Spirit has sealed your lips. He often does this so you will be still and allow him to speak for you.

O God, do not keep silent; be not quiet, O God, be not still.
PSALM 83:1 NIV

Friend, if another person is bent on accusing you of something you did not do, give God the opportunity to reveal the truth. You bear his name, and when you act in obedience to him, you can be sure he will defend you in a manner better than any other manner you could possibly imagine.

The Lord works in amazing ways and can change the course of any human plan. Be patient and trust him, because his vindication is coming.

*God, thank you for answering my prayers. Even when I
wait for you to defend me, I know that you will
be faithful to reveal the whole truth. Amen.*

August

*Don't ever
stop thinking
about what is
truly worthwhile
and worthy
of praise.*

PHILIPPIANS 4:8 CEV

ANY OTHER NAME

God said to Moses, "I AM WHO I AM." He said further, "Thus you shall say to the Israelites, 'I AM has sent me to you.'"

EXODUS 3:14 NRSV

Abraham planted a tamarisk tree in Beersheba and worshiped GOD there, praying to the Eternal God.

GENESIS 21:33 MSG

There is one God with many names. He has many names because there are many ways he wants to help you. For instance, when you need God's healing touch, call on *Jehovah-Rapha*, "the Lord your healer." When you are confused about something, call on *Jehovah-Shalom*, "the Lord your peace."

When you are short of energy or your finances are in bad shape, call on *Jehovah-Jireh*, "the Lord your provider." When you lack direction and don't know which way to turn, call on *Jehovah-Raah*, "the Lord your caring shepherd." When you are down in the dumps and can't get excited about anything, call on *Jehovah-Nissi*, "the Lord your banner." No matter what name you use, God is your God. Call on him. He is on call for you.

Dear God, you have a name I can call on for everything I need. Amen.

ENOUGH FOR TODAY

Blessed are those whose strength is in you. . . . They go from strength to strength, till each appears before God.

PSALM 84:5, 7 NIV

God has given his Word to you for several reasons. When you study it, you not only gain insight into his ways and principles, you also receive direction and encouragement. The psalms are an excellent source of hope and comfort, especially when you are battling some intense trial. David faced many challenges in his lifetime, but he always found the strength he needed to overcome every threat by recalling God's goodness and promises to him.

How lovely is Your tabernacle, O LORD of hosts! My soul longs, yes, even faints for the courts of the LORD; my heart and my flesh cry out for the living God.

PSALM 84:1–2 NKJV

Have you learned to do the same? When trouble comes, do you turn to the Bible and ask the Lord to speak to you, or do you rush to call a friend? The support of loved ones is essential, but the amazing love of an omnipotent God can never be replaced.

God, you know all things. Please help me to understand your Word and your will for me. Encourage me according to my deepest need. Amen.

YOU KNOW

If you only knew the gift God has for you and who you are speaking to, you would ask me, and I would give you living water.
JOHN 4:10 NLT

I know the one I have faith in, and I am sure that he can guard until the last day what he has trusted me with.

2 TIMOTHY 1:12 CEV

The world, in all its varied and lavish beauty, says that God loves you. Your own life, with its possibilities and blessings, indicates the source of the great love you are given. The story of God coming to earth in Jesus Christ paints a conclusive picture of God's love.

Jesus sat on the edge of a well one day and talked to a woman about the gift of God's love for her. She didn't understand at first, but after a while she came to know that it was God who loved her. "If you only knew," Jesus had said. Now, beyond doubt or speculation, she knew. God gives conclusive evidence of his love for you. It is all around you everywhere.

Dear God, thank you for all the ways I know that you love me with an everlasting love. Amen.

WORDS OF PEACE

I will hear what God the LORD will say; for He will
speak peace to His people, to His godly ones.
PSALM 85:8 NASB

Worrying is a difficult habit to break, especially because it's become such an inherent part of you. "Worrying—a habit? Impossible! It's part of my nature!" you may exclaim.

No, friend. Worrying reflects how your mind has been conditioned—not the way you've been created. Remem-

The LORD will indeed give what is good, and our land will yield its harvest. Righteousness goes before him and prepares the way for his steps.

PSALM 85:12–13 NIV

ber that when you worry, you're declaring that God is not going to help you. You doubt him, his character, and his love.

However, God wants you to trust him, and his message to you is peace. He doesn't want you to worry but to be confident in his care. So listen to his words and learn from him. He'll help you break that bad, worrisome habit and live with confidence.

God, please forgive me for doubting. I want to trust you.
Please transform the way I think so I won't fret
but will always hope in you. Amen.

GOD IS MOVING IN YOUR LIFE

He who calls you is faithful; he will surely do it.
1 THESSALONIANS 5:24 ESV

God is able to make all grace abound to you, so that in all things at all times, having all that you need, you will abound in every good work.

2 CORINTHIANS 9:8 NIV

Quiet time is a good time to see more clearly what God is doing in your life. With interference shut down and interruption shut out, the fog of busyness lifts and you see what God is about on your behalf. Without people and issues to claim your time and attention, you can look beyond the immediate scene to the larger picture of how God is moving in your life to fulfill his will for you.

See his action in your daily events; see his purpose in the happenings of every day. What was previously confused becomes clear to you. You understand what God is doing and how he is doing it. God is doing good things in your life. Look around and see what they are.

Dear God, thank you for working behind the scenes to help me perform your will on the stage of my life. Amen.

HIS LOVELY DWELLING PLACE

A day in your courts is better than a thousand elsewhere.
PSALM 84:10 ESV

You've thought about God entering into your situation. Now imagine dwelling in his. Picture his glorious home in heaven where there's no suffering or sadness—no tears, troubles, or regrets. It's far more lovely, wondrous, and opulent than anything could ever be here on earth.

How lovely is your dwelling place, O LORD Almighty! My soul yearns, even faints, for the courts of the LORD; my heart and my flesh cry out for the living God.

PSALM 84:1–2 NIV

Contemplate living in God's joy and peace for all eternity. You will be together with loved ones, and you'll never be separated from them again. Visualize praising him with people from every nation who are also filled with adoration for him. God is preparing you for his everlasting kingdom and constructing a special place for you that you can forever call home. So begin knowing and worshiping him now—you can't ever have too much practice!

You are the living God, and I praise you! I yearn to live in your presence and worship at your footstool, my glorious God. Amen.

WHAT YOU CAN DO

*If any want to become my followers, let them deny
themselves and take up their cross and follow me.*
MATTHEW 16:24 NRSV

*He went out and saw
a tax collector named
Levi, sitting at the tax
office. And He said to
him, "Follow Me." So
he left all, rose up,
and followed him.*

LUKE 5:27–28 NKJV

Finding leads to following. When you find the ways in which God is working in your life, pay attention and follow his lead. Where is he leading you? In your quiet moments, consider the shape that God's purpose is taking in your mind and heart. Seek to fulfill that purpose with who you are, what you do, and where you're going.

A man stopped at a traffic light behind another car. While waiting for the light to change, he noticed a bumper sticker on the car in front of him. It read, *Are you following Jesus this close?* That's a good question, isn't it? What would your answer be? Just as important as experiencing God is what results from that experience.

*Dear God, help me to do with my life what
you are doing in my life. Amen.*

PLACING YOUR HOPE IN GOD

The LORD God is a sun and shield; the LORD bestows favor and honor.
No good thing does he withhold from those who walk uprightly.
PSALM 84:11 ESV

At times your life is filled with the darkness of a polar night, with icy winds blowing across the frozen reaches of your heart. In these times, you must place your hope in God, for he will not allow the icy darkness to reign forever in your life. Eventually the sun will shine again, melting your ice-locked emotions.

Light is sown for the righteous, and gladness for the upright in heart.
PSALM 97:11 KJV

The promise of renewed life comes with the sunlight of his love. You feel an unrestrained urge to turn your face upward into its brilliance. The sunlight illuminates your heart and chases away the long, cold night. You find that once again you are able to love and laugh and live; once again you are able to appreciate the good things God has placed in your life. His mercy will bring you a bright, new morning tomorrow.

God, thank you for bringing sunlight to my
soul and warming my frozen heart. Amen.

CONSIDER IT AGAIN

This book of the law shall not depart from your mouth,
but you shall meditate on it day and night, so that you may
be careful to do according to all that is written in it.

JOSHUA 1:8 NASB

The Spirit will give him wisdom and understanding, guidance and power. The Spirit will teach him to know and respect the LORD.

ISAIAH 11:2 NCV

To contemplate something is to consider it until you understand it. For instance, when you sit quietly in a garden for a long time and watch a butterfly move among the flowers, you come to understand the beauty, grace, and purpose of butterflies.

Or if a builder stands in front of large piles of rocks studying their size and shape, he or she begins to get an image of a grand cathedral. You see what you look at repeatedly. Repetition leads to insight and knowledge. You come to know in your heart what you consider in your mind. You come to recognize in your will what you contemplate in your heart.

There are great lessons in contemplating what has happened and pondering why it has happened.

Dear God, I will consider repeatedly the counsel
and direction you give me. Amen.

YOU ARE RIGHT TO ASK

Protect me and save me because you are my God.
I am your faithful servant, and I trust you.
PSALM 86:2 CEV

Why must you pray? If God already knows all your needs and heart's desires, why is it necessary to ask him to fill them?

Friend, God wants you to ask for his help because it opens the lines of communication. He wants to have a relationship with you. If he were to satisfy your needs without your ever asking, you'd never remember to interact with him. Yet when you pray to him, you open yourself to his love and provision.

Be kind to me! I pray to you all day. Make my heart glad! I serve you, and my prayer is sincere. You willingly forgive, and your love is always there for those who pray to you.

PSALM 86:3–5 CEV

☾

So pray—and do it often. Get to know the Lord God and let him into your life. He'll not only be your Provider, he'll be your Counselor, Confidant, King, and Friend.

God, thank you for wanting a relationship with me. I want to know you too. Help me to seek you and love you more every day. Amen.

HELP ON THE WAY

GOD is good, a hiding place in tough times.
He recognizes and welcomes anyone looking for help.
NAHUM 1:7 MSG

She came and,
kneeling, worshiped
Him and kept
praying, Lord,
help me!

MATTHEW 15:25 AMP

During the filming of the movie *Quo Vadis*, there was a scene in which actress Deborah Kerr was exposed alone to a whole pride of lions. Afterward she was asked by reporters covering the making of the movie if she had been afraid. With a glint in her eye, she replied, "Oh no, I had read the script and knew that Robert Taylor would come and save me."

When you get into some kind of trouble and call on God for aid, be assured that help is on the way. You can count on it. God comes quickly and promptly to give you assistance. It is God's intention to rescue and deliver you. No matter where you are when you call on God for help, he hears and comes.

Dear God of instant help, thank you for coming
to me any time and every time. Amen.

WHEN YOU MESS UP

You, O Lord, are good, and ready to forgive [our trespasses, sending them away, letting them go completely and forever]; and You are abundant in mercy and loving-kindness to all those who call upon You.

PSALM 86:5 AMP

The enemy's goal is to tempt you to yield to sin. He knows that even the smallest failure can cause guilt to rise up within you. If he can lead you to stumble spiritually or morally, he can further crush you with the lie that God wants nothing

Every time I'm in trouble I call on you, confident that you'll answer.

PSALM 86:7 MSG

more to do with you. Yet nothing could be further from the truth. The Lord hates sin because he loves you—because sin devastates your soul. However, when you confess your failings to him and turn away from them, God embraces you with deep affection and support.

Never allow the enemy's accusations to keep you from experiencing God's forgiveness. The devil may want you to fall, but the Lord can lift your soul. He will never leave you, so call upon him and receive his pardon.

Teach me, God, to call out to you for help and strength rather than yield to temptation. And thank you for forgiving me when I mess up. Amen.

ALWAYS MORE

Now we see a dim reflection, as if we were looking into a mirror, but then we shall see clearly. Now I know only a part, but then I will know fully, as God has known me.
1 CORINTHIANS 13:12 NCV

Great indeed, we confess, is the mystery of godliness: He was manifested in the flesh, vindicated by the Spirit, seen by angels, proclaimed among the nations, believed on in the world, taken up in glory.

1 TIMOTHY 3:16 ESV

Your eyes are made to take in a wide range of colors that span the spectrum of your consciousness and awareness, from red at one end of the spectrum to violet at the other end. But this is not all the color there is. There is infrared beyond the red and there is ultraviolet beyond the violet. Your eyes are not made for these colors, but they are there all the same.

Likewise, there is more to God than you know or understand. Beyond what you know and understand about God, there is great mystery, unparalleled majesty, unspeakable glory, and immeasurable love. Beyond your perceptions and understandings of God, there is God himself. No matter how much you know about God, there is always more than you perceive or comprehend.

Dear God, thank you for the ever-expanding glory of who you are to me. Amen.

UNDIVIDED, UNENCUMBERED

Teach me Your way, LORD, and I will live by Your truth.
Give me an undivided mind to fear Your name.
PSALM 86:11 HCSB

You've heard it said that you cannot serve two masters. And it's true. When your heart is divided between two goals—or two leading influences—you will not have peace. They'll always battle against each other to hold you, which will encumber you with inner conflict.

There is no god like you and no works like yours. Lord, all the nations you have made will come and worship you. They will honor you. . . . Only you are God.

PSALM 86:8–10 NCV

Friend, do you have something in your life that is competing with God for your affections? Ask yourself what it offers that God cannot provide. What need does it fill that God cannot satisfy better?

You'll undoubtedly find that whatever your second master is, it falls short of God's promises to you. So leave it behind. You'll only be truly free when your devotion is completely undivided.

God, give me an undivided heart to love and obey you.
May nothing ever come between us, but help
me to honor you with my life. Amen.

JUST DO IT

Peter and the other apostles replied:
"We must obey God rather than men!"
ACTS 5:29 NIV

Because you listen to these rules and keep and do them, the LORD your God will keep with you the covenant and the steadfast love that he swore to your fathers.

DEUTERONOMY 7:12 ESV

Obedience is the shortest distance to who God is, the quickest way to know his presence in your life. You come to more truth about God in one instant of implicit obedience than in days of mulling over in your mind what you think or suppose he wants you to do about something.

There is no substitute in the Christian life for obedience. It brings the blessing of God's presence and power to you. When you do what God wants, you know God is present within you to make you strong for your life. You are assured of God's strengthening company, and you go forth in confidence. Obedience opens the door to God's presence and power in your life.

Dear God, when I trust and obey,
the way to you is clear to me. Amen.

DO YOU REALIZE IT?

Wonderful things are told about you.
PSALM 87:3 CEV

It's interesting that people who genuinely follow God often don't know what a blessing they are to others. They've been taught to be humble—to hold God as their standard instead of others—so they're modest about their graces and abilities.

Of Zion it shall be said . . . "the Most High himself will establish her."

PSALM 87:5 ESV

Friend, if you've been seeking God obediently, he's been shining through you. His unique qualities of love, joy, peace, patience, kindness, gentleness, and faithfulness have encouraged others and inspired them to seek God. The humility you experience isn't about feeling worthless; it's about attributing the glory in you to God. So if you're feeling down about yourself—stop it. You just can't see what others can. God is working through you, and that's truly praiseworthy.

Wow, God. Thank you that the good others see in me is you! Thank you for shining through me and giving me your beautiful attributes. Amen.

465

PRACTICE YOUR PRAYERS

The LORD does not listen to the wicked,
but he hears the prayers of those who do right.
PROVERBS 15:29 NCV

The LORD is near to
all who call upon Him,
to all who call upon
Him in truth.

PSALM 145:18 NKJV

Out of your prayer life comes a desire to love people. When you talk with God about yourself, he talks to you about others. He points out whom you are to love and how you are to love.

During World War II, a soldier was by his bunk in the barracks saying his prayers just before taps. Another soldier, bothered by the show of piety, threw his heavy combat boot and hit the praying man on the head, knocking him down. The first soldier said nothing. The other soldier laughed and went to bed, forgetting to retrieve his boot. The next morning, he found both of his boots by his bed, beautifully spit-shined. The two soldiers ended up praying together. Talking to God sends you out to love other people.

Dear God, as I speak to you, speak to me about
those you want me to love today. Amen.

THAT'S HIS JOB

The Most High Himself will establish her.
PSALM 87:5 AMP

Do you ever think about how much God loves you? Some people rarely take time to do this. They are burdened by their problems, stresses, and shortcomings. They tell themselves that if they lived a better life, God would love them more.

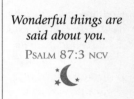

Wonderful things are said about you.
PSALM 87:3 NCV

This simply is not true! God loves you with an undivided love. Nothing you do can cause him to care for you any more or less. Rather, he accepts you just the way you are, and his ultimate goal is to build you up in his image.

God created you for a relationship with him, and he gently and compassionately molds you into all you were created to be. Therefore, rejoice! Because he is establishing you by his loving hand and will shine through you with his everlasting love.

God, I'm humbled by the fact that you love me and that you have a plan for my future. Thank you for molding me in your image. Amen.

WHAT GOD IS DOING

*I am the vine, and you are the branches. Those who remain in me, and
I in them, will bear much fruit; for you can do nothing without me.*
JOHN 15:5 GNT

*God has made us what
we are. In Christ Jesus,
God made us to do
good works, which
God planned in
advance for us to
live our lives doing.*

EPHESIANS 2:10 NCV

Your challenge each day is to find
out what God is doing in the
part of the world where you live and
join him in doing whatever that is.
How can your personal thoughts and
actions, even attitudes, relate to the
activity of God? How is God moving
today in the place where you are?

You know what God is doing by
looking around you for evidence of
his activity. You see God involved in institutions that care for
people. He is obvious in causes that promote good values and
strong principles. Be aware of where God is working, and join
him there. Discern the divine in everyday life, and join forces
with God in what he is doing. Give yourself to God's work.

*Dear God, show me what you are doing so I can
help accomplish your will in the world. Amen.*

ENDING THE DAY WITH HIM

O LORD, the God of my salvation . . .
at night I am in Your presence
PSALM 88:1 AMP

I f you were a combat soldier, you would not sleep at night without knowing you were battle ready. You'd be sure you had your orders and all the equipment you needed to engage the battles successfully when you awake.

Lord, you are the God who saves me. I cry out to you day and night. Receive my prayer, and listen to my cry.

PSALM 88:1–2 NCV

Though you may not be a conventional warrior, you faced conflicts— struggles you weren't quite sure how to handle—today. You had unforeseen skirmishes with others, and you wrestled with strategic situations that required ingenuity, strength, and wisdom. God was with you for these conflicts and skirmishes. That's why you can rest tonight knowing that you can commit all your troubles to his hands. Remember that all your battles belong to him. As your Commander, he'll always lead you safely to triumph.

God, I'm glad you are present with me tonight. Thank you for equipping me with everything I needed to face everything I encountered. You're truly wonderful! Amen.

MADE LIKE GOD

God created humankind in his image, in the image of God he created them; male and female he created them.
GENESIS 1:27 NRSV

They will take root in your house, LORD God, and they will do well. They will be like trees that stay healthy and fruitful, even when they are old.

PSALM 92:13–14 CEV

When sixteen-year-old Dan entered an elevator in a department store, a woman stared at him, looking him over from head to toe. She made Dan nervous. After looking at him three or four times, the woman explained the reason for her scrutiny. She said to him, "You're Erick's boy, aren't you?" She recognized him from knowing his dad.

You are made in the image of God and resemble your maker. You have inherited God's essential qualities of love and joy. You have within you characteristics that speak of God's passion and faithfulness. Who you are has the print of God all over it. You are made in the image of God. You come from God. You are unmistakably his.

Dear God, I am lovingly conceived, masterfully created, and wonderfully made. Amen.

AVAILABLE

My eyes are weak from crying. LORD, I have prayed to you
every day; I have lifted my hands in prayer to you.
PSALM 88:9 NCV

Disappointment can strike suddenly, and your first reaction may be one of defensiveness. You may feel angry and hurt; however, do not lash out. Your best course of action is always to step away from the situation and ask God to show you what to do.

LORD, God of my salvation, I cry out before You day and night. May my prayer reach Your presence; listen to my cry.

PSALM 88:1–2 HCSB

The wonderful thing about God is that he is always accessible and willing to receive you. He will show you what you need to do and comfort your aching heart. Has discouragement assailed you? Are your eyes weak from crying and your heart tender and grieved? God will find a way to encourage you and admonish you not to give up. So turn to him—because even at this moment, he is listening for your call.

I know that when I keep my eyes on you, God, you will
give me the comfort, the strength, and the understanding
I need. Thank you for your unfailing love. Amen.

YOUR FATHER

The time is coming when the true worshipers will worship the Father in spirit and truth, and that time is here already. You see, the Father too is actively seeking such people to worship him.

JOHN 4:23 NCV

When Jesus had spoken these things, He lifted up His eyes to heaven and said, Father, the hour has come.

JOHN 17:1 AMP

In the entire Old Testament God is referred to as Father only six times, and then not very personally. But in the Gospels, Jesus speaks of God as "my Father" or "our Father" more than sixty times. When Jesus came to earth, he reversed the traditional concept of God. God is no longer removed and remote. There is every reason for you to refer to him as your Father.

There is something very concrete, nothing abstract, about talking to God your Father. It's a sit-down, face-to-face, close-enough-to-touch kind of thing. Talking to God as your Father is the most intimate of conversations. When you talk to God your Father, you speak with someone you know and someone who knows you.

Dear Father, I come to you as a child waiting for you to speak your will and show your way to me. Amen.

GOD'S STRENGTH IS ENOUGH

Powerful is your arm! Strong is your hand!
Your right hand is lifted high in glorious strength.
PSALM 89:13 NLT

To small children, an adult must look like a giant. You loom over them and stoop down to pick them up in your arms. In the instant you do, however, your intimidating strength blurs into a single gesture of tenderness. Sometimes that's how you see God—vast and mighty and towering in strength high above you. The moment he folds you in his arms, however, you remember that he is, after all, your loving God.

With a strong hand, and with a stretched out arm: for his mercy endureth for ever. To him which divided the Red sea into parts: for his mercy endureth for ever.

PSALM 136:12–13 KJV

✴☽

When you grow weak and afraid, the image of God's strong arms brings a fresh reminder of his nearness. God promises to keep you in the palm of his hand. There, safe in his grasp, you find the strength to do whatever he asks of you.

You are able, dear God, to do far more with me than I am able to do with myself. I trust your power, seek your wisdom, and surrender to your leading. Amen.

GOD IS GREAT

The LORD your God is supreme over all gods and over all powers.
He is great and mighty, and he is to be obeyed.

DEUTERONOMY 10:17 GNT

> *God thunders wondrously with his voice; he does great things that we cannot comprehend.*
>
> JOB 37:5 NRSV

If you close down interferences and interruptions to be alone with God, nothing detracts you from God. He is in front of you. He alone is there.

At the funeral of Louis XIV, the light of many candles, symbolizing the brightness and greatness of the king, filled the room. At the appointed time, the court preacher stood to address those who had come to honor the king. He nodded his head toward several attendants, who in turn snuffed out every one of the candles. The cathedral was now completely dark. Out of that darkness, the court preacher spoke. "God only is great," he said. None is as great as God. Only he creates and sustains the world. Only God has you in the palm of his hand.

Good and great God, you are everything to me.
You set the stars in place. You live in my heart. Amen.

YOUR LIFE IS A PSALM

Happy are those who hear the joyful call to worship,
for they will walk in the light of your presence, LORD.
PSALM 89:15 NLT

When you believe in God, your life is a psalm—one that will be read throughout eternity. It will record your downbeats of doubt as you cry out to God with your troubles. And it will chronicle your songs of exultation as he helps you and gives you the desires of your heart.

Because of you they rejoice all day long, and they praise you for your goodness. You give us great victories; in your love you make us triumphant.

PSALM 89:16–17 GNT

The theme of your life will be God's faithfulness to you, for when all your days have been documented, you will undoubtedly report that he never failed you.

Your life is a song of praise to God that's being written through your circumstances. Today find peace in the knowledge that he's making your life into a beautifully intricate work of art.

God, thank you that every exultant high note and dissonant chord in my life is making a beautiful song of praise to your faithfulness. Amen.

HOW YOU LOOK AT IT

He said to them, "Come, and you will see." So they came and saw where He was staying; and they stayed with Him that day.
JOHN 1:39 NASB

He is not here, for He has risen, just as He said. Come, see the place where He was lying.

MATTHEW 28:6 NASB

The closer you get to God, the more your perspective about God changes. Through the eyes of reverence, God comes across in a different way. Who he is becomes clearer. It was said of an early-twentieth-century photographer that he had "the ability to see beyond the lens." So also can you.

God is like a prism. What you see depends on how you turn the glass. Turn it in faith and see the greatness of God. Turn it in love and see the warmth of God. Turn it in hope and see the promises of God. Turn it in anticipation and see the guidance of God. Turn it in assurance and see the eternity of God. The closer you get to God, the more of him you see.

Dear God, how wonderful and exciting to see you now as I have not seen you before. Amen.

HE KEEPS HIS PROMISES

No, I will not break my covenant;
I will not take back a single word I said.
PSALM 89:34 NLT

One of the deepest hurts you can experience is betrayal. Discovering that a friend, co-worker, or loved one has acted treacherously can tempt you to feel defeated and rejected. Imagine what Jesus felt when he saw Judas walking toward him that night in the garden of Gethsemane.

LORD God of Hosts, who is strong like You, LORD? Your faithfulness surrounds You.

PSALM 89:8 HCSB

Yet you can know that God would never betray your trust by breaking his promises to you. Not only would it contradict his holy character, but it would also violate his perfect love for you. Is there some precious promise that is long in being fulfilled? God has not forgotten his word to you. On the contrary, what he is providing is too wonderful to create quickly. Therefore, wait upon him with confidence and hope, because he would never betray your trust.

God, it is very difficult to wait for my dreams and
hopes to come to fruition. Yet I have confidence
that you will keep all your promises to me. Amen.

FENCES DOWN

*Faith in Christ Jesus is what makes each of you equal
with each other, whether you are a Jew or a Greek,
a slave or a free person, a man or a woman.*
GALATIANS 3:28 CEV

*How wonderful,
how beautiful, when
brothers and sisters
get along!*

PSALM 133:1 MSG

When you take time and make room to get close to God, you acquire a more inclusive attitude toward other people. You see that God loves everybody and wants you to do the same. Divisions between you and others melt away before the bright and warm glow of God's universal embrace.

A man stood up in church after a terrible hurricane hit his city and talked about his backyard fence. Ferocious winds had blown it into splintered fragments and left him exposed to a neighbor he'd never met. It wasn't long before they were barbecuing together, a result of taking time and making room for each other. Unity is the birthplace of God's purpose for you. It is where you feel God's love in its richness.

*Dear God, in your love, my arms are wide open to other
people. In you, we have much in common. Amen.*

GOD'S DIFFERENT PERSPECTIVE

*To you, a thousand years is like the passing of
a day, or like a few hours in the night.*
PSALM 90:4 NCV

G od has not failed you. Though every human indicator may suggest that God is absent from your situation, the reality is far from it. The problem is that the full panorama has yet to be seen—your complete situation still hasn't been unveiled.

Give us gladness in proportion to our former misery! Replace the evil years with good. Let us, your servants, see you work again; let our children see your glory.

PSALM 90:15–16 NLT

☽

Why has God allowed these trials to come into your life? It's not because he is letting you down. Rather, he's teaching you that he makes all your circumstances work together for your good—even the waiting.

So don't fret. Hang on to him as tightly as you can and trust that he's working out something important. Because when you see what he sees, you're going to love the big picture.

God, I know you won't ever let me down. Help me hang on until I can see your answer to my prayers. I know you're faithful. Amen.

THE WEIGHT OF YOUR WORRY

*The eternal God is your refuge and dwelling place,
and underneath are the everlasting arms; He drove
the enemy before you and thrust them out.*

DEUTERONOMY 33:27 AMP

*Humble yourselves,
therefore, under
the mighty hand
of God so that at the
proper time he may
exalt you, casting
all your anxieties
on him, because
he cares for you.*

1 PETER 5:6–7 ESV

In an early manuscript of the Christian era, there is a record of a man named Titedios Amerimnos. The first part of that name is a proper name, but the second part is made up of the Greek word for *worry* plus the prefix meaning *never*.

This man is thought to have added the second part of his name after he became a Christian. He was then "Titedios, the man who never worries." A life of worry is on the natural plane, but the Christian life is on a spiritual plane. There is no need to worry when one trusts in God. Put the weight of your worry on God. Give him your tomorrows, and trust them to his care and wisdom.

*Dear God, I will quit wringing my hands and place
them in yours for you to hold and guide me. Amen.*

BETTER THAN A BEDTIME SNACK

Let the favor of the Lord our God be upon us.
PSALM 90:17 NASB

A healthy snack at bedtime can be beneficial. Yet there's nothing as positive or satisfying as feeding on God's Word.

Lord our God, may your blessings be with us. Give us success in all we do!

PSALM 90:17 GNT

God knows what you need before you ever say your bedtime prayer and climb into bed. When you spend time with him, he nourishes you with the perfect diet of joy, wisdom, and strength to comfort you during the night and fuel you the next day.

So before you have a handful of popcorn or drink that hot cocoa, remember that your spirit needs to be fed too. Enjoy a hearty helping of God's presence each evening. You really will be ending your day in the very best way.

God, thank you for nourishing my spirit with the perfect diet. May I honor you with my confidence in your soothing comfort. Amen.

DON'T BE AFRAID

Jesus spoke to them, saying, "Take heart;
it is I. Do not be afraid."
MATTHEW 14:27 ESV

I am the LORD your God, who holds your right hand, and I tell you, "Don't be afraid. I will help you."

ISAIAH 41:13 NCV

When Rodney was eight years old, he attended a professional football game in a large stadium in a big city with his dad and some of his dad's friends. When they were leaving the stadium, Rodney was separated from the others. When he realized what had happened, tears flooded his face and sobs convulsed his small body. In full-blown panic, he had no idea what to do.

Just then, Rodney spotted his dad running rapidly down a ramp in his direction. As soon as he saw his dad, Rodney was no longer afraid. Now in his forties, Rodney says that's the day he began to understand who God is to him. Knowing God is near, you are better able to manage your fears. The presence of God encourages an absence of fears.

Lord God, quiet the wind and waves
of my anxieties and fears. Amen.

EVERLASTING CONFIDENCE

*Those who live in the shelter of the Most High
will find rest in the shadow of the Almighty.*
PSALM 91:1 NLT

The word *danger* raises your anxiety level because of its dire implications. Dangers threaten your life and those of your loved ones. Dangers shake your world and destroy your security. Dangers make you question everything—especially why God would allow them.

*You have made the
LORD, my refuge, even
the Most High, your
dwelling place. No
evil will befall you,
nor will any plague
come near your tent.*
PSALM 91:9–10 NASB

Yet when you know God and trust him for salvation, perils can only come so near to you because God protects your eternal destination. Though hazards may trouble you on earth, you can be confident that they won't follow you into heaven. So don't fear the dangers. Rather, thank God that the worst that can happen is limited—and it's nothing compared to the wonderful things he's planned for you.

*God, I face many dangers every day, but none is stronger
than you are. Thank you for protecting my loved
ones and me daily and for eternity. Amen.*

RAISED UP

*When you were baptized, it was the same as being buried
with Christ. Then you were raised to life because
you had faith in the power of God.*
COLOSSIANS 2:12 CEV

*If you have been raised
up with Christ, keep
seeking the things
above, where Christ is.*
COLOSSIANS 3:1 NASB

Paul did not speak of a future resurrection. He spoke of the present experience of living a resurrection life. You die to the pain of troubles, and you rise to the life of new opportunity.

During World War II, a London church prepared for a harvest thanksgiving service. Among the bounty in the sanctuary was a sheaf of corn. An enemy air attack destroyed the church before the service could be held. Months passed, spring came, and someone noticed that on the bomb site where the church had been there were shoots of green. Summer arrived, the shoots grew, and in the fall a flourishing patch of corn grew in the midst of the rubble. Your trust in the resurrected Christ sends you out as one who believes life is stronger than death.

*Dear God, thank you for resurrection power in each day,
and for its power in the midst of challenge. Amen.*

SAFE AND SOUND

You will not fear the terror of the night,
or the arrow that flies by day.
PSALM 91:5 NRSV

The eyes of the mother lion never leave her cubs as they scuffle playfully in the underbrush. Her instinct to guard and protect her little ones is intense and constant. She leaves them only long enough to secure food in the darkest hours of the night.

The LORD will keep you from all evil; he will keep your life.

PSALM 121:7 NRSV

God watches over you more carefully than the most attentive lioness watches over her cubs. His eyes are on you as you move through your days. Under his constant watchfulness, you can find safety and wholeness. In the midst of danger and chaos, you will find that his presence is a source of hope and peace. When you call on him for help, be assured that he will come quickly to rescue you and show you the way to safety.

I often feel fearful and insecure as I search for safety and protection for those I love and for me. From this day forward, I will place my trust in you, God, and hope in your faithfulness and love. Amen.

KNOW WHO KNOCKS

Look at me. I stand at the door. I knock. If you hear me call and open the door, I'll come right in and sit down to supper with you.
REVELATION 3:20 MSG

After this, I looked and saw a door that opened into heaven.

REVELATION 4:1 CEV

A pastor took money to a woman who was in need of help for herself and her family. He knocked on the door, but there was no answer. He knocked again, more forcefully this time, and no one came to the door. Another day and still another day he repeated his effort, but to no avail.

Eventually, he was able to get the money to her. When he did, she confessed that she had heard him knocking on the door every time he'd been there, but she had thought it was a bill collector. Instead, someone had come to give money to her. God knocks on the door of your heart to give you gifts of grace and joy.

Dear God, it is you I hear knocking on the door of my heart. I am coming. Amen.

PRAISE ALL DAY?

Lord Most High! It is wonderful each morning to tell about your love and at night to announce how faithful you are.
PSALM 92:1–2 CEV

When speaking with others, do you assume the best—or the worst? Are you pessimistic in your discourse or positive? Friend, your conversation is self-fulfilling.

You made me so happy, God. I saw your work and I shouted for joy. How magnificent your work, God! How profound your thoughts!

PSALM 92:4–5 MSG

If you complain—emphasizing the negative aspects of your life—you'll always be governed by your problems. Your trials will set the tone of your life. Yet if you consciously praise God in all things, you'll find a new confidence and strength that nothing can take away. With him, truly nothing will be impossible for you.

This isn't naive optimism. Rather, it's the deep-seated understanding of God's unfaltering love and faithfulness. So yes, friend, praise him all day, because every day you experience God's presence is a good one.

God, I do praise you! Thank you for working through my positive attitude to bring glory to yourself—and strength and joy to me. Amen.

SOW THE SEED

God is the One who gives seed to the farmer and bread for food.
He will give you all the seed you need and make it grow
so there will be a great harvest from your goodness.

2 CORINTHIANS 9:10 NCV

Sow fields and plant vineyards, and gather a fruitful harvest.

PSALM 107:37 NASB

God gives the seed and God makes the seed grow, but God doesn't sow it. Sowing the seed is what you do. You take God's gifts and invest them in your every day. You put the seed in the ground for God to grow.

A woman dreamed of entering a large store in which the gifts of God were kept. Behind one of the counters was an angel dispensing something to those who stood in line. The woman waited her turn and, when it came, said to the angel, "Please give me the fruit I need for my life." The angel responded, "I'm sorry. We don't stock fruit. All we have is seed." You receive rich possibilities from God and make them richer by what you do with them.

Dear God, thank you for the seed you give to me.
May I sow faithfully and wait expectantly. Amen.

THE BLESSINGS OF LONG LIFE

The righteous flourish like the palm tree, and grow like a
cedar in Lebanon. . . . In old age they still produce fruit.
PSALM 92:12, 14 NRSV

Occasionally you may spot an elderly couple holding hands and gazing into each other's eyes like newlyweds. *What's their secret?* you wonder. If you investigate a little more deeply, you'll usually find two people who are lifelong examples of the second greatest commandment: Love your neighbor (or spouse) as yourself. Time has etched deep lines on their faces and stooped their bodies, and yet their spirits remain sound and supple—and as full of life as when they first caught sight of each other and recognized a kindred spirit.

He will call upon me,
and I will answer him;
I will be with him in
trouble, I will deliver
him and honor him.
With long life will I
satisfy him and show
him my salvation.
PSALM 91:15–16 NIV

The quintessential ingredient to every good relationship is a servant's heart, each person holding out the light of Christ for the other.

Everything I know, O God, I know because I love. To love is to live,
and to live is to love. Thank you for loving me in Jesus Christ. Amen.

A SWEET SMELL

The fig tree forms its early fruit; the blossoming vines spread their fragrance.
SONG OF SOLOMON 2:13 NIV

He appointed twelve, that they might be with Him and that He might send them out to preach.

MARK 3:14 NKJV

In California there is a lovely place called the Valley of Roses. For many miles, lush roses bloom on both sides of the road. There are many varieties, and each one is as beautiful and sweet smelling as the next. They pervade the air with pleasant scents. Travelers driving through the Valley of Roses open the windows of their cars so they won't miss the full aroma of the magnificent flowers. The fragrance saturates even the clothes they wear. When they get home, people know where they have been from their fragrance

People know when you have been with God. When you make the effort to draw close to God, it is obvious to others. Time spent with God gives you a sweet fragrance of love, joy, and peace.

Dear God, as I move through each day, may it be known that I have been with you. Amen.

UNCHANGING

*God is King, robed and ruling, God is robed and surging
with strength. And yes, the world is firm, immovable,
Your throne ever firm—you're Eternal!*
PSALM 93:1 MSG

It seems that everything changes—and, in a sense, everything in this world is fleeting. Earthly things just weren't intended to last forever.

What you say goes—it always has. "Beauty" and "Holy" mark your palace rule, God, to the very end of time.

PSALM 93:5 MSG

Like a flower, we see living things germinate, grow, bloom, and then begin the process of decay. Even our lives are ruled by time—births and deaths, beginnings and endings. The cycles of change are inherent in our nature.

Yet God isn't subject to any such phases or cycles. Immune from time, God's character is completely unchanging and his nature is eternal. That's why as things start, finish, and change in your life, you can always hope in him. God will always be steadfastly faithful to you—today, tomorrow, and always.

*How I need you, God! Thank you for being unchanging,
immovable, and wise. Thank you for always providing
stability and strength to my life. Amen.*

HE IS ALIVE

Jesus came and stood among them and said,
"Peace be with you."
JOHN 20:19 NRSV

Jesus came near and started walking along beside them.

LUKE 24:15 CEV

God raised Jesus from the grave so the spirit and strength of the risen Lord could be with you. He is alive in your relationships and activities. He is available to you in everything you do.

For years, R. W. Dale, an able scholar and a renowned preacher, was a follower of Christ. As he was preparing an Easter sermon for his congregation at Carr's Lane Church in Birmingham, England, the reality of the presence of Jesus swept over him so strongly that he began to pace and shout, "He is alive! He is alive!" Every Sunday thereafter, an Easter hymn was sung in Dale's church. Every Sunday became to him a resurrection day. Everywhere you go, God goes with you.

You are alive, Lord Jesus, in my heart and in my life. I am never alone. Amen.

492

YESTERDAY, TODAY, AND FOREVER

Your throne, O LORD, has stood from time immemorial.
You yourself are from the everlasting past.
PSALM 93:2 NLT

When you acknowledge God's power and might, he pours his encouragement into your heart. A simple prayer, "Lord, I need your help," speaks volumes to him. He hears your confession and moves into action. Yet there will be times when you do not have days or weeks to pray about what you are facing. An emergency will arise, and within a few minutes or even seconds, you will need his comfort and direction. Can God help you in such urgent situations?

Lord, your laws
will stand forever.
Your Temple will be
holy forevermore.
PSALM 93:5 NCV

Yes, he is perfectly able to provide all you need the moment you cry out to him.

So take heart, friend, in your faithful God. He is as faithful to you today as he has been from time immemorial. And he will surely come to your aid as soon as you call.

God, you are truly faithful—as you were yesterday, you
will be today and forevermore. Thank you that I can
always trust your mighty, loving hand. Amen.

GOD IS AFTER YOU

This is what the Lord God says: I, myself,
will search for my sheep and take care of them.
EZEKIEL 34:11 NCV

God understands
the way to it, and he
knows its place. For
he looks to the ends
of the earth and sees
everything under
the heavens.

JOB 28:23–24 ESV

You are on God's to-find list. God is after you. He seeks you until he finds you. One person who understood this was C. S. Lewis. He used a number of metaphors to describe God's relentless pursuit of him.

He likened God to a great angler playing his fish and a cat chasing a mouse. Perhaps Lewis's most remembered metaphor is that of a divine chess player maneuvering him into the most disadvantageous positions until in the end he had to concede. He wrote to a friend who was trying very hard to avoid God in his life, "I think you are already in the meshes of the net. You will not escape." God wants you. God knows where you are. God is after you. You won't get away.

Dear God, thank you for seeking me out no matter
where I am or how far that is from you. Amen.

SPIRITUAL WORKOUT

How blessed the man you train,
GOD, the woman you instruct in your Word.
PSALM 94:12 MSG

Spiritual lessons require practice —that's the truth of the matter. You may believe you know everything necessary about faith or obedience; yet almost as soon as you express your confidence about that area, you're plunged headlong into a situation that puts your understanding to the test. Don't be surprised—it's through this process

The minute I said,
"I'm slipping, I'm fall-
ing," your love, God,
took hold and held me
fast. When I was upset
and beside myself, you
calmed me down and
cheered me up.

PSALM 94:18–19 MSG

that what you've learned intellectually becomes a practical reality in you. Tonight thank God for training you through your trials and strengthening your spiritual muscles. It's preparation that you'll certainly be glad to have.

God, thank you for stretching my faith in you and
making it real. Thank you for always loving me and
comforting me in every circumstance. Amen.

GOD SENDS YOU

Go, then, to all peoples everywhere and make them my disciples.
MATTHEW 28:19 GNT

You will tell everyone about me in Jerusalem, in all Judea, in Samaria, and everywhere in the world.

ACTS 1:8 CEV

It is God's desire that you take love for him from your heart and put it into the hearts of other people.

Years ago, in West Africa, a man lay on a hospital cot on a suffocatingly hot day. He had been sick for a long time and was extremely weak from the surgery just performed on him. But he was not without hope. In fact, it surged in his heart. A man in a doctor's coat stood over him and smiled. It was the man who had operated on him and saved his life. "Who sent you?" he asked the doctor. "The Lord Jesus Christ sent me," answered Albert Schweitzer.

God has been sending his servants into the world for a long time. He sends you now.

Dear God, I listen for your call. I am ready to go where you send me. Amen.

FACING THE FUTURE

When anxiety was great within me,
your consolation brought joy to my soul.
PSALM 94:19 NIV

A giant tortoise lumbers contentedly along on its way to nowhere, stopping often to nibble on the grass. A loud noise pierces the air, and a shadow crosses the tortoise's path. The tortoise stops right where it is, pulls its head into its shell, and shuts out the world.

Create in me a clean heart, O God; and renew a right spirit within me.

PSALM 51:10 KJV

You may experience times when you wish you could pull inside yourself to avoid emotional pain, fear, or disappointment. Brief periods of solitude can often help you process your thoughts and gain inner strength. It would be tempting to stay there. However, just as the tortoise would soon starve if it remained in its shell indefinitely, so, too, would you starve emotionally if you remained walled up within yourself. God can help you face your circumstances and walk forward with confidence and hope.

Gracious God, thank you for drawing me out of my
fearful, anxious shell and into the light of your love.
Thank you for new promise and purpose for my life. Amen.

WHAT GOD CAN DO

*I commend you to the care of God and to the message of
his grace, which is able to build you up and give
you the blessings God has for all his people.*

ACTS 20:32 GNT

*He did not waver at
the promise of God
through unbelief, but
was strengthened in
faith, giving glory to
God, and being fully
convinced that what
He had promised He
was also able
to perform.*

ROMANS 4:20–21 NKJV

When you put yourself in God's hands, you are in a place where great things can be accomplished in your life.

Stuart Hamblen was a radio disc jockey in Los Angeles in 1949 at the time of the first large-scale Billy Graham crusade. Liquor had come to dominate his life, but after several visits to crusade meetings, he was converted and lost his appetite for alcohol. A friend asked, "Have you not wanted one drink?" Hamblen replied, "No, John, it is no secret what God can do." His friend, knowing Hamblen's interest in music, said, "Stuart, you ought to write a song about that." Stuart Hamblen wrote a song about what God can accomplish in your life. He said it is no secret what God can do.

*Dear God, you are more than able to do all
in my life that needs to be done. Amen.*

WHAT IS WORSHIP?

Come, let us worship and bow down; let us kneel before the LORD our Maker. For He is our God, and we are the people of His pasture.
PSALM 95:6–7 NKJV

Some people talk about being in a great house of worship and sensing God's presence. The towering spires, stained-glass windows, and deeply carved wooden altar where private confessions are made are elements that can stir your heart with thoughts of his unconditional love, mercy, and grace.

> *Let us come before him with thanksgiving and extol him with music and song. For the LORD is the great God, the great King above all gods.*
> PSALM 95:2–3 NIV

Many times, however, the most sacred place is found in the quietness of your own room and in the stillness of your heart. This is where God personally meets with you, reveals himself to you through his Word, and teaches you how to live each day with hope and a sense of victory. The Lord of heaven is omnipresent—everywhere at all times. He is awesome in nature, and he is near to you right now.

God, I am in awe and wonder at your greatness. Thank you for extending your personal love to me and for the opportunity to live each day for you. Amen.

STRAIGHT WITH CROOKED LINES

In all your ways acknowledge him, and he will make your paths straight.
PROVERBS 3:6 NIV

Listen! It's the voice of someone shouting, "Clear the way through the wilderness for the LORD! Make a straight highway through the wasteland for our God!

ISAIAH 40:3 NLT

A young boy had a rough home life and grew up to write books that blessed thousands of people. A fledgling musician had his violin stolen, found a used trumpet for sale cheap, and became an outstanding band leader. A woman had to drop out of college to care for her mother but later became a doctor because of that experience.

God sometimes uses unlikely means to get to desired ends. He takes something that doesn't look like it would do and makes it work. In his hands, the improbable makes a good outcome possible. God writes straight with crooked lines. God can see beyond what you can see. He knows what will work in your life better than you do.

Dear God, you see beginnings where I see endings, possibilities where I see problems. Amen.

BE WILLING

If you hear his voice, do not harden your hearts.
PSALM 95:7–8 ESV

You may think, *No way!* It may be the first thing you think when you understand God's will for you. Maybe that's because his plans seem overwhelmingly difficult, or because they involve too many of your weaknesses. Perhaps it's because God's directions seem counter to your own ideas or prejudices. Whatever the reason, you really don't want to do as God says.

The LORD is a great God and a great King above all gods. . . . Come, let us worship and bow down, let us kneel before the LORD our Maker.

PSALM 95:3, 6 NASB

Reconsider, friend—don't be so quick to say no. God wants to do great things through you—endeavors that will astonish your eyes and bring true joy to your soul. True, it's going to take faith, but if you're willing to do whatever God says, you're sure to be blessed. So say yes, and trust him.

God, I do want to obey you, but I'm afraid. Fill me with confidence in your ways so I may serve you faithfully and please you. Amen.

GOD WASTES NOTHING

Whatever is true, whatever is honorable, whatever is right,
whatever is pure, whatever is lovely, whatever is
of good repute . . . dwell on these things.
PHILIPPIANS 4:8 NASB

When you give to them, they gather it up; when you open your hand, they are filled with good things.

PSALM 104:28 NRSV

✴

Bad things that happen in your life wake you up to the good stuff you may not otherwise attend to. Problems bring with them an invitation to explore new territory and discover what God has put there for your benefit and the blessing of others.

As a young man, Arturo Toscanini played the cello. His eyesight was poor and he could hardly see the music in front of him, so he had to memorize it. One evening, the orchestra conductor became ill, and Toscanini was the only one who knew the musical score. He conducted the entire program without once referring to the music. His performance was flawless, and his career was underway. God wastes nothing. He can use anything to bring good to your life.

Dear God, help me look far enough in my life to see the good things you have put there. Amen.

NATURE DECLARES HIS PRAISE

Let the heavens be glad and the earth rejoice; let the sea and all that fills it resound. Let the fields and everything in them exult.
PSALM 96:11–12 HCSB

It is easy to think, *When I see the Lord, I'll do this or say that.* The truth is that when you see him face-to-face, the only thing you will want to do is bow down and worship him. Words, if they are spoken, will only be those of praise and adoration. You will not be able to contain yourself or the love you feel for him. In fact, all of creation will exalt his holy name.

The LORD is great! He should be highly praised. He should be feared more than all other gods because all the gods of the nations are idols. The LORD made the heavens.

PSALM 96:4–5
GOD'S WORD

★ ☾ ★

This is why it is so necessary to learn to praise him now. It is practice for what you will be doing for eternity. Honor him for his goodness, faithfulness, long-suffering, and provision for your every need. Sing songs of glory to his name—for surely he is worthy both now and forevermore.

God, there are times when I overlook all that you have done for me. Right now I want to thank you for taking care of all that concerns me. Amen.

WHEN YOU STUMBLE

I, your GOD, have a firm grip on you and I'm not letting go.
I'm telling you, "Don't panic. I'm right here to help you."
ISAIAH 41:13 MSG

*The nations will walk
in its light, and the
kings of the world
will enter the city in
all their glory.*

REVELATION 21:24 NLT

A mother of a toddler watches her child. When he stumbles and is about to fall, she reaches out her hand to catch him. When he trips over his feet, she restores his balance. As the child moves around the room, she lets him do all he can on his own. When he falters, she is there in a flash. She is always ready to move to his side and give him the assistance he needs.

God gives you that kind of ongoing care when you invite him into your life. He lets you walk when you can, but when you get into difficulty, he is there promptly to give you a helping hand. God has his eye on you. He knows when you need him to come and help.

*Thank you, dear God, for catching me when I stumble
and putting me upright when I fall. Amen.*

UNPREDICTABLE

Clouds and darkness are round about Him [as at Sinai];
righteousness and justice are the foundation of His throne.
PSALM 97:2 AMP

God is never surprised by the unpredictable events of this world. He is never shaken, and he is never changed by anything that happens. He is the same today, tomorrow, and forever, and he is in control of all things.

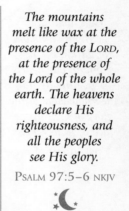

The mountains melt like wax at the presence of the LORD, at the presence of the Lord of the whole earth. The heavens declare His righteousness, and all the peoples see His glory.

PSALM 97:5–6 NKJV

Why can you face the future with a clear sense of hope and promise? Because he takes care of all that concerns you. Whether the stock market rises or falls, God remains the same. Though health issues come and go, he will always prove to be faithful.

You have a sure hope for your life that holds steady no matter how stormy or bright life becomes—and that is the hope you have in Jesus Christ.

God, I praise you because nothing is beyond your control.
If I have an unexpected challenge, please remind
me of your constant and unyielding love. Amen.

FOLLOW THE LIGHT

*About noon when I came near Damascus, a bright
light from heaven suddenly flashed all around me.*
ACTS 22:6 NCV

*God, who said,
"Let light shine out
of darkness," has
shone in our hearts
to give the light of
the knowledge of the
glory of God in the
face of Jesus Christ.*

2 CORINTHIANS 4:6 ESV

From the book *Living Love* by Saint Francis de Sales comes this story. One day a group of travelers took a nap under a large tree. Because the location was cool and they were tired, the travelers slept well.

After a while, the shade moved and the sun awakened them. Some of the travelers got up and resumed their journey. Others turned their backs on the sun and went back to sleep. When they woke up again, night had fallen and they resumed their journey in the dark. They strayed in various directions in the forest and soon were hopelessly lost. As you draw close to God, you will experience divine light upon your path. When that light comes, follow it.

*Dear God, may I always follow light that
comes from you and is for me. Amen.*

SCARY WORLD, STRONG GOD

Love the LORD and hate evil! God protects his loyal people and rescues them from violence.
PSALM 97:10 CEV

The pressure is always there—you must play along to get along. You do things that you aren't comfortable with in order to please others. You know that what you should do is stand up for what's right, but you feel so helpless. What choice do you really have? Friend, understand that you're never alone. Though you're afraid of crossing someone who could hurt you or mess up your future, realize that God will always honor you for doing what is right.

If you obey and do right, a light will show you the way and fill you with happiness. You are the LORD's people! So celebrate and praise the only God.
PSALM 97:11–12 CEV

God is with you and he's powerful. The people harassing you may prosper in the short term, but not forever. So trust God and obey him. He'll surely show himself mighty on your behalf.

God, thank you for being with me in this situation. It's difficult to obey you, but I will. Protect me and help me do what's right. Amen.

SMALL THINGS COUNT

Having obtained help from God, I stand to this day testifying both to small and great, stating nothing but what the Prophets and Moses said was going to take place.
ACTS 26:22 NASB

Though your beginning was small, yet your latter end would increase abundantly.

JOB 8:7 NKJV

✸

When God asks you to do something for him, your call might seem small. Often God asks you to do something quite unspectacular, minuscule in scope, and not particularly noteworthy. You want to play first violin, would even be willing to play second violin, but God asks you to pull the curtain.

Pulling the curtain is not at all what you had in mind. Nevertheless, be the best curtain puller you can be. The concert will not go on without you. When the orchestra members are seated and looking spiffy in their tuxedos and gowns, they can't be seen if you don't do your job. The maestro won't mount the podium and conduct the symphony without you. Give what you have to God. Nothing is too small for God's hands.

Dear God, you use whatever I give, and I thank you for recognizing who I am and what I have. Amen.

REASON FOR REJOICING

*O sing to the L*ORD *a new song, for He has done wonderful things, His right hand and His holy arm have gained the victory for Him.*
PSALM 98:1 NASB

The giant oak tree outside the bedroom window was home to a vocal mockingbird. In the silver darkness just before dawn, the bird would throat up, mimicking the songs of other birds and singing a full repertoire of tunes. After the mockingbird had whistled its way through every one, it would start all over again. At first nearby residents considered the repetitive singing loud and obnoxious. Then they realized that the mockingbird's predawn song made them smile. In the end, listeners thought that it was a rare treat to wake to the sound of singing so vibrant that it stirred the neighborhood to spirited wakefulness. Who but God could stir the mockingbird to such a songfest, day in and day out?

Hallelujah! Yes, let his people praise him as they stand in his Temple courts. Praise the Lord because he is so good; sing to his wonderful name.
PSALM 135:1–3 TLB

☽

Dear God, help me not to sin by failing to rejoice in all you are to me and all you give to me. May I not take any of the gifts of life for granted. Amen.

GOD CARRIES YOU

He tends his flock like a shepherd; he gathers the lambs
in his arms and carries them close to his heart.
ISAIAH 40:11 NIV

He took a child and had him stand in front of them. He put his arms around him and said to them, "Whoever welcomes in my name one of these children, welcomes me."

MARK 9:36–37 GNT

Do you remember what it was like when you were little and someone picked you up and carried you somewhere? What a comfortable and secure feeling when a parent or an older sibling reached down to your small frame, lifted you into strong and capable arms, and carted you across the room or around the yard or up the street. It was good to be held and carried like that. You knew everything was okay.

Let God carry you each day. You will feel safe and secure in the arms of God's compassion and concern. You will be comfortable everywhere you go because the eternal arms of God's power and might are underneath you. You are God's child. God always takes care of his children.

Dear God, thank you for supporting me in
ways I can feel, know, and trust. Amen.

HIS LOVE IS WITH YOU

He has remembered his love and his loyalty to the people of Israel.
All the ends of the earth have seen God's power to save.
PSALM 98:3 NCV

God loves you, and that love is unlimited. You may have to earn love from others—or even work hard to maintain it. But not for God's love. He offers it to you freely and never stops caring for you.

> *Sing a new song to the LORD, for he has done wonderful deeds. His right hand has won a mighty victory; his holy arm has shown his saving power!*
>
> PSALM 98:1 NLT

Always remember that you are the one who rejects or turns away from God. He'll never forsake you or withhold his love from you. That's the nature of unconditional love—it's given because it flows from God's character and has absolutely nothing to do with your actions. His love is always with you, in hopes that you'll receive it.

So embrace God's love. Forget your fears and feel its overwhelmingly wonderful power. Then, love him back.

My God, I do love you! Thank you for loving me
unconditionally and for giving me the victory and
salvation because of your powerful love. Amen.

September

*Wisdom brings
strength, and
knowledge gives
power.*

PROVERBS 24:5 CEV

THE NEW YOU

If anyone is in Christ, there is a new creation: everything old has passed away; see, everything has become new!
2 CORINTHIANS 5:17 NRSV

The former things have come to pass, and new things I now declare; before they spring forth I tell you of them.

ISAIAH 42:9 AMP

Shortly after his conversion, Saint Augustine was walking down the street when he met a woman who had been a mistress to him in his rebellious days. He turned abruptly and walked quickly in the other direction. Surprised at his action but thinking he did not recognize her, she cried out to him, "Augustine, it is I!" Augustine, increasing his speed, continued walking away from her and cried back over his shoulder, "Yes, but it is not I."

He meant there was a new Augustine. Since taking God into his life, his actions were different and his behavior had changed. He was not the person he had been. When God comes into your life, he changes and transforms you. You are not the same.

Thank you, dear God, for inviting me to change and for helping me do it. Amen.

WORSHIPING HOLINESS

*Exalt the LORD our God, and worship at his holy
mountain; for the LORD our God is holy!*
PSALM 99:9 ESV

God is holy—he embodies holiness. Several words may come to your mind such as *sacred*, *blessed*, and *virtuous*. Yet you may also wonder what exactly all that means.

God's holiness means that he's free from problems common to humankind and earthly limitations. He has no imperfections. Also, God is diametrically opposed to evil—he always does what is good and loving and never has moral dilemmas. Though he allows bad things to happen for now, he won't permit them forever. God faithfully fulfills all his promises. God is set apart—higher, purer, and more wonderful than all you know. And yet he still loves and helps you. Surely, that makes him worthy of your worship.

The Lord is great in Zion, and He is high above all the peoples. Let them confess and praise Your great name, awesome and reverence inspiring! It is holy, and holy is He!

PSALM 99:2–3 AMP

*Yes, God, you are worthy of my worship and awe.
I praise you for being sacred, blessed, virtuous, pure,
perfect, and good. Truly, you are holy! Amen.*

WHAT'S ALREADY HAPPENED

I will sing to the Lord, for He has triumphed gloriously; the horse and his rider or its chariot has He thrown into the sea.
EXODUS 15:1 AMP

Moses said to the people, "Remember this day in which you came out from Egypt, out of the house of slavery, for by a strong hand the LORD brought you out from this place."
EXODUS 13:3 ESV

✺

The children of Israel, beginning with Moses and Miriam, were able to glance into the past and remember their great escape from the Egyptians. Looking to the past, they could document their deliverance. They could recall and rehearse the past from their memory. Knowing God's past mercies allowed them to praise God and to look forward to his continuing presence.

Knowing that God had been with them in the past gave them assurance that he would walk with them in the present and accompany them into the future. They believed he would continue to act on their behalf. A good memory increases gratitude and assurance. You thank God for what he has done, and you look forward to what he will do.

Dear God, I remember how you have come time and again to hold and lift me up. Thank you. Amen.

A GLOBAL SONG

Shout triumphantly to the LORD, all the earth.
Serve the LORD with gladness; come before Him with joyful songs.
PSALM 100:1–2 HCSB

Who could imagine one thing that everyone on earth could agree upon? With all of the cultures, languages, and traditions—how could we come to an understanding about anything?

Yet we are told that one day every knee will bow and every tongue will confess Jesus as Lord. One day we will join hearts and hands with brothers and sisters across the world

> *Acknowledge that the LORD is God. He made us, and we are His—His people, the sheep of His pasture. Enter His gates with thanksgiving and His courts with praise.*
>
> PSALM 100:3–4 HCSB

with one purpose: to praise the One who saves us. What economics, politics, and diplomacy could never achieve will happen naturally because of God's extraordinary love.

So anticipate the global chorus by praising him today. And thank him that one day it'll be a song the whole world will sing.

God, I praise you that the day is coming that people from every nation will sing your praise! You are truly worthy, my Savior! Amen.

LIVE WHERE YOU LAND

*I have learned how to be content (satisfied to the point where
I am not disturbed or disquieted) in whatever state I am.*
PHILIPPIANS 4:11 AMP

*Give thanks for
everything to God the
Father in the name of
our Lord Jesus Christ.*

EPHESIANS 5:20 NLT

✷

Years ago, a hot air balloonist was going to make a long trip over a vast area. He planned his itinerary carefully, knowing exactly where he would stop on which day. He took off, confident he would be able to stick to his plan and follow his itinerary.

However, he had not planned adequately for the wind from the mountains. For the first four days, the wind blew him off course. He ended up in towns he'd never been to and didn't know anything about. But in each town where he landed, the hot air balloonist was heard to say, "Had I known about this place I would have planned all along to land here." Life sometimes takes you off course. Enjoy where you end up. Live where you land.

*Dear God, may I stand in awe and appreciation
before the surprises of my life. Amen.*

THE GOOD LIFE

I will give heed to the blameless way. When will You come to me?
I will walk within my house in the integrity of my heart.
PSALM 101:2 NASB

King David knew what it was like to be a poor shepherd boy and a wealthy king. He'd experienced what it was to have nothing and to have everything—to be lowly and unnoticed and to have the respect and love of a nation.

> *I will sing of your love and justice; to you, O LORD, I will sing praise.*
>
> PSALM 101:1 NIV

Yet through it all, there was one thing that defined the worthwhile life to David—a healthy relationship with God.

No matter how you define "the good life," one thing is certain: It's always better with God. As David discovered, possessions and power will fail to satisfy your soul, but God never will.

God can fill you with more joy and purpose than anything you can imagine. So follow him to the best life.

God, you make my life so much better. Lead me to the life you have for me—I know it's more wonderful than I can imagine! Amen.

WITH UTMOST CONFIDENCE

*In Whom, because of our faith in Him, we dare to have the
boldness (courage and confidence) of free access (an unreserved
approach to God with freedom and without fear).*
EPHESIANS 3:12 AMP

*We say with
confidence, "The
Lord is my helper;
I will not be afraid.
What can man
do to me?"*

HEBREWS 13:6 NIV

You don't have to wait for an invitation to talk to God. You have had a standing invitation since the beginning of time. Just as God made himself available to the couple in Eden's garden on a moment's notice, so also is he available to you.

God is available when things aren't going well in your family. He is available when you are disappointed because you haven't met a goal you set for yourself. God is ready to listen to your every word when someone you care about has let you down or when you have let someone down. Nothing is outside of God's ability and willingness to listen to you and to hear you. God's door is always wide open. God is always in for you.

*Dear God, I come boldly into your presence
and stand confidently before your love. Amen.*

WHAT YOUR EYES TAKE IN

I will search for faithful people to be my companions. Only those who are above reproach will be allowed to serve me.

PSALM 101:6 NLT

Have you ever experienced that pang of longing in your heart that comes after an especially beautiful love story? Or the grumbling of your stomach after a particularly delectable cooking demonstration? The things you watch, read, and listen to greatly influence the way you think and react to situations.

I will ponder the way that is blameless. . . . I will walk with integrity of heart within my house; I will not set before my eyes anything that is worthless.

PSALM 101:2–3 ESV

☾

God wants to fill you with good things that will bring joy to your soul and strengthen your heart. Therefore, if you think he would disapprove of something that is influencing you— let it go.

God, please show me if there is anything in my life that is influencing me in a negative way. I know that you will always keep me from harm. Amen.

FALLING DOWN

Humble yourselves [demote, lower yourselves in your own estimation] under the mighty hand of God, that in due time He may exalt you.

1 PETER 5:6 AMP

Respecting the LORD and not being proud will bring you wealth, honor, and life.

PROVERBS 22:4 NCV

The best position from which to see God is on your knees, humbled before God's majesty and magnificence. From your knees you can look up to the greatness and grandeur of God and gain perspective on how splendid and wonderful God is.

Prayer puts you on your knees to receive the fullness of God. Mother Teresa said that prayer "enlarges your heart until it is capable of receiving God's gift of himself." Prayer spoken humbly before God creates many rooms in your heart for God to occupy with his great power and immense love. He comes into those rooms to listen, understand, and speak. Prayer positions you to receive the gifts of God. It opens your heart to who God is and what God has.

Teach me, dear God, that I cannot be on my knees and on my high horse at the same time. Amen.

THE TIME FOR FAVOR

I pray to you, LORD! Please listen. Don't hide from me in my time of trouble. Pay attention to my prayer and quickly give an answer.
PSALM 102:1–2 CEV

If you've ever seen a baby bird wrestling free from its egg or a butterfly escaping its cocoon, you know it's a long, arduous process. Yet it's completely necessary because the creatures must become strong enough to endure conditions outside of their protective coverings.

You will arise and have compassion on Zion, for it is time to show favor to her; the appointed time has come.

PSALM 102:13 NIV

✦☾✦

Friend, have you likewise suffered a lengthy, difficult delay in seeing God's promises fulfilled? Understand that God doesn't make you wait in vain—it's necessary for you to be prepared for your blessings. The longer you wait, the more precious and beautiful God's provision will be. So count this time as one of training and favor—because you can be sure that God is doing wonderful and important things in your life.

God, help me to trust you and persevere during this time.
It's really been a struggle, but I know that your
blessings are worth the wait. Amen.

A THANK-YOU OFFERING

*Through him, then, let us continually offer a sacrifice of praise
to God, that is, the fruit of lips that confess his name.*
HEBREWS 13:15 NRSV

*Since we are
receiving a kingdom
that cannot be shaken,
let us be thankful,
and so worship God
acceptably with
reverence and awe.*

HEBREWS 12:28 NIV

Your blessings from God make you grateful. The extent and extravagance of God's gifts make you thankful. When you acknowledge how good God is in your life, you let him know how much you appreciate what he does for you. You come before him in great thanksgiving.

Thanksgiving is the constant and characteristic note of the Christian life. In happy moments, praise God. In difficult moments, seek God. In quiet moments, worship God. In painful moments, trust God. In every moment, thank God. As J. B. Lightfoot said, "Thanksgiving is at the end of all human conduct, whether observed in words or works." Giving thanks is the very life of prayer. Tell God how grateful you are for the fruit that falls from your tree.

*Dear God, you are the origin of my blessings
and the cause of my bounty. Amen.*

TIME IS HIS TOOL

It is time to be gracious to her,
for the appointed time has come.
PSALM 102:13 NASB

D o you ever feel as if time is your enemy? There is either too little of it when deadlines assail, or too much when waiting for some blessed hope. Yet understand—time is a precision instrument that God uses to develop your potential. Through abbreviated seasons— when there isn't enough time to get everything done—he shows you his mighty wisdom, power, and mercy. During the long years of waiting

Long ago you laid the foundation of the earth. Even the heavens are the works of your hands. They will come to an end, but . . . you remain the same, and your life will never end.
PSALM 102:25–27
GOD'S WORD

he molds your faith and character. Time is merely a tool in God's hand to reveal himself to you in a new way. His grace is sufficient for every moment of your life.

God, even though time is a driving factor in my life, I thank
you that I don't have to fear it. I praise you for your
lovingkindness every moment of every day. Amen.

THE POWER WITHIN YOU

You have already won a big victory over those false teachers, for the Spirit in you is far stronger than anything in the world.

1 JOHN 4:4 MSG

I pray that out of [God's] glorious riches he may strengthen you with power through his Spirit in your inner being.

EPHESIANS 3:16 NIV

Because God made you, there is a great power within you. Hudson Taylor, a nineteenth-century missionary to China, said, "All giants have been weak people who did great things for God because they reckoned on his power within them."

Did you ever buy something that ran on batteries but you didn't know it? You took your purchase out of the bag when you got home, and there it was right in front of your startled eyes: *Batteries not included*. You couldn't use what you bought because it had no source of power. Your personal source of power is God. He brings his strength to your weakness and enables you to rise above what holds you down. What is before or beyond you fades when approached by what is within you.

*Dear God, let your Spirit have his way within me.
Guide me and teach me along the way. Amen.*

SAY THANK-YOU

Bless the LORD, O my soul; and all that is within me, bless His holy name! Bless the LORD, O my soul, and forget not all His benefits.
PSALM 103:1–2 NKJV

When you were young and someone gave you something, your dad or mom would remind you, "Now, what do you say?" They wanted you to express gratitude for what you had received. Think of how generous God is to you and how grateful you are to

They must thank the LORD for his constant love, for the wonderful things he did for them.

PSALM 107:8 GNT

him. Take out a pencil and paper and write down a list of your blessings. The psalmist tells you not to forget any of them.

Gratitude comes when you take time to count your past and present gifts and benefits. It is a fundamental response to God's grace. Prayer reaches its highest level as gratitude. Gratitude is the heart's memory of what God has done for you. The most complete prayer is a grateful thought toward heaven.

Dear God, when I think of what you do for me, my heart is lifted in gratitude and my voice in praise. Amen.

FROM BUD TO BLOSSOM

*We are to grow up in all aspects into
Him who is the head, even Christ.*
EPHESIANS 4:15 NASB

*Brothers and sisters,
we taught you how to
live in a way that will
please God, and you
are living that way.
Now we ask and
encourage you in the
Lord Jesus to live that
way even more.*

1 THESSALONIANS 4:1
NCV

The spiritual life is one of becoming. It is more process than event, and the process is always going on. The spiritual life is not so much reaching a destination as it is being on the road. You are on the road to a deeper understanding of who God is, to a more personal acceptance of God in your life, and to more joy and love than you have known before.

Whistler, the great painter, once lost a shipment of blank canvases. A friend asked him if they were of any great value. The master artist pulled on his chin, his eyes twinkled, and he said, "Not yet, not yet." The spiritual life is one of expansion and extension. There is always room for more.

*Dear God, keep me unhappy enough with who I am
to grow toward who you want me to be. Amen.*

CLAIMING GOD'S BLESSINGS

He fills my life with good things.
PSALM 103:5 NLT

God's blessings are available to you as you put your trust in him and keep his commandments. His abundance is beautiful and simple. His promises are everywhere in Scripture. He will be your God if you will be his child; if you honor and obey him, he will withhold nothing from you. All you have to do is ask.

See for yourself the way his mercies shower down on all who trust in him. If you belong to the Lord, reverence him; for everyone who does this has everything he needs.

PSALM 34:8–9 TLB

God forgives your trespasses and provides righteousness and justice when you are treated unfairly; he is merciful and gracious; he is slow to get angry and full of unfailing love. Sin and despair are the only obstacles between you and God's many blessings. They can cloud your vision and prevent you from seeing things as they are. But God understands and is eternally patient with you. He will give you the grace to overcome your weaknesses.

God, thank you for the blessings you have placed in my life. Cleanse my heart so that I can receive all you have provided for me. Amen.

INSIGHT IS BETTER

If any of you lack wisdom, you should pray to God, who will give it to you; because God gives generously and graciously to all.
JAMES 1:5 GNT

> *To the one who pleases him God has given wisdom and knowledge and joy.*
>
> ECCLESIASTES 2:26 ESV

Insight is more potent than eyesight. The famous singer Ray Charles had no sight, but he possessed remarkable insight. Insight enables you to see the big picture and read between the lines of the little one. It helps you take things apart to analyze, and put them together to actualize.

Hindsight shows you where you have been and foresight shows where you are going, but insight helps you understand and comprehend all the movements of life. Someone who understood this placed this bumper sticker on her car: *I brake for insights*. Insight occurs when God's wisdom comes to your mind. The gift of God's wisdom makes the path before you both clearer and brighter. You see more, you see better. Insight helps you search within so you can see ahead.

Dear God, thank you for the insight that enables me to follow you and your will for me more closely. Amen.

ARE YOU MAD?

*The Lord is merciful and gracious, slow to anger
and plenteous in mercy and loving-kindness.*
PSALM 103:8 AMP

Do you know people who are angered by the littlest things? It seems like they're always offended about something, and you're never sure how to please them.

Sometimes that kind of personality is attributed to God because of his multitude of instructions in the Bible. Yet nothing could be further

> *The LORD is like a father to his children, tender and compassionate to those who fear him. For he knows how weak we are.*
>
> PSALM 103:13–14 NLT

from the truth. God gives you rules because he loves you—not because he's easily offended. He knows a holy life will ultimately be happier and healthier for you.

God doesn't get angry as quickly or easily as people do. Rather, he always treats you with compassion and grace. So don't fear that you've made him mad. Instead, rejoice that he loves you deeply.

*God, thank you for your love, compassion, and grace.
Thank you for being patient with me and for always
forgiving me when I confess my offenses. Amen.*

COMING IN TO GO OUT

Come, see the place where the Lord lay. And go quickly
and tell His disciples that He is risen from the dead,
and indeed He is going before you into Galilee.
MATTHEW 28:6–7 NKJV

Little children, let us
not love with word or
with tongue, but in
deed and truth.

1 JOHN 3:18 NASB

The spiritual life is a coming in and a going out. When Jesus' friends went to the empty tomb to honor his memory, they were greeted by an angel who told them to *come* into the tomb where Jesus had been placed. Next, he told them to *see* that Jesus was not in the tomb anymore. Then, they were to *go* from the empty tomb into the world to *tell* the good news of the resurrection of Jesus Christ from the dead. Come in and see, go out and tell.

God wants you to have inward and outward movements. Go inside yourself to be with God, and go out to others to take God to them. Retreat to the sanctuary, and then advance to the streets where people need God.

Dear God, may I be with you in prayer and meditation
so I can be with others in love and service. Amen.

FAR ENOUGH

How far has the LORD taken our sins from us?
Farther than the distance from east to west!
PSALM 103:12 CEV

You fail and it plagues you. You make a mistake and cringe at what God must think. Other people don't let you forget your wrongdoing, so why should God?

Friend, once you confess your offenses to God and turn away from them, they're completely gone. In fact, they're the only thing about you that God will ever forget. You may remember how you've disobeyed him and

Let all that I am praise the LORD; may I never forget the good things he does for me. He forgives all my sins and heals all my diseases. He redeems me from death and crowns me with love and tender mercies.

PSALM 103:2–4 NLT

☽

may even have to face some consequences, but God forgives you completely and refuses to recall the iniquities you've committed.

East and west will never meet, and you'll never have to face your sins again. So forgive yourself and thank God that when he removes your transgressions, they're erased forever.

God, thank you for forgetting my wrongs and treating
me with mercy and grace. Thank you for your
unconditional love and unfailing forgiveness. Amen.

SPIRITUALLY CORRECT

Do not conform yourselves to the standards of this world, but let God transform you inwardly by a complete change of your mind.

ROMANS 12:2 GNT

You shall do no unrighteousness in judgment, in measures of length or weight or quantity.

LEVITICUS 19:35 AMP

☀

When you are socially correct, you use respectful words to refer to particular people and topics. You conform to a certain standard. When you are spiritually correct, you conform to God's standard. You say and do what God expects you to say and do. There are words and actions that are acceptable and unacceptable to God. There is a prescribed way to conduct yourself as a Christian. As one popular admonition phrases it, "Live so the preacher won't have to lie at your funeral."

Take the high road of word and deed. Be fair to other people. Practice honesty in all your transactions. Hold yourself to the standard God has for you. Follow God's moral compass. Do what is right. Live by God's code of conduct. And be spiritually correct.

Dear God, keep my feet on the path of what is right and good. May I be true to you and to myself. Amen.

SECOND CHANCES

The LORD has mercy on those who respect him,
as a father has mercy on his children.
PSALM 103:13 NCV

Mistakes are inevitable; everyone makes them at some time or another. Sometimes the consequences of these mistakes are far-reaching, even irreversible. You may feel you are doomed to a life of frustration and despair, enslaved by the misdeeds of the past and the shadows of yesterday. In those difficult times, you can turn for help to the God of the rainbow, the God of second chances.

He brought me up also out of an horrible pit, out of the miry clay, and set my feet upon a rock, and established my goings.

PSALM 40:2 KJV

Even when your mistakes are so devastating that you cannot return to the life you once knew, God's light can break through the threatening clouds. God can add his miraculous touch and help you to build something new.

You are the God of second chances. Grace my life with the miracle of your touch, and help me to begin again beneath the rainbow of your faithful love. Amen.

WHY YOU ARE

We are God's workmanship, created in Christ Jesus to do good works, which God prepared in advance for us to do.
EPHESIANS 2:10 NIV

We know that God is always at work for the good of everyone who loves him. They are the ones God has chosen for his purpose.

ROMANS 8:28 CEV

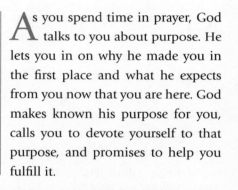

As you spend time in prayer, God talks to you about purpose. He lets you in on why he made you in the first place and what he expects from you now that you are here. God makes known his purpose for you, calls you to devote yourself to that purpose, and promises to help you fulfill it.

God has a rationale for your life that fits his will. He has a reason for your life that pleases him. He has a cause for your life that helps him get his work done. You do not live randomly or aimlessly. You live according to God's purpose for you. God has something better than a wonderful plan for your life. He has a wonderful purpose for your life.

Dear God, I am grateful for a purpose in my life that clearly comes from you. Amen.

GOD'S GREATNESS AND MAJESTY

My whole being, praise the LORD.
LORD my God, you are very great.
PSALM 104:1–2 NCV

The best way to appreciate the grandeur and glory of God is to shed your weariness and worldly wisdom and begin to see things through childlike eyes. Doing so returns to you your sense of wonder and awe. Christ said as much when he encouraged you to become as a little child, awed by life, but trusting nonetheless in God.

O Lord my God, many and many a time you have done great miracles for us, and we are ever in your thoughts. Who else can do such glorious things? No one else can be compared with you.

PSALM 40:5 TLB

God's majesty is evidenced everywhere, if you look with childlike eyes—birds fly from branch to branch, fishes swim in the sea, and stars shoot across the night sky. A child has no difficulty believing that God made all these things. When you become as a child, you will have no difficulty either.

God, help me never to become so grown up that I no longer revel in the glory of your creation or accept your unconditional love for me. Amen.

GOD KNOWS THE WAY

I am the way, the truth, and the life.
No one can come to the Father except through me.
JOHN 14:6 NLT

Whether you turn to the right or to the left, your ears will hear a voice behind you, saying, "This is the way; walk in it."

ISAIAH 30:21 NIV

Imagine riding on a train through a difficult mountain passage. A lot of things could happen to the train. At the most it could derail and bring great harm to you. At the least you might be late for an important appointment. But you are not worried because your best friend is the engineer. Everything will be all right because he knows the way to where you are going and knows how to get you there.

When you become friends with God, you develop confidence in him. You have faith that he understands where you need to go and knows how to get you there. God is in charge, and everything is all right. When you travel with God, don't worry. You won't get lost. God knows the way.

Dear God, thank you for showing me the way and going with me in it. Amen.

UNLIMITED, BREATHTAKING WISDOM

O LORD, how manifold are your works! In wisdom have you made them all; the earth is full of your creatures.
PSALM 104:24 ESV

Currently, there are an estimated nine thousand species of birds known in the world. What is more, there are more than fifteen thousand kinds of mammals, in excess of twenty-nine thousand types of fish, and more than thirty million varieties of insects.

These all wait for You, that You may give them their food in due season. . . . You open Your hand, they are filled with good. . . . May the glory of the LORD endure forever.
PSALM 104:27–28, 31 NKJV

Though these numbers are bound to increase as new discoveries are made, God knows them all and provides for their needs. Nothing is born, nothing grows, and nothing dies without God's knowledge of it. Yet there's a magnificent creature that gets God's special attention—you. He's as careful with the minutiae in your life as he was in creating the attributes that make one species different from another.

God, I'm in absolute awe of your great wisdom, understanding, and creativity. Thank you for being so profoundly involved in every area of my life. Amen.

JOY PROVES IT

I have told you these things, that My joy and delight may be in you, and that your joy and gladness may be of full measure and complete and overflowing.

JOHN 15:11 AMP

Light is sown for the righteous, and joy for the upright in heart. Rejoice in the LORD, O you righteous, and give thanks to his holy name!

PSALM 97:11–12 ESV

Joy in your life indicates you belong to God. The Queen of England's standard flies over Buckingham Palace as a sign that the queen is in residence there. Similarly, the joy you show and share is evidence that God lives in your heart. Someone asked Joseph Haydn, the famous composer, why his music was so cheerful. He replied, "I cannot make it otherwise. When I think upon God, my heart is so full of joy that the notes dance and leap from my pen."

Joy is an infallible and undeniable sign of the presence of God in your life. It indicates you have a relationship with God founded on faith and nurtured in love. Joy in your life leaves no doubt about whom you belong to.

Dear God, I celebrate a life lived in the joy of your presence and the pleasure of your company. Amen.

RULE NUMBER ONE

Seek the LORD and his strength;
seek his presence continually!
PSALM 105:4 ESV

As David wrote this psalm about Israel's journey to the Promised Land, he knew one very important thing to be true: Whenever people would turn to God and obey him, he would help them achieve victory. This was a principle that David was committed to because he'd seen God lead him to so many triumphs. That's why rule number one for you is this:

> *Sing to Him, sing praise to Him; tell about all His wonderful works! Honor His holy name; let the hearts of those who seek the LORD rejoice.*
>
> PSALM 105:2–3 HCSB

Seek God and do as he says. Not only will God guide you in your circumstances, but also you'll know him even better.

So as situations arise today—negative or positive—look to God and obey him. It's a simple rule, but it's one that will assuredly bring you joy and success.

God, help me to love you so much that I automatically
seek and obey you in every circumstance. Thank you
for showing me the way to victory. Amen.

WHAT IT MEANS

*God, who is rich in mercy, out of the great love with which
he loved us even when we were dead through our
trespasses, made us alive together with Christ.*
EPHESIANS 2:4–5 NRSV

*How great is the
love the Father has
lavished on us, that
we should be called
children of God!*

1 JOHN 3:1 NIV

Think about what it means for God to love you. Think about God in heaven loving you enough to make you the unique and wonderful person you are. Think about God coming to earth as Jesus Christ so he could get close enough to love you even more. Think about God loving you to such a degree that he walks with you every step you take in life.

God's love for you is just plain wonderful, isn't it? Nothing can bring you greater joy than the conviction that God loves you. Don't lose sight of that truth. Pound it into your mind and heart every day. The foundation of faith is God's love for you. God's love for you always comes first.

*Dear God, thank you for loving me more than
I can understand or comprehend. Amen.*

PROVISION FROM HEAVEN

He brought quail and satisfied them with bread from heaven.
He opened a rock, and water gushed out; it flowed like a
stream in the desert. For He remembered His holy promise.
PSALM 105:40–42 HCSB

Many people are tangled up in their thoughts because they have forgotten what God has promised them in the Bible. You do not have to follow the same path. God wants you to understand that his mercies are new every morning and that he will provide for you in miraculous ways as you travel through life.

He brought Israel out with silver and gold, and no one among his tribes stumbled. . . . He spread out a cloud as a protective covering and a fire to light up the night.

PSALM 105:37, 39
GOD'S WORD

One way he does so is through the Bible, which contains all the hope and wisdom you need for each day. Do not think that the Bible was written for someone else. The Bible was written for you, and the truth is just as powerful today as when it was first penned. When God promises to love, provide for, and guide you each day, he means it.

Thank you, God, that your mercies are new every day and your care for me never changes. Teach me through the Bible how to walk in your way. Amen.

MEETING JESUS

Some Greeks had gone to Jerusalem to worship during Passover.
Philip from Bethsaida in Galilee was there too. So they went
to him and said, "Sir, we would like to meet Jesus."
JOHN 12:20–21 CEV

My sheep hear my voice. I know them, and they follow me. I give them eternal life, and they will never perish. No one will snatch them out of my hand.

JOHN 10:27–28 NRSV

Some Greek philosophers came one day to a celebration in Jerusalem. They sought out one of Jesus' close associates and requested to meet with Jesus. They knew about Socrates, but they wanted to see Jesus. They knew about Aristotle and about Plato, but they wanted to see Jesus. They knew about Homer, but they wanted to see Jesus. They believed that Jesus was whom they truly needed in their lives.

You, too, will have no greater encounter than a meeting with Jesus. No coming together with anybody else measures up. Think of the celebrity you'd most like to meet, and compare that to meeting Jesus. There is no comparison. When you are ready to meet Jesus, he is ready to meet you.

Lord Jesus, I will meet you today in many places.
You will be there with me. Amen.

BELIEVING THE BIBLE

He saved them for his name's sake, that he might make known his mighty power. . . . Then they believed his words; they sang his praise.
PSALM 106:8, 12 ESV

Perhaps you've wondered: *What if I make the wrong choice? What if I make a terrible mistake?* You have stayed awake at night pondering the right way to handle some difficult decision, and you are fraught with anxiety.

God knows all that you are facing, and he knows how you should handle the situation. Will he help you with the decision that you need to make? Will he show you how to make the right choice? The answer is yes, when you ask him to show you what is best and you believe him. He may speak to you through the Bible or through a trusted Christian friend. Listen for his answer to your prayers, and be confident that he will lead you in the right way.

> *Hallelujah! Give thanks to the LORD, for He is good; His faithful love endures forever. Who can declare the LORD's mighty acts or proclaim all the praise due Him?*
> PSALM 106:1–2 HCSB

God, I greatly admire your power. I am amazed how you never become weary or tired of teaching me how to live each day. I believe you, God. Lead me. Amen.

YOU KNOW THE NAME

To the church of God which is at Corinth, to those who are sanctified in Christ Jesus, called to be saints, with all who in every place call on the name of Jesus Christ our Lord.

1 CORINTHIANS 1:2 NKJV

Through [Jesus], therefore, let us constantly and at all times offer up to God a sacrifice of praise, which is the fruit of lips that thankfully acknowledge and confess and glorify His name.

HEBREWS 13:15 AMP

A woman sat behind the driver on a sightseeing bus in the Detroit area. "On the right is the Dodge mansion," said the driver. "John Dodge?" inquired the woman. "No, Horace Dodge," the driver corrected. A few minutes later, the driver said, "The house on the left is the Ford home." The woman asked, "Henry Ford?" The driver replied, "No, Edsel Ford."

Another few blocks and the driver called out, "On the left is Christ Church, the largest church in the city." After a couple of minutes, a passenger nudged the woman and said, "Go ahead, lady, you can't be wrong all the time." You can count on the name of Jesus. The name of Jesus in your life brings purpose, power, and peace.

Dear God, thank you for the name of Jesus in my heart and in my life. There is no greater name. Amen.

GOD SATISFIES THE SOUL

*He satisfies the longing soul, and fills
the hungry soul with goodness.*
PSALM 107:9 NKJV

Holidays and special occasions are universally celebrated by feasting. Imagine a birthday party without cake, the Fourth of July without watermelon, Thanksgiving without pumpkin pie. Sharing food around a table bonds people together, and "Pass the peas, please" branches into warm and meaningful conversation. The sharing of food leads to the sharing of words and the sharing of hearts.

*I have trusted in thy
mercy; my heart shall
rejoice in thy salvation.
I will sing unto the
LORD, because he hath
dealt bountifully
with me.*
PSALM 13:5–6 KJV

In the same way, when you feast on the goodness of God, which you can do as often as you like, your soul-hunger is satisfied in a way that nothing else can match. Out of that fullness comes a desire to feed others with the blessings God has showered on you. When you give out of your abundance, you are filled even more.

*At every meal, God, I am reminded of the many ways
you feed my heart. Thank you for the other kind of bread,
the kind with which you nourish my very being. Amen.*

WATCH JESUS PRAY

I pray for these followers, but I am also praying for all those who will believe in me because of their teaching.

JOHN 17:20 NCV

You will call upon me and come and pray to me, and I will listen to you. You will seek me and find me when you seek me with all your heart.

JEREMIAH 29:12–13 NIV

As you develop your own prayer life, consider the prayer life of Jesus. The Bible records the words of five of Jesus' prayers and shows him praying on nineteen different occasions. Jesus called on the power of prayer for what God wanted him to say and do.

Jesus began his day in prayer. When you begin your day in prayer, you get it started in the right direction. You connect to God as a power source for your daily encounters and experiences. You take God with you into your relationships and transactions. Starting your day in prayer is the best way to have a good one. Jesus began his ministry at the Jordan with prayer and ended it on the cross with prayer.

*Dear God, as I watch Jesus pray
I learn how to talk to you. Amen.*

548

OUT OF TROUBLE

They cried to the Lord in their trouble, and he saved them
from their distress. He brought them out of darkness and
the deepest gloom and broke away their chains.
PSALM 107:13–14 NIV

Have you ever felt like giving up? Most people have. The truth is, if you live long enough, you will battle thoughts of discouragement, but you do not have to give in to them. There is hope even when the landscape of your life appears dark and stormy. The psalmist cried out to God, and he was saved from his distress.

By the power of his own word, he healed you and saved you from destruction.

PSALM 107:20 CEV

What was the key to his turnaround? He acknowledged his situation to God and proclaimed his faith in God. Instead of being "me focused," he was God focused. When you are tempted to keep going, pushing to resolve a difficult issue—stop. Go to God in prayer and cry out to him. You will find that clouds of disheartenment quickly evaporate in his presence.

God, I know there are times when I have not trusted
you fully and have been discouraged because of it.
Forgive me, God, and help me to have hope in you. Amen.

MORE ABOUT JESUS

*Then we will be mature, just as Christ is,
and we will be completely like him.*
EPHESIANS 4:13 CEV

Leaving the elementary teaching about the Christ, let us press on to maturity.

HEBREWS 6:1 NASB

A wonderful old hymn—"More About Jesus Would I Know"—sings its way into your heart and invites you to grow and mature in your relationship with Jesus. Its words speak of advancement, escalation, and increase.

The time you spend with God provides an opportunity to develop your spiritual life. It invites you forward to larger places of understanding and awareness. Time spent with God is time well spent because it shows you more of who God is and what God can do in your life. Time spent with God brings you closer to him and him nearer to you. The largest room in your spiritual life and journey is the room for improvement in your relationship with God.

Dear God, may I always be moving up and onward toward your grace and call. Amen.

HIS HEALING WORD

He sent His word and healed them, and
delivered them from their destructions.
PSALM 107:20 NASB

The heart is a strange thing—it seems like nothing can heal it and there are no words for the depth of it.

You were in serious trouble, but you prayed to the LORD, and he rescued you. He brought you out of the deepest darkness and broke your chains.

PSALM 107:13–14 CEV

Yet when you read the Bible, somehow your heart is always helped. You continually find messages of encouragement that your heart drinks in the way a desert traveler gulps down water. So why is God's Word different from other things you read? Friend, through the Bible, God not only speaks to your mind, but also to your heart, soul, and spirit. His truth heals you.

Yes, the Bible is different from other reading materials because it's a balm to your spirit. So take a healthy dose—you'll feel better in no time.

God, grow my love for your Word and heal me with it. Thank you for speaking to my mind, heart, soul, and spirit with your truth. Amen.

SOUND OF SANDALED FEET

So it was, while they conversed and reasoned,
that Jesus Himself drew near and went with them.
LUKE 24:15 NKJV

Strolling along, he saw Levi, son of Alphaeus, at his work collecting taxes. Jesus said, "Come along with me." He came.

MARK 2:14 MSG

☀

Jesus pulled up next to people and walked with them. He did it with Matthew at the tax office, Peter and his fishing partners along the sea, the women from Galilee who worked and traveled on his behalf. He walked with Zacchaeus to his house for supper. After Jesus was raised from the dead, he put his stride next to two people walking from Jerusalem to Emmaus. They heard the sound of sandaled feet.

You know Jesus' presence when you give him permission to live in your heart. You know he is there to begin and end each day with you. You are aware of his touch in all aspects of your life. Jesus came into history and stayed. He is with you now.

Dear God, you are always ready to come and make your presence known to me. Amen.

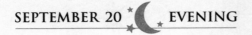
CALM

He made the storm stop and the sea be quiet.
PSALM 107:29 CEV

Your heart roars wildly in your chest, like a flag flapping violently on a turbulent day. Chaos surrounds you. There's no time to think—just react to the tornado of troubles that hit.

There's only one to cling to because only God can quiet this tumultuous maelstrom.

So friend, pray. Repeat to yourself the things you know: God loves you

They were glad when it grew calm, and he guided them to their desired haven. Let them give thanks to the Lord for his unfailing love and his wonderful deeds for men.

PSALM 107:30–31 NIV

and can handle this situation. God is in control and will help you. He has never let you down, and he never will. The tempest may not pass immediately, but he'll infuse you with his wonderful peace and empower you with his strength. Then you'll know what it is to have calm in the midst of the storm.

God, I need your calming voice in my troubles. Please help me. I will praise you because you give me your peace and strength. Amen.

GO HIS WAY

Jesus said to him, "Go your way; your faith has made you well." And immediately he recovered his sight and followed him on the way.
MARK 10:52 ESV

He had been taught about the way of the Lord and was always very excited when he spoke and taught the truth about Jesus.
ACTS 18:25 NCV

Jesus told the previously blind Bartimaeus to get on his way. Go home, get back to where you were. Bartimaeus didn't go home. He went with Jesus. That's because he understood that Jesus' way was also his way. He knew that when he was with Jesus he was truly at home. Having felt God's healing touch on his eyes, he used his sight to see where Jesus was going so he could follow him there.

You belong with Jesus. That is where you are most at home. That is where life makes more sense, agendas are clearer, power and strength more available. The best way for you to go is the way of Jesus. When you go the way of Jesus, everything is brighter and better.

Dear God, open my ears so I may hear when you come near to lead me in your way. Amen.

YOUR HAVEN IN HIM

They were happy that it was quiet,
and God guided them to the port they wanted.
PSALM 107:30 NCV

One of the irresistible things about God is how he often gives you the desires of your heart. When your life is fully committed to him, he blesses you. This is because the closer you are to him, the more you realize the things of the world are unworthy of your attention. Rather, you want to enjoy his pleasures. You will also notice that the more you surrender your life to him, the more you sense his personal care for you. You experience his blessings in a new way, and may even begin to wonder what you have done to receive so much from him.

He hushes the storm to a calm and to a gentle whisper, so that the waves of the sea are still.

PSALM 107:29 AMP

That is the way he is—God gives good things to his children. When your life is committed to him, he provides for every need you have and much more.

> *God, I want to know you better—not just so I can receive*
> *your good gifts, but also so I can truly know and enjoy*
> *you more. You are my peaceful place of refuge. Amen.*

JESUS PRAYS FOR YOU

He is always living to make petition to God and intercede with Him and intervene for them.
HEBREWS 7:25 AMP

After [Jesus] had sent them away, he went by himself up into the hills to pray. It was late, and Jesus was there alone.

MATTHEW 14:23 NCV

✵

Close your eyes and imagine Jesus on his knees praying for you. His lips move, and it is your name he speaks. He talks about your tasks, relationships, and needs. He knows who you are. Jesus prays that your sickness will be healed, your hurt assuaged, and your brokenness mended.

As he prays for you, Jesus commends your desire and compliments your effort. He applauds your accomplishments and achievements. He speaks of your dreams and asks that you have the courage to pursue them. Jesus sets his heart on what is best for you and prays that you be immensely blessed.

The Bible says praying for you is so important to Jesus that he lives in order to do it.

Nothing strengthens me more, dear God, than to perceive that Jesus is on his knees praying for me. Amen.

DESERT STREAMS

He turns a desert into pools of water,
a parched land into springs of water.

PSALM 107:35 NRSV

On your journey, you sometimes pass through desert areas filled with nothing but uninviting cacti and sun-scorched sands as far as the eye can see—seemingly barren wastelands on the landscape of your life. What you do not see so easily is that the desert is teeming with robust life. Underground streams support a variety of hearty vegetation and lively creatures. God has not lessened the intensity of the sun's rays for their benefit. The sun shines on, but God has equipped the desert's flora and fauna to withstand the extremities of their home.

O God, thou art my God; early will I seek thee: my soul thirsteth for thee, my flesh longeth for thee in a dry and thirsty land, where no water is.

PSALM 63:1 KJV

You pass through dry, parched areas in your journey through life. When you do, you must remember that God will faithfully provide for you, just as he has for the plants and creatures of the desert.

God, when I need streams in the deserts of my life, I will place my hope in your faithfulness and love for me. Amen.

UNDER SAME MANAGEMENT

Jesus Christ is the same yesterday, today, and forever.
HEBREWS 13:8 NLT

[God] who began a good work in you will carry it on to completion until the day of Christ Jesus.

PHILIPPIANS 1:6 NIV

Spending time with God underlines his constancy in your life. When you meet God on a regular basis, you feel the strong thread of his presence weaving itself through the fabric of your efforts and endeavors. Your sense of his being with you and for you does not come and go. It comes and stays.

God's constancy enables you to make good decisions because you know you can count on his help with what you decide. It gives you courage of conviction because you are assured God will be with you as you respond to what you believe. With God at your side, you have a lifelong supply of confidence. God never goes away. He is with you to stay.

Dear God, you are my constant companion. You are with me all the time everywhere I am. Amen.

A BOUNTIFUL CROP

They sowed fields and planted vineyards that yielded a fruitful harvest; he blessed them, and their numbers greatly increased, and he did not let their herds diminish.

PSALM 107:37 NIV

American writer George Grant wrote a letter home to his wife about what he called "one of London's most delightful gardens" nestled within the tiny churchyard of Saint Mary's parish. Most intriguing of all was a bronze plaque in one corner that declared a good theology would invariably produce a good garden.

Every one of these depends on you to give them daily food. You supply it, and they gather it. You open wide your hand to feed them and they are satisfied with all your bountiful provision.

PSALM 104:27–28 TLB

☾

Grant later realized that the words conveyed a scriptural worldview: a solid theology always takes into consideration the link between the profound and the ordinary. Indeed, the spiritual results are bountiful.

Thank you, God, for the accomplishments of small beginnings. Thank you for great journeys from first steps and large harvests from tiny seeds. Amen.

WHAT FAITH SEES

[Jesus said,] "If you have faith and don't doubt, I promise that you can do what I did to this tree. And you will be able to do even more. You can tell this mountain to get up and jump into the sea, and it will."

MATTHEW 21:21 CEV

I have been crucified with Christ; and it is no longer I who live, but Christ lives in me; and the life which I now live in the flesh I live by faith in the Son of God, who loved me and gave Himself up for me.

GALATIANS 2:20 NASB

✳

Faith helps you see more than you think you can. Faith makes you a visionary. It puts concepts and precepts in your mind by which you can build your life beyond what you thought possible. Faith enables you to look farther than you can see and see more than you thought you could.

By faith, Thomas Edison saw light in the darkness. By faith, the Wright brothers saw a way for humans to fly. By faith, Martin Luther King Jr. saw a road to freedom and equality that was hidden to others. By faith, you stare up the steps until you have the courage to step up the stairs. What you see in your mind and heart is what you get in your life.

Dear God, I praise you for letting me hear what you hear and see what you see. Amen.

GOD REVEALS HIMSELF IN YOUR DAILY LIFE

Those who are wise will take all this to heart: They will see in our history the faithful love of the LORD.
PSALM 107:43 NLT

Although you sometimes feel that you are alone and he is far away, God is not a distant power. He is an active presence in your life. When you develop the habit of reading the tone and incidents of your days as if he shaped them, you gain insight into how to draw closer to him.

I remember the days of old, I think about all your deeds, I meditate on the work of your hands.
PSALM 143:5 NRSV

Things don't just happen. Those things you may call "accidents," "surprises," or "discoveries" are actually revelations of God's love and constant concern for you. If you keep your faith and trust in God, the meaning of these things will become clear. When you expect each new day to reveal the glory, power, and love of God, your hours will be filled with joy and awe. His mystery will lead you toward him.

God, help me see your hand in all the events of my life. I know you are with me, giving my life meaning and purpose. Amen.

FOLLOW THE LEADER

*You are blessed, because you see with your
eyes and hear with your ears.*
MATTHEW 13:16 NCV

*Turning to the disciples
[Jesus] said privately,
"Blessed are the eyes
that see what you see!"*

LUKE 10:23 ESV

Several years ago, an advertisement showed a symphony orchestra with the eyes of every musician focused on the conductor. No one was looking anywhere else. The caption on the advertisement said: "The eternal importance of a leader." The advertising company was selling a series of books on management and wanted to make an impression about the importance of leadership.

Your quiet time with God helps you keep your eyes on Jesus. You can see more clearly in him your call and purpose. You can take from him cues and signs that direct you to God's will for your life. Jesus is your leader. Follow him closely. When your eyes are on Jesus, you know where to go and what to do.

*I put my eyes on you, dear Lord, and keep them
there so I might follow where you lead. Amen.*

A STEADFAST HEART

My heart is steadfast, O God;
I will sing and make music with all my soul.
PSALM 108:1–2 NIV

Tomorrow, plan to take time before daily responsibilities demand your attention. Stand on your porch with eyes lifted to the trees and you can easily see why the psalmist chose to "awaken the dawn." Breezes are blowing, colors are varied and vibrant, and life is stirring all around you. Song is filling the air—birds are singing, cicadas are shrilling, crickets are chirping. Do

Birds build their
nests nearby and
sing in the trees.
From your home
above you send
rain on the
hills and water
the earth.
PSALM 104:12–13 CEV

☆🌙

these creatures know instinctively that God put music in their bodies? Do they make melody to him?

Whether you choose to sing aloud your own song to God or to praise him in silence from your heart, God can hear and enjoy the music of a happy soul that is unwavering and resolute in him. Sing and make joyous music to your God.

Dear God, help me always to rejoice
in the melody you put in my heart. Amen.

OPEN EVERY DOOR

[Pray] that God will open up to us a door for the word,
so that we may speak forth the mystery of Christ.
COLOSSIANS 4:3 NASB

I have set before you
an open door, and no
one can shut it.

REVELATION 3:8 NKJV

Listen for the knock of opportunity on the door of life. God sends opportunity because he loves you and wants the best for you. You are his child and he will provide you with occasions to do well. He has many wonderful places for you to be, and he will provide you the means to get to them.

Open every door on which you hear a knock because behind each door is a fresh possibility. Wayne Gretzky, the great hockey player, said that "you miss one hundred percent of the shots you don't take." The best way to live your life fully is to be ready, when opportunity knocks, to open the door and enter the room. God sends opportunity to knock on your door.

Dear God, when you open a door, no room is small.
Thank you for all my opportunities. Amen.

YOU CANNOT IMAGINE

Your love reaches higher than the heavens,
and your loyalty extends beyond the clouds.
PSALM 108:4 CEV

Think of the person you love most—the person you'd do anything for. Examine the depth of your love for him or her. Do you love that person more than you love yourself? Perhaps the one you love deepest is you.

Answer us and save us by your power so the people you love will be rescued.

PSALM 108:6 NCV

Please understand that any love you could feel for another—or even for yourself—pales in comparison to the love of God. There's a limit to your love, but God's is unlimited. There are conditions to your love, but God's is unconditional. God's love is so vast, noble, and astounding that it's on a completely different level.

You cannot imagine how amazingly powerful and profound God's love is for you. So then rejoice that nothing can ever separate you from it.

God, I can't figure out or measure your love, but I can thank you
for it. Help me to trust the height and depth of it. Amen.

GET YOUR FAITH LIFTED

*When Jesus heard this, he was astonished and said to those
following him, "I tell you the truth, I have not found
anyone in Israel with such great faith."*

MATTHEW 8:10 NIV

*You have accepted
Christ Jesus as your
Lord. Now keep on
following him. Plant
your roots in Christ
and let him be the
foundation for your life.
Be strong in your faith,
just as you were taught.
And be grateful.*

COLOSSIANS 2:6–7 CEV

When Jesus commended the soldier for his great trust, he was making a faith comparison. By applauding the military commander for believing his servant could be healed, Jesus was saying that some people have more faith than others do. To increase your faith, spend time with God and draw close to him.

The important thing in faith development is not to compare where you are to others but to compare it with yourself. Where are you now in comparison to where you were before? Is your faith being lifted to a higher level? In your faith, be superior to your previous self. In your Christian life, have a faith that regularly increases and steadily rises. Your faith increases as you focus more and more on who God is to you.

*Dear God, thank you that I do not have to stay where I
am in my faith. I can go deeper and rise higher. Amen.*

LISTEN EXPECTANTLY

God spoke in holy splendor.
PSALM 108:7 MSG

Have you ever prayed for God to meet a need in a certain way but the answer did not come immediately? You continued to seek his will, but it appeared that he was silent about the matter.

> *With God we will gain the victory.*
> PSALM 108:13 NIV

God is always at work. However, you may not see the many ways he is orchestrating the blessings he sends. How should you wait for your prayers to be answered? One of the best ways is to wait with confident expectation, knowing that he is the God of the universe and that he is intimately involved in your life.

Never be quick to jump ahead of him. Waiting with patience and with hopeful expectation of his provision is a demonstration of your faith in his ability to meet every need you have.

God, I proclaim my faith in you. You set the heavens and the earth in place, and I know you will meet every need I have with your great power and wisdom. Amen.

PRAYER POWER

Confess your sins to one another and pray for one another, so that you will be healed. The prayer of a good person has a powerful effect.

JAMES 5:16 GNT

The Lord is far from the wicked, but He hears the prayer of the [consistently] righteous.

PROVERBS 15:29 AMP

Prayer changes things. Prayer has power. When John Knox got on his knees to pray, the queen feared his prayers more than she did all the armies of Scotland. When John Wesley prayed, life-changing renewal came to England. When Jonathan Edwards said his fervent prayers, a great revival spread throughout the American colonies. Repeatedly, history relates and records the wonderful and magnificent power of prayer.

Your prayers have power. God works through praying people. He makes his way known to those who submit themselves prayerfully to him. He accomplishes his purposes through those who offer their urgent and sincere prayers to him. God sends your prayers out with power to affect, change, and bless. On every day and in every hour, your prayers have power.

Dear God, I believe that you give your power to my prayers. Amen.

OTHER PEOPLE'S FAILINGS

In return for my love they accuse me,
but I continue to pray.
PSALM 109:4 HCSB

Whenever someone hurts you, you can choose to take one of two paths. The first is the road of bitterness. You ruminate on their wounding words and actions until they paralyze your heart.

The second is the road of blessing. This option leads you to God, to whom you release their cruelty against you. You realize that God has forgiven you of the wrongs you've done, and to be like him you must forgive them. This path brings you closer to God and develops his character within you.

People's failings can either draw you closer to God or paralyze your heart against him and others. Friend, you know the better path—so take it.

> *I will give repeated thanks to the LORD, praising him to everyone. For he stands beside the needy, ready to save them from those who condemn them.*
> PSALM 109:30–31 NLT

God, I've been harboring unforgiveness in my heart.
Please forgive me and help me forgive those who've
harmed me. Thank you for your love. Amen.

MOVE FORWARD

I run straight toward the goal in order to win the prize,
which is God's call through Christ Jesus to the life above.
PHILIPPIANS 3:14 GNT

He was looking forward to the city that has foundations, whose designer and builder is God.

HEBREWS 11:10 ESV

God accepts and loves you as you are, but he doesn't want you to stay there. God is interested in your moving forward to new places of opportunity and influence. He wants you to see what you are able to accomplish for his kingdom and for his people. He equips you with what you need to accomplish that to which he calls you.

Someone asked David Livingstone where he was prepared to go, and he replied, "Anywhere, as long as it is forward." He understood that the Christian life is one of forward movement on behalf of what God wants done in the world. Walk toward the dreams, visions, and goals God puts before you. God invites you to walk through open doors that lead to large rooms.

Dear God, in the same way that Jesus walked
out ahead of his disciples on the way to Jerusalem,
I see where you are in my life. Amen.

570

A PRIEST TO YOU ALWAYS

The LORD made a solemn promise and will not take it back: "You will be a priest forever."
PSALM 110:4 GNT

In the Old Testament, a priest would represent the people before God, teach them about him, and offer sacrifices for their sins. Unfortunately, earthly priests were restricted in what they could do, and their sacrifices were only temporary.

Yet Psalm 110 speaks of the great High Priest who isn't limited in saving his people—that's Jesus. When Jesus came, he not only became the flawless, everlasting sacrifice for your offenses, he became your eternal High Priest. He constantly teaches you about God, and he prepares you to be close to God. Jesus is your High Priest forever, and he's ideal for the job. Trust him with your deepest needs because he'll always represent you perfectly.

The LORD (God) says to my Lord (the Messiah), Sit at My right hand. . . . Your people will offer themselves willingly in the day of Your power, in the beauty of holiness.
PSALM 110:1, 3 AMP

God, I thank you that Jesus is my High Priest—that Jesus reconciles me to you and forgives me of my offenses. Truly, Jesus is worthy of praise! Amen.

THE CHALLENGE OF IT ALL

Because the Sovereign LORD helps me, I will not be
disgraced. Therefore have I set my face like flint,
and I know I will not be put to shame.
ISAIAH 50:7 NIV

Commit your way to
the Lord . . . trust
(lean on, rely on, and
be confident) also in
Him and He will bring
it to pass. And He will
make your uprightness
and right standing
with God go forth as
the light, and your
justice and right as
[the shining sun
of] the noonday.

PSALM 37:5–6 AMP

☀

Leave your comfort zone and move out into new territory on behalf of God's kingdom. You grow in Christ when you do something for God beyond what you've already mastered. You sense God's presence with you in personal and intimate ways.

When you attempt something difficult for God, you discover God's resources. For instance, if you make a witness speech in church even though that makes you uncomfortable, you discover abilities previously unknown to you. It is not necessary to wait until you think you are ready to do something for God. Do it, and God will make you ready. Nobody would have heard of Saint George if he had slain a dragonfly instead of a dragon.

Dear God, disturb me when I am too pleased
with what I do for you. Amen.

IN GOD'S PRESENCE

The Lord is beside you to help you.
PSALM 110:5 NCV

There is never a time when you are not with God. He is infinitely aware of your every move, thought, desire, and request. Still, one of the greatest joys you can ever experience is being in God's presence—those special moments when he seems closer, when the answers you receive from him

Your people will join you on your day of battle. You have been dressed in holiness from birth; you have the freshness of a child.

PSALM 110:3 NCV

profoundly affect you. In times like this, you feel as if you are sitting at God's feet, listening to his every word with a heart of intense devotion and peace.

The psalmist learned that there was joy, wisdom, and strength to be gained by drawing near to God. Have you experienced the wonder of his presence? Have you opened your heart to his eternal love? There is no better place to be.

God, I am listening. Help me to experience your awesome presence and mold my life into a vessel of honor that will draw others to you in a personal way. Amen.

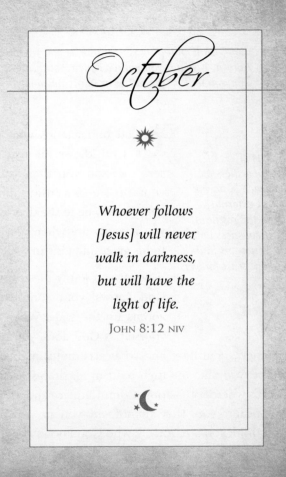

October

*Whoever follows
[Jesus] will never
walk in darkness,
but will have the
light of life.*

JOHN 8:12 NIV

WHO YOU ARE

*What's more, I am changing your name. It will no longer be
Abram. Instead, you will be called Abraham,
for you will be the father of many nations.*
GENESIS 17:5 NLT

*The effect of
righteousness will
be peace [internal
and external],
and the result of
righteousness will
be quietness and
confident trust forever.*

ISAIAH 32:17 AMP

God understands who you are. God knows the real you. He sees more in you than you see in yourself. He sees inside the person you seem to be to the depths of who you actually are when you respond to his grace and gifts in your life.

When you know the real you that God knows, your confidence level zooms up the scale. When you see yourself as God does, you recognize what strengths you have and what accomplishments you are capable of. You take the high road in all things because you know that's where you belong. Commonplace and ordinary no longer appeal to you. They are not who you are. You are more than you think you are. You are who God knows you to be.

Dear God, give me the ability to see myself as you see me. Amen.

TO BE WISE

Respect and obey the LORD! This is the first step to wisdom and good sense. God will always be respected.
PSALM 111:10 CEV

There are some people who are quite scholarly—they read all of the most prestigious journals and can thoroughly bewilder you with their lofty words and theories. They seem to know everything. However, for all their knowledge, they don't always act in the wisest ways. Yet there's great wisdom in this psalm, which declares we are to respect and obey God. After all, he really does know everything and never steers you wrong.

I will praise the LORD with my whole heart, in the assembly of the upright and in the congregation. The works of the LORD are great, studied by all who have pleasure in them.
PSALM 111:1–2 NKJV

The basis of wisdom is to realize you don't know it all, but you do know the One who does. So to be wise, follow him. In the end, all the other sources of knowledge will pass away, but he will remain.

God, I don't know it all, but I'm thankful that you do. Help me to respect and obey you so I can have true wisdom. Amen.

DON'T MISS IT

People do not live by bread alone, but by every
word that comes from the mouth of God.
MATTHEW 4:4 NLT

The thing you should
want most is God's
kingdom and doing
what God wants. Then
all these other things
you need will be
given to you.

MATTHEW 6:33 NCV

Jenny Lind was a talented opera
singer known as the Swedish
Nightingale. She performed all over
the world and toured the United
States in the 1850s under the
management of P. T. Barnum. She
thrilled thousands.

Surprising everyone, Jenny Lind retired at the pinnacle of her career to
live in quiet seclusion with her hus-
band. She never returned to the stage. A friend went to visit her
and found Jenny Lind on the beach with a Bible on her lap. Her
eyes were focused on a sunset. When asked why she had retired
so early, she pointed to the Bible and said, "Because every day
made me forget this." Then she pointed to the sunset. "And
that." Nothing in life is as important and precious as your appreciation of God.

Dear God, I appreciate the many and creative
ways in which you are known to me. Amen.

LIGHT ALWAYS COMES

Even in darkness light dawns for the upright, for the gracious and compassionate and righteous man.

PSALM 112:4 NIV

There's fear in the unknown: how you'll pay your bills or reconcile that relationship; whether or not you'll recover from this illness or overcome that obstacle. As if darkness covers your view, you cannot see what's ahead—or why this is happening to you.

He will never be shaken. The righteous will be remembered forever. He will not fear bad news; his heart is confident, trusting in the LORD.

PSALM 112:6–7 HCSB

Yet when you look to God, he sheds light on your situation. He'll not only give you assurance of his help, but more important, he'll show you the good that can come from your difficulties if you'll only focus on him.

Friend, no matter how dark and confusing your situation, God can illuminate it. So trust in him with all your heart and you'll be sure to see the light.

God, I need wisdom and understanding in this dark situation. Thank you for shedding light on it and showing me the good that'll come of it. Amen.

KNOW WHAT'S COMING

*God raised the Lord from death, and
he will also raise us by his power.*
1 CORINTHIANS 6:14 GNT

*You are from God and
have overcome them,
for he who is in you is
greater than he who
is in the world.*

1 JOHN 4:4 ESV

When you get to know God, you come to trust his power in your life. When disappointment pulls a cloud over your heart, you know God is able to bring you again to a clear and bright day. When you fail at something you were determined to achieve, you know God is able to move you forward in hope and confidence. Whatever happens, you know God is with you to help you.

When you are certain of God's help, you can face anything. When you know God's power is your strength, you can stand anything. You can fall and not despair because you know God will lift you up. God, who raised Jesus from the dead, brings you the victory of new life every day.

*Dear God, thank you for coming to
me when I need you most. Amen.*

NOTHING TO FEAR

Good people will always be remembered. They won't be afraid of bad news; their hearts are steady because they trust the LORD. They are confident and will not be afraid.

PSALM 112:6–8 NCV

When your life is committed to Jesus Christ, you have nothing to fear. Though you face disappointment and hardship, the one thing that never changes is God's love for you. Difficulty comes, but you can be certain that he will never fail you. Why does the opposite seem true at times? Often because the last thing you want to do is deal with the serious problems that confront you. However, God uses adversity to prepare you for greater blessings. He stretches your faith in him—not to harm you, but to teach you to draw near to him.

Light shines in the darkness for the upright. He is gracious, compassionate, and righteous.

PSALM 112:4 HCSB

Your trials can make you bitter or better. Set your heart on becoming better by drawing near to God. Determine to stay courageous by focusing on him.

God, I know the only way I can know you better is by allowing you to teach me what is right. Please give me the strength and courage to follow you always. Amen.

GLOW AS YOU GO

*It came about when Moses was coming down from
Mount Sinai . . . that Moses did not know that the skin
of his face shone because of his speaking with Him.*

EXODUS 34:29 NASB

*There in front of his
disciples, Jesus was
completely changed.
His face was shining
like the sun, and
his clothes became
white as light.*

MATTHEW 17:2 CEV

God's glory shines through you, and you are a joyous reflection of his splendor and character. As Michael Caine said of his profession, "A bad actor is a picture. A good actor is a reflection." You are God's reflection.

Stand outside on a clear night and watch the moon illuminate an entire landscape. By its light you can see all around and know what is there and what isn't. Yet the moon has no light of its own. It reflects the brightness of the sun. It mirrors the light the sun makes. You reflect the glory that comes from God. He is the source of all light and life.

*Dear God, put your glory on me and
help me to show it to others. Amen.*

NOT PERMANENT

He lifts the poor from the dust and the needy from the garbage dump.
He sets them among princes, even the princes of his own people!
PSALM 113:7–8 NLT

One of the worst things about a hopeless situation is just that—it lacks any hope. You can't see any evidence that things will ever get better. The same difficulty dogs you incessantly, wearing you down without any apparent possibility of reprieve.

Blessed be the name of the LORD from this time forth and forevermore! From the rising of the sun to its going down the LORD's name is to be praised.
PSALM 113:2–3 NKJV

Friend, the worst thing you can do is to assume your bad situation will never change—that it's beyond God's reach to improve. Yet your life can be transformed in an instant. From one moment to the next, God can lift you out of your bad circumstances.

Your situation is not permanent, but the love and grace of God is! So follow him. And praise God that he's going to transform your life for good.

God, thank you that this situation will not last forever,
but your goodness to me does. I praise you for
being my hope in every situation. Amen.

WORSHIP IS RESPONSE

GOD passed in front of him and called out, "GOD, GOD, a God of mercy and grace, endlessly patient—so much love, so deeply true."
EXODUS 34:6 MSG

Since we are receiving a Kingdom that is unshakable, let us be thankful and please God by worshiping him with holy fear and awe.

HEBREWS 12:28 NLT

Hearing the word that God had spoken about himself, Moses bowed his head, bent his knee, and worshiped the one who had shown his presence. Your response to God's awesome presence is worship. Worship is the only reasonable response when you begin to know God.

Worship is an offering of your life to God in response to his life in you. When Nehemiah asked Ezra to read holy Scripture, the people responded by bowing low and worshiping God with their faces to the ground. The truth of God in their minds and hearts led them to bow their knees in worship. Worship is a response to who God is to you and what he does in your life.

When God passed in front of Moses, God chose to talk about his incredible mercy, his infinite patience, and his awesome love. How can we help but respond to "so much love, so deeply true" in our worship?

Dear God, when I consider all you are to me,
I worship and exalt your holy name. Amen.

FROM BARREN TO FRUITFUL

*He grants the barren woman a home, like a joyful
mother of children. Praise the LORD!*
PSALM 113:9 NKJV

Rejoice that God always provides exactly what you need. Even if you long for children, but haven't had any, don't fret. God has a marvelous plan for you. It all hinges on maintaining the right attitude. Set a goal to become involved in the lives of others—especially young people, who will remember you as a godly role model.

*He raises the poor
from the dust; he lifts
the needy from their
misery and makes
them companions
of princes.*

PSALM 113:7–8 GNT

Years ago a young woman established a school for students who didn't have the financial ability to attend college. She believed all students should become all God wanted them to be. Years later students continue to remember this woman's commitment to their future. While she never had children of her own, there is an army of young people who saw her as a caring and godly surrogate mother. She was exactly what they needed, just as you can be.

*God, there are times when I doubt your purpose, especially
when it involves my desires. Give me insight into your
will so I can rejoice in all you have given me. Amen.*

585

WHY YOU DO IT

Martha was distracted with all her preparations; and she came up to Him and said, "Lord, do You not care that my sister has left me to do all the serving alone?"
LUKE 10:40 NASB

Everything comes from him; everything happens through him; everything ends up in him. Always glory! Always praise! Yes. Yes. Yes.

ROMANS 11:36 MSG

Jesus went to the Bethany home of Mary, Martha, and Lazarus for dinner. Martha was in charge of preparing the meal, and she wanted everything to be perfect. She spent time deciding what would be on the menu. She made certain she had all the necessary ingredients. She prepared the food with care, concern, and precision. She served it on a table creatively set according to the highest protocol. Imagine her shock when Jesus suggested she'd done it all for the wrong reason.

When you do something for God, remember that you are doing it for him. Remember why you do it. You do it to honor and glorify God. You do it to make his name known. Do the work of God for the sake of God.

Dear God, may everything I do for you be done on behalf of your glory. Amen.

THE EARTH'S TRUE MASTER

Tremble, O earth, at the presence of the Lord.
PSALM 114:7 ESV

The earth is full of the glory of God—his absolute majesty inhabits every corner. Nothing you face today can or will change this truth—no heartache, no sorrow, and no disappointment. This may be a fallen world, one that has been tainted by sin, but soon God will return in power and might. He will restore all that has been broken.

God brought his people out of Egypt. . . . When the sea looked at God, it ran away, and the Jordan River flowed upstream.

PSALM 114:1, 3 CEV

Every created thing is subject to his command because he is the Maker and King of all that exists. So regardless of how disjointed life seems, remember he is greater than all you fear. You can rest in his presence and find all the goodness, love, mercy, gentleness, kindness, and blessing you need. The sovereign God of the universe watches over you.

God, forgive me for becoming so concerned about my problems and fearful of earthly threats. Your love is awesome; teach me to worship only You. Amen.

LET THEM KNOW

*While there, he encouraged the believers
in all the towns he passed through.*
ACTS 20:2 NLT

*Joseph . . . whom
the apostles called
Barnabas (which
means "One who
Encourages"), sold a
field he owned, brought
the money, and turned
it over to the apostles.*

ACTS 4:36–37 GNT

Perhaps the deepest human need is the need to be appreciated. Love the people God gives you, and let them know you love them. Affirm who they are. Encourage who they can become. Give them your backing. Be generous with tokens of appreciation. Be slow to correct and quick to praise. Treat people as ends in themselves, not as means to an end.

Make someone's day by sending him or her a little note of appreciation. Call someone on the phone and speak of your affection. Send an e-mail that supports someone. Because of what you say, people feel better about their lives and live more confidently. Your words of encouragement put them on their feet and get them on their way. In the strength of your affirmation, people become themselves.

*Dear God, lead me to those who need encouragement.
When they are down, I will lift them up. Amen.*

ROCK TO WATER

He turned the rock into pools of water; yes,
a spring of water flowed from solid rock.
PSALM 114:8 NLT

As the Israelites fled from Egypt across the desert, they were weary and parched—yet there was no water to quench their thirst. So Moses prayed, and God instructed him to strike a particular rock with his staff. Moses obeyed the strange command, and the water flowed out. This unimaginable miracle is your encouragement today: Whatever you yearn for, don't despair when you don't see it. God will use unexpected things in your path to provide for your needs. Your responsibility is to obey his commands and trust his promises.

Earth, you will tremble, when the Lord God of Jacob comes near.

PSALM 114:7 CEV

It'll take faith, friend, but God will help you. So do as he says. He'll transform your situation in a way you could never have dreamed.

God, thank you for the reminder that you can do miracles in my situation. Lead me, and I'll follow. Thank you for your love and power. Amen.

THE DIVINE GATEKEEPER

*The LORD is thy keeper: the LORD is
thy shade upon thy right hand.*
PSALM 121:5 KJV

*The LORD shall
preserve your going
out and your coming
in from this time forth,
and even forevermore.*

PSALM 121:8 NKJV

Throughout history, gatekeepers have filled a crucial role. From their lookout, they could see who was approaching the city and determine whether that person—or group of people—should be allowed inside the city walls. They kept out and ushered in as they saw fit, all with the best interests of the city's inhabitants in mind.

Your step becomes sure when you know that God is your gatekeeper—the one who allows you to come and go in safety. He allows you to pass through. It's comforting to know that this same gatekeeper also bars your entry to any place that might bring you harm. He knows when to open doors and when to close them. With God as your gatekeeper, you need never fear where your foot may fall.

*I praise you, God, that you are my on-time God. You come exactly
when I need you, even when I don't know I need you. Amen.*

GETTING OVER YOURSELF

Not for our sake, God, no, not for our sake, but for your name's sake, show your glory. Do it on account of your merciful love, do it on account of your faithful ways.

PSALM 115:1 MSG

You may be tempted to believe your life is no more than a mundane, ordinary routine. You may do your daily tasks the same way every day, and mediocrity may characterize your tiresome existence. However, you don't have to stay in a rut. God is creative. He wants you to grow beyond the boundaries you have set for yourself and experience the abundant life he created.

Our God is in heaven doing whatever he wants to do. . . . May you be blessed by GOD, by GOD, who made heaven and earth.

PSALM 115:3, 15 MSG

☆☽☆

When you see limitations, he sees gateways to new opportunities. God challenges you to view life from his perspective. Trust him to use you to encourage others and to expand your narrow limits, because there are exciting opportunities for you to enjoy when you place your faith in him.

God, help me to accept new challenges so I can grow in my faith in you. Open doors so that I can become all that you want me to be. Amen.

REAL AUTHORITY

Our God is in heaven; He does whatever He pleases.
PSALM 115:3 NKJV

Trust in the LORD, all you that worship him. He helps you and protects you. The LORD remembers us. . . . He will bless everyone who honors him, the great and the small alike.

PSALM 115:11–13 GNT

It's common to look up to those who are famous and wealthy and imitate how they behave in order to achieve what they have. Yet when you do so, you're allowing them to influence you. Do they really deserve that power?

The truth is that only God rightfully warrants that kind of authority in your life. When you focus on him and consider what behavior would please him, you're acting wisely. By studying his Word, praying for wisdom, and considering his viewpoint, you set yourself on the path to real success.

Friend, always seek God and make choices that honor him. He is the only One who's truly worthy of a say in your life.

God, please help me to understand how you would handle my situation. Please reveal yourself to me so that I can act like you. Amen.

MORE THAN YOU THINK

How sweet your words taste to me;
they are sweeter than honey.
PSALM 119:103 NLT

A faithful churchgoer had to miss the Sunday service one week. On Monday morning, he asked his neighbor for a report on church. He asked questions about the anthem, the Bible reading, the sermon. To each question, she replied, "I don't remember."

I will sing to the LORD as long as I live; I will sing praise to my God while I have my being.
PSALM 104:33 NASB

"What good did it do for you to go church?" he said. "You don't remember a thing." His neighbor thought about that and then reached down and picked up a wicker basket and asked him to bring her a basket of water. He told her it was impossible to carry water in a wicker basket. "I know it is," she said. "But don't you think the basket would be cleaner afterward?" Your faithfulness to the priorities of God washes across your heart in love and renewal.

Dear God, as I pray to you and praise you,
I am transformed and made new. Amen.

OPEN THE BOOK

Your word is a lamp to my feet and a light to my path. I have sworn and confirmed that I will keep Your righteous judgments.
PSALM 119:105–106 NKJV

God's words are pure words, pure silver words refined seven times in the fires of his word-kiln.

PSALM 12:6 MSG

You have a readily available manual for the time you spend close to God. In that manual there are instructions about prayer, meditation, and reflection. In that same manual you will learn what it means to have a heart for God. On the pages of this manual are clear directions for a life lived with God.

You will read about the spiritual journeys of very real people, just like you, and you can discern from their stories how to feel the closeness of God. In this manual, you will find directions and signposts for your walk with God. This manual is the Bible, the greatest how-to book ever written. Read of God's love, affection, and desire for you in the Bible.

Dear God, I open your book and find in it your word, your way, and your will for me. Amen.

GOD'S MERCY AND COMPASSION

The Lord is kind and does what is right; your God is merciful.
PSALM 116:5 NCV

God's mercy and compassion make life bearable and invest it with meaning. You pray to him for aid, and he answers you. You ask him, the God of light, to protect you, and he does just that. You implore him for wisdom and guidance, and he gives it freely. His deep and abiding concern for you as his children is manifest in the steadfast love he shows you.

> *As a father has compassion on his children, so the Lord has compassion on those who fear Him.*
> PSALM 103:13 HCSB

How comforting it is to rest in God's mercy—to know without any doubt that no matter where you fail, no matter where you might be fearful, his mercy abounds. It never ends. It is infinite. How reassuring it is to know that he feels compassion for you and intervenes in your everyday life, with the blessings of his divine mercy.

God, thank you for your mercy that is poured out on me. Teach me to reach out to others as you have reached out to me. Amen.

GIVE GOD GLORY

Hallelujah! It's a good thing to sing praise to our God; praise is beautiful, praise is fitting.

PSALM 147:1 MSG

The LORD is my strength and song, and He has become my salvation; He is my God, and I will praise Him; my father's God, and I will exalt Him.

EXODUS 15:2 NKJV

A secretary, who had been especially busy, bowed her head at her desk and said, "God, I think the stapler is your greatest invention." A good use of your time with God is to praise him for everything. Praise God, who gives you all you have.

A minister had just started his Sunday sermon when it started to thunder and lightning. Rain poured down in wild torrents. "God is wonderful!" he told the congregation. "While all of us are sitting here dry and comfortable, he's out there in the parking lot washing our cars for us!" Find phrases for your praises. Create many and varied ways to say thank-you to God. You can't say enough praises to God.

Dear God, I raise my praise to you for all you do for me and all you are to me. Amen.

596

BELIEVE IN MIRACLES

The Lord has done this wonderful miracle for me. . . .
I shall live! Yes, in his presence—here on earth!
PSALM 116:7, 9 TLB

Miracles happen every day. Some are extraordinary acts of God that alter the natural course of events, and some consist of situations where individuals have overcome tremendous odds to achieve their goals. But no matter

I sought the LORD,
and he answered
me, and delivered me
from all my fears.

PSALM 34:4 NRSV

how you define them, miracles happen. No situation is so dire, no goal so remote, that you cannot expect God's help and intervention on your behalf.

Miracles are unexplainable, but so are the other aspects of your relationship with God. You don't know why God loves you unconditionally and completely, but he does. You don't know why he listens to and answers your prayers, but he does. You don't know how miracles happen any more than you know how God created you in the first place. But you don't have to understand; you only have to believe.

God, thank you for the miracles you have brought to my life.
As I look around me, I see all that you have done
and am humbled by your goodness to me. Amen.

HEAVEN IN YOUR HEART

Our hearts brim with joy since we've taken
for our own his holy name.
PSALM 33:21 MSG

I, through the abundance of your steadfast love, will enter your house, I will bow down toward your holy temple in awe of you.

PSALM 5:7 NRSV

You can have a little piece of heaven right now. Go somewhere to be alone with God. Talk with and listen to him, and he will put his joy in your heart. When you are with God, you will experience the spark of his love and the promise of heaven in your life. That spark will warm your spirit when you feel cold and weary, and it will provide a light to your path when you are confused and misdirected.

The joy of God's presence knows no boundaries. You can experience it anytime and anywhere and enjoy God's love and grace. You can taste a bit of heaven when you intentionally put yourself before God. God will visit you in that moment and suffuse your heart with his love.

Dear God, when I know your presence in my heart and life,
all the way to heaven is heaven. Amen.

LIVE!

You have delivered my soul from death, my eyes from tears, and my feet from falling. I will walk before the Lord in the land of the living.
PSALM 116:8–9 NKJV

Are you a procrastinator? Do you get things done at the last minute? Friend, there's no procrastination for living—you either live or you don't. If you're hiding from life out of fear of what will happen, you'll never live at all.

Yet God created you to have the abundant life. He wants you to be full of joy, and there's no better way to do that than loving and serving him with your whole heart, mind, soul, and strength.

O Lord, truly I am Your servant. . . . You have loosed my bonds. I will offer to You the sacrifice of thanksgiving and will call on the name of the Lord.
PSALM 116:16–17 AMP

It's understandable that you don't want to be hurt or rejected, but realize that you'll never lose God's love. So step out in faith—take the leap God's calling you to. Your abundant life awaits.

God, I don't want to procrastinate anymore. Please calm my fears, show me how to really live, and teach me how to serve you well. Amen.

ASK GOD FOR HELP

*Rescue me from my enemies, O LORD, for I hide myself
in you. Teach me to do your will, for you are my God.*
PSALM 143:9–10 NIV

*Ask, and it will be
given to you; seek,
and you will find;
knock, and it will
be opened to you.*

MATTHEW 7:7 NASB

✴

Asking is God's plan to get you to go to him for help. The Bible clearly emphasizes the importance of asking in order to receive. The repetition of this in word and story leaves no doubt as to how God wants you to act when you have a need. God wants you to ask. Charles Spurgeon said, "Whether we like it or not, asking is the rule of the kingdom."

There is always something to be gained when you ask God for help. Cry out your need to God. He will honor your request. He will strengthen you for your tasks, give insight for your relationships, enlighten your mind, and fill your heart. In the Lord's Prayer, you are encouraged to ask God for help six times.

*Dear God, I am grateful that you are ready to
give when I am ready to ask. Amen.*

OUT OF THANKFULNESS
OR OBLIGATION?

How can I repay the LORD all the good He has done for me?
PSALM 116:12 HCSB

There will certainly be times when God requires you to obey him in something that you find extremely challenging or unpleasant, and you will be tempted to abandon what he has called you to. This is a test of your heart—of how you really view your relationship with God.

> GOD, *here I am, your servant, your faithful servant: set me free for your service! I'm ready to offer the thanksgiving sacrifice and pray in the name of* GOD.
>
> PSALM 116:16–17 MSG

☾

Are you serving him out of a thankful heart—willing to do whatever he tells you to? Or are you serving him out of obligation—with limits on what you will do on his behalf? Are you committed to him because of your overflowing love? A difficult assignment can leave you wondering why you should continue trusting and serving him. But when you do, you become an authentic, living example of true praise and thanksgiving to God.

*God, I want to serve you out of love and thanksgiving—
not out of obligation. Help me to offer myself wholeheartedly
no matter what you call me to do. Amen.*

IT TAKES BOTH

Trust in the LORD and do good; dwell in the land and enjoy safe pasture. Delight yourself in the LORD and he will give you the desires of your heart. Commit your way to the LORD; trust in him and he will do this.

PSALM 37:3–5 NIV

Teach me to follow you, and I will obey your truth. Always keep me faithful.

PSALM 86:11 CEV

When a fine artist takes the hand of a promising student and guides it on the canvas, the brushstroke is more the teacher's than the student's. The student holds the brush and makes a motion of the hand, but the teacher's touch comes through to the painting. Much honor and praise belong to the teacher.

But there is honor and praise for the student as well. The student has put himself in the teacher's capable hands, has made himself malleable to the teacher's touch. The student has yielded to the motion and direction of the teacher. The surrender of the student to the teacher brings wonderful and beautiful results. Your attitudes and actions are always better when you let God guide them with his hand and heart.

Dear God, I feel the inspiring and directing touch of your hand on mine. Amen.

LOVE THAT COVERS THE WORLD

Praise the LORD, all you nations. Praise him, all you people of the earth.
PSALM 117:1 NLT

Praise God that he loves all the people of the world. Exalt him because he cares for the young and the old, the poor and the wealthy, the weak and the strong, the helpless and the powerful.

He loves us with unfailing love; the LORD's faithfulness endures forever. Praise the LORD!

PSALM 117:2 NLT

Every person, adore him—whether you're red, yellow, black, brown, or white; whether you're in Europe, Africa, Asia, Australia, or the Americas. In every language and dialect—from every urban, suburban, and rural house, apartment, farm, and hut—worship the Lord God Almighty!

He loves and accepts us all and waits for us to receive him by faith. So rejoice in him and let songs of praise cover the earth. Hallelujah! He loves us! Glory to his name!

God, the scope of your love is so deep, so wide, so great, so powerful, so all-encompassing! How faithful you are! Glory to your name! Amen.

STRAIGHT TALK

When they call to me, I will answer them; I will be with them in trouble, I will rescue them and honor them.
PSALM 91:15 NRSV

Call on Me in the day of trouble; I will deliver you, and you shall honor and glorify Me.

PSALM 50:15 AMP

When Bill Moyers was a special assistant to President Lyndon Johnson, he was asked to say a prayer at a dinner held at the White House for visiting dignitaries. Moyers began his prayer by speaking softly to God. President Johnson, sitting several seats away at a long table, said, "Speak up, Bill. I can't hear you." Moyers, an ordained minister, stopped in midsentence and without looking up, said, "But, Mr. President, I wasn't addressing you." He was addressing God.

When you pray, talk directly and specifically to God. Tell him how it is with you, how you want it to be, and how he can help you. Talk to him from your heart. When talking to God, speak clearly, boldly, and expectantly.

God, thank you for hearing me whether I talk to you silently or aloud. Amen.

A PERSON HE LOVES

Great is His faithful love to us.
PSALM 117:2 HCSB

You don't need to worry about the future. God is in control, and he will provide his very best for you—a child he loves dearly. He knows what you will face today, tomorrow, and forever, and how you should navigate through every twist and turn that life holds. He has a

Praise the LORD, all you nations! Praise him, all you people of the world!
PSALM 117:1
GOD'S WORD

wonderful plan for you, but you must accept it. You do so by asking him to keep you in the center of his will, and trusting him as he trains you to see your life and circumstances from his loving perspective.

While problems that stretch your faith will come, you can learn to look beyond them to when God triumphantly fulfills his purpose for your life and lovingly blesses you with his great and precious promises. Truly, you will never regret trusting him.

*God, teach me to be still before you and wait for your
leading before I move forward. I know it is in times
of quiet that you whisper truth to my heart. Amen.*

IT TAKES TIME

I pray to you, LORD. So when the time is right,
answer me and help me with your wonderful love.
PSALM 69:13 CEV

Go into the city to a certain man and tell him, "The Teacher says: My appointed time is near. I am going to celebrate the Passover with my disciples at your house."

MATTHEW 26:18 NIV

Quiet moments in God's presence may need scheduling. Put your time with God on your calendar and stamp it nonnegotiable. When someone asks you to do something that conflicts with that time, say, "Sorry, I already have an appointment." Have respect for what you set aside for God. Understand it as holy time.

Meeting God is about time. It is about understanding minutes and hours, and knowing what *daily* means. It is about labeling your time "God" and defending your choice against all competitors. It takes time to pray and meditate. It takes time to remember and reflect. It takes time to know God as he can be known. Time is an irretrievable resource. Plan your time wisely. Use it prudently. Spend it with God.

Dear God, my time is in your hands.
Put your presence in my heart. Amen.

STEADFAST PROMISES

*It is better to trust in the LORD
than to depend on people.*
PSALM 118:8 GNT

What is it that you're waiting for today? Perhaps you've been disillusioned by people who've pledged to help you but have failed to carry through. They may have even tried their best for you, but you're left disheartened all the same.

Friend, if God has given you a promise, then look to him to deliver it—he won't go back on his word. The people around you just don't have his power, wisdom, and creativity. Though they want to help you,

The LORD is my strength and my song; he has given me victory. Songs of joy and victory are sung in the camp of the godly. The strong right arm of the LORD has done glorious things!
PSALM 118:14–15 NLT

they can never do so as perfectly as God can. So trust God's promise to you, and don't despair if you have to wait for it. Know that it's absolutely assured, and rejoice!

God, it's easier to have faith in someone I can see than in someone I can't. Please help me to trust your steadfast promises. Amen.

YOUR TIME IS NOW

*This is the day that the LORD has made.
Let us rejoice and be glad today!*
PSALM 118:24 NCV

*You know how
to interpret the
appearance of
earth and sky, but
why do you not know
how to interpret the
present time?*

LUKE 12:56 ESV

The past and the future are good places to visit, but you live in the present. This minute is a rich gift God puts in front of you. See it gratefully, and enter it expectantly. This minute is filled with potential. The minute before you right now invites you to meaningful movement, fervent hope, and forthright effort. It is, for you, a golden opportunity.

Be good at now. It is God's gift, and it is your time. Use the past to inform and correct; regard the future with hope and vision; live in the now. There is no greater power than to live in the present tense.

Live more fully in the present. Receive the present as the great and rich blessing it is.

*Dear God, thank you for the gift of now. Lead me
to fruitful action in the present moment. Amen.*

YIELDING TO TRUST

I was pushed back and about to fall,
but the LORD helped me.
PSALM 118:13 NIV

News of a sudden sorrow or a shift in the way you live life can cause you to feel shaken. You may wonder if you'll be able to make it through another day. Frustration, stress, and pressure can overwhelm you, but you don't have to yield to discouragement. The psalmist placed his trust in God and found the help that he needed. You can too. It may

I was right on the cliff-edge, ready to fall, when God grabbed and held me. God's my strength, he's also my song, and now he's my salvation.
PSALM 118:14–15 MSG

be tempting to charge ahead in your thoughts and begin to consider all that you can do to make life easier and better. However, moving forward without God's guidance will bring you even more disappointment.

The best way to proceed is to seek God's will. Listen to him and trust him to guide your every step, because you will surely enjoy his untold blessings.

God, thank you for guiding and comforting me through every decision and distress. I acknowledge that the best plan for my life is yours—in your timing. Amen.

A CHILDLIKE CONTENTMENT

I have calmed and quieted my soul, like a weaned child with its mother; my soul is like the weaned child that is with me.
PSALM 131:2 NRSV

You had my mother give birth to me. You made me trust you while I was just a baby. I have leaned on you since the day I was born; you have been my God since my mother gave me birth.

PSALM 22:9–10 NCV

Small children have the ability to go with the moment, their imaginations seizing the opportunities of whatever little joys they happen upon. Nothing is too small or too insignificant for their wonder: a dandelion, a pile of crisp leaves, a tiny worm, or an unexplored mud puddle.

Watching children romp, you're reminded that play is their "work." Play is a time for unleashing imagination and creative energy. The heart of a child seems to embody all that God finds best about humankind. Maybe that's why David likened himself to a "weaned child," gladly deferring thoughts of things "too marvelous" for him to God. What greater image of contentment is there than that of a young child resting with complete trust on the shoulder of the one who loves him best?

Dear God, I am in awe of your presence everywhere. I will dance before your goodness and sing a song of gladness for your grace. Amen.

THE LIGHT OF GOD'S LOVE

*The LORD is God, and he has made
his light shine upon us.*
PSALM 118:27 NIV

Problems always seem most daunting just before the dawn —right before the morning light climbs above the horizon and slips quietly into the room. In that darkest hour, shadows of fear and discouragement may threaten to overwhelm you. But the morning

> *The LORD is my light
> and my salvation;
> whom shall I fear? the
> LORD is the strength of
> my life; of whom
> shall I be afraid?*
>
> PSALM 27:1 KJV

light chases away the nighttime, restoring your perspective, filling you with hope, and offering you the promise of a bright new day! The light of God's love is much like the morning sunlight. It dispels darkness from your heart and sweeps away shadows of fear and discouragement. It renders harmless specters of condemnation that would harshly remind you of past failures. God's wondrous light allows you to see yourself as he sees you—a new creature, forgiven, ready to begin again.

*God, I thank you for flooding my heart with the light of your
love and for illuminating the shadows and bringing a
bright, shining morning of hope to my life. Amen.*

HARD TIMES FAITH

Look at the proud! Their spirit is not right in them,
but the righteous live by their faith.
HABAKKUK 2:4 NRSV

Be alert, stand firm in the faith, be brave, be strong.

1 CORINTHIANS 16:13
GNT

The prophet Habakkuk lived in hard times. Babylon was threatening Judah, and God didn't seem to be doing anything about it. Habakkuk asked God to address the problem, and then he waited. At last God spoke. God told Habakkuk that to get through hard times, he had to have faith.

When you have a problem, you probably wish God would ride in on a champion horse and slay your difficulty. "Take away my problem," you plead with God. But removing your problem is not always best for you. God may have something else in mind, because problems bring you opportunities to do and be your best. Solving problems is not as important as trusting God in the midst of them.

Dear God, thank you for being with me
when I need you the most. Amen.

PRAYER HELPS YOU MAKE DECISIONS

*With my whole heart have I sought thee:
O let me not wander from thy commandments.*
PSALM 119:10 KJV

Throughout the days of your life, you are presented with moral choices to make. And those choices are not often simple issues of all right and all wrong. Indeed the most difficult situations you face have to do with choosing from a variety of possibilities, with varying shades of good and bad.

Thy word have I hid in mine heart, that I might not sin against thee.

PSALM 119:11 KJV

Fortunately, you do not have to deal with difficult choices alone and unaided. If you ask God, he will enlighten you. He will show you the way to go. He has already given you his commandments to light your way through the maze of facts and emotions. And he waits patiently for you to bring each one before him. He will help you do what is right for your life and the lives of those you love.

God, thank you for the direction you give and the way you fill my heart with quiet assurance. Amen.

WHEN IN TROUBLE

I will call to you whenever I'm in trouble,
and you will answer me.
PSALM 86:7 NLT

Take my yoke upon you and learn from me, for I am gentle and humble in heart, and you will find rest for your souls.

MATTHEW 11:29 NIV

✳

A band of ruffians rose up against David, and he was in big trouble. The insurrectionists tried to assassinate him, but the man whose heart resembled God's knew where to go. He went to God. He prayed. His prayer was made in the confidence that God would respond.

When trouble comes to you, you can't tell trouble your schedule is full. But God knows what to do when you have troubles and difficulties. God is on the job, and things are getting better already. When trouble comes to your life, you know where to go. You know whom to ask for help. When trouble comes, prayer gets simple. Without enough power of your own, you ask for the power of God.

O Lord God, let your presence be my promise
and your power my strength. Amen.

FORTIFIED IN SPIRIT

I will meditate in thy precepts, and have respect unto thy ways.
I will delight myself in thy statutes: I will not forget thy word.
PSALM 119:15–16 KJV

The word *library* calls to mind a variety of images—a large room with floor-to-ceiling shelves, tables with people sitting hunched over their books, numbered signs directing you to a plethora of subjects, a row of computers, a small section devoted to new arrivals, and nothing but the sound of rustling pages, soft hums, and gentle whispers—the sounds of studying. A quiet time of contemplation and study is consoling and satisfying. You feel that you've found some answers you've been seeking.

You made me willing to listen and obey. And so, I said, "I am here to do what is written about me in the book, where it says, 'I enjoy pleasing you. Your Law is in my heart.'"

PSALM 40:6–8 CEV

When the words you meditate on come from God, you are fortified in your spirit as well as your mind. If you continue to meditate, you will discover that what started as a discipline has turned to a delight.

Thank you, God, for all the times I hear you speak
when I meditate on your word. Through faith and
practice, keep me within hearing distance. Amen.

HE IS THE POTTER

*He used that clay to make another
pot the way he wanted it to be.*
JEREMIAH 18:4 NCV

*We are the clay, and
you are our potter; we
are all the work of
your hand.*

ISAIAH 64:8 ESV

Jeremiah went to the potter's shop one day to watch the potter make pots. He was a good potter, and his pots were the most beautiful anywhere around. But something went wrong as the potter worked on a particular vessel. The potter was dissatisfied with the way that vessel looked.

Jeremiah watched what happened next. The potter did not set the unacceptable item aside. He did not throw it away. He took the still soft clay, plied it into a shapeless lump, put it on his wheel, and remolded it until it was beautiful and perfect. Jeremiah then understood how God works in the lives of his people. God is the potter of your life. You are the clay in his hands. You are the vessel in his heart.

*Dear God, I am ready and willing for
you to shape me and use me. Amen.*

SEEKING SUCCESS

Deal bountifully with your servant, so that
I may live and observe your word.
PSALM 119:17 NRSV

The word *success* means different things to different people. To one the word means wealth and fame; to another it means comfort and contentment; to yet another it means accomplishment and fulfillment. You measure success by the degree to which you obtain the things that are most important.

Lead me in the path of your commands, because that makes me happy. Make me want to keep your rules instead of wishing for riches. Keep me from looking at worthless things. Let me live by your word.

PSALM 119:35–37 NCV

But even when you achieve the goals you've set, you sometimes arrive at the finish line only to feel that your victory is empty and meaningless. Too late you realize that your furious run was in the wrong direction, and you experience feelings of sorrow and regret. God measures success in terms of faith, hope, and love. It is never too late to begin following his lead. Your consequent victory will bring lasting satisfaction and a sense of true success.

Help me, God, to measure success by your standard, trusting you to keep me headed in the right direction. Amen.

SHOUTING NEWS

Be glad in the LORD and rejoice, O righteous,
and shout for joy, all you upright in heart.
PSALM 32:11 NRSV

There came from the throne the sound of a voice, saying, "Praise our God, all his servants and all people, both great and small, who have reverence for him!"

REVELATION 19:5 GNT

Get a pencil and paper and write down everything for which you are grateful to God. Every gift, each blessing, anything you can think of. After a while you'll run out of paper and your pencil will wear down to a tiny nub, but keep going as long as you can.

Then take your list and, item by item, tell God how much you appreciate what he has done in and through your life. Be excited about your gifts and talents, your abilities and assets. Be exuberant in your praise. Don't hold anything back. Unplug all the stops and let praise pour forth. Your blessings are wonderful news. Know how much you are blessed, and then show that you know.

Dear God, when I consider my blessings one by one,
I shout to you with exceedingly great joy. Amen.

ABSOLUTES

I have chosen the way of truth;
Your judgments I have laid before me.
PSALM 119:30 NKJV

As you get to know God and learn to love him more, he'll teach you the truth that sets you free. Though you're liberated immediately from sin by believing in him, he must continue to unshackle you from the harmful attitudes that have been deeply ingrained within you.

I am eager to learn all that you want me to do; help me to understand more and more. Point out your rules to me, and I won't disobey even one of them.

PSALM 119:32–33 CEV

You must learn that there's one absolute reality—and it's based on God. This doesn't happen overnight. Rather, it's the passionate pursuit of a life dedicated to him. And every day, God is working toward that goal—setting you increasingly free by the truth he reveals to you. So stick close to God, and rejoice in the liberty you're gaining today. He will make you truly free, indeed!

God, you know the destructive attitudes that continue
to hinder me. Thank you for teaching me the truth
that heals and liberates me from them. Amen.

LAUGH OUT LOUD

We laughed, we sang, we couldn't believe our good fortune.
We were the talk of the nations.
PSALM 126:2 MSG

[There is] a time to weep and a time to laugh; a time to mourn and a time to dance.

ECCLESIASTES 3:4 NASB

Laughter is a precious gift that comes to you from heaven. Laughter is God reaching down to you with delight and gladness. Laughter is a wonderful blessing from God.

God gives laughter because it is good for you. It treats you kindly with healing, wellness, and wholeness. An old Jewish proverb says, "When you are hurt, laugh." Good side-shaking laughter can transform pessimistic diagnosis into hopeful prognosis. It is cheaper and quicker to laugh aloud than to reach into the medicine cabinet or check in to the hospital. Maybe it's a laugh a day rather than an apple a day that keeps the doctor away. If you laugh a lot, when you get older, your wrinkles will be in all the right places.

Dear God, thank you for giving me so many reasons to laugh.
I hear the angels in heaven laughing with me. Amen.

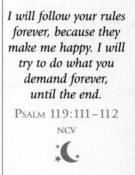

ALONG THE FOOTPATH

Make me go in the path of thy commandments;
for therein do I delight.
PSALM 119:35 KJV

In his poem "The Road Not Taken," Robert Frost wrote about two paths that diverge in a wood and how he chose the "one less traveled by." He ended the poem with these words: "and that has made all the difference." Similarly, you may ponder what may have happened if you had veered down another life path. Ultimately, however, it's the path taken that molds you into the person you turned out to be—for better or for worse. How blessed you are when you choose the path that leads to God.

I will follow your rules forever, because they make me happy. I will try to do what you demand forever, until the end.
PSALM 119:111–112
NCV

Just as a footpath through the woods winds its way past twisting roots and low-hanging branches, the narrow way that leads to God may be full of obstacles. Someday you'll be able to look back and rejoice over the road not taken.

Dear God, I choose the abundant life you offer and the eternal life you promise. I have decided to follow you in all things. Amen.

ALWAYS REMEMBER

Remember the wonders he has performed,
his miracles, and the rulings he has given.
PSALM 105:5 NLT

You shall remember that you were a slave in the land of Egypt, and the LORD your God redeemed you.

DEUTERONOMY 15:15
NKJV

A good way to deepen your spiritual life is to remember when you felt especially close to God. Keep your mountaintop experiences with God fixed in your mind and planted deep in your heart. They will renew your faith and refresh your commitment.

When Blaise Pascal died, a friend found a piece of paper sewn into the lining of a jacket the great saint and scientist had worn. On it was scribbled a description of a night when he perceived the fire of God had come down to him. He had never told anyone about that extraordinary night, but with each crinkle of the paper he remembered the glory of it. You always have with you the memory and reminder of the work of God in your life.

Dear God, thank you for all the times you came to me in your presence and power. I remember them well. Amen.

THE SHELTER OF HIS PROMISES

*Even in my suffering I was comforted
because your promise gave me life.*
PSALM 119:50 GNT

When the sun is shining, it's hard to imagine the approach of a violent storm. However, a change in environment can take place quickly. What begins as a beautiful morning may become a dark and threatening day.

*Remember your
promise to me,
your servant; it
has given me hope.*
PSALM 119:49 GNT

☾

However, you don't have to allow a sudden shift in climate to cause you to feel discouraged or defeated. God has vowed never to leave your side, and he is always at work on your behalf. He knows your struggles, and has promised to provide the wisdom, strength, and courage you need to stand firm in your faith.

Therefore, hide his promises and principles within your heart so you'll have the hope you need for times of tempest. Because then, no matter how strong the winds of adversity blow, the Word of God will guide you to safety.

*God, whenever pressures build and the storms of life
assail, help me to recall your wonderful promises so
that I will not be tempted to give up. Amen.*

SURRENDER ALL

I trust in you, O LORD; I say, "You are my God." My times are in your hand; deliver me from the hand of my enemies and persecutors.

PSALM 31:14–15 NRSV

The eyes of the LORD range throughout the earth to strengthen those whose hearts are fully committed to him.

2 CHRONICLES 16:9 NIV

Give your problems, challenges, and difficulties to God, but make sure there are no claw marks on them. The great missionary Jim Elliot once prayed, "Father, let me lose the tension of the grasping hand." Give God your situations willingly, without disclaimer or condition. Without reservation, give God your relationships, employment issues, and inner struggles. Give God all your choices and say to him, "It's your call."

Turn things over to God. He knows better what to do with them than you do. Let God carry you. He is better able to do that than you are. It is letting go, not holding on, that makes you strong. It is coming to God with full hands and leaving with empty ones. Give control to God. Make him Lord of your life.

Dear God, thank you for receiving what I bring and giving what I need. Amen.

THE EYES OF UNDERSTANDING

*Thy hands have made me and fashioned me: give me
understanding, that I may learn thy commandments.*
PSALM 119:73 KJV

The sunset is one of God's magnificent wonders. Sweeping across the horizon as if painted by God's own hand, it imbues the receding sunlight with indescribable splendor and signals that one day is giving way to another—a celestial changing of the guard.

*Long ago you laid
the foundation of
the earth and made
the heavens with
your hands.*

PSALM 102:25 NLT

Your life is full of days as well, but you seldom pass as smoothly from one to the other. You fail to view the sunsets in your life in the same way you do the sunrises. Endings can be just as beautiful as beginnings if you allow God to open the eyes of your understanding. When you truly realize the miracle of the sunset, you will no longer cling to the remains of the day. You will instead revel in its beauty, celebrating life to its fullest.

*Great Creator, open the eyes of my understanding
to appreciate the sunsets in my life. Amen.*

STANDING TALL

All the nations you made will come and bow before you,
LORD; they will praise your holy name.
PSALM 86:9 NLT

Humble yourselves
under the mighty
hand of God, that He
may exalt you at the
proper time.

1 PETER 5:6 NASB

You can stand tall in the world when you bow low in the presence of God. You can be a giant wherever you are if you are a child before God. Humility is a condition that acknowledges how great God is and how dependent you are on him. You are dependent enough to accept the power and strength he offers. You are needy enough to receive God's resources and gratefully watch him elevate your efforts and endeavors.

Knowing how great God is and giving yourself over to his power bring potency and fervor to the life you live each day. You are more able and more effective when you are in the hands of God. God makes everything you do better. Humility puts both you and God in proper perspective.

Dear God, as the stars fade in brightness when the
sun comes out, you exceed all things. Amen.

ENCOURAGING OTHERS' SOULS

May those who fear You see me and be glad,
because I wait for Your word.
PSALM 119:74 NASB

Today you utilized talents that benefit your work and life. Those have been given to you for your own survival and improvement.

Yet you also have spiritual gifts that are specifically entrusted to you for the sake of others. God imparted those gifts so you could be his instrument of blessing and encouragement to those in need. Whether you

Let your steadfast love comfort me according to your promise to your servant. Let your mercy come to me, that I may live; for your law is my delight.

PSALM 119:76–77 ESV

helped, gave, taught, prayed, or served, you represented God's comfort and provision to them. Friend, understand that you've been given the wonderful privilege of showing God's love to all the people who cross your path. So use your God-given gifts for his glory! Others will undoubtedly be encouraged and glad to have you around.

God, how would you have me encourage others?
Please empower me tomorrow to bless those around
me mightily with my spiritual gifts! Amen.

TROUBLESOME ATTRACTIONS

*Take away my desire to do evil or
to join others in doing wrong.*
PSALM 141:4 NCV

*My eyes are upon You,
O GOD the Lord; in
You I take refuge.*

PSALM 141:8 NKJV

No one denies that temptations are truly tempting! The promise of immediate gratification will always be dangerous as long as you live on this earth. How do you stop falling prey to the things that lure you into sin? You know Jesus has already broken the power of sin over you, but why is it still so attractive to you? How do you stop *wanting* the things that harm you?

Romans 12:2 (NLT) instructs, "Let God transform you into a new person by changing the way you think." Temptation begins in your thoughts; you must therefore change what you set your mind on. Focus on God, and allow him to cleanse you with the Bible. Those troublesome temptations will not go away immediately, but over time, you will find that your desire to do wrong will certainly diminish.

*God, I know that I have often focused on the very things
that make me stumble and sin. Transform me, God,
because I want to honor you with my whole life. Amen.*

GROWING WISER

Thou through thy commandments has made me wiser than mine enemies: for they are ever with me. I have more understanding than all my teachers: for thy testimonies are my meditation.
PSALM 119:98–99 KJV

The passing down of wisdom from parent to child, like cultural links in ancestral succession, gives character a chance to take root in each new generation. If watered, nourished, and pruned regularly, this heritage seedling will grow into a beautiful tree—broad, tall, and capable of withstanding the forces of nature and contributing to its environment. Its canopy of shade will protect all those who gather under its leafy branches. So also does a child grow into and then give back his or her wisdom.

> *A good person speaks with wisdom, and he says what is fair. The teachings of his God are in his heart, so he does not fail to keep them.*
> PSALM 37:30–31 NCV

Wisdom shows up best, not in the things you choose, but in the things you don't choose. That's when your legacy comes into fruition. With God as your gardener, you flourish in the place where he plants you, enriching your own life and the lives of others.

Dear God, give me wisdom to know what to look over and what to overlook. Teach me that the greatest wisdom is a loving heart, and when I am afraid, make me wise beyond my fears. Amen.

ALONE

When I look beside me, I see that there is no one to help me,
no one to protect me. . . . Lord, I cry to you for help; you,
Lord, are my protector; you are all I want in this life.
PSALM 142:4–5 GNT

Set me free from my prison, that I may praise your name. Then the righteous will gather about me because of your goodness to me.

PSALM 142:7 NIV

There are struggles that are so deep and hurt so badly that you cannot share them with someone else. Uncertainty, insecurity, hurt, fear, shame, and confusion cloak your situation in darkness, hindering you from bringing the issue into the light of another's love and counsel. The loneliness of this area infects your whole life, and soon enough the feeling of alienation consumes you. You're not alone, and this issue is not too awful for God to deal with. He knows that it's debilitating you from experiencing his best for your life.

It's scary, but you must allow him to illuminate the situation so that he can set you free of the prison it has become to you. He is already working in you, so don't go through this alone. Trust him.

God, I recognize that I need your healing, but it's difficult to let go of this painful issue. Please help me. Thank you for not abandoning me in this area of need. Amen.

SWEETER THAN HONEY

How sweet are Your words to my taste,
sweeter than honey to my mouth!
PSALM 119:103 NKJV

Curling up with a good novel on a quiet day is one of life's underrated pleasures. You open the pages, and the world around you fades away while you're drawn, willingly, into the story before you. The author's words weave their magic, changing you if only slightly.

I will sing unto the LORD as long as I live: I will sing praise to my God while I have my being. My meditation of him shall be sweet: I will be glad in the LORD.
PSALM 104:33–34 KJV

Who can deny the power of words to inspire, to deflate, to encourage, to discourage, to help, to hurt? The psalmist found the words of God "sweeter than honey." Unlike your own words, his words are always life-giving. Though you may find pleasure in other books, the one God wrote has the power to transform you from the inside out. No wonder this perennial bestseller has stood the test of time.

Thank you, dear God, for the words of life you speak to me.
By your words I am named and claimed. By your words
I am held, molded, and sent out. Amen.

THE WORD THAT ENDURES

*What you have done will be praised from one generation
to the next; they will proclaim your mighty acts.*
PSALM 145:4 GNT

*Everyone will know
the mighty things you
do and the glory and
majesty of your
kingdom. Your
kingdom will go
on and on, and you
will rule forever. The
Lord will keep all
his promises.*

PSALM 145:12–13 NCV

People do different things to have a lasting influence on others' lives. Many volunteer, some provide meals for families in crisis, and others offer advice. All these things are good, but do they count for eternity? Do they have a lasting effect? There is something you can do that God promises will endure—and that is telling others about him and directing them to the Bible.

"The rain and snow come down from the heavens and . . . water the earth. They cause the grain to grow, producing seed for the farmer and bread for the hungry. It is the same with my word. I send it out, and it always produces fruit. It will accomplish all I want it to, and it will prosper everywhere I send it" (Isaiah 55:10–11 NLT).

*God, I want to have an eternal influence on this world
for your name's sake. Please teach me the Bible so I can
instruct others and lead them to you. Amen.*

QUESTIONS AND DOUBTS

Sustain me according to your promise,
and I will live; do not let my hopes be dashed.
PSALM 119:116 NIV

In the utter stillness of a cavern deep underground, a single drop of water falls onto the surface of a small pond—and then another and another and another. With time, the pond swells until the entire chamber is underwater. Doubt enters your life in the same way—one drop at a time.

When doubts filled my mind, your comfort gave me renewed hope and cheer.
PSALM 94:19 NLT

☆☽☆

When you experience loss or disappointment, it is natural for you to have questions and experience doubt. But you can bring your questions and doubts to God. He will help you resolve your doubts and find the peace you seek. It may take longer than you expect for the answers to come, but they will come. You can know God's true and lasting peace as you allow your doubts to flow out into the river of God's love.

God, I bring my questions and doubts to you, and I trust
that you will sustain me, for my hope is in you. Amen.

WHEN OTHERS DISAPPOINT

Do not trust influential people, mortals who cannot help you. When they breathe their last breath . . . their plans come to an end.
PSALM 146:3–4 GOD'S WORD

The LORD sets prisoners free and heals blind eyes. He gives a helping hand to everyone who falls. . . . He defends the rights of orphans and widows. . . . The LORD God of Zion will rule forever! Shout praises to the LORD!

PSALM 146:7–10 CEV

Don't get caught in the trap of thinking others will fulfill you or give you the joy you long for. Whether you're hoping for someone to love, help, or honor you for some achievement, it's possible that they will let you down. That disillusionment could crush your spirit.

Your first reaction may be to blame God. Understand, however, that he was not the one who disappointed you. In fact, if you had kept your eyes on him instead of that person, your heart would not be broken. Rather, you would be growing deeper in your relationship with him.

When others fail you, use it as an opportunity to refocus on God, who will always lead you in the best way possible.

God, I acknowledge that I put too much emphasis on the help and opinion of others. Please help me to trust you and look only to you for help and approval. Amen.

UNDERSTOOD BY THE SPIRIT

The unfolding of your words gives light;
it imparts understanding to the simple.
PSALM 119:130 ESV

S ome call it the "Aha!" moment. You study a principle and still don't comprehend it. Then, one day, in the midst of common activities, you suddenly get it. "Aha!"

This happens many times with spiritual concepts because God's principles are not only learned by your intellect, but also by your willing spirit. We think of God's truth as lofty and ethereal, but in reality, his precepts must be understood in a practical way. You must be able to live out his precepts from deep within.

Your promise has been tested through and through, and I, your servant, love it dearly. . . . The way you tell me to live is always right; help me understand it so I can live to the fullest.
PSALM 119:140, 144 MSG

Friend, the God who is able to save your soul is able to instruct you in his ways. So listen and learn from him. He'll undoubtedly lead you to many profound "Aha!" moments.

God, thank you for teaching your wisdom to my spirit. Teach me your truth so that I can always follow you well and praise you. Amen.

HE PREFERS YOUR TRUST

The Lord takes pleasure in those who reverently and worshipfully fear Him, in those who hope in His mercy and loving-kindness.
PSALM 147:11 AMP

How good it is to sing praises to our God, how pleasant and fitting to praise him! . . . Great is our Lord and mighty in power; his understanding has no limit.

PSALM 147:1, 5 NIV

✺

It is easy to be stuck on a certain idea of what the Christian life should be. Going to church, reading your Bible, having a prayer time—it becomes a burdensome routine. Somehow, God is left out.

However, the purpose for fellowshiping with other believers, studying the Bible, and praying should be so you can know him better—not so you can check off a list of what it means to be a "good Christian." God wants a living, growing, personal relationship with you that leads to loving obedience, not meaningless ritual. He wants your trust.

So be willing to give up your religious practices and pursue a deep relationship with God. Then you won't just have an idea of the Christian life—you'll be experiencing it abundantly.

God, I want to know you in an authentic, profound relationship. Teach me to have full confidence in you, my God, for you are surely worthy of all my trust. Amen.

PROMISES TO KEEP

My eyes stay open through the watches of the night,
that I may meditate on your promises.
PSALM 119:148 NIV

What would life be like without spring's warmth after a long and cold winter, rest after an exhausting and difficult day, achievement after an intense and tiring struggle? Promises of the reward to come mark your life. In fact, life is a promise in the process of being kept.

Your promise revives me; it comforts me in all my troubles.

PSALM 119:50 NLT

You may wonder at times if your life is no longer a bright promise. You may lie awake in the night hours rehearsing your regrets that this may be so. But God is the great promise keeper. You can count on what he has promised. He is already aware of every poor choice, every lost opportunity, and every wasted second. He knows, and your mistakes grieve him. He takes you as you are and restores hope to your life.

God, I will focus my eyes on your faithfulness rather
than on my own failures. I will look to you to help me
fulfill the promise of all that my life can be. Amen.

November

*Because of all that
the Son is, we have
been given one
blessing after
another.*

JOHN 1:16 CEV

GOD'S DELIGHT

*The LORD takes pleasure in His people; He adorns the
humble with salvation. Let the godly celebrate in
triumphal glory; let them shout for joy.*
PSALM 149:4–5 HCSB

*Sing to the LORD
a new song, and
His praise in the
congregation of
the godly ones.*

PSALM 149:1 NASB

There may be times in your life when you feel as if you're on your own—it seems that no one understands or cares for you, and you can't do anything right. These are the times it is most important to remember your Creator. God loves you, cares for you, and works through you to fulfill his purpose for your life. Of course, he does not approve of your sins, because when you commit them you hurt yourself. That's why he empowers you to turn from them and triumph over them.

Are you feeling like a failure today? Rejected, unloved, and unworthy? Then it's time to give up your opinion of yourself and embrace God's vision for your life. He delights in you and will lead you to victory if you will follow him.

*God, in you is all my worth, glory, and joy. I thank you
for accepting and loving me. I praise you for delighting
in me and leading me to victory. Amen.*

WORDS THAT RESTORE

I rejoice at Your word as one who finds great treasure.
PSALM 119:162 NKJV

At the end of Mark Twain's classic *Tom Sawyer*, the boy hero of Hannibal, Missouri, uncovers a treasure buried in the cavern that nearly claimed his life. The town rejoices at Tom's good fortune, and you, the reader, get to peek over his shoulder, vicariously experiencing the thrill of finding something of great worth long buried.

Your goodness continues forever, and your teachings are true. I have had troubles and misery, but I love your commands. Your rules are always good. Help me understand so I can live.
PSALM 119:142–144
NCV

That's just the sort of word picture that David painted in Psalm 119. God's words fill you with joy and the promise of lifelong provision. You become heir of a fortune that transcends earthly values. To your surprise, you find that for the first time in your life your cup runs over, just as the psalmist said it would.

Through your word of encouragement, dear God, I become myself. Thank you for looking far enough in me to see strengths and skills I don't know are there. Amen.

PRAISE TO THE END

Praise the LORD! Praise God in his sanctuary; praise him
in his mighty heaven! Praise him for his mighty works;
praise his unequaled greatness!
PSALM 150:1–2 NLT

Let everything that has
breath praise the LORD.
Praise the LORD.

PSALM 150:6 NIV

The book of Psalms begins: "Happy are those who . . . love the LORD's teachings" (1:1–2 NCV), and ends: "Praise the Lord!" (150:6 NCV). In between is every situation you might experience on the journey of life—trials, losses, betrayals, joys, hopes, promises, and desires. The Psalms represent the whole spectrum of human experience, and the faithfulness of God to walk with you through each one.

Hopefully you have not missed this precious truth: When you begin with faith in God—reading the Bible and trusting his love—you end with praise for him

So adore him! Worship him! Express your love for him from the depths of your soul! Because he will never let you down, and surely he is worthy.

How blessed and fitting to praise you, God! May my life
be a psalm of adoration to you from this time forth and
forevermore. I'll love you always, my God. Amen.

AN ENDURING PEACE

Great peace have they which love thy law:
and nothing shall offend them.
PSALM 119:165 KJV

The starry grandeur of a mid-summer night. The gentle gurgle of a languid river. The majestic stillness of a desert vista. The rolling wave of unharvested grain. The cleansing rain on a warm day. These are but a few of the natural expressions of peace and constancy that God has placed in the world.

In times of turmoil and distress, you can find moments of comfort and solace by gazing at the ageless beauty of a snowcapped mountain or by walking along a shell-strewn beach. You hope that when you return to your everyday life the peace you found will remain with you. God alone can offer you lasting peace in your heart.

You make springs pour water into the ravines, so streams gush down from the mountains. They provide water for all the animals, and the wild donkeys quench their thirst. The birds nest beside the streams and sing among the branches of the trees.
PSALM 104:10–12 NLT

God, bring peace and constancy to my heart, where pain and hope-lessness now reside. I will hope in your goodness. Amen.

THE SHEPHERD'S REPUTATION

*He renews my soul. He guides me along the paths
of righteousness for the sake of his name.*

PSALM 23:3 GOD'S WORD

*The LORD is my
shepherd; I have
everything I need.
. . . I know that
your goodness and
love will be with me
all my life; and
your house will be
my home as long
as I live.*

PSALM 23:1, 6 GNT

One can generally deduce the skill of the shepherd by the condition of his sheep. Is the flock cared for? Healthy, well-fed, free of parasites and injuries? This is due to the shepherd's watchful leadership. He nurtures his lambs with skill and understanding and gladly gives his life to rescue them from danger.

The same is true for your shepherd—the Lord God. He nourishes your soul through his Word and Spirit. He protects you from paths that would destroy you, and exercises your faith so you can grow strong and healthy. He guides you through the perils of life to places of peace. How well you are cared for reflects on his name, so he is not going to let you down. Therefore, trust the Shepherd. With him, you shall surely never want.

*God, you are my wonderful shepherd. Thank you for
leading me so faithfully. May my life bring praise
to your good, holy, and merciful name. Amen.*

WHAT'S WRONG HERE?

Deliver me, O Lord, from lying lips
and from deceitful tongues.
PSALM 120:2 AMP

As you're talking to someone, you feel it—like a sudden pause in your spirit. Something with what they're saying makes you feel uneasy, though it all appears right. What's going on?

When I am in trouble, I pray.
PSALM 120:1 CEV

Sometimes when you feel a hesitation about others, God may be cautioning you about their true intentions. Old-time believers called that a "check in the spirit." It's a divine signal that alerts you concerning some danger or deceit.

Friend, don't disregard God's warning, no matter how attractive or convincing the person. Pay attention to the "checks." Step back from the situation and watch it unfold. Certainly, God will show you what he's protected you from, and you'll be glad you listened to him.

God, thank you for warning me about the things that can harm me. Help me to heed your warnings and pay attention to the "checks." Amen.

HIS CHERISHED NAME

I will give thanks to your name, O LORD, for it is good.
For he has delivered me from every trouble.
PSALM 54:6–7 ESV

God, save me by Your name, and vindicate me by Your might!

PSALM 54:1 HCSB

✺

William Shakespeare wrote, "What's in a name? that which we call a rose by any other name would smell as sweet." Yet when considering God's name, it carries with it meaning that should not only give you comfort, but confidence as well. Take heart that when you read the Bible and see "LORD" in all capitals; it is an indication that it is a transliteration of *Yahweh*, which means, "I AM." In God's name is his character—the declaration that he is the ever-present Lord, who will never fail you.

He is faithful, wise, all-powerful, loving, and able to help you no matter what happens—just as he has been throughout history and will always be forevermore. What is in his name? Everything, for in his wonderful name is the assurance that the One you love is truly worthy of all your adoration.

My God, the great I AM, thank you for being faithful and trustworthy in my life and in the lives of all your people. May your name be cherished forever. Amen.

SEARCHING FOR ANSWERS

I look up to the mountains; does my strength come from mountains? No, my strength comes from GOD, who made heaven, and earth, and mountains.

PSALM 121:1 MSG

Answers to some questions are difficult to find. Why are you here? What purpose does your life serve? Why is the life of a child cut short? Why is a strong and decent man cut down in his prime? Why must a young mother care for her children alone? Why do evil people prosper? Why do the ravages of war seem never to end?

I truly believe I will live to see the LORD's goodness.

PSALM 27:13 NCV

You may never know the answers to these questions or the thousands of others drawn from the circumstances of your life and from those around you. You can but place your hand in the hand of God and place your hope in his great wisdom and eternal love. You can rest in the knowledge that his intention for you is always good.

God, settle my heart and help me to rest in the hope that one day all my questions will be answered as I stand in your presence. Amen.

NEVER ALONE

I am continually with thee: thou hast holden me by my right hand. Thou shalt guide me with thy counsel, and afterward receive me to glory.
PSALM 73:23–24 KJV

I love the LORD because he hears my voice and my prayer for mercy. Because he bends down to listen, I will pray as long as I have breath!

PSALM 116:1–2 NLT

A solitary tree standing in the middle of a field may appear to be deserted by all else. In fact, however, it is not. The warmth of the sun kisses that tree; the gentle breezes caress it; the fellowship of birds on the wing gladden it; and a small underground universe of lively creatures stimulate it.

At some time in your life you experience loneliness. Loneliness is natural and should be appreciated rather than feared. In seasons of loneliness, you discover that you are never truly alone—no more than that solitary tree. People you barely notice during times of social prosperity surround you and can become valuable friends. But the greatest discovery is that God is constantly with you, warming you with his love, and you can learn to hope in him.

God, during those times when I feel the ache of loneliness, help me to remember that you are never more than a whispered prayer away. Amen.

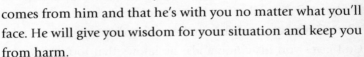

GOD IS GUARDING YOU

*The LORD is your protector, and he won't
go to sleep or let you stumble.*
PSALM 121:3 CEV

Anxious about tomorrow? Are your concerns keeping you awake? Fears can rob you of the rest you know you need and make you even weaker.

*The LORD will protect
you and keep you
safe from all dangers.
The LORD will protect
you now and always
wherever you go.*
PSALM 121:7–8 CEV

Yet you can sleep peacefully knowing that God is guarding you. So turn your thoughts and prayers to him. Remember that your help comes from him and that he's with you no matter what you'll face. He will give you wisdom for your situation and keep you from harm.

Though you're concerned for what will develop as you slumber, understand that God is watching the situation closely. He is your guard—observing what you cannot and preparing you for what's ahead. So remember your Protector and sleep well.

God, thank you for protecting me while I sleep. Please help me turn my concerns over to you, knowing you'll help me in every situation. Amen.

THE ESTABLISHMENT OF BOUNDARIES

You set all the limits on the earth.
PSALM 74:17 NCV

You have been our king from the beginning, O God; you have saved us many times.

PSALM 74:12 GNT

Fire is a wonderful thing—especially when cooking food or keeping warm. Unfortunately, if a fire gets out of control in your home or a forest, it can be devastating. The flames quickly consume everything in their unhindered path.

To avoid disaster, one must only build fires within the confines of a suitable fireplace or pit, where they can be easily managed. Likewise, boundaries keep the resources and relationships of your life from becoming damaging. That's why God gives you his commands; he knows that too much of a good thing can be harmful, and he wants you to flourish rather than self-destruct.

So don't be afraid of his laws—they'll always keep you safe.

God, thank you that your boundaries are meant to protect me rather than limit me. Help me to always abide by your life-giving commands. Amen.

WHOLESOME PRESERVATIVES

The LORD shall preserve thee from all evil: he shall preserve thy soul. The LORD shall preserve thy going out and thy coming in from this time forth, and even for evermore.
PSALM 121:7–8 KJV

Patrick was sold into slavery as a teenager when marauding Irishmen raided the English coastal regions where he lived. During his years as a slave, this son of a deacon turned to God with zeal. After escaping to England, he dreamed that an Irishman begged him to return and preach to his countrymen. Patrick did return to Ireland as a missionary and became the Emerald Isle's most beloved saint—Saint Patrick.

You go before me and follow me. You place your hand of blessing on my head. Such knowledge is too wonderful for me, too great for me to understand! I can never escape from your Spirit! I can never get away from your presence!
PSALM 139:5–7 NLT

We read much about the preservatives that go into your food, stripping them of their organic value. One kind of preservative, however, is good for your body as well as your soul: God. As Patrick discovered, what comes disguised as evil, God often uses for good.

God, I am grateful that you are always with me, protecting me from evil. Amen.

AN ISSUE OF TIME

He remembered that they were only human,
like a wind that blows and does not come back.
PSALM 78:39 NCV

They repented and sought God earnestly. They remembered that God was their rock, the Most High God their redeemer.

PSALM 78:34–35 ESV

Have you ever faced a puzzle that seemed completely unsolvable—but then something shifted your perspective and altered your understanding of it? Suddenly, you saw the answer clearly. It was there all along, but you couldn't grasp it until your vantage point changed.

Often, we cannot understand God's direction because of our perspective on time. We deal with issues in the present and are quick to categorize things as "deal with now" or "wait until later." Unfortunately, that's not always the right viewpoint.

What God is doing in you isn't about "now versus later," but "temporary versus eternal." So don't fight him—he's teaching you to see life as you've never understood it before.

God, thank you for showing me that my human viewpoint
is limited. Please help me to see all of my circumstances
from your outlook—the eternal perspective. Amen.

LIKE-MINDED

I rejoiced with those who said to me,
"Let us go to the house of the LORD."
PSALM 122:1 HCSB

Do your friends love God and teach you about his goodness? Do they encourage you to know him better through Bible study and prayer? Do they help you make godly decisions?

For my brothers and companions' sake I will say, "Peace be within you!"

PSALM 122:8 ESV

Your friends will either bring you closer to God or make it harder for you to remain faithful to him. That's not to say you should abandon the friends that don't know God, but you must be careful about how they influence you—and how you inspire them.

It's wise to spend time with people who also love God—so seek out and befriend those who serve him. They'll undoubtedly bless you and help you grow in your relationship with him.

God, thank you for my godly friends. Please help me befriend more people who honor you and will help me grow closer to you. Amen.

ONLY ONE WILL DO

You are great and do wondrous things; you alone are God.
Teach me your way, O Lord, that I may walk in
your truth; unite my heart to fear your name.
PSALM 86:10–11 ESV

I will give thanks to
you with all my heart,
O Lord my God. I will
honor you forever
because your mercy
toward me is great.
You have rescued me
from the depths of hell.
PSALM 86:12–13
GOD'S WORD

At times you may be tempted to think that God is not intimately aware of the dreams you have for the future. But he is. He knows the deepest desires of your heart because he has placed many of them within you. However, he will not compete with the desires of your heart—he wants to be your priority. If you place anything above him, he will remove it because only he deserves first place in your life.

Are the desires of your heart united to honor him? Or are they divided between him and some other person or object of desire? Remember that it is God who gives you life and everything you have, so honor him above all else. You may be very surprised by how he rewards your faithfulness.

God, I want you to be first in my life. Though it is painful, please remove anything that hinders me from honoring you first. Amen.

IT'S WHAT YOU LOOK TO

Unto You I lift up my eyes, O You who dwell in the heavens.
PSALM 123:1 NKJV

We will keep looking to you, O LORD our God.
PSALM 123:2 GNT

Whatever fills your eyes will permeate your thoughts and ultimately affect your behavior. Continually view destructive content, and eventually you'll be either likewise aggressive in your dealings with others or too afraid to venture out. Yet if your focus is continually on God, you'll resemble him more and have increasing confidence in his power and goodness. That's why it's so important to concentrate your attention on God and pray to him continually—because he strengthens your soul.

Friend, what do you set your focus on? Consider it carefully because it'll affect you profoundly. So lift your gaze to the One enthroned in heaven, and fill your eyes and heart with the only One truly worthwhile.

God, I want you to fill my eyes, permeate my thoughts, and change my behavior to be like you. I will focus on you, God—now and always. Amen.

FROM ETERNITY

*From everlasting to everlasting, You are God. . . . For a thousand
years in Your sight are like yesterday when it passes by.*
PSALM 90:2, 4 NASB

*Teach us to number
our days aright, that
we may gain a heart
of wisdom. . . . Satisfy
us in the morning with
your unfailing love,
that we may sing
for joy and be glad
all our days.*

PSALM 90:12, 14 NIV

There is no one like the Lord God.
Nothing on this earth compares
to his greatness. He can easily deal
with the ongoing operation of the
universe, and at the same time be
intimately interested in every detail
of your day—no matter how great or
small it may be.

God knew you before he formed
the foundation of the earth. He is
omniscient—he knows the desires of your heart and the prayers
you will pray even before you lift your eyes to heaven in hopeful
expectation of his answer. As you begin your day and before you
turn your light out at night, take time to thank him for caring for
you so dearly and completely. His love for you is everlasting, so
make sure you praise his wonderful name.

*God, you set the heavens in place and know every star
that shines. Yet you also know the slightest detail of
my life, and I praise you for your care. Amen.*

DON'T LOSE YOUR FOCUS

Our eyes look to the LORD our God.
PSALM 123:2 ESV

E verything changes when you set your focus on God. You filter every situation through the knowledge you have of him.

I lift my eyes to You, the One enthroned in heaven. . . . Show us favor, LORD.

PSALM 123:1, 3 HCSB

Is any problem too hard for him? No. Can he use every circumstance for your good and his glory? Yes. Because nothing is impossible for God, every challenge you encounter is just another opportunity to see his mighty work in your life—building your confidence in him. Unfortunately, sometimes you lose your focus. It's so easy to do—especially when trouble arises that you didn't expect. It can even be something small—a flat tire, a bill that's difficult to pay, an irritating issue. Suddenly you're wondering, *God, where are you?* God hasn't moved; your focus has—and you must turn your attention back to him. Because he's *still* bigger than your problems and will certainly help you.

God, help me to keep my eyes on you! I praise you that nothing is ever too difficult for you and that you use everything for my good and your glory. Amen.

WHAT CAN'T HE DO?

Ascribe to the LORD, you families of the peoples,
ascribe to the LORD glory and strength.
PSALM 96:7 HCSB

Sing to the LORD and praise his name; every day tell how he saves us. . . . He is coming to judge the world; he will judge the world with fairness and the peoples with truth.

PSALM 96:2, 13 NCV

✸

It might surprise you to find out that there are things God cannot do. Though God is all-powerful, there are certain acts he won't commit because of his character.

For example, God is holy, so he cannot lie or break his promises to you. He'll never use his knowledge for evil—he'll only use his great wisdom to help you. God cannot stop loving you either, because love is his nature. Yet because of that, he can't stand silently by when you take a destructive path. That's why he offers you his salvation—because he wants you to spend eternity with him.

So embrace God and trust his ways. He can't fail you—isn't that wonderful?

God, I praise you for your holy, loving ways. Thank you that I can always count on you. You couldn't be more wonderful! Amen.

THINGS COULD BE WORSE

*What if the LORD had not
been on our side?*
PSALM 124:1 GNT

It happens without fail. Some extra money comes your way, and you know just what to do with it. Then your car breaks down. There goes your bonus. Or you finally take a day off work, and you look forward to relaxing. Then a loved one has an emergency. There goes your vacation. In a sense, you may feel as if you were robbed of a blessing. However, what you need to remember is that things could have been much worse. Imagine not having the money to pay for that repair, or taking that loved one to the doctor during high-pressure deadlines.

*Blessed be God! He
didn't go off and leave
us. He didn't abandon
us defenseless. . . .
GOD's strong name is
our help, the same
GOD who made
heaven and earth.*
PSALM 124:6, 8 MSG

You had other plans, but God was providing for what he knew was ahead. Therefore, embrace it as a special blessing and praise him for helping you.

*God, please forgive me when I have a bad attitude.
Thank you so much for providing for me. I don't know
what I would do without your wonderful grace! Amen.*

TRUST TAKES TIME

*Then they believed his words were true
and broke out in songs of praise.*
PSALM 106:12 MSG

*O LORD, in Your favor
toward Your people;
visit me with Your
salvation, that I may
see the prosperity of
Your chosen ones,
that I may rejoice
in the gladness of
Your nation.*

PSALM 106:4–5 NASB

It's profoundly freeing when you realize, "God, I never want to be without you. I know you'll always love and help me." It takes time to internalize that God will never lie to you. It requires many instances of experiencing his faithfulness to understand that God is absolutely unlike the people who've let you down.

Friend, truly trusting God is never automatic, but he's a patient and wise teacher. So set your heart on realizing the truth about him, and rejoice as you discover your best hopes are true. Undoubtedly, when you learn to trust him and see his faithful activity in your life, you'll want to sing and shout for joy.

*God, "I never want to be without you. I know you'll
always love and help me." Please make
this prayer true in me. Amen.*

HIS NAME IS OUR HELP

Our help is in the name of the LORD,
who made heaven and earth.
PSALM 124:8 NKJV

What sort of help do you need? Call upon God. He is:

The Great I AM—the God who is the same yesterday, today, and forever. As he's helped others in the past, he'll help you. *El Shaddai*—the Almighty God who defends you against every enemy or evil. *Yahweh Rapha*—the God who heals all of your wounds. *Yahweh Yireh*—he's your provider who cares for all of your needs. *Yahweh Shalom*—he himself is your peace. *Yahweh M'Kaddesh*—he's the one who makes you ready for salvation.

Oh, blessed be GOD! He didn't go off and leave us. He didn't abandon us defenseless.
PSALM 124:6 MSG

So call upon your wonderful God! He loves you greatly and he's always ready to help you, no matter what you need.

God, your flawless character and wonderful name always perfectly provide for all my needs. Your name is above every other, and I praise you forever! Amen.

WHY FEAR THE FORGIVER?

There is forgiveness with You,
that You may be feared.
PSALM 130:4 NASB

With all my heart, I am waiting, LORD, for you! I trust your promises. . . . Trust the LORD! He is always merciful, and he has the power to save you.

PSALM 130:5, 7 CEV

It seems like a paradox: God loves you and forgives your sins, but you're still supposed to fear him. Why should you dread someone who pardons you? Though fear and forgiveness seem like contradictory concepts, they actually go hand-in-hand. That's because godly fear is not terror; it's reverence.

When you truly respect God, you honor his commands. You also acknowledge when you violate his law because you want to maintain a good relationship with him.

Out of reverence to God, you confess your sins; out of love, he heals and pardons you. So ultimately, fear and forgiveness teach you the love of the Lord—and that, dear friend, is a very good thing.

God, thank you for teaching me about your healing
and forgiveness. I don't want to sin against you;
I want to have loving reverence for you. Amen.

A MOUNTAIN UNSHAKABLE

Those who trust in God are like Zion Mountain: nothing can move it, a rock-solid mountain you can always depend on.
PSALM 125:1 MSG

Tragedy strikes, but you have to be strong. The wind is knocked out of you, but you must stay steady for others. You try to be brave, but you just want to cry. Friend, the more you insist you're an unshakable mountain of strength, the more likely you are to crumble.

As the mountains surround Jerusalem, the LORD surrounds his people now and forever.

PSALM 125:2 NCV

☽

If you really want to be strong for those around you, then direct them to God and be honest about how he helps you in your weakness. It's your trust in God that makes you strong, not anything you can do on your own. So go ahead and weep, but also trust God to be strong enough for you—and everyone else as well.

God, thank you that I don't have to be the strong one, because you are strong enough for all of us. Thank you for your great comfort. Amen.

A WELCOME PURSUIT

Those who know your name will trust in you,
for you, LORD, have never forsaken those who seek you.
PSALM 9:10 NIV

The LORD has made
Himself known.
PSALM 9:16 NASB

✷

Chase fame, power, accomplishments, or social status, and you may discover that the more you have, the more unstable you feel. Try to fill your innermost needs with wealth, relationships, or activities, and you will probably find yourself with a greater sense of dissatisfaction than you have ever felt before. Attempt to escape your sorrows with food, alcohol, or other substances, and the gnawing emptiness within you will only increase.

Yet pursue God, and the doors of joy and fulfillment will spring open. Not only does he give you a firm place to stand and satisfy your soul, but he also fills your life with his presence, love, and purpose. Seek him with all of your heart, therefore, because you will certainly find what you are looking for.

God, I want to know you more—teach me your ways.
Thank you that when I seek you, I find everything
I need and all that my heart desires. Amen.

ENCIRCLED BY STRENGTH

As the mountains surround Jerusalem, so the LORD surrounds
His people from this time forth and forever.
PSALM 125:2 NKJV

The word *Jerusalem* may be translated "teaching or legacy of peace." Undoubtedly, the City of David was very tranquil when the psalmist lived there. Buttressed by Mounts Olivet and Scopus—as well as the valleys of Hinnom, Tyro-poeon, and Kidron—Jerusalem was virtually inaccessible to invading armies. She was, indeed, a place of peace. Sadly, enemies eventually found a way in—as is generally the case with any earthly defense. History bears witness that the tranquillity that once characterized Jerusalem is no more.

Those who trust the LORD are like Mount Zion, which can never be shaken. It remains firm forever.
PSALM 125:1
GOD'S WORD

Has this happened to you? Have your earthly defenses failed you? Remember, they are imperfect and may falter, but the living God is your true protection. He will teach your heart lasting peace that none can ever take away by surrounding you with his love, wisdom, and strength from this time forth and forevermore.

God, you are and always will be my perfect Defender!
I praise you for covering me with your wisdom, strength,
and love. May you be exalted forever! Amen.

A HEAVENLY PERSPECTIVE

The Lord is in his holy temple; the Lord is on his heavenly throne. He observes the sons of men; his eyes examine them.
PSALM 11:4 NIV

I trust in the Lord for protection.
PSALM 11:1 NCV

✲

Is safety important to you? Would you like to feel secure in your home, finances, relationships, and occupation? Are you ever afraid of the future—of being unprepared for the challenges ahead? Fears about the unknown can steal your peace. Yet understand that although your perspective is limited, God's is not. That is why your best safeguard is always to trust him.

From his heavenly throne, God sees the troubles on the path before you, and he can lead you through them unharmed. He also examines the dangers within you—the harmful behaviors that undermine your life—and frees you from them.

Therefore, be confident in God's unfailing perspective and discover real security in your relationship with him. There is no safer place to be than in his wonderful care.

God, you know my fears and my need for security. Help me to trust and obey you so that I can remain in the center of your perfect care. Amen.

TEARDROPS

They who sow in tears shall reap in joy and singing.
PSALM 126:5 AMP

God has not allowed one of your tears to drop to the ground—he's caught them all and made them into something beautiful. By all that you've been though, you've been uniquely trained to comfort those who are going through the same thing.

He who goes out weeping, carrying seed to sow, will return with songs of joy.

PSALM 126:6 NIV

You know what it is to hurt as they hurt, fear as they fear, and yearn as they yearn. You can show them how to survive and be comforted as you have been comforted.

The tears of your biggest hurts have been resoundingly transformed into your most amazing opportunities for ministry. So today praise God for helping you overcome your trials, and console others with the wisdom you have received.

God, I praise you for turning my biggest defeats into my greatest victories. Thank you for your marvelous comfort— help me to share it with others. Amen.

INTERMINABLE?

*How long, O Lord? Will you forget me forever? . . .
Consider and answer me, O Lord my God.*
PSALM 13:1, 3 ESV

*I've thrown myself
headlong into your
arms—I'm celebrating
your rescue. I'm
singing at the top of
my lungs, I'm so full
of answered prayers.*

PSALM 13:5–6 MSG

After weeks, months, perhaps even years of waiting for the Lord to work in a certain situation, you may feel weary and your hope may be fading. Maybe you are wondering, *Why is God taking so long? Why isn't he answering my prayers? Will this ever end?* Waiting is difficult, but it is also necessary because it builds your faith in him. That is because you resolve to trust him even when every circumstance tells you not to. God rewards you by fulfilling the desires of your heart in a way more wonderful than you ever thought possible.

Therefore, friend, do not be discouraged—your wait is not in vain. God's provision is coming, and when it does, you will truly have great reason to rejoice.

*God, thank you for this encouragement—I know you
have not forgotten me. Help me to wait patiently and
expectantly for your answer to my prayers. Amen.*

USELESS?

Unless the Lord builds a house, its builders labor over it in vain; unless the Lord watches over a city, the watchman stays alert in vain.
PSALM 127:1 HCSB

Solomon is known as the wisest man who ever lived, and he knew one thing to be absolutely true: Everything must have God at its foundation. Success, security, and joy all must be established through God's wisdom and power or they will fade away.

It is useless to work so hard for a living, getting up early and going to bed late. For the Lord provides for those he loves, while they are asleep.
PSALM 127:2 GNT

This is because anything that's not based on God returns to dust. Yet everything that God does lasts forever.

Friend, you're working hard for what you have, but if God isn't leading you, you're chasing the wind. So spend your life on things that will have everlasting results. Obey God and trust his superb plans for you—because when you work for him, you know it's never in vain.

God, I don't want to waste my life working for things that won't last. Please lead me and help me do whatever you ask. Amen.

AM I GOOD ENOUGH?

LORD, who can dwell in Your tent?
Who can live on Your holy mountain?
PSALM 15:1 HCSB

Such people will
stand firm forever.
PSALM 15:5 NLT

Psalm 15 goes to the heart of humanity's deepest problem—is anyone worthy of living in heaven with God? You are told that you must be honest and kind and that you must keep all the Lord's commands and never do wrong to others. Reviewing these requirements, you may question whether you can ever truly meet God's standards.

That is as it should be. The inability to be *good enough* makes you aware of your need for God's help, which he graciously provided through the death and resurrection of his Son, Jesus Christ.

When you trust him for salvation, God covers you with his righteousness and makes you worthy of dwelling with God for eternity. So believe in him, trusting his provision. Because then you can rest in *his* goodness forever.

God, I know I cannot make myself worthy of heaven, so I
trust you for salvation. Thank you for forgiving my sins
and covering me with your goodness. Amen.

BLESSED WITH REST

*It's useless to rise early and go to bed late, and work
your worried fingers to the bone. Don't you know
he enjoys giving rest to those he loves?*

PSALM 127:2 MSG

You know all there is to accomplish and how little time there is to finish it all; so you try to press on—straining your body and mind to continue. However, it is useless. You cannot go any further. The weariness has completely overtaken you.

*Unless the LORD
builds a house, the
work of the builders
is wasted. Unless the
LORD protects a city,
guarding it with
sentries will
do no good.*

PSALM 127:1 NLT

What can you do? First, you must accept that you need rest. Second, you must acknowledge that you're having so much trouble because you're trying to do everything in your own strength rather than God's strength. Express your faith in him by resting in his care. Give your burden to him, and trust him to renew you with his energy, wisdom, and efficiency. You will be amazed at all he will accomplish through you.

*God, it is challenging to give this burden to you, but I will
trust you with it. I rest with confidence knowing that with
your help so much more will be accomplished. Amen.*

GOOD BOUNDARIES

*LORD, you have assigned me my portion and my cup;
you have made my lot secure. The boundary lines
have fallen for me in pleasant places.*
PSALM 16:5–6 NIV

*I will praise the LORD
who counsels me—even
at night my conscience
instructs me. I keep the
LORD in mind always.
Because He is at my
right hand, I will not
be shaken.*

PSALM 16:7–8 HCSB

God created you at this appointed time in history and in your unique circumstances for a reason. Your experiences have not only shaped your personality and values, but they will also affect how you serve God and to whom you are able to minister. Although your life may be difficult at present, it is not a mistake that you are where you are.

God has set the boundaries of your life not for harm, but for good. Not to cause you pain, but to give you purpose. You may not understand how God could use your situation, but he will bless you abundantly if you will allow him to lead you. Therefore, listen to him and seek his wisdom in your circumstances. Then rejoice as he turns your limitations into wonderful opportunities.

*God, I praise you for working all things out for my good.
Thank you for using my life's boundaries for your glory,
the benefit of others, and my edification. Amen.*

RETURN FOR THE WORK

You shall eat the fruit of the labor of your hands;
you shall be blessed, and it shall be well with you.
PSALM 128:2 ESV

There's unacknowledged work that you do faithfully—at home, in your vocation, and in the community—because you want to honor God. It may not be glamorous or fun work—in fact, it's most likely humble and monotonous—but you do your

This is how the man who respects the LORD will be blessed.

PSALM 128:4 NCV

best at it because you know it's right. Friend, that work isn't for nothing. Though you may not see any fruit from your labor right now, the seeds of your loyal service are taking root and will soon produce wonderful results.

So continue being an exceptional family member, co-worker, mentor, and friend because your faithfulness is making a big difference in the lives of others. And be patient, because what will bloom is going to bless you.

God, thank you for rewarding the work I do every day
for my loved ones, friends, and co-workers. Though
they may not see it, you always bless me. Amen.

ALWAYS WITH YOU

I feel completely secure, because you protect me from the power of death. I have served you faithfully, and you will not abandon me.
PSALM 16:9–10 GNT

You have made known to me the path of life; you will fill me with joy in your presence, with eternal pleasures at your right hand.

PSALM 16:11 NIV

✦

Loneliness can strike for many reasons: loss, rejection, and separation from loved ones. Yet if you allow it to consume you, alienation, insecurity, and thoughts of unworthiness can become your private prison, one that is incredibly destructive and difficult to escape from.

Friend, God wants to free you from your loneliness through his enduring presence and healing care. With him, you never have to fear being alone, because he assures you of his unfailing love. As you grow closer to him, he not only teaches you to have a fulfilling relationship with himself, but with others as well.

So whenever the bondage of loneliness begins to close around your heart, trust the One who will never leave you or forsake you. You will be glad you did.

God, I thank you for never leaving or forsaking me. Thank you for freeing me from the bondage of loneliness and teaching me to love others as you do. Amen.

THE REWARDS OF OBEDIENCE

A man who obeys the Lord
will surely be blessed.
PSALM 128:4 GNT

Why not just do what you want—forgetting God's commands and following your own desires? You know the answer, because there have been times that you've done that very thing. You've gone against God's instruction and have caused your own grief. Your plans left you unsatisfied, lonely, and full of regret. Just the opposite has been true

Happy are those who respect the Lord and obey him. You will enjoy what you work for, and you will be blessed with good things.

PSALM 128:1–2 NCV

✴︎🌙✴︎

whenever you've submitted yourself to him. The tasks may have been difficult, but his presence energized you and filled you with his indescribable joy. You saw his amazing work in your life and experienced the blessings of being in his will.

You know how rewarding obedience can be—so do as he says in every situation! Because "God is fair; he will not forget the work you did and the love you showed for him" (Hebrews 6:10 NCV).

God, thank you for taking note of and blessing everything I
do in obedience to you. Thank you for always leading me
in the best way possible. I submit myself to you. Amen.

A REASON FOR CONFIDENCE

*May he give you what you desire and
make all your plans succeed.*
PSALM 20:4 GNT

*Some trust in their war
chariots and others in
their horses, but we
trust in the power of
the LORD our God.
Such people will
stumble and fall,
but we will rise
and stand firm.*

PSALM 20:7–8 GNT

Throughout the Bible, you read of people who had amazing challenges but were able to face them with astonishing confidence and assurance. Moses, Joshua, David, Paul—all faced terrible odds but did not falter. How was it possible?

The answer is not found in their strength, but in the might of the One they believed in wholeheartedly. They all trusted God and realized that no matter how bad the situation, he could overcome it. You should have confidence for the same reason. No matter what God calls you to do, you will see the victory and the wonderful blessings he has for you as long as you obey him. You may not have great earthly resources, but you have God, and he makes you a winner every time.

*God, thank you for giving me such a wonderful reason for confidence!
Help me to trust you wholeheartedly and obey you always. Amen.*

FROM CHILDHOOD

They have greatly oppressed me from my youth,
but they have not gained the victory over me.
PSALM 129:2 NIV

There are issues that have plagued you since you were young. Perhaps they developed because of how you were raised or because of your own insecurities, and maybe they've resulted in a poor self-image or the incorrect belief that somehow you're unlovable. If so, these issues will crop back up when you're under

The Lord is [uncompromisingly] righteous; He has cut asunder the thick cords by which the wicked [enslaved us].
PSALM 129:4 AMP

☾

pressure and cause you to doubt yourself and God. Yet they're not too difficult for God to overcome—he'll assuredly heal you from them and give you the victory.

Friend, whatever you've been struggling with can be conquered through God's power—so don't be afraid of those issues anymore. Claim the triumph over them and know that God makes you lovable, whole, and completely acceptable.

God, thank you that I don't have to live under the oppression of these issues any longer. Thank you for freeing and loving me, Lord God. Amen.

NEVER DESPAIR

*I would have despaired unless I had believed that I would
see the goodness of the LORD in the land of the living.*
PSALM 27:13 NASB

*Wait on the LORD; be
of good courage, and
He shall strengthen
your heart; wait, I
say, on the LORD!*

PSALM 27:14 NKJV

Despair can drive you to all sorts of destructive behaviors. You become so anxious to see your desires fulfilled that you turn to options that oppose God's best for you. You may even convince yourself that he has abandoned you.

Of course, that is untrue. God *will* help you, in his timing. Yet that is why you need to protect yourself from despair while you are waiting for him to work—so you do not miss his perfect will for you.

Therefore, meditate daily on his Word, on his promises, and on the occasions he has rescued you, because then it is so much easier to hold on to your hope. Wait expectantly for God's goodness no matter how long it takes, because that is the perfect position to be in to receive his very best.

*God, thank you for rescuing me when I have come
so close to despair. Help me to stay steadfast in hope
and to trust your perfect will always. Amen.*

A BRIGHT NEW DAY

If thou, Lord, shouldst mark iniquities, O Lord, who shall stand?
But there is forgiveness with thee, that thou mayest be feared.
PSALM 130:3–4 KJV

Past failures and disappointments can hover over you like leaden clouds, refusing to yield to the promise of sunlight and clear skies. When you find yourself surrounded by gray thoughts and gray feelings, it may seem difficult to dream of happier times. But there is

> *The salvation of the righteous is from the Lord; he is their refuge in the time of trouble.*
>
> PSALM 37:39 NRSV
>
> ✦☽✦

great hope. When you find yourself in such a situation, God is there to help. When you call out to him, he extends his hand to you and leads you out from under the foreboding clouds of the past and into the light of a new day. He offers hope for a new beginning. The journey into the sunlight is usually not an easy one, but God will walk with you every step of the way. A new life lies before you.

God, I will place my hope in you as you walk
together from beneath the dark clouds of the
past and into the promise of the future. Amen.

TOUGH WORLD, TENDER GOD

*You have seen my troubles, and you care about the anguish
of my soul. You have not handed me over to my
enemies but have set me in a safe place.*

PSALM 31:7–8 NLT

*Be strong, all who
wait with hope for the
LORD, and let your
heart be courageous.*

PSALM 31:24
GOD'S WORD

Trouble comes in many forms and finds everyone eventually. Some people feel like outcasts and never really learn to fit in. Others face financial, physical, or relational problems that keep them in constant chaos. The world offers no solutions or mercy. On the contrary, people must constantly beware of those who would take advantage of their weaknesses.

Unfortunately, instead of turning to God, people question why he allows so much suffering. Yet the reason there is such turmoil is that sin is a painful reality in the world.

Friend, God longs to show you his loving care, but you must stop clinging to the world and blaming him for your hardships. Rather, embrace him. He will reveal the truth and free you from your hurt.

*God, forgive me for blaming you for my troubles and turning
to the world for comfort. Help me to remember
that only you can truly heal my heart. Amen.*

PATIENCE AS YOU WAIT ON THE LORD

I wait for the LORD, my soul waits, and in his word I hope.
PSALM 130:5–6 NRSV

No one likes to be kept waiting. *The hold button on telephones ought to be outlawed*, you might sometimes think. The line at a popular restaurant, the crowded waiting room of a doctor's office, the plumber who is late, a lunch date who keeps you waiting—these are all time wasters.

> *I waited patiently for God to help me; then he listened and heard my cry.*
>
> PSALM 40:1 TLB

But waiting on God is a different matter. You may go through periods during which you feel he isn't listening to your prayers. Though you ardently beseech him, heaven is silent. During those times, it's important to understand that the "wait" is part of the answer God gives to you. Waiting is part of the mystery of his plan and the degrees by which it will be unfolded to you. God answers you in his time, not yours.

God, help me to be patient and to rest comfortably in the knowledge that you are taking care of all those things that concern me. Amen.

MENDED HEART

*The Lord is close to the brokenhearted and
saves those who are crushed in spirit.*
PSALM 34:18 NIV

*My flesh and my
heart faileth: but
God is the strength
of my heart, and
my portion for ever.*

PSALM 73:26 KJV

Few people pass through life without feeling the sting of betrayal, the loss of friendship, or the failure of important relationships. At those times, you may feel that the pain of a broken heart will cling to you for the rest of your days and that you will never be whole again. Sometimes you may even wonder if God still loves you.

God does love you, purely, simply, and unconditionally. Even if your pain is the result of your own actions, God's love does not condemn you. It urges you forward, calling you to forgive yourself, make amends, and become a better person. His love is constant and predictable. And with the assurance of his love comes hope—hope that you will love again, trust again, offer your heart again.

*Thank you, God, for the promise of your constant
love and the hope it brings to my life. Amen.*

STOP COMPETING

GOD, I'm not trying to rule the roost, I don't want to be king of the mountain. I haven't meddled where I have no business.
PSALM 131:1 MSG

Who is it that gets under your skin? You can't stand to see them achieve anything because you're convinced they don't deserve success as much as you do. When they do well, you're devastated.

Hope in the LORD from this time forth and forever.
PSALM 131:3 NKJV

You're struggling from a toxic mix of jealousy and pride—and no good can come of it. Even if that person is as rotten as you believe, you're only hurting yourself by harboring such bitter thoughts.

Friend, life isn't about competing with others, but about the purpose God has for you—and nobody can keep you from that except you. So stop competing and start praying for those people. God will change them through your prayers—and will certainly transform you as well!

God, please forgive me for being so negative about others. Teach me how to pray for them so that they'll know your love and salvation. Amen.

REAL, ABUNDANT LIFE

With you is the fountain of life;
in your light do we see light.
PSALM 36:9 ESV

Your love, O LORD,
reaches to the heavens,
your faithfulness to
the skies. . . . How
priceless is your
unfailing love! Both
high and low among
men find refuge in the
shadow of your wings.

PSALM 36:5, 7 NIV

What does the perfect life look like to you? Perhaps you picture a life of wealth and luxury. Or maybe you desire to be surrounded by loved ones, people who care deeply about you. Although there is nothing wrong with these dreams, when you finally reach them, you will most likely find that there is still something missing. John 17:3 explains, "Eternal life is to know you, the only true God, and to know Jesus Christ" (CEV). That is because when you seek God, you will find a truly worthwhile life, not only full of purpose but also full of love, hope, and meaning.

Friend, do you feel as if something is missing from your life? Pursue God. Love him. Devote yourself to him. He will satisfy your heart's deepest desires and never disappoint you.

God, I need you in my life. Your presence makes all
things more wonderfully satisfying—including family,
friendships, and all this life has to offer. Amen.

SLEEP WELL

I will allow no sleep to my eyes, no slumber to my eyelids, till I find a place for the Lord, a dwelling for the Mighty One of Jacob.
PSALM 132:4–5 NIV

Conrad had been sleeping better in the past few weeks. He no longer tossed, turned, and watched the clock tick slowly on. In the morning, the bedcover didn't look like there'd been a major wrestling match there the night before. Conrad, wondering why it had taken place, told his friend Randy about the improvement.

The night before Peter was to be placed on trial, he was asleep, fastened with two chains between two soldiers.

ACTS 12:6 NLT

☽

Randy asked Conrad if any significant changes had occurred in his home life. Was his job any different? Conrad answered no to both questions. Then Randy said, "How about your spiritual life? Are you praying more? Do you feel more of God's love in your heart?" Conrad smiled brightly and nodded knowingly. He was sleeping better because he was closer to God. When you make positive strides in your spiritual life, you sleep better.

Dear God, I rest in your arms, relax in your love, and sleep in your peace. Amen.

PATIENCE, FRIEND

Entrust your ways to the LORD. Trust him, and he will act on your behalf. . . . Surrender yourself to the LORD, and wait patiently for him.
PSALM 37:5, 7 GOD'S WORD

Trust in the LORD, and do good; dwell in the land, and feed on His faithfulness. Delight yourself also in the LORD, and He shall give you the desires of your heart.

PSALM 37:3–4 NKJV

It can be very frustrating. You get ready to work, but the inspiration is just not there. You need to get things done to stay on track, but something prevents you from moving forward.

Friend, God is waiting for you to get quiet before him, to cast aside your worries and seek the peace of his presence. After all, what you are doing is for him; he is not going to fail you.

However, learning to trust him is more important than whatever you must get done. Therefore, take a deep breath and calm your heart. Express your absolute confidence that he will do as he has promised. He will help you in your work and provide the desires of your heart. Then wait patiently for him to inspire you, because he will certainly do wonderful things on your behalf.

God, waiting is a challenge! Help me to be patient.
Help me to know you better and trust you more so that
I may serve you wholeheartedly and please you. Amen.

YOUR HEART, HIS HOME

This is my resting place forever. Here is where
I want to stay. I will bless her with plenty.
PSALM 132:14–15 NCV

When you accept Jesus as your Savior, he marks you as his own. Ephesians 4:30 (GNT) explains, "The Spirit is God's mark of ownership on you, a guarantee that the Day will come when God will set you free." In other words, God's own Holy Spirit dwells within you—connecting you to him forever. You cannot lose your relationship with God because it's not based on anything you can do or should refrain from. However, when you sin, you will recognize the dishonor of it because his Spirit is in your heart, saying, "Stop resisting me, beloved! Trust me. Rest in me. I will satisfy you and give you plenty."

O LORD, arise,
and come to
your resting place.
PSALM 132:8
GOD'S WORD

Your heart is his home, and he works to keep you spotless, pure, and beautiful. So don't fear losing him. Rather, acknowledge when your heart needs to be cleansed.

God, thank you that I don't need to fear losing you
when I sin. Help me to live a life of holiness and hope so that
your home in my heart can stay beautiful forever. Amen.

BEGINNING AGAIN

The steps of a good man are ordered by the Lord: and he delighteth in his way. Though he fall, he shall not be utterly cast down: for the Lord upholdeth him with his hand.
PSALM 37:23–24 KJV

Faithfulness will spring up from the ground, and righteousness will look down from the sky.
PSALM 85:11 NRSV

A tiny shoot thrusts itself through the crusty soil and pushes up into the sunlight. Fragile but determined, it presses on until one day it is covered with beautiful flowers. It stands glorious in triumph— until the cold winter winds extinguish its beauty and strip it of all it has worked so hard to accomplish. But the story does not end. In season, spring breezes blow across the forsaken ground and the sun once again warms the earth. Its hope restored, the little shoot, waiting beneath the soil, begins its journey again.

In many ways, your life is as fragile as that tiny plant. Cold winds may blow over you, leaving you feeling withered and ruined. But then God shines his light on your life and you can blossom once more.

God, help me push through the crusty soil of heartache and bloom again in the springtime of your love. Amen.

THE PROMISED ANOINTED ONE

My anointed one will be a light for my people.
PSALM 132:17 NLT

The Ark of the Covenant was important to Israel because God's presence would shine above it once a year on the Day of Atonement. Psalm 132 was written to commemorate the day when the Ark was brought back to Jerusalem after a long time away. Yet it also looked forward to the day when God's presence would constantly shine on his people.

> *Here I will dwell, for I have desired it. I will abundantly bless her provision. . . . Her priests also I will clothe with salvation, and her godly ones will sing aloud for joy.*
> PSALM 132:14–16 NASB

Friend, that day came when the anointed one—Jesus—came as the Light of the World. Because of him, you can constantly have God's presence in your life—every minute of every day. So embrace God's light by believing in Jesus, and thank him that you never have to live in darkness again.

God, I do believe in you! Thank you for sending Jesus to open the way to you and for constantly shining light on my life. Amen.

SOMEONE TO COUNT ON

*I have been young, and now am old; yet have I not seen
the righteous forsaken, nor his seed begging bread.*

PSALM 37:25 KJV

*Keep me safe, O God,
for in you I take refuge.*

PSALM 16:1 NIV

Life is a long and complex journey that includes the tragic and the sublime, the good times and the bad times. Where can you turn when the bad times come? Who will keep your feet from stumbling when your eyes are filled with tears?

Even your closest friends and family can disappoint you—just as you can disappoint them. You can be confident that there is someone who will never let you down, someone who will be there for you in every season of your life, someone who will lift your burdens and provide light for your feet as you walk along dark and lonely stretches of life's road. That someone is God. He has promised never to leave you nor forsake you. He will walk with you every step of the way.

*God, thank you for the comforting light of your presence
and the comforting strength of your arm that lead me
carefully through the dark places in my life. Amen.*

UNIFIED

How good and how pleasant it is for
brethren to dwell together in unity!
PSALM 133:1 NKJV

In the human body, muscles, bones, and tendons; glands and nerves; and the cardiovascular, digestive, immune, and respiratory systems all coordinate to comprise a living being. Though they are different in their functions, they all work together to keep you going.

The LORD
gives his
blessing of
life forever.
PSALM 133:3 NCV

Your body is truly amazing—and it's the perfect way to understand how we relate to each other as God's people. God doesn't want us to be exactly alike—he created us with special talents and unique strengths. Yet we all come together for the extraordinary purpose of serving him.

Love for God is the basis of our unity—not conformity. So serve God with your whole heart and you're sure to fit right in.

> *God, thank you for creating me with a unique*
> *purpose that fits right in with your people.*
> *I praise you for uniting us all in love. Amen.*

A DIFFERENT FOCUS

Lord, make me to know my end and [to appreciate] the measure of my days—what it is; let me know and realize how frail I am [how transient is my stay here].
PSALM 39:4 AMP

Lord, what do I wait for? My hope is in You.
PSALM 39:7 HCSB

Too often people base their happiness on a future experience —a career, a wedding, the birth of a child, or what have you. They are utterly convinced that they will not be content or complete without it. Unfortunately, they are so focused on tomorrow that they fail to make the most of today, and they miss the blessings God has for them.

Friend, is this you? Are you waiting for life to begin when you get that great job, meet the perfect man, or achieve some other goal? Then your focus is misplaced.

God has important things for you to do and people for you to love today. So do not waste your life on fantasies. Rather, devote it to the One who will make you truly joyful and whole. The rest will come in its time.

God, only you can truly make my life meaningful. Please help me to focus on honoring you today rather than the blessings of tomorrow. Amen.

A REASON TO LIVE FOREVER

Oh, praise the LORD, all you servants of the LORD,
you who serve at night in the house of the LORD.
PSALM 134:1 NLT

Forever—that's a long time. In fact, eternity is so overwhelming, many may wonder what we'll be doing. Other than eating at God's banquet and worshiping at his throne, won't we get bored? But heaven isn't just puffy clouds and flowing robes. Whatever your purpose is on earth, it'll be even more joyous and fulfilling in eternity—because there, you won't face any of the hindrances that you have here. Rather, you'll praise God in creative ways you've never dreamed of.

> *Lift your praising hands to the Holy Place, and bless GOD. In turn, may God of Zion bless you—GOD who made heaven and earth!*
> PSALM 134:2–3 MSG

★ ☾ ★

Friend, don't underestimate the overpowering awe of being in the magnificent presence of your Creator. He's more wonderful than you ever hoped. You're going to love heaven—and it's certain you'll never want to leave.

God, I don't know what we'll be doing in heaven, but as long as I'm in your presence, I'll have everything I need. Hallelujah and amen!

AN AMAZING FUTURE

You, LORD God, have done many wonderful things, and you have planned marvelous things for us. No one is like you! I would never be able to tell all you have done.
PSALM 40:5 CEV

I delight to do Your will, O my God; Your Law is within my heart.

PSALM 40:8 NASB

✸

This verse contains a wonderful promise: God has planned marvelous things for you. In fact, his vision for your future is infinitely higher and abundantly better than anything you could imagine. If you are somewhat confused about what he is doing in your life—it is no wonder. You are not supposed to figure it out or understand how all of your experiences fit together. Not yet, anyway. God is doing something through you that is so amazing it can only be achieved by his magnificent power and imagination.

Allow this hope to strengthen you today: Because of God's extraordinary love, the best is still ahead. His plans for your future are unfolding, and they are truly fantastic. So have faith, friend, honor him always, and praise his glorious name.

God, I can imagine some amazing things—but your plans are resplendently filled with your love, power, and brilliance. Praise your wonderful name! Amen.

DESTRUCTIBLE VERSUS ETERNAL

The idols of the nations are of silver and gold, made by human hands. They have mouths, but cannot speak, eyes, but cannot see.
PSALM 135:15–16 HCSB

When the people of Israel got impatient for God to act, they'd mold an idol and ask it for help. Of course, these lifeless statuettes couldn't hear, speak, or move—they were useless. But the Israelites wanted something they could put their hands on to trust.

Your name, O LORD, endures forever; your fame, O LORD, is known to every generation. For the LORD will give justice to his people and have compassion on his servants.
PSALM 135:13–14 NLT

The same is true when you base your security on your job, wealth, or some other tangible thing. You're trusting in something constructed with human hands that can also be destroyed by human hands. True, you cannot see God, but you're assured that your faith in him is well founded because he is faithful and everlasting.

Friend, don't give up hope; keep believing in God. He'll never disappoint you.

God, sometimes I wish I had something tangible to put my trust in, but I know you're the only One truly worthy of my faith. Amen.

REFLECTING HIS CHARACTER

Happy are those who are concerned for the poor;
the LORD will help them when they are in trouble.
PSALM 41:1 GNT

By this I know that You favor and delight in me. . . . You have upheld me in my integrity and set me in Your presence forever.

PSALM 41:11–12 AMP

✴

God has provided everything you have. When you needed salvation, he gave it to you freely. When you were desperate for his help and comfort, he sent it to you without reservation.

He does this not only for your sake, but for those around you as well. You see, it is his desire that as you receive his compassion and encouragement, they will transform you and you will grow in his character. You become kindhearted and giving because of your love and gratitude to the Lord.

Friend, do you give freely, reflecting God's character and provision to others? God is generous and loving, and he wants his people to be so as well. So today be his representative and care for those in need just as he would.

God, thank you for your mercy and generosity. Help me
to meet others' needs with your sincere compassion so that
they can know you and praise your name. Amen.

EXPRESSING YOUR GRATITUDE

*Give thanks to the Lord of lords. His love continues
forever. Only he can do great miracles.*
PSALM 136:3–4 NCV

It's customary to seek God when you're hurting and need his intervention—but how often do you simply communicate your thankfulness to him?

*O give thanks to the
God of heaven,
for His mercy and
loving-kindness
endure forever!*

PSALM 136:26 AMP

*🌙

Friend, you should show appreciation to God in every situation because it helps you rightly refocus your attention on him. Articulating your gratefulness strengthens your love for him and refreshes your soul. So stop what you're doing right now and praise God. Express your gratefulness to him for all the loving ways he's provided for you. Thank him for the good he's bringing out of your most difficult situations and the blessings he's creating that you cannot yet see. Then just worship him for who he is. Feels wonderful, doesn't it?

*God, it does feel fantastic to thank you and worship you
for your loving-kindness to me. You are utterly amazing
and worthy of all my gratefulness! Amen.*

DRAWING STRENGTH FROM STILLNESS

Cease striving and know that I am God; I will be exalted among the nations, I will be exalted in the earth.
PSALM 46:10 NASB

Come, behold the works of the LORD.

PSALM 46:8 NKJV

The swift pace and challenges of life can leave you weary and disheartened if you never take time to rest in your relationship with God. That is why it is crucial for you to be quiet before him, surrendering yourself and your struggles to him as an offering. Be silent and relax, confident that he can handle everything that concerns you. Meditate on his sufficiency. Surely nothing is impossible for Almighty God—the glorious Creator of heaven and earth. Enjoy his presence and allow his Spirit to encourage your heart. Receive his mighty strength and wonderful wisdom for every burden you carry.

It is in the stillness that God will give you the confidence and endurance for everything that comes your way. So know him, friend, and find peace.

God, I sit before you in quiet expectation. Please help me to be calm and focus on you. Fill me with your peace and strength and I will praise your name. Amen.

WHEN IT'S DIFFICULT TO PRAISE

How shall we sing the Lord's song in a strange land?
PSALM 137:4 AMP

When the inhabitants of Jerusalem were taken captive to Babylon, they lost absolutely everything. Their homes, families, and even the temple where they worshiped God were destroyed. It was as if their identity and security had been lost forever. How could they possibly praise?

> *Let my tongue stick to the roof of my mouth if I do not remember you, if I do not think about Jerusalem as my greatest joy.*
>
> PSALM 137:6 NCV

Perhaps you're experiencing a similar loss—your life's been destroyed and you don't know what to do. First, you must remember all the times God has been faithful to you in the past. Second, cling to the fact that God is still with you and is working on your behalf. God eventually brought the people back to Jerusalem and enabled them to rebuild the temple. He will restore you as well. Look forward to that time and praise him.

God, it is difficult, but I praise you for your faithfulness throughout history and your past goodness to me. I look forward to your deliverance and restoration. Amen.

December

*Not only is Christ
the key to God's
mystery, but all
wisdom and
knowledge are
hidden away
in him.*

COLOSSIANS 2:2–3 CEV

HIS RIGHTFUL PLACE

God is the king of the whole earth.
Make your best music for him!
PSALM 47:7 GOD'S WORD

Clap your hands, all you peoples! Shout to God with the voice of triumph! For the LORD Most High is awesome; He is a great King over all the earth.

PSALM 47:1–2 NKJV

When visiting heads of state, it is customary to bring a gift. Certainly no mediocre offering will do. You must present the dignitary with a meaningful item that represents your respect for them.

Unfortunately, most people do not approach God with the same reverence. Whereas people will offer their best to earthly leaders, they believe their Creator will be satisfied with the leftovers. They give him a few seconds of prayer, a minute or two of Bible reading, and an honorable mention now and again, and they think it is enough. Yet understand, there is no higher sovereign than God. When all other rulers have turned to dust, he remains Lord of all that exists. He deserves your absolute best. So stop presenting him with halfhearted offerings. Give God his rightful place in your life and truly honor him.

God, please forgive my not honoring you as I should. Help me to give you my very best today and every day—just as you deserve. Amen.

702

LOVE AND CREATION

The God whose skill formed the cosmos, His love never quits. The God who laid out earth on ocean foundations, His love never quits.
PSALM 136:5–6 MSG

Have you ever considered that the creation didn't have to be so spectacular? It wasn't necessary for there to be a full spectrum of fragrant flowers for you to admire or colorful birds to entertain you with their lovely songs. The mountains with their rugged heights, the valleys with their verdant panoramas, the briny beauty of the oceans—none of these landscapes had to exist. But they do.

> *Give thanks to the Lord of lords, for his steadfast love endures forever; to him who alone does great wonders, for his steadfast love endures forever.*
> PSALM 136:3–4 ESV

Why? God created everything for you to enjoy. In this way, he reveals himself to you and expresses his love for you. God always goes the extra mile to show you his love—and the creation is full evidence of this fact. So don't doubt him, friend. Surely he will always provide for your needs and satisfy your soul in a manner beyond all you could ask or imagine.

God, thank you for such an amazing world and for loving me so much! Help me to know your love and show you love in return. Amen.

WORTHY VENTURES

My mouth shall speak wisdom; the meditation of my heart shall be understanding. I will incline my ear to a proverb.
PSALM 49:3–4 ESV

> *See what happens to those who trust in themselves, the fate of those who are satisfied with their wealth—they are doomed. . . . But God will rescue me; he will save me from the power of death.*
>
> PSALM 49:13–15 GNT

For a beloved child of God, there are some activities that are not worthy of your time. Pursuing possessions that quickly perish, holding grudges, fretting over the future, and achieving ambitions by unjust means are all deeds that are unbecoming to one who belongs to the Lord.

Friend, you have goals more significant to accomplish. Strengthening your relationship with God through prayer and Bible study, representing him faithfully in the world, being a good example, and telling others about him so they can be freed from sin all have enduring results in eternity. You are a person of worth, so do not waste your precious life on unworthy pursuits. Do only things that honor God. Then you can be sure that every minute is time well spent.

God, I want to honor you. Please show me the activities that merit my time and the ones that do not so I can glorify you with my entire life. Amen.

REMEMBERING THE DREAM

May my tongue cling to the roof of my mouth if I do not remember you, if I do not consider Jerusalem my highest joy.

PSALM 137:6 NIV

When God's people went into captivity in Babylon, they kept their hopes up by remembering their capital city of Jerusalem. Thoughts of returning to Jerusalem motivated them to persevere and not succumb to despair.

May I never be able to play the harp again if I forget you, Jerusalem!

PSALM 137:5 GNT

Friend, when you lose sight of your dreams, your life can become drudgery. In fact, if you're struggling today, you may have forgotten the vision God has given you. Yet you should never get so discouraged by your circumstances that you disregard his promises.

Whenever you lose your passion for life, realize it's either because you've stopped pursuing your dreams or because you've forgotten that God empowers you to achieve them. So today get back on track by remembering.

God, thank you for reminding me of your promises and reenergizing my life. May I never forget the great dreams you're fulfilling in me. Amen.

WORTH REPEATING

God looked down from heaven on all people to see if anyone was wise, if anyone was looking to God for help.

PSALM 53:2 NCV

How happy the people of Israel will be when God makes them prosperous again!

PSALM 53:6 GNT

Whenever you read something more than once in Scripture, it is because it is important. This is the case with Psalm 53, which is strikingly similar to Psalm 14.

Its message is certainly worthy of repetition—God peers down from his throne in heaven, watching for people who are looking for him. He wants to answer the searching heart and show his love to any who call upon him.

Are you seeking God? Do you long to experience his presence in a deep, meaningful way? Then realize that this desire within you is one he answers with a resounding "Yes!" He is gazing at you, friend, and he is delighted that you want to know him. Surely he will reveal himself to you in a powerful way.

God, I want to love you with all my heart, soul, mind, and strength. Thank you for making yourself known to me and for teaching me your wonderful ways. Amen.

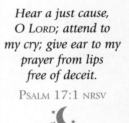
THE CONFIDENCE OF ANSWERED PRAYER

In the day when I cried thou answeredst me,
and strengthenedst me with strength in my soul.
PSALM 138:3 KJV

In the not-too-distant past, parents often summoned children for supper by means of a dinner bell. No matter where the children played, the sound of Mama's bell brought them scrambling toward home. Through the years, the pattern

Hear a just cause,
O LORD; attend to
my cry; give ear to my
prayer from lips
free of deceit.

PSALM 17:1 NRSV

remained the same: Mama called, and the children responded by showing up at the table. It was a summons not just to eat but to come *home*.

Now you are the one who often does the calling, and you wonder: Does God hear you? Will he answer your prayers? You can have confidence in the fact that God not only hears but is faithful to answer your cries for help. Knowing that God is always ready to respond when you call to him gives you boldness and strength. In him you find your true home.

God, I am glad I am a member of your family. I am listened
to and I am heard. You honor me with your patience
and encourage me with your faithfulness. Amen.

A FAITHFUL SOUNDING BOARD

Give ear to my prayer, O God. . . . Give heed to me and answer me; I am restless in my complaint and am surely distracted.
PSALM 55:1–2 NASB

I call to God; God will help me. At dusk, dawn, and noon I sigh deep sighs—he hears, he rescues.

PSALM 55:16–17 MSG

✴

The troubles come from every side, leaving you almost paralyzed due to their intensity. You try to concentrate—to get something done. However, the problems you face bombard your thoughts until you cannot separate one from another.

You are weary but cannot sleep. You want to escape but feel so bound by the situation that you cannot take your mind off it. You think no one could possibly understand the toll it is taking on your soul. However, there is One who does. Friend, no matter what troubles you are facing, there is no reason for despair. God hears you and will help you. Call to him—lay your burdens at his feet. He never tires of hearing you and is always available to speak peace to your soul.

God, thank you for understanding the terrible stress I am experiencing and for listening to my prayers. And thank you, dear Lord, for helping me as only you can. Amen.

708

HOPE AND HUMILITY

Though the Lord is supreme, he takes care of those who
are humble, but he stays away from the proud.
PSALM 138:6 NCV

Many people believe that such things as money, posses-sions, good looks, intelligence, and even power are the measure of their lives. None of these is inherently bad, yet none can predict happiness or instill a lasting sense of worth. What if you were to awaken one morning to find that your personal wealth and power had vanished?

God, examine me and know my heart; test me and know my nervous thoughts. See if there is any bad thing in me. Lead me on the road to everlasting life.
PSALM 139:23–24 NCV

☾

What if your attractiveness failed and your intelligence faltered? Would hopelessness and despair overcome you?

God places little importance on outward appearances or the size of bank accounts. He measures your life and hearts by a different standard. He teaches you that humility leads to greatness and that you achieve true success when you give yourselves to others. No measure other than the eternal love of God is a true measure.

God, help me measure my life by your standard so that my
hope may shine brightly and never be disappointed. Amen.

LET GO

Give your burdens to the LORD, and he will take care of you.
He will not permit the godly to slip and fall.
PSALM 55:22 NLT

He will redeem my soul in peace from the battle which is against me.

PSALM 55:18 NASB

Are some issues so personal that you feel you cannot give them up—not even to God? The thought of entrusting your beloved burden to his care is more than you can handle. It is as if you would be allowing a piece of your heart to be torn from you.

Friend, let go. You have made this situation an idol, and you are clinging to it as if it could make you happy. Yet all that it has brought you is heartache.

Your battle is not with God, it is with yourself. Moreover, if you release this burden to him, he will take care of it better than you ever could. He will also heal you of all the pain it has caused you.

So let go. And let God show you how sufficient he truly is.

God, it is so difficult for me to relinquish control in this area. Nevertheless, I also know it will destroy me if I do not. Please help me—overcome my fears and teach me to trust. Amen.

A WORK OF HIS HANDS

The LORD will fulfill his purpose for me;
your love, O LORD, endures forever.
PSALM 138:8 NIV

Are you pondering what God is doing in your life? You may not know, and that is okay. However, the real question is this: Do you have confidence that God knows where he is leading you?

Many, O LORD my God, are the wonders you have done. The things you planned for us no one can recount to you; . . . they would be too many to declare.

PSALM 40:5 NIV

Your hope should not be based on your understanding of God's purpose for you. Rather, your faith should be firmly grounded in God, who is bringing it about in you. Even if that purpose seems distant, you still trust him to bring you to the destination successfully.

It is his able hand that works out his plans—not yours. Trust him to do exactly what is needed to bring them to fulfillment.

Dear God, I trust that you are a faithful and able leader. Thank you that my future is a work in your hands. Amen.

THROUGH HIM YOU WON'T FAIL

O my Strength, I watch for you; you, O God, are my fortress, my loving God. God will go before me.
PSALM 59:9–10 NIV

You've been a safe place for me. . . . Strong God, I'm watching you do it, I can always count on you—God, my dependable love.

PSALM 59:16–17 MSG

You face many challenges every day—some are exciting, some routine, and others may be quite difficult. While there are times of instability that will assail your life, there is one truth that never changes: God is your eternal strength and your present help. Nothing you face takes him by surprise.

God has never been unfaithful to you, and he never will be. If he has asked you to wait for his answer to come, then it is because he has something far better for you than you can imagine.

Thoughts of doubt may tempt you to believe that he is not watching over your life; however, if he knows when a sparrow falls to the earth, then he certainly knows your every need.

God, thank you for loving me and for walking with me each moment of every day. No matter what I face, I know that you will help me through the day. Amen.

PROFOUND KNOWING

O Lord, you have searched me [thoroughly]
and have known me.
PSALM 139:1 AMP

You can keep up a front with other people—it's a way to protect yourself when you feel insecure. You conceal your flaws and fears so people can't hurt you. Unfortunately, your defenses also stop you from receiving their love.

Where could I go to escape from you? . . . If I flew away beyond the east or lived in the farthest place in the west, you would be there to lead me, you would be there to help me.

PSALM 139:7, 9–10
GNT

Yet you cannot hide from God. He knows you completely and is aware that those defenses are stopping you from having the life you were created for. That's why he chips away at them until you can fully experience his love. Friend, God knows you more profoundly than you know yourself—and he's declared that you're worth loving. Therefore, let him tear down those defenses so that others can know and love you as well.

God, you're my Protector—not the defenses I've built up.
Please tear down the harmful walls in my life so I
can fully experience your love. Amen.

A DAILY NEED

For God alone, O my soul, wait in silence, for my hope is from him. He only is my rock and my salvation, my fortress; I shall not be shaken.
PSALM 62:5–6 ESV

Trust God, my friends, and always tell him each one of your concerns. God is our place of safety.

PSALM 62:8 CEV

Every day, you will face challenges—some of them are simple to solve, while others are more trying. There will be times when you will want to rush ahead of God, even though you do not have a clear plan.

However, he has allowed that difficulty so that you will learn to trust him at a deeper level—seeking him consistently for your needs. His timing in your situation is perfect, and if you move too quickly, you risk missing his best.

If you seek him daily and wait for him to work on your behalf, you will discover that your waiting is not in vain. Therefore, when trouble comes, ask him to show you how to deal with the matter and allow him to draw you even closer through it.

God, teach me to wait for your very best and to rest in the safety of your care. Every day I will seek your face and trust you to lead me. Amen.

EVERYWHERE YOU ARE

With your powerful arm,
you protect me from every side.
PSALM 139:5 CEV

Having returned from Sunday school, a little boy was playing with his dog in the front yard of his house. A neighbor, the local cynic, walked by and stopped to visit with the boy. He asked him what he'd been doing that morning, and the boy told him he'd been to Sunday school where he'd learned a lot about God.

Let me hear what God the LORD will speak, for he will speak peace to his people.

PSALM 85:8 NRSV

★ ☾ ★

The neighbor laughed derisively and challenged the boy, "Well, if you can tell me where God is, I'll give you a quarter." The boy responded in a polite and calm voice, "Sir, if you'll tell me where God isn't, I'll give you a dollar."

God is everywhere you are. For the most difficult day, God is your stay. For the darkest night, God is your light. God is with you in all things to bring you peace.

Dear God, I can't go anywhere today that you won't be there to greet me with peace. Thank you for the peace you give when I come to you. Amen.

HIS TO LOVE

The God who is in his holy dwelling place is the father of the fatherless and the defender of widows. God places lonely people in families.
PSALM 68:5–6 GOD'S WORD

Thanks be to the Lord, who daily carries our burdens for us. God is our salvation.

PSALM 68:19
GOD'S WORD

Have you truly opened your heart to the wondrous love that God has for you? You may say, "Oh, I know he loves me," but do you realize that his love for you is so great that he thinks about you constantly? He longs to give you good things, and when your heart is turned toward him in devotion, he is blessed.

You do not have to wait until you "feel" the love of God—his love is a reality that is always present with you. No sin can prevent him from loving you, and nothing is greater or has more power than his love. Rather, he gives his wonderful love to you freely, unconditionally; and the closer you grow in your relationship with him, the more you learn how faithful, strong, and true his care for you really is.

Draw me ever nearer to you, God, so that I will know the fullness of your love. In you I hope, and I give myself to you wholeheartedly. Amen.

THE DIVINE MYSTERY AT THE HEART OF LIFE

Such knowledge is too wonderful for me,
too great for me to understand!
PSALM 139:6 NLT

God's power and love are too great for you to fully comprehend in this life. Great art, poetry, and music perhaps best convey God's mind-numbing majesty. When you pause from your daily routine of activities, struck by the intensity of a sunset or majesty of a tree or the beauty of a butterfly,

O give thanks to the Lord of lords, for his steadfast love endures forever; who alone does great wonders, for his steadfast love endures forever.

PSALM 136:3–4 NRSV

you catch a glimpse of the divine mystery at the heart of life. And it only whets your appetite for more. It is a glimmer of God's handiwork, vanishing as quickly as it has captured your attention.

The attitude of awe is a powerful reminder of your littleness and God's greatness. Reacquire the receptive mind of the child so that you may never lose the "wow" you feel for the stunning beauty of God's grandeur in the world.

God, give me the heart of a child, a heart that is constantly amazed and awed by your greatness. Amen.

BE CAREFUL WHOM YOU FOLLOW

Give the gift of wise rule to the king, O God. . . . May he judge your people rightly, be honorable to your meek and lowly.
PSALM 72:1–2 MSG

Praise be to the LORD God, the God of Israel, who alone does marvelous deeds. Praise be to his glorious name forever; may the whole earth be filled with his glory.

PSALM 72:18–19 NIV

Every day you receive many messages—people expressing their opinions on the television and radio and in conversation. Many have strong views and make viable cases for why you should have the same outlook as theirs. God cautions you to be wise and not believe all you hear.

God is straightforward in his approach to right and wrong—and you can be sure that anything that contradicts his Word is false and destructive. So do not get caught in the trap of thinking he does not really care what you do. He will not ignore your unfaithfulness. The Lord has only the best in mind for your life, and he is motivated to see you enjoy it. However, it all begins with your obedience to him. Therefore, do as he says, because he really is worth following.

God, you are truly a worthy leader, and I love your ways. Please help me to embrace your truth and to apply it correctly to my life. Amen.

LORD OF THE NIGHT

Even the darkness is not dark to you; the night is as bright as the day, for darkness is as light to you.
PSALM 139:12 NRSV

Waking up in the wee hours of the night, you find that all is still and black as pitch. As you walk to the refrigerator for a drink, your eye peeks outside at the night sky, the backyard, and the woods that fringe the edge of the lawn. What is it about nighttime that calls the spirit toward fear or peace, anxiety or calm?

By day the LORD directs his love, at night his song is with me—a prayer to the God of my life.
PSALM 42:8 NIV

☾

When he penned the lines of Psalm 139, David prefaced them with these rhetorical questions: "Where can I go from your Spirit? Where can I flee from your presence?" (v. 7 NIV). David knew that even the darkness could not hide him from God's watchful eyes and blanketing care. The darkness need not hold fear for you; God always watches over you. And that is reason enough to find peace in the night.

Dear God, may I walk straight into my darkness and trust that your light will chase it away. And when darkness comes again, may I remember what I learned in the light. Amen.

PROACTIVE OR REACTIVE?

We will tell to the generation to come the praiseworthy deeds of the Lord, and His might, and the wonderful works that He has performed.
PSALM 78:4 AMP

He commanded our fathers, that they should make them known to their children . . . that they may set their hope in God, and not forget the works of God, but keep His commandments.

PSALM 78:5, 7 NKJV

Your life is a testimony of the way God works. People will learn whether they can truly trust the Lord by observing how you handle moments of joy as well as times of sorrow.

Friend, when you battle hardships and obstacles, do you still demonstrate faith in your unshakable God? There were times when Moses, David, Paul, and the disciples experienced terrible pressure. However, each one of them refused to give up or react negatively to their circumstances. Rather, they were proactive—they not only honored the Lord and grew in their faith, but many others came to know him through their excellent example. The same can be true for you, but you must decide to trust him in every situation. Will you honor him no matter what happens? Will you be his faithful witness as well?

God, I choose to trust you today and refuse to believe or respond to any and every thought of spiritual defeat.

HIS WORK IS WONDERFUL

You knitted me together in my mother's womb. I praise you,
for I am fearfully and wonderfully made.
PSALM 139:13–14 ESV

You are God's special creation. When he formed you, he was delighted to give you all the qualities that make you unique—your traits and talents. Yet even the things you consider flaws and weaknesses were all part of his perfecting you—his wonderful one.

With your own eyes you saw my body being formed. Even before I was born, you had written in your book everything I would do.

PSALM 139:16 CEV

✦☾✦

He made no mistakes in constructing you. In fact, those aspects you feel are errors are actually his mark on your life— what he used in a powerful way to make himself known to you.

This morning, rejoice that you have been excellently formed by your wonderful maker, and fulfill that precious part of his great plan that has been specially created for you.

Dear God, thank you for creating me the
way I am. I praise you that all of your
works are truly wonderful. Amen.

BREAKING DESTRUCTIVE CYCLES

Do not hold us guilty for the sins of our ancestors! Let your compassion quickly meet our needs, for we are on the brink of despair.

PSALM 79:8 NLT

Then we, your people, the ones you love and care for, will thank you over and over and over. We'll tell everyone we meet how wonderful you are, how praiseworthy you are!

PSALM 79:13 MSG

You can change the way you respond to life's trials and temptations, but you cannot do it alone. You need God's encouraging truth to make the switch from failure to success. Many people think this is impossible. They look at the shortcomings of their parents or other family members and are tempted to think, *I am just like them. I will never change.*

God did not want the nation of Israel to be defeated by the sins of their ancestors. He had a better plan in mind for them. Because of his great love and mercy, they could overcome every obstacle, and you can do the same when you surrender your life to him.

God, I want to be the very best I can be. Therefore, I choose not to dwell on thoughts of defeat or failure. Rather, I rejoice that your life flows through me. Amen.

WOVEN IN SECRET

*My frame was not hidden from you when I was made in
the secret place. When I was woven together in the depths
of the earth, your eyes saw my unformed body.*
PSALM 139:15–16 NIV

A butterfly slips slowly from its cocoon and flutters away on a gentle breeze. Hidden from sight, it passes through a transforming process known only to God, its Creator. In the same way that God made the butterfly, God fashioned you in secret—adding, subtracting, and shaping as only the great Creator can.

*He brought me out
into a broad place; he
delivered me, because
he delighted in me.*

PSALM 18:19 NRSV

When you are tempted to question your inherent worth or to see yourself as ugly and ungainly, you must remember that you are a treasured piece of God's own handiwork. You are an expression of the same creative force that placed the stars in the sky, strewed the flowers along the path, and raised up dry land in the midst of the sea. It is in the hand of the Artist that you have reason to hope.

*Great God, when my failings cause me to lose a sense of my
own value, I will hope in you, for you made me. Amen.*

A PERSONAL RESPONSIBILITY

*Defend the weak and the orphans; defend
the rights of the poor and suffering.*
PSALM 82:3 NCV

*Rescue weak and needy
people. Help them
escape the power of
wicked people.*

PSALM 82:4
GOD'S WORD

The enemy of your soul cannot defeat you—not as long as Jesus is guarding your life. Nothing is more powerful than Christ's ability to sustain you. He is all-knowing and all-powerful. No force on this earth can overwhelm you when you are walking in fellowship with him.

However, when you choose to disobey him and strike out on your own, you will receive only what you can produce. You also will expose yourself to the enemy's sinister attacks.

Jesus promises to defend you and to fight on your behalf, but only if you are surrendered to his manner of protecting you. Therefore, do not put yourself in harm's way. Seek the Savior, who has promised to bless and keep you, because he is faithful to give you the victory.

*God, keep me close to you. Make me aware of my
weaknesses so I can surrender them to you. Amen.*

A NEW NAME

He put a new song in my mouth, a song of praise to our God;
many will see and fear and will trust in the LORD.
PSALM 40:3 NASB

There is a town in England named Christchurch, and it received its name in a most interesting way. Many years ago, some men were building a church there and were joined in their work by a stranger who was an excellent carpenter. He

Create in me a clean heart, O God, and put a new and right spirit within me.

PSALM 51:10 NRSV

★ ☾ ★

worked harder than anyone else but would never accept any pay. When the church was completed, a dedication service was held, but the stranger did not attend. He was never seen in their town again. As the townspeople pondered this mystery, they decided the stranger was none other than Jesus, the carpenter from Nazareth. After only a little deliberation, they voted to change the name of their town from Twineham to Christchurch.

When Jesus comes to your heart, nothing stays the same. He revives you and then he revises you.

Dear God, you change my fear to faith, my reluctance
to resolve, and my uneasiness to peace. I give thanks
for your transforming power in my life. Amen.

OKAY NOW

*Your presence fills me with joy and
brings me pleasure forever.*
PSALM 16:11 GNT

*Even when the way
goes through Death
Valley, I'm not afraid
when you walk at
my side. Your trusty
shepherd's crook makes
me feel secure.*

PSALM 23:4 MSG

Circumstances can be dire and forecasts bleak, but when you are close to God, you can be secure enough to step forward in your life with purpose and courage. You can have confidence to move toward goals and objectives, and know that God is with you.

As God accompanies you, he gives wisdom to your mind, resolve to your will, and joy to your heart. He reinforces that you belong to him. He makes known the many and varied resources he makes available to you. God's presence guarantees that you will never be alone and that you will never have to face anything by yourself. You can stand tall because God lifts you up. You can stride confidently because God walks with you.

*Dear God, in your presence I am in a large place of
purpose and possibility, power and provision. Amen.*

726

THOUGHT-ATTACK

Lord GOD, my strong Savior,
You shield my head on the day of battle.
PSALM 140:7 HCSB

You've heard of psych-ops, the strategy of waging war within the mind and intimidating enemies by undermining what they believe. That's essentially what happens in your spiritual life—your old, destructive thoughts battle against God's truth and the good he's doing in you. God

Surely the righteous shall give thanks to Your name; the upright shall dwell in Your presence.

PSALM 140:13 NKJV

☽

promises you success, but those thoughts predict failure. God says he loves and accepts you, but you only remember when others rejected you.

But God transforms your mind and cleanses it of negative thoughts when you study his Word. Whenever the bad thoughts return, you subdue them by repeating his promises. That's why you should continually focus on God—because with him, eventually you'll be truly victorious on the battleground of your mind.

God, please help me to get rid of those negative and untrue thoughts. Remind me of your Word so that I can think triumphantly. Amen.

PEACE, IF . . .

I am listening to what the Lord God is saying; he promises peace to us, his own people, if we do not go back to our foolish ways.
PSALM 85:8 GNT

God will soon save those who respect him, and his glory will be seen in our land. Love and truth belong to God's people; goodness and peace will be theirs.
PSALM 85:9–10 NCV

A deep sense of peace is yours when you turn your thoughts to God. There is always hope when you choose to listen to him instead of to the negative messages of the world.

God's Word reminds you that when you draw near to him, you will find the comfort you need. When you are still in his presence, he provides the wisdom and insight to meet every challenge victoriously. King David knew that with God's aid he could advance against a mighty army and subdue his enemies. Because of his faith, the Lord strengthened him and gave him many astounding triumphs.

Not every day brings an emergency or a call for action, but many do bring a need to remember how greatly God loves you. So seek him, and receive his peace.

Thank you, dear God, for the times you express your unconditional love toward me. Teach me your ways so I can always abide in your peace. Amen.

A TROUBLING TONGUE

Set a guard, O LORD, over my mouth;
keep watch over the door of my lips.
PSALM 141:3 NKJV

Do you say, "I can't" or "God can"? Do you declare, "I'm not strong enough" or "I can do anything through him who strengthens me"? Do you proclaim, "It's impossible" or "With God everything is possible"?

Think about what you articulate—do you focus on your weaknesses or God's power? It's no wonder your speech is negative when you're constantly mea-

GOD, come close. Come quickly! Open your ears—it's my voice you're hearing! Treat my prayer as sweet incense rising; my raised hands are my evening prayers.
PSALM 141:1–2 MSG

★ ☾ ★

suring your burdens against your ability to handle them. However, when you focus on God, you realize that he can handle anything you face.

Friend, you can either talk yourself into defeat or call upon God for the victory. So voice your praises to God's amazing power and perfect wisdom. It's the surest way to triumph!

God, I praise you! I will speak out my confidence in your love, wisdom, and power, because you truly deserve it. Thank you for the victory. Amen.

RESPITE FOR THE WEARY SOUL

*He who dwells in the shelter of the Most High
will rest in the shadow of the Almighty.*
PSALM 91:1 NIV

*He will cover you
with his feathers. He
will shelter you with
his wings. His faith-
ful promises are your
armor and protection.*

PSALM 91:4 NLT

How does one rest in the shadow of the Almighty? The idea presented is this: You are in the presence of God no matter where you are or what time of the day it happens to be. God is always with you, and his presence brings you an undeniable sense of peace.

This means that you can literally abide in his shelter at all times—sensing His closeness and deep affection no matter the situation. Whether you are shopping, in a business meeting, talking with a friend, or praying at home in your quiet time, he is with you.

When heartache threatens or trouble approaches, his protective cover drops down over your life, providing the spiritual comfort you need amid every storm.

*God, thank you for protecting me from the troubles that assail me. I am
tired, God, but I am thankful that with you I can find true rest. Amen.*

CONSTRUCTIVE REBUKES

If a good person punished me, that would be kind. If he corrected me, that would be like perfumed oil on my head.
PSALM 141:5 NCV

The person who talks too loud may not realize she has a hearing problem. The person who stands too close when conversing with others may not realize that he's making people feel uncomfortable. You may not even realize that you have broccoli in your teeth after lunch unless a friend points it out to you.

I look to you for help, O Sovereign LORD. You are my refuge.
PSALM 141:8 NLT

At times, there will be things about you that you won't realize are amiss, counterproductive, and even destructive. These foibles are blind spots that are impeding your progress.

Thankfully, God wants you to succeed, so he reveals those issues to you. Listen to him when he rebukes you, because he wants you to reach your full potential.

God, thank you for revealing my weaknesses, sins, and blind spots. Thank you for loving me enough to help me be all that I can be. Amen.

AN ATTITUDE OF ADORATION

It is good to give thanks to the LORD, to sing praises to your name, O Most High; to declare your steadfast love in the morning, and your faithfulness by night.
PSALM 92:1–2 ESV

You, O LORD, have made me glad by what You have done, I will sing for joy at the works of Your hands.

PSALM 92:4 NASB

✷

Battling difficulties can be draining and may alter the way you view your circumstances. Instead of seeing the potential of your life, you begin to feel that you are not special and that God has forgotten you. His good plan for your life seems more and more unlikely every time you think about it.

However, remember that his goal for you is always geared for ultimate victory and success. Therefore, the best remedy for your heart is to sing songs of praise to remind you of his goodness. No matter what you are facing, God will lift your spirit when you worship him. This is what the psalmist did, which is why he wrote confidently and with great joy, "It is good to give thanks to the LORD."

God, you are my salvation and my source of joy and gladness. Truly it is good to praise you; and no matter what happens, I'll rejoice in your love for me! Amen.

PERSONAL PRISONS

Rescue me from this prison, so I can praise your name.
And when your people notice your wonderful
kindness to me, they will rush to my side.
PSALM 142:7 CEV

Your troubles surround you like an army—driving you forward though you long to rest. You feel like you have no choices—you tackle your day, trying to survive all the things that have to be done.

Lord, I cry out to you. I say, "You are my protection. You are all I want in this life."

PSALM 142:5 NCV

☽

Personal prisons take many shapes and sizes, but they're limiting all the same. Perhaps yours is due to illness or finances; or maybe there's a demanding relationship that requires your continual attention and care.

Friend, your situation is difficult, but it won't last forever. God will eventually set you free. But in the meantime, allow him to be your freedom. Even if your time and activities are restricted, your spirit isn't. So focus on him and discover true liberty.

God, I don't know how to be free with all I have to do,
but I know you can teach me your liberty. Thank you. Amen.

DISCIPLINE OF THE HEART

How blessed the man you train,
God, the woman you instruct in your Word.
PSALM 94:12 MSG

When I felt my feet slipping, you came with your love and kept me steady. And when I was burdened with worries, you comforted me and made me feel secure.

PSALM 94:18–19 CEV

Have you ever considered whether you are a living reflection of God's mercy and grace to others? If not, then you should ask God to teach you how to be an instrument of his love and understanding.

Each day you must deal with all kinds of situations—such as rude store clerks who test your patience and irate drivers in traffic who make your blood boil. However, each of these is an opportunity for you to demonstrate your true character—to show what is really in your heart. To react in a manner that honors God takes discipline. So the next time you are annoyed, angered, or aggravated, think of it as an opportunity to share his grace with the offender. Certainly God will bless your efforts to be more like him.

God, there are times when I need a firm reminder that
I belong to you and my actions reflect what is hidden
in my heart. Please help me to honor you. Amen.

DIRECTION

Teach me to do Your will, for You are my God;
let Your good Spirit lead me on level ground.
PSALM 143:10 NASB

There are times when God will give you ease in your journey—like a falcon effortlessly gliding over a forest with no concern for the problems below. These are the blessed moments when you truly believe anything's possible with God.

> *I trust in You; teach me the way in which I should walk; for to You I lift up my soul.*
>
> PSALM 143:8 NASB

There will also be seasons when you feel like an ant—small and challenged by obstacles. Every pebble on the path will require an arduous climb, and it'll be difficult to make progress. These are also blessed moments because you'll learn to rely on God.

Whether simple or difficult, on the heights or in the depths—when God is directing you, you're always on stable, level ground. So proceed with confidence. He'll protect and teach you wherever you go.

God, whether easy or difficult, I'll follow wherever you
lead. Truly, you are perfect and wonderful. Thank you
for delighting in me and directing my path. Amen.

HE HAS NOT FORGOTTEN

He has remembered his steadfast love and faithfulness to the house of Israel. All the ends of the earth have seen the salvation of our God.

PSALM 98:3 ESV

The LORD has made His victory known; He has revealed His righteousness in the sight of the nations.

PSALM 98:2 HCSB

There will be times when you wonder if God has forgotten his promises to you. He never does. Months or years may pass, but regardless of the length of time, always remember the plans he has for you. God does not operate according to anyone's schedule. Joseph spent years in Egyptian exile before he realized what the Lord wanted to do in his life. The time he spent in prison was not wasted. God was preparing him for an even greater purpose, and only time would reveal what this was. His responsibility was to wait obediently for the Lord to work.

This same principle applies to you. The next time you are tempted to become anxious or impatient, remember God always blesses those who are committed to waiting for and trusting him.

God, I want to honor you with my life. Please forgive me for pushing forward when you want me to wait, and help me to know when you want me to advance. Amen.

TRAINED AND READY

Blessed be the LORD, my rock, who trains my hands for war, and my fingers for battle.
PSALM 144:1 ESV

The obstacles in front of you will not defeat or destroy you, but they will be the vessels by which God brings you to your ultimate goal.

He is my loving God and my fortress, my stronghold and my deliverer, my shield. . . . the One who gives victory to kings, who delivers his servant David from the deadly sword.
PSALM 144:2, 10 NIV

Recall David's battle against Goliath and how Israel's army was afraid to confront the nine-foot Philistine giant. Even the gargantuan Goliath could not overcome David. David gained the victory through God's help, and eventually Israel recognized David's leadership because of it. Friend, do not fear your obstacles. Though you're overwhelmed right now, you will not succumb to them. Rather, thank God that he'll use them to fulfill his promises to you. He's training you for a great victory, so face those obstacles with courage.

God, thank you that these obstacles are really your way of preparing me for your great promises to me. I'll trust you through them all. Amen.

THE IMPORTANCE OF HOLINESS

*Exalt the LORD our God, and worship at
His holy hill; for the LORD our God is holy.*
PSALM 99:9 NKJV

*Mighty King, lover
of justice, you have
established fairness.
You have acted
with justice and
righteousness.*

PSALM 99:4 NLT

People often think that doing a certain activity will make them holy. There is only one way to begin the journey into holiness, and that is through a personal relationship with Jesus Christ.

Even though the Lord spent three years with the disciples, they still had problems that they had to overcome. Peter was impetuous, and Thomas was doubtful. The others worried whether Jesus would do what he had promised. However, when the Holy Spirit came and he renewed their minds, they began to respond to problems and difficulties the way Jesus had. They drew even nearer to him and sought to be holy—just as he is holy.

The same is true for you. The closer you grow to Christ, the more you will be inspired to live a pure life that honors him.

*God, remove everything within my life that would
prevent me from becoming like you. I love you and
want my life to honor you in every way. Amen.*

GOD IS IN THE DETAILS

I will meditate about your glory,
splendor, majesty, and miracles.
PSALM 145:5 TLB

God is evident in a tear or in a far-off whistle. He is in the twinkle of a stranger's eye and in a certain shade of blue. He is in the warmth of a handshake and in the missing front teeth of a five-year-old. He is between the lines of handwritten letters and in the nervous laughter of teenage girls. He is in the invisible

This is the LORD's doing; it is marvelous in our eyes. This is the day that the LORD has made; let us rejoice and be glad in it.
PSALM 118:23–24 NRSV

arc made by a hawk on a fine autumn day. He is the energy you use to write your to-do lists, and he is in the itch to take a break in the middle of the day.

God surrounds you with reminders of his presence. He is in kept promises and acts of love and mercy. God is in every sigh, whisper, and exclamation. God is by you now.

God, thank you for your presence in my life.
Give me eyes to see the many things you do for me. Amen.

A SONG TO SING TOGETHER

Shout praises to the LORD, everyone on this earth.
Be joyful and sing as you come in to worship the LORD!
PSALM 100:1–2 CEV

Realize that the LORD alone is God. He made us, and we are his. We are his people. . . . Enter his gates with a song of thanksgiving. Come into his courtyards with a song of praise. Give thanks to him; praise his name.

PSALM 100:3–4
GOD'S WORD

Nothing binds individuals together like a vibrant faith in Jesus. In fact, the normal things that divide people tend to melt away when they allow the abundant love of Christ to flow through them.

Believers were always meant to be unified. In fact, Revelation 7:9–10 says that one day people from "every race, tribe, nation, and language" will together call "out in a loud voice: 'Salvation comes from our God, who sits on the throne, and from the Lamb!'" (GNT). So next time you feel lonely or as if you don't belong, reach out to other Christians and ask what Jesus is doing in their lives. Soon enough, you will find your hearts knit together in songs of praise to the Lord.

God, thank you that I have a song to sing with every
other believer—a song of praise to you! Truly, you
are worthy of all honor and glory! Amen.

740

GOD'S JOY AND DELIGHT IN YOUR LIFE

The Lord is good to everyone;
he is merciful to all he has made.
PSALM 145:9 NCV

W hen you think of those you love—family and friends, mentors and heroes—joy and affection fill your heart. Because they are in the world, your life is brighter and more meaningful. You watch for opportunities to show them how much you care for them and value them. You jump at chances to nourish and to sustain them, to cheer them

The Lord himself
is my inheritance,
my prize. He is my
food and drink,
my highest joy!
PSALM 16:5 TLB

☾

and to make their hearts glad. Their very existence is a cause for celebration. When they are happy, you are happy.

As children of God, you mimic him in these feelings for your loved ones, feelings that are dim reflections of his profound delight in you as his children. He wants to see you happy and fulfilled, and he wants you to know he is the source of the abundant blessings in your life.

Knowing that I am your child brings me great joy and delight, God.
Help me to be happy and to achieve all that I was created to do. Amen.

FORGET IT

*As far as the east is from the west, so far has
He removed our transgressions from us.*
PSALM 103:12 NKJV

*Praise the LORD, my
soul, and do not forget
how kind he is. He
forgives all my sins
and heals all my
diseases. He keeps
me from the grave
and blesses me with
love and mercy.*

PSALM 103:2–4 GNT

There may be people in your life who never allow you to forget what you have done wrong. Every time you make a mistake, they are quick to pounce—reminding you of the ways you have failed.

However, God isn't like that. Whenever a believer repents he says, "I'll wipe the slate clean. . . . I'll forget they ever sinned!" (Jeremiah 31:34 MSG).

Of course, maybe the person who is always reminding you of your faults is . . . you. Don't do this to yourself. God forgives you, and when he says your sins have been erased forever, there isn't a trace of them left in your life. Therefore, pardon yourself and learn from your errors. Then praise him for all the grace he has shown you.

*God, thank you for forgiving all my sins and never
reminding me of the way I have failed. You are truly
loving and merciful, and I praise you! Amen.*

GOD'S TENDER MERCIES

*The LORD is good to all: and his tender
mercies are over all his works.*
PSALM 145:9 KJV

No one knows you like God;
every secret wish, shameful
weakness, latent talent, or buried
pain is plainly displayed before him.
He loves you in the fullness of who
you are, forgiving you of every sin,
protecting you from every adversity.
He is there to pick you up and dust
you off. He is there to guard and
protect you.

*Surround me with
your tender mercies so
I may live, for your
instructions are
my delight.*
PSALM 119:77 NLT

You may think you need more money; he may know that
what you really need is to reorient your priorities. You may be
disappointed because you didn't get a job or you missed an
opportunity; he may know that what you think you need is not
in your best interest. His mercies are mighty. If you let him, he
salves all your hurts in an intimate, knowing, and kind way.

*God, I place myself in your care and thank you for your tender
love that brings me all that you know I need. Amen.*

A MESSAGE FROM CREATION

What a wildly wonderful world, God! You made it all, with Wisdom at your side, made earth overflow with your wonderful creations.
PSALM 104:24 MSG

I will sing to the LORD as long as I live; I will sing praise to my God while I have my being. May my meditation be sweet to Him; I will be glad in the LORD.

PSALM 104:33–34 NKJV

✴

There will be times when your day seems flat and even dull. You start your daily routine and find yourself wondering why your attitude toward it has changed. Was there a time when it felt special, when the routine was easy and the pace of your life enjoyable?

Everyone feels this way at some point—it is as if life has lost its luster. However, there is a solution: Recall the awesome, creative power of God—surveying his handiwork and enjoying the world he has designed. The psalmist realized that when he praised God for his wondrous works, his heart lifted to new heights. You can do the same. Discover fresh hope for your day and expectancy for the future by remembering all the awesome things God has done.

God, please draw me near to you today so that I may see you and your creation in a new way. Truly you are infinite in nature and loving in all your ways. Amen.

744

YOUR ATTENTION PLEASE

They will speak of the glory of Your kingdom and will declare
Your might, informing [all] people of Your mighty acts.
PSALM 145:11–12 HCSB

You have within your grasp the greatest message ever known: There is one God who loves you and forgives your sins. He saves you if you'll only believe in him.

My mouth will declare
the LORD's praise;
let every living thing
praise His holy name
forever and ever.

PSALM 145:21 HCSB

Throughout history, the bravest, most compassionate people have proclaimed God's Word despite persecution, pressure, and terrible consequences. It was worth it because the message is true—and it transforms the life of whoever accepts it.

You may be fearful of the attention God's message will bring you, but understand that you're not alone—you're part of an excellent history of people who trusted God and told others about him. So join the boundless throng of people who proclaim God's salvation. You're truly in great company!

God, thank you for your saving word and for all who've proclaimed it.
Thank you for teaching me the greatest message ever known. Amen.

THE RIGHT STEP

Wisdom begins with respect for the Lord; those who obey his orders have good understanding. He should be praised forever.
PSALM 111:10 NCV

> *All he does is just and good, and all his commandments are trustworthy. They are forever true, to be obeyed faithfully and with integrity.*
>
> PSALM 111:7–8 NLT

Have you ever longed to know what was going to happen in the future? You may be facing a problematic situation and want to make the best choice in the matter. Or perhaps you have been given an exciting opportunity and question whether moving forward is the right thing to do.

God's will is not a mystery. He has a wonderful path that he wants you to follow, but you must be willing to do two things: First, ask him to reveal his plan to you. Second, be committed to obeying him even if it means making a difficult decision.

You may be tempted to move forward without him, but don't. Wait until you know his will, because he will certainly show you the right step to take.

Thank you, God, for revealing your will to me when I fully place my trust in you. You are faithful and true, and worthy of all praise. Amen.

THE KINGDOM OF GOD IS NOW

*Your kingdom is an everlasting kingdom, and your
dominion endures throughout all generations.*

PSALM 145:13 NRSV

Heaven is usually spoken of as a faraway place that you reach only at the end of a godly life. But God's reign over all that he created is right here in the present day, before your eyes and under your nose. Place your trust in him and in his commandments.

*I extol you, my God
and King, and bless
your name forever
and ever.*

PSALM 145:1 NRSV

You don't have to wait for heaven to draw near to God, to experience his love, and to do his will. Everything you need is available by faith and grace. God has given you the tools to know him—Scripture, prayer, communities of faithful believers, acts of love, peace, and mercy. All of these pull you toward your true center and spiritual home with God. The foretastes of heaven are abundant if you open your heart to see them.

*God, open my eyes to see your goodness and mercy in
the midst of this life. Thank you for giving me
a taste of the good things yet to come. Amen.*

SET ME FREE

I run in the path of your commands, for you have set my heart free. Teach me, O Lord, to follow your decrees; then I will keep them to the end.
PSALM 119:32–33 NIV

I have gained perfect freedom by following your teachings.
PSALM 119:45 CEV

Have you ever yearned to be free from your responsibilities? It isn't unusual for you to feel this way—especially if the tasks you've been doing haven't been initiated by God. When you fail to follow God's course for your life, the activities that were once enjoyable may become burdensome obligations.

However, Jesus said, "Take my yoke upon you and learn from me, for I am gentle and humble in heart, and you will find rest for your souls. For my yoke is easy and my burden is light" (Matthew 11:29–30 NIV). The work he gives you to do sets you free because he takes the responsibility for its success upon himself. Are you wearied from burdens and obligations? Then trade your yoke for his and do as he says. Surely you'll find freedom for your soul.

God, help me to keep in step with your plan by doing what you have given me to do. Strengthen me to do your will, my God, so I don't become weary. Amen.

GOD IS LOVE

The Lord watches over all who love him.
PSALM 145:20 NRSV

The New Testament reduces the laws of the Old Testament to one overriding rule: love. If you want to know what true love is, you only need to study God's behavior toward you. God is generous, forbearing, kind, faithful, supportive, nurturing, forgiving, and just. He is everything you want and need.

How I love your laws! How I enjoy your commands!

PSALM 119:47 TLB

You exist in God and know God through your own acts of love in the world. He is in the face of everyone you reach out to, no matter from what station in life he or she might come. His love is in your gentle word to a friend in pain, in the simple work of making a home for your family, and in the kindness you show to a stranger. When you live in love, you become more and more like God.

God, fill my heart with love for you and for those whose lives I touch each day. Thank you for first loving me and showing me how to love others. Amen.

SOMETHING TO OFFER

*Those who fear You will be glad when they see me,
because I have hoped in Your word.*
PSALM 119:74 NKJV

*I rejoice at Your
word, as one who
finds great spoil.*

PSALM 119:162 NASB

When you hear the testimony of other believers, do you ever wonder, *God, why haven't I told others what you've done for me?* Or do you think, *My story isn't as exciting as his. I really have nothing to offer.*

Friend, this simply isn't true. Jesus wants you to lift him up so he can draw people to his side, and one of the ways you exalt him is by telling others what he's done for you. The very anecdote that seems so insignificant to you could be exactly what someone else needs to hear to have faith in him.

Always remember that the hope you have in Jesus Christ is like a cool drink of living water to dry and thirsty souls. So offer all you have and trust him to satisfy them.

*God, there are so many things you have done for me that
need to be told. Teach me to tell others about you
so they will have faith in you as well. Amen.*

YOUR HOPE IS IN GOD

Joyful are those who have the God of Israel as their helper,
whose hope is in the LORD their God.
PSALM 146:5 NLT

Hope is a quality you are so accustomed to living with that only in its absence do you truly understand its importance. Hope is what enables you to get out of bed in the morning and get your family off to school and work. Hope is the strength in your backbones that allows you to withstand storms of trouble and pain. Hope keeps you going.

I will keep on hoping for your help; I will praise you more and more. I will tell everyone about your righteousness. All day long I will proclaim your saving power, though I am not skilled with words.

PSALM 71:14–15 NLT

Your grounds for hope is in God's Word and in his promises, in the history of steadfast love he has shown toward you and in the constant care and comfort he gives to all who trust in him. Hope is your reliance on God's blessing and provision for you. Hope puts the smile on your face as you go forward.

God, I want to put you first in my life. Keep your hand on me and don't let me stray from your will, for you are the source of my hope. Amen.

DISCERNMENT

LORD, save me from liars and from those who plan evil.
PSALM 120:2 NCV

In my distress I cried to the Lord, and He answered me.

PSALM 120:1 AMP

Not all the blessings God sends your way are material in nature. In fact, one of the greatest blessings he gives is a spirit of discernment. This one gift will help you make wise choices at every turn.

Of course, you may wonder: *How do I gain this wonderful gift?* You begin by spending time with God in prayer and the study of the Bible.

The more you know about him, the more you will understand his ways, desires, and plans. He also will open your eyes so you're prepared for the challenges that come your way.

When you have his discernment, you have a greater sense of confidence and hope because you know that God is sovereign—ready, willing, and able to reveal his will to you and protect you in every situation.

God, open my eyes so I can see what is right and true according to your principles. I don't desire worldly wisdom. I desire your truth for my life. Amen.

SEEING GLORY CLEARLY

He judges in favor of the oppressed and gives food to the hungry.
The LORD sets prisoners free and . . . lifts those who have fallen.
PSALM 146:7–8 GNT

It's true that you'll always have troubles, but can you imagine what you'd miss out on if you never experienced pain or challenges? Life would be extremely different, but it wouldn't necessarily be better. Your trials, though difficult, teach you what's important in life. Your afflictions confirm that God is real—because through them, his profoundly deep, healing comfort transforms your soul.

Happy is the one whose help is the God of Jacob, whose hope is in the LORD his God, the Maker of heaven and earth, the sea and everything in them. He remains faithful forever.
PSALM 146:5–6 HCSB

Friend, if you never face an impossible situation, how could you ever see God's glory or experience the power of his presence? You couldn't. So thank God that even your troubles have a wonderful purpose when you see them through his love.

God, thank you that through my trials I can see your glory.
I praise you that even my suffering can become a
blessing through your healing touch. Amen.

WORSHIPING TOGETHER

I was glad when they said to me,
"Let us go to the house of the Lord."
PSALM 122:1 NASB

Because of my friends and my relatives, I will pray for peace. And because of the house of the LORD our God, I will work for your good.

PSALM 122:8–9 CEV

Why is it important to go to church—to worship and serve God with other believers? It is important because you were created for deep fellowship with God and with his people. Unfortunately, sometimes we think that "church" is merely singing a few hymns and listening to a sermon. Although that is part of it, what's missing is how you discover and implement God's purpose for your life in partnership with those who will love, encourage, and equip you. It is in relationship with other believers that God helps you become all you were created to be.

Church isn't a country club for Christians; it is a living community that exists to edify its members and glorify God. Don't avoid it! Join your brothers and sisters in Christ, and worship him together as you were created to do.

God, I thank you for the church—for sisters and brothers
to share with, learn from, relate to, and depend upon.
Develop your love for the church within me. Amen.

NO HIGHER FRIEND

He counts the stars and calls them all by name. How great is our Lord!
His power is absolute! His understanding is beyond comprehension!
<small>PSALM 147:4–5 NLT</small>

Understand that there are things you cannot determine. No matter your wisdom or expertise, there's an entire universe of information that's completely unknowable to the human mind. Science cannot measure heaven, and literature has yet to faintly imagine it.

Yet God comprehends it all, for it comes from his making. And he's also aware of each breath you take, every

Sing to GOD a thanksgiving hymn, play music on your instruments to God, who fills the sky with clouds, preparing rain for the earth, then turning the mountains green.
<small>PSALM 147:7–8 MSG</small>

hair on your head, and all the cells in your body. No one has such complete and lofty understanding as God does. So ask yourself: Where can you go for counsel that is better than God's? You may be limited, but God isn't. Truly, he is your wisest and most wonderful Friend.

God, sometimes it's hard for me to remember that
I don't know everything, but you do. Teach me your
wisdom so I can walk in your ways. Amen.

A FLAME REKINDLED

I wait for the LORD, my soul waits, and in his word I hope.
PSALM 130:5 NRSV

Why am I discouraged? Why is my heart so sad? I will put my hope in God!

PSALM 43:5 NLT

A blazing wood fire is glorious, but when it's spent, nothing remains but white-gray ash—a somber contrast to the rough-cut log that once lay on the hearth and the colorful flames that danced high in the air, filling the room with warmth.

At times you may feel that your life is reduced to ashes, that your strength is gone, and that the flame you once carried inside is cold and colorless. But God promises that even at your lowest point, even when you feel there is nothing left with which to rebuild your life, he is there to rekindle the flame within you. His indwelling Spirit offers hope and strength for you to begin again, and his never-failing love shines brightly on your path, illuminating each step you take.

God, I thank you that the fire of your Spirit brings new life to my body and soul. I will place my life in your hands and my hope in your faithfulness and love. Amen.

THE CREATION SPEAKS OF HIM

*Praise him, you highest heavens, and you waters above
the heavens! Let them praise the name of the LORD!
For he commanded and they were created.*
PSALM 148:4–5 ESV

Why does the psalmist tell the creation to praise God? Do the heavens have a voice? Can the sun and moon declare God's glory? In a sense, the answer is yes.

Let them all praise the name of the LORD. For his name is very great; his glory towers over the earth and heaven!

PSALM 148:13 NLT

✦🌙✦

Consider the question this way: When you go to a gallery, do you commend the artwork or the painter? When you eat a delicious meal, do you extol the food or the expertise of the chef? Is it the overture or the composer that inspires your awe? The creation reflects the brilliance of the Creator—it doesn't draw attention to itself.

Remember that the next time God works through you to do something wonderful—and direct all the glory, honor, and praise to him.

*God, you are the source of everything lovely that comes
from me. May my life reflect your glory, wisdom,
and honor—and always bring you praise. Amen.*

HUMBLED

My heart is not proud, O Lord. . . . I do not concern myself
with great matters or things too wonderful for me.
But I have stilled and quieted my soul.
PSALM 131:1–2 NIV

Hope in the Lord
from this time
forth and forever.

PSALM 131:3 AMP

There's a pride problem whenever you imagine that you know better than God does. Unfortunately, it's an easy trap to fall into. From your point of view, you know exactly how things should work out. You pray and tell God your plans and how you would like everything to fall into place. But God says, "No" or "Wait." It frustrates you.

Friend, you don't know better than God does because your perspective is limited. You have absolutely no idea about what's ahead or what he has in mind. Therefore, whenever you start to believe you've got your plans all figured out—stop. Back up. Humble yourself before him and acknowledge that he is the One in control. Because "God resists the proud, but gives grace to the humble" (James 4:6 GNT).

God, I acknowledge that I've tried to wrestle control
from your omnipotent hand. Please forgive me.
Teach me to humbly accept your will. Amen.

ALL CREATION PRAISES GOD

All creation, come praise the name of the LORD.
Praise his name alone.
PSALM 148:13 CEV

In the fullness of summer, in all of its green lushness, you can sometimes hear a noisy symphony of natural sounds. Crickets, frogs, cicadas, birds, dogs, and cows all contribute to the song of praise to God the Creator. How can they keep from singing?

Shout to the LORD, all the earth. Serve the LORD with joy; come before him with singing.

PSALM 100:1–3 NCV

The other seasons have their own harmonies and melodies of praise. In autumn the owl at night and the crow in the morning raise their voices in the crisp breezes; deer, rabbits, raccoons, and other game rustle in the dry foliage. Winter's cool silence and keening winds make their own frosty music, slow and majestic. Then spring, on the rebound from winter's solemnity, sings in full throat with the sounds of a schoolyard at recess. Praise is a natural activity that issues from life filled with God.

God, my heart is filled with praise and my lips with thanksgiving.
I am in awe of your creation. Thank you for your tender
care over all that you have made. Amen.

AN INTERDEPENDENT PURPOSE

*How good and how pleasant it is for
brethren to dwell together in unity!*
PSALM 133:1 AMP

*The LORD has
promised to bless
his people with
life forevermore.*

PSALM 133:3 CEV

☀

It's God's desire that harmony be a characteristic of his people. Unfortunately, sometimes the church becomes confused about how to go about achieving it. Instead of striving for authentic unity, it settles for uniformity—a human understanding of what the church should look like. This falls short of God's will. Rather, there is only one way to be truly unified, and that is for each person to be wholeheartedly obedient to God. God never contradicts himself, so when everyone is doing as he says, they're actually working toward the same goal—an interdependent purpose—whether they realize it or not.

Therefore, friend, realize that the best way for you to preserve the harmony of the church is to focus your heart, soul, mind, and strength on God. He will take care of the rest.

*God, I pray that my church would be devoted to serving you whole-
heartedly—so that we would have the peace,
harmony, and unity that glorify you. Amen.*

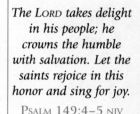
YOUR INSTRUMENT OF CHOICE

Praise the Lord! Sing to the Lord a new song. . . . Praise his name with dancing, accompanied by tambourine and harp.
PSALM 149:1, 3 NLT

What's the right way to praise the Lord? Do you use a stringed instrument or a tambourine? Do you sing a beautiful melody or recite an eloquent speech? Do you bow your head or raise your hands?

The Lord takes delight in his people; he crowns the humble with salvation. Let the saints rejoice in this honor and sing for joy.
PSALM 149:4–5 NIV

First and foremost, praise to God must come from the heart—with an attitude of joy, honor, and love for him. After that, your praise can express itself in countless ways.

David himself praised God on an instrument, with dancing, and through writing psalms. He didn't limit the creative ways he could express his adoration for God. Neither should you. So exalt God in everything you do and with everything you have. Truly, your loving God deserves it.

God, I praise you with all my heart, soul, mind, strength, and talent. You are honorable and worthy of all my love and thankfulness. Amen.

THE SONG OF YOUR LIFE

Come, praise the Lord, all his servants.
PSALM 134:1 GNT

Lift up your hands to the holy place and bless the Lord!

PSALM 134:2 ESV

☀

There are certain tunes that immediately stir your soul. The music is uplifting, the lyrics inspiring, and for some reason it touches your heart whenever you hear it.

Some people have the same effect on your life. A smile spreads across your face whenever you see them, and a sweet melody of faith, kindness, and joy follows them even during the most difficult times. They've set their heart on God—and it resonates to all who know them.

What does your life tell people about God? Do you inspire others to follow him? Is your life a praise hymn—or a dirge? An overture of peace and trust—or a lament of pain and tragedy? You can choose the tune. What will the song of your life be?

God, I want my life to be a song of worship and thanksgiving to you! Please show me how to be a person of praise. May all who meet me want to know you. Amen.

WITH EVERY BREATH

Let every living, breathing creature praise GOD! Hallelujah!
PSALM 150:6 MSG

In life, all things come to an end—except, of course, your relationship with God. That continues for all of eternity. When your circumstances seem hopeless, he shows you the victory. When everything else fails, his love remains steadfast.

Praise the LORD! Praise God in His sanctuary; praise Him in His mighty firmament! Praise Him for His mighty acts; praise Him according to His excellent greatness!

PSALM 150:1–2 NKJV

That's why it's wonderful when you learn to walk with him and praise him with every breath you take. You're building the most important relationship—the one that lasts forever. You discover how to rely on him and trust him no matter what challenges may come.

Friend, today—and for all of your days—praise God with every breath and continue on in the blessing of his presence. For that truly is a life well spent.

God, thank you for never leaving me! Teach me to praise you so that each day I will grow closer to you and love you more. Amen.

Seek the LORD and his strength;
seek his presence continually.

PSALM 105:4 NRSV

The LORD is good, a strong refuge when trouble comes. He is close to those who trust in him.

NAHUM 1:7 NLT

Give all your worries and cares to God,
for he cares about you.

1 PETER 5:7 NLT

My peace I give you. I do not give to you as the world gives. Do not let your hearts be troubled and do not be afraid.

JOHN 14:27 NIV